D1380675

OXFORD STUDIES ON THE ROMAN ECONOMY

General Editors
Alan Bowman   Andrew Wilson

OXFORD STUDIES ON THE ROMAN ECONOMY

The innovative monograph series reflects a vigorous revival of interest in the ancient economy, focusing on the Mediterranean world under Roman rule (c.100 BC to AD 350). Carefully quantified archaeological and documentary data will be integrated to help ancient historians, economic historians, and archaeologists think about economic behaviour collectively rather than from separate perspectives. The volumes will include a substantial comparative element and thus be of interest to historians of other periods and places.

The Roman Agricultural Economy

Organization, Investment, and Production

Edited by
ALAN BOWMAN
and
ANDREW WILSON

OXFORD
UNIVERSITY PRESS

OXFORD
UNIVERSITY PRESS

Great Clarendon Street, Oxford, OX2 6DP,
United Kingdom

Oxford University Press is a department of the University of Oxford.
It furthers the University's objective of excellence in research, scholarship,
and education by publishing worldwide. Oxford is a registered trade mark of
Oxford University Press in the UK and in certain other countries

First Edition published in 2013
Impression: 2

British Library Cataloguing in Publication Data
Data available

ISBN 978–0–19–966572–3

Printed in Great Britain by
CPI Group (UK) Ltd, Croydon, CR0 4YY

Preface

This, the third volume in the series Oxford Studies on the Roman Economy, like its two predecessors, originates in the research programme entitled *The Economy of the Roman Empire: Integration, Growth and Decline*, funded by the Arts and Humanities Research Council in 2005–10 and directed by the Series Editors. The aims and nature of the research project are described in the preface to the first volume, *Quantifying the Roman Economy: Methods and Problems* (eds A. K. Bowman and A. I. Wilson, 2009), to which the reader is referred for more details. This volume focuses on the Roman agrarian economy, and in particular on systems of organization, and the nature and scale of agricultural production, and investment in it. Most of the chapters were originally delivered as papers at a conference on 'The Agricultural Economy' held in Oxford on 3 October 2008, and the introduction also reflects discussion there and at a workshop session on the following day.

We thank the AHRC for the award of the grant that supported the research programme. The project has also benefited greatly from the interest and support of Baron Lorne Thyssen, which have enabled us to continue the research programme well beyond the period funded by the AHRC. We are grateful also to the project's postdoctoral research assistants, Drs Myrto Malouta and Annalisa Marzano, who did much of the conference organization, to the staff of the Stelios Ioannou Centre for Research in Classical and Byzantine Studies, where the conference was held, and to all those who contributed to the discussion at the conference and the following workshop.

Andrew Wilson
Alan Bowman
December 2011

Contents

List of Contributors

Katherine Blouin, Assistant Professor in Greek and Roman History, University of Toronto, Canada. Her work centres on Roman Egypt, and more specifically on issues dealing with multiculturalism, cultural identities, and ancient environments. Publications include: *Le Conflit judéo-alexandrin de 38–41: L'Identité juive à l'épreuve* (Paris, 2005); 'Environnement et fisc dans le nome mendésien à l'époque romaine: Réalités et enjeux de la diversification', *Bulletin of the American Society of Papyrologists*, 44 (2007), 135–66; and 'La Révolte des *Boukoloi* (delta du Nil, Égypte, *ca*.166–172 de notre ère): Regard socio-environnemental sur la violence', *Phoenix*, 64/3–4 (2010), 386–422.

Alan Bowman, Principal of Brasenose College, and Camden Professor Emeritus of Ancient History, University of Oxford. His areas of research are the social and economic history of the Roman empire, Ptolemaic and Roman Egypt, papyrology and the Vindolanda writing tablets. Publications include: *Agriculture in Egypt from Pharaonic to Modern Times* (ed. with E. Rogan; London, 1999); *Life and Letters on the Roman Frontier: Vindolanda and its People* (rev. edn; London, 2003); *Quantifying the Roman Economy: Methods and Problems* (ed. with Andrew Wilson; Oxford, 2009) and *Settlement, Urbanization, and Population* (ed. with Andrew Wilson; Oxford, 2011).

Mariette de Vos, Professore di Archeologia classica, Dipartimento di Filosofia, Storia e Beni culturali, Università degli Studi di Trento, Italy.

Hannah Friedman, Assistant Professor of Classics in the Department of Classical and Modern Languages and Literature at Texas Tech University, USA. Her interests include the ancient Roman economy, industry and technology, mining and metal supply, and the application of modern geospatial technologies to archaeology. She is a co-investigator of the Barqa Landscape Project in southern Jordan. She has published on viewsheds and observational control in Roman mining ('Imperial Industry and Observational Control in the Faynan Region, Southern Jordan', *Internet Archaeology*, 27) and excavations of Islamic farmhouses (R. Adams, J. Anderson, J. Grattan, D. Gilbertson, L. Rouse, H. Friedman, M. Homan, and H. Toland, 'Report on First Season of the Barqa Landscape Survey, South-West Jordan', *ADAJ* 54).

Helen Goodchild, Project and Fieldwork Officer, Department of Archaeology, University of York, UK. Her research interests include geophysics, topographic and field survey, and computer modelling in landscape archaeology. Publications include: 'Agriculture and the Environment of Republican Italy', in J. D. Evans (ed.), *Companion to Roman Republican Archaeology* (Blackwell Companions to the Ancient World; Chichester and Malden, MA, in press); 'Modelling the Agricultural Landscapes of Republican Italy' (with R. Witcher), in J. Carlsen and E. Lo Cascio (eds), *Agricoltura e Scambi nell'Italia tardo repubblicana* (Bari, 2010), 187–220; and *Spatial Data Quality: From Process to Decisions* (ed. with R. Devillers; London, 2009); and V. Gaffney and R. White, with H. Goodchild, *Wroxeter, the Cornovii, and the Urban Process: Final Report on the Wroxeter Hinterland Project 1994-1997*, i. *Researching the Hinterland* (Journal of Roman Archaeology Supplementary Series 68; Portsmouth, RI, 2007).

Dennis Kehoe, Professor, Department of Classical Studies, and Andrew W. Mellon Professor in the Humanities, 2010–13, Tulane University, USA. His research interests include the economy of the Roman empire, especially as it was influenced by law and legal institutions. His publications include: *Law and the Rural Economy in the Roman Empire* (Ann Arbor, 2007); 'The Early Roman Empire: Production', in W. Scheidel, I. Morris, and R. Saller (eds), *The Cambridge Economic History of the Greco-Roman World* (Cambridge, 2007), 543–69; 'Law and Economic Institutions' (with B. W. Frier), ibid., 113–43, as well as 'Food Production in the Long Term (Roman World)', forthcoming in A. Bresson, E. Lo Cascio, and F. Velde (eds), *Oxford Handbook of Economies in the Classical World*.

Myrto Malouta, Lecturer in Greek Papyrology, Ionian University, Corfu. Her research interests are documentary and literary papyri, the history of Ptolemaic and Roman Egypt, and Roman social, cultural, and economic history. Publications include: 'Families, Households, and Children in Roman Egypt', in C. Riggs (ed.), *Oxford Handbook of Roman Egypt* (Oxford, 2012); 'Talei: A Methodological Case Study in Papyrological Topography', in T. Gagos (ed.), *Proceedings of the 25th International Congress of Papyrology* (Ann Arbor, 2010); 'Fatherlessness and Formal Identification in Roman Egypt', in S. Hübner and D. Ratzan (eds), *Growing up Fatherless in Antiquity* (Cambridge, 2009); and 'Antinoite Citizenship under Hadrian and Antoninus Pius, 130–161', *BASP* 46 (2009).

Annalisa Marzano, Reader in Ancient History, University of Reading. Her main areas of interest are Roman social and economic history, the utilization of marine resources and aquaculture in antiquity, and the archaeology and socio-economic function of villas. Publications include: *Roman Villas in Central Italy: A Social and Economic History* (Leiden and Boston, 2007); 'Trajanic Building Projects on Base-Metal Denominations and Audience Targeting', *PBSR* 77 (2009), 125–58; 'Costly Display or Economic Investment? A Quantitative Approach to the Study of Roman Marine Aquaculture' (with G. Brizzi), *JRA* 22 (2009), 215–30.

Andrew Wilson, Professor of the Archaeology of the Roman Empire, University of Oxford. His research interests include the economy of the Roman empire, ancient technology, ancient water supply and usage, Roman North Africa, and archaeological field survey. Recent publications include: *Quantifying the Roman Economy: Methods and Problems* (ed. with Alan Bowman; Oxford, 2009); *Settlement, Urbanization, and Population* (ed. with Alan Bowman; Oxford, 2011); *Alexandria and the North-Western Delta* (ed. with Damian Robinson; Oxford, 2010); *Maritime Archaeology and Ancient Trade in the Mediterranean* (ed. with Damian Robinson; Oxford 2011); and chapters on 'Hydraulic Engineering', 'Machines', and 'Large-Scale Manufacturing, Standardization, and Trade', in J. P. Oleson (ed.), *Handbook of Engineering and Technology in the Classical World* (Oxford, 2008).

List of Figures

List of Tables

1

Introduction: Quantifying Roman Agriculture

Alan Bowman and Andrew Wilson

INTRODUCTION

This volume has its origin in the third annual conference of the Oxford Roman Economy Project, on *The Agricultural Economy*, held on 3 October 2008, of which the theme was the agrarian economy between *c.*100 BC and AD 350.[1] It includes the nine papers from the 2008 conference, which exemplify a range of possible approaches to studying and, within limits, quantifying aspects of agricultural production in the Roman world, and casting light on the structure and performance of that sector of the economy, on the basis of widely different sources of evidence—historical, papyrological, and archaeological—for the modes of land exploitation and the organization and development of, and particularly investment in, agricultural production in the Roman world. It aims to move substantially beyond the simple assumption that agriculture was the dominant sector of the ancient economy, and to explore what was special and distinctive about the Roman economy in terms, for example, of state involvement and institutional infrastructure, elite investment in agricultural improvements and processing plant, or the phenomenon of market-oriented surplus production based around the villa system.

It will be obvious from the size and the content of the book that it makes no claim to a macroeconomic quantification of all agricultural activity over the whole of the Roman empire in a period of almost five centuries. Since our approach in this project has been to proceed on the basis of collections of quantifiable data from archaeological and documentary sources, it is evident

[1] We gratefully acknowledge the support of the Arts and Humanities Research Council, which funded the Oxford Roman Economy Project (OXREP) with a grant from October 2005 to September 2010. We also thank Baron Lorne Thyssen for his generous continued support of the Project.

that we cannot hope to produce a quantification of the whole agricultural economy on this basis, and we remain in doubt as to whether it is in practice possible to do that to any significant extent at all. Even given the huge amount of data, which has often been undervalued by ancient historians, there are too many gaps in the evidence and too many uncertainties about basic features such as population size[2] to produce reliable and robust results. That is not to say that we see no value in attempting to quantify the agrarian regime on the broadest macroeconomic scale, simply that this is not what we feel able to offer here. Rather, the focus is on marshalling a large quantity of evidence (chiefly archaeological and papyrological) to address large questions of the structure and performance of the agricultural economy of the Roman world. In particular, the papers collected here offer a means of analysing investment in agricultural facilities, and tracking variation in patterns across time and across regions within the empire.

A brief review of recent approaches to the Roman agricultural economy may set the scene for what we are attempting to achieve in this volume. If we look further back to the pioneering era, it is appropriate to acknowledge the work of Max Weber, though he paid virtually no attention to scale and volume of agricultural production or consumption in the Roman economy, emphasizing in his chapters on the late Republic and the empire rather the struggles for ownership and control of land and the comparison between Roman and medieval cities, particularly in respect of the character and role of the peasantry and the urban guilds.[3] A considerable quantity of economic hard data was compiled in the various volumes of Tenney Frank's *Economic Survey of Ancient Rome*, which represented a characteristic (for the period) American empiricist approach to the economy, and still has much useful material to offer, even if the emphasis is rather on accumulation than analysis and the macroeconomic estimates and conclusions now look rather dated.[4] From the 1960s onwards, works in English that commanded attention included the well-received book by K. D. White on Roman farming and J. M. Frayn's slighter work on Roman subsistence farming in Italy. These tended to rely heavily on literary evidence (Cato, Varro, Columella, and so on) and to avoid detailed quantified analysis of scale, although the choice of 'subsistence' farming as a subject, even if not very precisely defined, has an obvious implication of smallness of scale.[5]

In the context of Roman Italy, from our point of view the book by M. S. Spurr on arable cultivation marked a real advance, using a great deal

---

[2] See Bowman and Wilson (2011: ch. 1).
[3] Weber (1924/1976: chs 6 and 7).
[4] Frank (1933–40). The density of quantifiable evidence naturally varies significantly by region and period.
[5] White (1970); Frayn (1979).

of literary evidence, dealing in detail with the technology and considering the characteristics of different crop regimes, as well as paying some attention to livestock, labour, and markets. Although Spurr found it quite difficult to draw quantified conclusions from his ancient evidence, the book is notable for its attempts to utilize medieval and modern evidence as comparanda for crop yields, in particular.[6] Recent decades have seen considerable intensification of quantified studies of various aspects of Mediterranean agriculture, particularly olive oil and wine, whereas the third member of the triad has proved generally more intractable.[7] This is perhaps not surprising, given the greater availability of useable archaeological evidence for wine and oil presses, while milling and storage facilities for cereals have proved harder to exploit.[8] Naturally the evidence for wine and oil production exhibits considerable regional bias and reminds us that there are significant differences in the characteristics of the agrarian regime between different parts of the empire, not least in the comparative ratios of arable, livestock, and oleo- and viticulture.

From the point of view of quantification, Jongman's study of Pompeii marked an advance with a somewhat different focus, attempting a holistic picture of a single, well-attested town in its regional context.[9] Conscious of the influence of Finley's *Ancient Economy* and alert to the possibilities offered by the methodology of the social sciences, Jongman reacted strongly against the overemphasis on the textile trade in the Pompeian economy[10] and produced a more pluralistic analysis with a significant emphasis on the agricultural economy of town and region.[11] His detailed calculations deserve careful consideration and emphasize the necessity of achieving plausible estimates for population, land under cultivation, and crop yields in order to understand the balance between production and consumption and the likelihood of surpluses. The robustness of the exercise depends, as he concedes, on the plausibility of estimates of each of the three different variables that need to be combined, and none of these can be regarded as better than consistent. He estimated a territory of 200 km^2, populated at a density of 180/km^2, yielding a total population of 36,000 of which 8,000–12,000 (25–33 per cent) will be urban, a high but not impossible ratio, as he puts it.[12] More recent work, however, suggests a very different balance of land use from Jongman's

[6] Spurr (1986), acknowledged by Scheidel (1994).

[7] e.g. Tchernia (1986); Mattingly (1988a, 1988b); Hitchner (1993); Ruffing (1999). But see Erdkamp (2005).

[8] Moritz (1958); Rickman (1971); Wilson (2002: 9–15).

[9] Jongman (1988).

[10] Moeller (1976).

[11] Jongman (1988: ch. 3).

[12] Jongman (1988: 108–12). Pompeii offers more possibilities than other towns in Italy and most provinces, for the obvious reasons, but there have been a number of studies of the agricultural economy of individual towns and villages in Ptolemaic and Roman Egypt (see Bowman, Chapter 7, this volume).

estimates, and a reconstruction of the original morphology of Vesuvius with significantly more available land for vines, leading to a greater local surplus; moreover, Jongman's calculations do not take full account of the possibility that the region produced a surplus in cash that was exported in return for staples.[13] We also note, from the point of view of our interest in change and development, that Jongman's calculations offer a snapshot of a period just before the destruction of the town in AD 79 and therefore give no insight into the development of the town from the second century BC onwards, as the archaeology of the urban buildings can help to do.

We are fortunate in that the recently published *Cambridge Economic History of the Greco-Roman World* provides some excellent overviews of the character and the development of the agrarian sector of the empire and indicates some of the ways in which the subject has developed in the two decades since Jongman's book, in an organizational format that is largely dictated by region and by period.[14] To oversimplify, prominent questions and themes that run through the contributions of the different authors include the crop regimes and diet (self-evidently the 'Mediterranean triad'), the balance of production and consumption within which levels of 'subsistence' and surplus might broadly be calculable.[15] The approach itself suggests (and we would concur) that such analysis will not yield any sort of a comprehensive picture or widely applicable scenario of the 'agrarian sector' in the Roman Mediterranean, since regional and ecological diversity is so important. Only on the most general level can one envisage an order-of-magnitude estimate in terms such as agriculture accounting for (say) 80 per cent of the value of 'production' in the empire as a whole, the proportion of that value needed to feed the population at subsistence level (if one could be sure of the size of that population over time), and the overhead costs of the institutions and mechanisms needed to make sure that that the food was available when and where required.[16]

Kehoe's contribution to *The Cambridge Economic History* succinctly describes the essential features of the agrarian regime.[17] Wheat, the basic staple crop in regions with a Mediterranean climate, was mainly cultivated on the two-field system, perhaps with some progress towards more productive methods and some degree of integration of livestock farming.[18] The Roman

---

[13] De Simone (forthcoming).

[14] Scheidel, Morris, and Saller (2007).

[15] e.g. Scheidel, Morris, and Saller (2007: 597–600, 656–9, 678–82).

[16] This would fit within the parameters of 75–85% that most scholars seem to envisage, but that are no more than plausible guesses. Representative are the statements of Jones (1974), that the vast majority of the empire's population were peasants (p. 30), that agriculture produced twenty times as much income as trade and industry in the sixth century and the proportion had not changed much (pp. 36–7), that about 90% of the national income was derived from land (p. 83). Population size is still robustly debated (see Bowman and Wilson 2011: ch.1).

[17] Kehoe (2007).

[18] Some contrast here with Pleket (1993: 329).

period is certainly marked by intensification of vine and olive culture. Modes of private land tenure and agricultural management naturally vary from region to region in configuration and balance, but the two predominant types of unit of management were the villa estate, especially in Italy and the west, and (increasingly from the second century AD in the west) large estates consisting of agglomerations of individual farms, with parcels let out to tenants or exploited through a combination of tenancy and free or slave labour. Until the third century AD, alongside private land, there was a very significant amount of publicly and imperially owned land, generally managed through a system of small-scale tenancy.[19] The quantity of such land certainly increased in the early empire and significantly decreased after the third century.

Such a broad summary of the most general kind obviously tends to gloss over significant regional differences. On the larger scale, the most obvious emerge from the comparison between eastern and western parts of the empire,[20] between the development of a more intensive villa-based agriculture corresponding to demographic expansion[21] in North Africa, Spain, Gaul, Germany, and Britain, and a lesser degree of growth in the east, where the complex patterns of landownership and exploitation were well established by the Hellenistic period. Nevertheless, there too one can observe the expansion of site numbers, with settlements appearing in previously unoccupied areas, the development of technology, particularly in irrigation, and increased agricultural activity in the early Roman Imperial period.[22] It is obviously difficult to offer any general propositions that can characterize the agrarian economy as a whole across such a diverse empire and a long chronological span. Scholars who have addressed the issues on this scale have tended to think about the essential and defining characteristics of growth and development, which might then be identified (or not) to greater or lesser degrees in different regions. Pleket has usefully identified some of these characteristics that are germane to our discussion:[23]

- increase in the quantity of land under cultivation, noting the importance of 'marginal' lands brought into cultivation;
- better methods of cultivation and crop rotation, decreasing fallow and increasing cultivation of fodder crops;
- increased output and high yield ratios;
- increased specialization and commercialization of expanding markets;

---

[19] Imperial estates were effectively tenanted public land, although classified differently, at least in Egypt, from the category of public land, which comprised both *demosia ge* and *basilike ge* (former Ptolemaic royal land).

[20] See Alcock (2007); Leveau (2007).

[21] Cf. Pleket (1993: 329).

[22] Certainly in Egypt (see Bowman, Chapter 7, this volume), but clearly not only there.

[23] Pleket (1993).

- the rise of larger, more efficient estates and its corollary, the decline of the peasant economy.

It should be emphasized that we see these as propositions for testing, not necessarily accepting, and there are clearly significant modifications or nuances to be applied to all of them, in particular the last, which we do not think applicable as it stands to the agrarian economy of late antiquity; larger estates are not necessarily consolidated, not necessarily more efficient, and do not necessarily entail the 'decline' of the peasantry.[24] In any case, we should not fall into the trap of assuming that the rise of the large estate is a purely late antique phenomenon; scholarly focus on the large estates of late antique Egypt is chiefly a result of the abundant papyrological evidence, but the archaeological evidence of pressing facilities in North Africa, Gaul, and Istria implies very large consolidated villa estates in the western provinces in the second and early third centuries AD. Indeed, the villa system was a distinctive and crucial element of Roman agriculture in the western provinces, sometimes as a kind of plantation agriculture concentrating on cash-crop production for market sale. The capital-intensive nature of these enterprises may be judged from the degree of investment in, for example, large-scale wine- or oil-pressing facilities (discussed in the chapters by Marzano and by de Vos),[25] in the channel irrigation systems of Iberia and North Africa,[26] or cisterns for irrigated horticulture in the hinterland of Rome.[27] The need to commercialize agricultural surplus on a large scale meant that villa organization and urban markets were therefore closely linked, and villas tend to cluster more densely around towns. The system of intensive villa agriculture flourished under conditions of security and access to large overseas markets, but in the long run proved less resilient than the more diversified and often village-based systems of exploitation in the east, when these conditions broke down.

On cultivation and rotation we would certainly be more emphatic about improved technology and the failure by some ancient economic historians to recognize the existence of various rotation systems.[28] Pleket's provisional conclusion, however, that there is no justification for seeing a gap between a

---

[24] Dossey (2010: 41–54) proposes to identify a large sector of 'subsistence' farmers, defined as peasants with little or no access to the market, in north Africa, but we would not want to see this phenomenon generalized without detailed demonstration; and cf. in any case the arguments against 'subsistence' farming propounded by Horden and Purcell (2000: 272–4). Scheidel and Friesen's contention (2009) that archaeologically identifiable sites represent an upper echelon of settlement and that we are missing the vast majority of rural settlements that existed at subsistence level with no access to diagnostic material culture (pottery, coins, even durable building materials) is problematic and risks circular reasoning, which first postulates absence of evidence and then takes it as evidence of absence.

[25] See also Wilson (2002: 5–6).

[26] See, e.g., du Coudray la Blanchère (1895); Shaw (1982); Beltrán Lloris (2006).

[27] Wilson (2009b).

[28] See Kron (2000).

'primitive' Roman level and a more advanced 'protocapitalistic' level of medieval and early modern European agriculture in a highly diversified agrarian
world is of interest to us and is broadly consonant with our position.[29]

MACROECONOMIC MODELS OF THE ROMAN ECONOMY

Jongman's study of Pompeii and much recent work by Scheidel, including the
contributions to *The Cambridge Economic History*, exemplify the increased
focus on the construction of quantified models of the performance of the
Roman economy in particular, for which Hopkins's well-known taxes-and-
trade model had already blazed a trail a decade before Jongman's book
appeared.[30] In fact, such an approach should ideally be applicable to the
ancient Mediterranean and the Near East on a broader geographical and
chronological scale, but has perhaps proved most attractive for the Roman
empire because of its perceived political (and eventually) economic unity. For
all its weaknesses, Hopkins's model has been very influential, not least meth-
odologically, and it certainly deserves credit for addressing, among other
matters, the issue of how the political unity of the empire stimulated economic
growth and 'smoothed' inequalities in production and consumption across a
vast geographical area. This has stimulated scholars to consider how the
economy of the empire can be addressed as, in some sense, a coherent entity,
through quantification. Hopkins himself modified his position in response to
criticisms, and there have been numerous recent attempts to refine and
develop this kind of approach. From our present perspective, intensification
and decline of trading activity must be related in some way to stimulation,
growth, and depression of agricultural production, and we perhaps do not
need to be too concerned to weigh the importance of taxation as a driver of
trade.[31] We do, however, need to consider the parallel issue of rent structures
as mechanisms that might either stimulate or inhibit agricultural production,
an issue explored in Kehoe's chapter. But we should question whether the level
of cash-crop market-oriented surplus production, linked to villa culture, that
we do see particularly in the western empire between the first century BC and
the third or fourth centuries AD is explicable solely by the taxes-and-trade
model; the villa phenomenon reflects a profit mentality that exploited the
accessibility of larger distributed markets resulting from the lowering of
transaction costs with the development of empire-wide political and economic
institutions.

---

[29] Exemplified by Rathbone (1991).
[30] Hopkins (1980), with revisions in Hopkins (2002).
[31] More in Wilson and Bowman (forthcoming).

Most of the recent attempts to gauge orders of magnitude of production and consumption on an empire-wide scale have adopted a top-down rather than bottom-up approach, as is characteristic of the *Cambridge Economic History*.[32] That is to say, they make no attempt to identify and aggregate individual local or regional productions but assess, for example, what would be required for basic subsistence needs in wheat equivalent of a population of (estimated) given size. Thus, for example, the most recent attempt to model income distribution makes estimates of GDP in wheat equivalent consumption, at various levels, which can then be aggregated for (estimated) population figures and quantified by applying a cash value (again uncertain) within parameters.[33] Expressed in this way, such a calculation obviously has limited value as an actual quantification of the agricultural production of the empire as a whole. Estimates based on minimum subsistence for a hypothetical population figure do not, of course, tell us anything about the size of surplus that the Roman economy was actually capable of producing beyond supporting a population at a level above subsistence. Another analogous approach would be to construct an argument based on the assumption of the relative reliability of (for example) Duncan-Jones's estimate of annual turnover in the Roman imperial budget in the second century AD at 832 million sesterces, rounded up for the sake of simplicity to 900 million sesterces.[34] On the assumption that the generation of wealth through agriculture constituted something in the range of 75–85 per cent of the 'productive sector', as envisaged above, we could then calculate its value in the budget at *c.*675 million sesterces per annum and convert that to a wheat equivalent by applying an average or median cash equivalent value to the *modius* of wheat.[35] Some further calculation can be made as to what proportion of the diet wheat actually constituted (about 70 per cent?), and this will allow inferences about other sources of foodstuffs, including meat and fish but always bearing in mind that agricultural, or, perhaps more accurately, rural production is largely but not totally accounted for by foodstuffs (consider, for example, flax, flowers, sources of drugs, building materials such as reeds, balsam groves, and so on). Any such further calculation would also be in the nature of a guess-estimate and is bound to obscure significant regional diversity. But such an attempt at quantification would have no evidential value, being a product entirely of the assumptions used as inputs, and in fact would tell us nothing beyond what the model is assuming.

---

[32] The most significant of these, by Hopkins (1980), Goldsmith (1984), Temin (2006), and Maddison (2007), are cited and discussed by Scheidel and Friesen (2009), along with references to many other relevant books and articles.

[33] Scheidel and Friesen (2009).

[34] Duncan-Jones (1994); cf. Scheidel and Friesen (2009: 68 n. 26).

[35] Cf. Scheidel and Friesen (2009: 68), using values of 2, 2.5, and 3 sesterces per *modius*, thus admitting the uncertainty of such average values.

Nevertheless, scholarly activity along the lines of macroeconomic quantification in the last twenty years or so has been noticeably increasing with some powerful advocates for its usefulness.[36] There is a tendency in some quarters to see this as a necessary initiative in a field regarded as 'under-theorized', sometimes without explicitly explaining or justifying the need for more modelling and theorization. Perhaps it is regarded as self-evident that such large-scale models are really the only useful tools for comparing agricultural or agrarian economies in different empires, regions, and periods and are the only way of doing this in contexts where (as in the Roman empire) some absolutely crucial factors (size of population, level of yields, and so on) can be estimated only with varying degrees of 'notionality'.[37] Likewise, the greater the degree of notionality or the wider the parameters of the estimates, the more inevitable it is that the model will expand to allow for a wider range of possible scenarios that must take us further away from the empirical (and now to a large extent unrecoverable) reality. There are three further comments we would make about this. First, that such models of very large units such as the Roman empire often pay too little attention to regional or chronological variation, although we naturally recognize that some theoretical models such as Hopkins's 'taxes-and-trade model'[38] do recognize diversity within the whole (that, indeed, is a large part of the point of the model), as do the surveys in the *Cambridge Economic History*. Second, that they tend to ignore much of the actual evidence, particularly the archaeological evidence that is very much at the centre of our concerns. Third, that the actual figures used in the models are often, perhaps even usually, extremely fragile.[39] According to Scheidel, this does not matter (although the danger of subsequent misuse or misunderstanding of such figures seems to us to be a very real danger).[40]

That said, we do recognize and acknowledge the usefulness of some models (not all of them) in advancing our understanding of the Roman agricultural economy, and this volume contains one contribution by Goodchild that explicitly discusses and offers a model-based approach to understanding Italian agriculture through the evidence of archaeological survey. We are convinced that some models of this sort can lead us to a sharper definition and comprehension of the key structural features (markets, mechanisms of exchange, land use, investment, vertical integration, and so on). We can refine

---

[36] Hopkins (1980, 1983, 2002); Goldsmith (1984); Manning and Morris (2005); Temin (2006); Maddison (2007); Scheidel (2007).

[37] Though this is not the approach of Pleket (1993).

[38] Hopkins (1980, 1983, 2002).

[39] For example, population estimates, but not only those.

[40] Scheidel (2009: 60–1). There is a clear example of such misuse in the quantified data for ancient shipwrecks compiled by Parker (1992), which have often been used by others to draw flawed conclusions in ways not intended by the author (for discussion, see Wilson 2009a, 2011).

our analysis of the institutional role of the state and of the balance of production, distribution, and consumption, which will in turn allow some estimate of the distribution of resources and of wealth in the society. We can gauge the value of proxy evidence in the debate about economic growth or decline.[41] We can better understand the relationships between different factors or elements such as population, urbanization, state revenues, modes of production, and labour relations. Although we eschew an explicitly theoretical or model-based approach on the scale of the whole empire in this volume, many of these relationships are implied or discussed in the various contributions and will affect our estimates of macroeconomic features such as aggregate GDP, use of surpluses, tax revenue, and so on.

Furthermore, the actual figures used do matter to us, as Goodchild's contribution exemplifies. This, we emphasize, *is* built on hard archaeological evidence. Indeed, her chapter shows very clearly why the estimates produced to date for Roman GDP in wheat equivalent are largely pointless, since at some stage they involve a largely arbitrary multiplier of production as a factor above bare subsistence, and thus they assume precisely one of the most important things we would like to find out—how well did Roman agriculture do in producing a surplus? It matters greatly what data one plugs into such models, and Goodchild illustrates the very different results obtained, in terms of surplus production, by assuming a series of different models of landscape exploitation (farm size, crop monoculture, or polyculture) for the same region.

THE CONTENT OF THIS VOLUME

Having identified some of the obstacles to broad and robust macroeconomic quantification, we may now attempt to indicate positively how the contents of this volume might contribute to progress in understanding the agricultural economy. A brief synopsis will help to focus the discussion.

In Chapter 2, Dennis Kehoe analyses the institutional and political context by examining two main aspects of the Roman agrarian economy in relation to the state: the state as landowner and economic actor; and the various legal and administrative policies that the state developed for the rural economy.[42] Under the first heading, Kehoe considers the effect of state taxes and of rents on imperial estates on the rural economy. Under the second, he analyses Roman legal policy in relation to private land tenure, including incentives for the exploitation of marginal land, and measures for safeguarding property

---

[41] Cf. Lo Cascio (2007: 621–5).

[42] Different aspects of the role of the state will be analysed in more detail in our volume on trade (Wilson and Bowman forthcoming).

rights and encouraging investment. He also examines state policy in relation to commerce in agricultural products, arguing that Roman rule developed more responsive legal institutions that provided protection not only to the wealthy and well connected, but also to the economically less advantaged.

Goodchild's chapter summarizes recent research on the use of GIS computer models for quantifying agricultural output, discussing the purpose of such modelling in archaeological research, and demonstrating where such models can contribute to historical debates. She applies multi-criteria modelling techniques to investigate Roman agricultural production in the middle Tiber valley in central Italy, and compares farm and villa production in the region under several different production regimes.

In the first of her two chapters, Marzano examines the intensity and organization of wine and olive oil production in the *suburbium* of Rome, by analysing the distribution of 169 oil and wine presses in the region. The density of presses per unit of area suggests that production of oil and wine in the region was considerable and supports de Sena's argument[43] that a significant proportion of the wine and oil consumed at Rome came from the surrounding hinterland. The lack of amphora evidence from the region suggests the products were transported to Rome in skins. The *suburbium* of Rome, in addition to *pastio villatica* and market gardening of fruit, vegetables, and flowers for the city of Rome, appears also to have been involved in intensive viticulture and even olive cultivation. The recognition of this phenomenon and the chronology of the sites also cast doubt on the idea of a crisis in Italian viticulture under competition from the provinces; Rome was absorbing a large proportion of Italian surplus.

In Chapter 5, Marzano extends the analysis of oil and wine presses as indicators of capital investment in agricultural crop processing to three areas exhibiting signs of large-scale production facilities; Gaul, the Iberian peninsula, and the Black Sea. Looking at sites with multiple presses, as an indicator of investment in very large-scale production, she reveals different investment chronologies in the three areas, especially with varying patterns in different areas for the third century. She also identifies, in Gaul, a different pattern between wine and oil investment. The chronology of multiple-press installations in the three regions shows that the second century is the period when the highest number of presses was in operation, and in Gaul and the Black Sea the decline in the fourth century is steep. The cumulative known installation dates for the press facilities indicate that the peak in investment in the creation of multi-presses occurred in the first two centuries of the empire; in both Spain and the Black Sea region, this is paralleled by the development and peak of the fish-salting industry.

[43] De Sena (2005).

The chapter by de Vos presents the results of archaeological survey in the well-preserved North African landscape of the middle Medjerda (Bagradas) valley, and also draws some comparisons with survey work in Algeria. The abundant epigraphic and archaeological record enables an extraordinarily rich analysis of the agricultural exploitation and landholding patterns: individual farms and villas with oil or wine presses can be situated within estates whose boundaries are known from marker stones; the development of the estates of T. Statilius Taurus into the imperial estate of the *saltus Neronianus* can be traced, and the landscape exploitation related to the *lex Manciana* and the *lex Hadriana de rudibus agris*, referred to on the well-known inscriptions governing tenancy rights on imperial estates (which are discussed in Chapter 2), a new copy of which was found at one site.[44] The chapter also examines irrigation infrastructure, and transport networks for conveying the surplus production to distant markets. This chapter presents much new material for the first time and provides an exceptionally rich analysis of a Roman agricultural landscape, both linking well with Kehoe's chapter and providing a wider landscape context for the kinds of large-scale oil and wine production analysed for other provinces in Marzano's chapters. The potential for connecting epigraphic and archaeological evidence for this area has long been recognized, and de Vos's chapter marks a significant step towards realizing this.[45]

Three chapters focusing wholly or partly on Egypt follow. Bowman's study analyses various strands of quantifiable evidence for the scale and range of agricultural scenarios in regions, towns, and villages in Egypt. This includes an analysis of nome (district) sizes, and areas devoted to cultivated area, grain-land, gardens, and vineyards; calculations of grain yields and tax income for the Arsinoite Nome for the year AD 184/5; the distribution of land among landowners on the basis of tax registers and legal declarations for the nome capitals, and the rather different (and less unequal) patterns of distribution of landownership in village communities. At the village level, case studies are possible for intensive wine production at Philadelphia in the third century BC; land use at Theadelphia in the second century AD; and the sale and leasing of land at Tebtunis in the second century AD. Data from several regions indicate severe decline in agricultural production and tax revenues between the second and fourth centuries AD.

In Chapter 8, Blouin examines the fiscal and cadastral documentation for the Mendesian Nome in the Nile Delta, significant because documentary material from this fertile area is very rare and provides an important counterpoint to most papyrological studies of Egypt, which focus on evidence from the Nile valley. Using the carbonized archives from Thmuis, she identifies the

---

[44] See also Kehoe (1988).
[45] Hitchner (1995).

chief characteristics of the Mendesian agricultural economy, while an analysis of *P. Oxy.* XLIV.3205 offers a unique glimpse into the agrarian reality of a Mendesian village at the turn of the fourth century AD. The comparison of data from *P. Oxy.* XLIV.3205 with the agrarian and fiscal terminology in the Mendesian papyri shows that the agricultural economy of this region in the Roman period was characterized by a preponderance of cereal farming, with vine cultivation in second place. There are relatively few data relating to the growing of fruits and vegetables (including olives), lentil, and flax, but this is probably due to documentary bias as well as to the particular conditions in which these activities were practised and taxed. The diverse economic practices of the region, which also included livestock and fisheries, hunting and gathering, probably resulted, as in the Fayum and the Nile valley, from 'opportunistic' adaptations to the local deltaic environment. They are also symptomatic of a rivalry between the interests of those who held economic power (the state, large property owners, and merchants) and those of the small owners and managers, for whom diversification for domestic needs was advantageous, or even essential.

Malouta and Wilson compare the archaeological, literary, and papyrological evidence for water-lifting devices across the empire in an attempt to situate the evidence that we have for investment in irrigation machinery within the wider picture of evidence survival. Collection of the literary, documentary, and archaeological evidence for water-lifting devices over time shows a clear difference between the two categories of evidence, each of which is individually problematic; but comparison between the categories is revealing about the nature of the datasets. In the papyri, irrigation machinery constitutes the overwhelming bulk of attestations of water-lifting devices, whereas irrigation machines are rarely traceable archaeologically. The archaeological evidence increases sharply in quantity before the literary evidence does, in the second century BC, consistent with seeing the widespread diffusion of these technologies under the conditions of political unity and increased communication enabled by the Roman empire. The quantity of archaeological evidence drops considerably after the fifth century AD—in sharp contrast with the papyrological evidence for Egypt, which shows a major peak in the sixth and seventh centuries. The fifth- and sixth-century papyri contain proportionately more references to water lifting than before, perhaps for reasons connected with the type of document containing the evidence. Because of different biases in the different kinds of evidence, and the changing visibility threshold of different devices over time, it is clear that no single type of evidence—archaeological, literary, or papyrological—gives a reliable picture of the trends in usage of water-lifting technology (and, by extension, probably of other technologies too), and that any real understanding of the phenomenon must come from an analysis of all the types of evidence. What is, however, evident from the papyri is that artificial irrigation was not only a significant component of agriculture in

Byzantine Egypt, as is commonly thought, but also a prominent feature of the Egyptian agricultural economy of the Roman period, given the very large number of references to water-lifting machines in the second and third centuries AD. Where the context is given, the irrigation machines mentioned in the papyri were frequently watering intensively cultivated plots of high-value crops—orchards and vineyards.

In the final chapter, Friedman examines the relationship between industry and agriculture, which are too often viewed as separate 'sectors', showing how the integration of both provides insights into the operation of mining regions. The study focuses on the agricultural field systems associated with Khirbet Faynan, a settlement associated with the smelting activities for the nearby important copper mines of Faynan (ancient Phaeno). An analysis of the development and chronology of the field system produces a series of phased calculations over time for the number of people that could be supported from it; the effects of pollution from smelting in the agricultural activity of the region are also considered. The centralization of the field systems and creation of larger more sophisticated irrigation systems coincides with the periods of most intensive Roman period copper production. Food production was increased to supply the needs of the non-subsistence populations such as miners and smelters. The first means of accomplishing this was to import food; the second was to restructure the resources within the region. In practice, this second response resulted in the most important piece of arable land in the southern 'Arabah being changed dramatically through the implementation of a single, carefully constructed and executed plan of land usage. If the central-ized field system was created to supply the industry, the abandonment of this type of agriculture in the Late Byzantine period probably coincides with a downscaling of that industry. Greater food production benefited the supply of the region, supporting an increase in the size of populations devoted to mining and smelting, but this in turn led to more pollution and less food, thus adversely affecting the industry it was intended to sustain.

Plainly these studies will not amount to a quantified account of the whole agrarian regime of the Roman empire, which is beyond reach or plausibility for the reasons we have explained. They do, however, point up regional variations and also share common themes in their analysis of surplus produc-tion, and directed investment by the state, elite landowners, or even tenant farmers under rental arrangements designed to incentivize investment to increase output. We conclude this introduction by offering some suggestions as to how they might add up to more than the sum of the parts and illuminate some critical aspects of the agricultural economy, in the hope that the methods and perspectives can be applied to other kinds and other sets of data and to other areas that are not treated here.[46]

---

[46] We recognize that three crucial elements must be central to any discussion of economic structures: capital, land, and labour. For a good summary discussion, See Erdkamp (2005: 12–54).

REGIONAL DIVERSITY

It will be observed that it is difficult, though in our view not impossible, to attempt economic quantification with any evidential basis except for a limited number of places. As Goodchild's chapter suggests, we can consider how to achieve something in the nature of a quantified model of the relationship of various factors in the agricultural sector focusing on a micro-region. We suggest, however, that the contents of this volume show that the limitations are not quite so severe as has often been alleged. For example, for Egypt, Rathbone's study of the Appianus estate along with Bowman's chapter in the present volume do offer some calculations along these lines.[47] More robustly, Van Minnen has suggested that Egypt is the only area for which one can construct a reliable and quantified 'taxes-and-trade model', although he has not actually done so.[48] It will, however, be obvious that any such Egyptian model will yield a result that generally shows substantial surpluses, with some temporal variation, across long periods of time. Van Minnen's position may seem too aggressive to those who are not Egyptian specialists, especially if they misunderstand him to mean that Egyptian conditions are replicated and applicable elsewhere. But there is a more nuanced expression of that position that would suggest that the Egyptian evidence does allow some quantification in the relationship between agricultural production, state revenues, and the movement of goods and financial resources around the empire: that is, although its agriculture was, atypically, based on the annual Nile flood, Egypt was not atypical in the structure of agricultural management, development of markets, level of monetization, and extraction of revenue by the state, only in the extent to which we can put some detail into the structural picture.

In contrast, there is as yet relatively little good archaeological evidence for Egypt, and we rely mainly on the documentary evidence in the papyri for a regrettably isolated glimpse of conditions of land use in the Delta in the second century (which will in due course be supplemented by a more detailed analysis[49]) and for an attempt to analyse the scale and patterns of production in the Fayum villages and in the nomes of Middle Egypt. The evidence for yields, returns, and surpluses, as well as the changing patterns of land tenure and ownership, is more detailed than anything that can be derived from other sources and regions, but the trends that it suggests cannot be ignored in dealing with contemporary evidence from other places. In this respect, the contrasting study of the Wadi Faynan offered by Friedman is illuminating. The agricultural economy of the region responds specifically (and in quantifiable terms, within parameters) to the increase in mining activity, which must

---

[47] Rathbone (1991).
[48] Van Minnen (2000).
[49] Blouin (forthcoming); cf. Blouin, Chapter 8, this volume.

be directed by the central government. The region is very different from the agglomerations of agricultural villages in Egypt, but comparison of the governmental, technological, and economic drivers is nevertheless significant; the mining activities in the Egyptian eastern desert and the Red Sea quarries created a need to which the response took a very different form, dictated by total lack of a local agricultural infrastructure and the presence of developed communication routes and trading facilities.[50] Both cases emphasize the impossibility of making a clear demarcation between the agricultural economy and other kinds of economic activity.

The essence of the 'taxes-and-trade model' (discussed above) is, of course, that, in addition to supplying food to the megalopoleis, such surpluses will be directed towards making up for shortfalls in less productive areas, which have been identified in a general way as the less developed and more militarized frontier provinces, but it is not to be assumed that such provinces or regions could not have been self-sufficient if one discounted the costs of the military protection. Generally speaking, we lack the evidence to demonstrate this empirically. But Kristina Glicksman's recent thesis produces quite an optimistic picture of the economy of the province of Dalmatia,[51] and we should remember that even in Moesia a governor of the reign of Nero, Plautius Silvanus, was able to settle 100,000 *transdanuviani* with their families *ad praestanda tributa*.[52] Another approach might be through some case studies of particular crops or other types of foodstuffs such as meat and fish, for which pioneering exemplars already exist:[53] there are well-known studies of North African olive oil, but wine production, where there is surely significant expansion in several areas over the Roman period, partly but not solely in response to increased demand from large metropoleis, perhaps deserves more attention from this point of view.[54]

Goodchild's chapter in this volume also articulates much more explicitly the nature of GIS-based models and the ways in which they can be used to model the agricultural economy of a specific region in the Tiber valley, using robust archaeological evidence derived from surveys that reveal farm and villa sites in the hundreds. It will be seen that the evidence offered for other regions by other contributors to this volume shows both similarities and contrasts and is not systematically modelled in the manner of Goodchild's material; the evidence is now becoming available to make this a possibility for some areas of North Africa in the future (De Vos's survey region around Dougga would

---

[50] Cuvigny (2003); Schörle (2008, 2011).
[51] Glicksman (2009).
[52] *ILS* 986.
[53] Meat: King (1999). Fish: Marzano and Brizzi (2009).
[54] Olive oil: Mattingly (1985, 1988a, 1988b, 1994, 1996); Mattingly and Hitchner (1991, 1993); Hitchner (1993, 1995); Brun (2003b, 2004). Wine: Tchernia (1983, 2006); Panella and Tchernia (1994); Brun (2003a, 2003b, 2004); Banaji (2002) for late antique Egypt.

be amenable to this kind of treatment). However, for many regions the methods of approach to different bodies of evidence and the aspects of the agricultural economy that they illuminate are different. Egypt, of course, benefits from a quantity of detailed papyrological evidence unparalleled elsewhere in the empire, but the relatively underdeveloped state of the archaeology of rural or village settlement pulls in the opposite direction; as Malouta and Wilson's chapter shows, the picture one might draw of certain phenomena, such as the chronology and extent of the use of water-lifting devices for irrigation, might differ considerably if one looked only at the papyrological or the archaeological dataset in isolation. The comparison of the detailed evidence for the Thugga region in North Africa presented in the chapter by de Vos, where the archaeological survey material can be linked to the epigraphic record, with that from the Tiber valley is suggestive. Here we have, once again, a large amount of quantifiable archaeological evidence derived from intensive survey and excavation that can be amplified by the epigraphic evidence to show, *inter alia*, intensive development of oleoculture, the history of family ownership of estates and the balance between public/imperial, private, and urban land, the survival of different regional technological traditions well beyond the period that we treat here. It is worth emphasizing that, with this valuable material, De Vos enables us for the first time to get to grips with fleshing out the picture for which the well-known Bagradas valley inscriptions yield valuable and well-known evidence for the management of imperial estates in the second and early third centuries.[55]

INVESTMENT AND INTENSIFICATION

The archaeological evidence for agriculture consists chiefly of farms or villas, field systems, irrigation infrastructure, and the buildings and equipment used to process and store crops.[56] While buildings or irrigation systems may give a general indication of levels of investment, if we want to examine trends in what kinds of crops were produced, the evidence for processing equipment is most informative. However, our picture is directly influenced by the archaeological visibility and survival of different types of processing infrastructure. Some crops—for example, beans and pulses—do not require archaeologically distinctive equipment to grow, process, or store, and appear to have been transported in sacks that leave no archaeological trace. Grain production, as

[55] Kehoe (1988).
[56] Archaeological finds of carbonized or desiccated seeds, finds of agricultural tools and implements, or iconographic representations of agricultural activities may indicate a range of crops grown or harvested but can hardly form the basis for an assessment of scale.

opposed to consumption, is also difficult to trace archaeologically, since grain mills reflect processing into flour, which usually happened closer to the consumer than the producer. By contrast with the relative archaeological invisibility of grains, pulses, fruit, and vegetable production,[57] the archaeological durability of the infrastructure used to process olives and grapes—presses, mills, treading floors, and vats—leads to much greater visibility of the evidence for oleoculture and viticulture, which is reflected in the quantity of scholarship on these subjects.[58]

That this volume emphasizes the spread and intensification of olive and vine culture in the Roman Mediterranean therefore comes as no surprise. After the pioneering work of Mattingly and Hitchner in particular,[59] the investment in oil- and wine-pressing technologies can be quantified in places other than North Africa. Marzano's two contributions to this volume emphasize, first, that the intensity and quantity of production in the hinterland of Rome is greater than has hitherto been thought, and, second, that the patterns of investment vary somewhat across the regions studied. While the data for construction and use of multi-press sites for olive oil and/or wine suggest a general picture of prosperity in the first and second centuries AD, there are significant differences between regions. In Gaul, the main wave of construction comes in the first to early second centuries, with no new installations after the second century; the peak in the operation of sites lasts from the second half of the first to the first half of the third century AD. In the Iberian peninsula, the vast majority of the multiple press sites were built in the first half of the first century AD, and there was a sustained plateau of use through to the late fourth century, with reduced but still significant levels of operation through the fifth century. In the Black Sea one double-press site dates from the first century BC, but the main periods of construction of multi-press sites are the first and second centuries AD, but with a sustained plateau of use through the third century, and some reduced operation in the fourth. To a certain extent this picture parallels the levels of investment and use of large-scale fish-salting factories, at least in Iberia and the Black Sea.[60]

These analyses are based on robust quantifiable data for production sites with multiple presses, producing large-scale surpluses, albeit that the chronological evidence is frequently not as secure as one would wish. While a complete analysis of patterns of rural investment in olive oil and wine

---

[57] But see Wilson (2009b) for an attempt to link large rural cisterns to intensive horticulture or arboriculture in the hinterland of Rome.

[58] Cf. Durand and Leveau (2004: 204–6) on how the greater visibility of olive oil processing equipment led in the 1980s to an overestimation of the importance of olive growing in southern Gaul.

[59] Mattingly (1985, 1988a, 1988b, 1994, 1996); Mattingly and Hitchner (1991, 1993); Hitchner (1993, 1995).

[60] Wilson (2006).

production would, of course, include the sites with single presses, which are by far the most common, these run into the thousands, and such a study is beyond the scope of what can be accomplished here, although studies are in hand that move towards this goal.[61] Instead, the focus on the multiple-press sites concentrates on the very large-scale production stimulated by conditions of long-distance trade and access to overseas markets that were particular to the Roman world. It should be emphasized here that the phenomenon of large estate centres with batteries of presses for the bulk processing of agricultural surplus destined for market sale and even inter-provincial export is a special characteristic of the Roman period, largely unparalleled again until early modern plantation agriculture. It represents an intensification of cash-crop production well beyond even the levels of the market-oriented production that were normally characteristic of the villa system. It is important to note, however, that, while the chapters by Marzano focus on Italy, Gaul, Spain, and the Black Sea region, because the chronology is better understood here than in North Africa, it is in North Africa that the largest number, and the biggest, of the multiple olive oil and wine-pressing installations are found (for example, Kherbet Agoub in Numidia, with thirteen wine-treading floors and nine wine presses, and at least two olive oil presses; Henchir Sidi Hamdan with nine presses and Senam Semana with seventeen presses, both in Tripolitania and presumed to be for olive oil[62]). On the basis of general association with surface ceramics, the Tripolitanian sites are generally thought to have been particularly active in the second and third centuries AD, although those in Africa Proconsularis and Numidia go later: Kherbet Agoub was in fact in use from the third to the fifth centuries AD, and any real assessment of the chronology of their establishment and lifespan of such sites must await excavation. Indeed, much of rural Africa seems to have seen continued—or even increased—prosperity in the fourth century. The African multiple-press sites attest a massive degree of large-scale investment for cash-crop agriculture and market-oriented surplus in the mid-Roman Imperial period, but little is known concretely about their management or operation, whether they were directly managed through a bailiff, or rented to tenants, or even acted as central processing centres for crops produced by tenant farmers. Henchir Sidi Hamdan, occupied by the early second century AD,[63] may have been owned by one of the Lepcitanian elite and managed by a *vilicus* (given the lack of luxury accommodation at the site). Henchir el-Begar, a ten-press site in southern Tunisia, seems to have been owned by the senator Lucilius Africanus,

---

[61] Hobson (2012); cf., for earlier studies, Mattingly (1988a, 1988b, 1988c, 1988d).

[62] Kherbet Agoub: Meunier (1941) (incorrectly interpreting the main building as for olive oil pressing) and Brun (2004: 233–8); Henchir Sidi Hamdan: Oates (1953: 97–9); Senam Semana: Cowper (1897: 279–82).

[63] Oates (1953: 99); Kenrick (2009: 165–7).

who received permission in AD 138 to hold a rural market there, on his estate the *saltus Beguensis*.[64] Some may have been, or have eventually become, imperial estates—the study of the Thugga region by de Vos shows very clearly the expansion of imperial estates swallowing up private land, with the emergence of the *saltus Neronianus* from the estate of T. Statilius Taurus.

LAND AND LABOUR

This volume contains no study that focuses exclusively on the critical factors of land and labour, but they recur, explicitly or implicitly, throughout. In particular, Malouta and Wilson's study considers the effect of irrigation technologies on the availability and efficient exploitation of agriculturally useable land, while the effect of institutional arrangements on tenant labour is a leitmotif of Kehoe's chapter. Moreover, there is a great deal of recent scholarship that has advanced our understanding of the control, distribution, and modes of exploitation of the land that produced agricultural wealth. Ownership, control, and distribution of land are naturally inextricably linked to diverse settlement patterns, in which large-scale estates, villas, or village communities with multiple small-scale holdings might occur in varying proportions, with variation in the relative predominance of arable, pastoral, and oleo-/viticultural activity.[65] Large-scale private ownership and capital investment are reflected alongside direct ownership by the state (including the imperial authority), where there is also significant capital investment, and more modest medium-sized or small farms, with a substantial sector of farmers economically positioned between the wealthy elite landowners and the small peasantry; nor should we forget the existence of small plots 'farmed', or better 'cultivated', by those who were not exclusively agriculturalists (though, like peasant smallholdings, impossible to quantify outside Egypt). We have moved away from some traditional notions of a general linear progression towards 'latifundists' absorbing the independent peasantry, and an increase over time in the phenomenon of *agri deserti*. Although an appreciable amount of land changes hands, traditional patterns stubbornly persist in most rural areas. But, where there is quantifiable evidence, it suggests an increase (or at least no decrease) in the inequality of distribution of privately owned land and a clear trend away from state ownership and direct exploitation to private control, though caution is required in linking this to the

---

[64] *CIL* 8.270 = 11451; cf. Suppl. IV, p. 2358; Merlin (1906).

[65] We refrain from citing extensive bibliography here. For good summaries, with the recent bibliography, see Erdkamp (2005: 18–22); Kehoe (2007: 553–7). See also Bowman (1985); Bagnall (1992); Thonemann (2007).

supposed spread of 'feudalism' and the 'colonate', whatever we think these might be. In several areas, evidence for capital investment shows a peak in the second century AD and varying levels of decline from this peak in the third and fourth centuries, though many areas clearly remained prosperous and well populated, especially in North Africa and the East. Indeed, in some areas of the East, notably Syria and Egypt, archaeological data somewhat impressionistically collected also suggest a peak in rural prosperity in the fifth and sixth centuries AD. More work on the excavation of rural sites in these regions, and much more systematic rural survey, is required to see whether the surface evidence for Byzantine prosperity is mantling and hiding a general mid-imperial picture of prosperity too (certainly the urban wealth of sites in these regions suggests a considerable agricultural surplus, although it is unclear how far the countryside shared in the fruits of this), or if the late antique period here saw greater prosperity than under the High Empire (as the villages of the Syrian limestone massif at first sight seem to suggest[66]).

Size, control, and configuration of landholdings are naturally intimately related to modes of exploitation and to the issue of subsistence and surplus. Definition of the composition of the labour force is essentially reducible to the categories of tenancy (private or state), free labour, and slave labour.[67] Apart from the regional variations, there are complexities involved in estimating the balance of these categories. Tenants might range between poor sharecroppers and relatively prosperous individuals who behaved in an economically rational manner as both lessors and lessees of plots.[68] The gradual withdrawal of the state from direct ownership and leasing of land presumably meant that the class of state tenants was transformed over time either into one of private tenants (not necessarily *coloni*) or small-scale owners. Calculation of the economic advantages of slave labour to the detriment of the small peasantry and seasonal free labour is by no means straightforward; wage labour may be specialized (as in viticulture) and can also be seasonally supplied.

Any attempt to quantify production and consumption in relation to subsistence and surplus has to take into account the kinds of variations in crop regimes and yields explored by Goodchild, and labour productivity, and is therefore extremely difficult for most periods and areas in antiquity. It is axiomatic that a significant proportion of what was produced was consumed in the unit where it was produced, thus effectively constituting a significant part of the subsistence requirements for the population that produced it. But this does not in our view equate to what is sometimes described as a straightforward scenario of 'subsistence farming'—it is clear that even small-scale agriculturalists cumulatively produce a significant surplus, represented by the difference between 'gross' and 'net' agricultural surplus (that is, the value of

---

[66] e.g. Tchalenko (1953–8).   [67] Cf. Whittaker (1980).
[68] On tenancy, see Foxhall (1990); Erdkamp (2005: 23–33); Kehoe (2007: 557–9).

the product net of labour and other 'overhead' costs).[69] Moreover, as Horden and Purcell have cogently argued, peasants certainly did not aim at subsistence, for in a bad year they would starve; aiming to produce a surplus, that could be stored or traded, is the only sensible strategy.[70]

AGRICULTURE, INDUSTRY, AND COMMERCE

Any discussion of the factors involved in realizing the value of the agricultural product will naturally lead to an attempt to estimate the role of industrial and commercial activities: transport, the pottery industry, food processing, marketing, and the provision of financial services (financial capital and liquidity becoming more crucial as one increases the scale and complexity of production). Hannah Friedman's chapter in this volume explores the development of agriculture specifically to support a mining settlement in the Jordanian desert, and the effects of the mining pollution on the agriculture. The mutual interdependence of agricultural and artisanal activities has recently been stressed in relation to the 'industrie agro-alimentaire',[71] and we will have more to say on the relationship between agriculture and craft production in a future volume. For the moment it will suffice to point out that we have to take account of 'industrial' production in the countryside and of food processing in the towns, as well as the needs of other specifically non-agricultural sectors such as the military, mining, and quarrying operations. In the countryside, certain types of pottery production show a tendency for co-location with agriculture, possibly employing seasonal labour. Besides the obvious instances of amphora production as packaging for agricultural produce (oil and wine), the production of African Red Slip table pottery at sites in inland Tunisia is of interest, as it may well be linked to rural estates, making use of seasonally available labour in slack periods of the agricultural year.[72] Moreover, in a region where good firewood was scarce, co-location with agriculture offered the possibility of using the residue from olive pressing as fuel. Some stages of textile production also occurred in the countryside, and, even where it was predominantly urban based, the town played a vital role in the process of converting the wool or flax produced in the countryside into textiles for sale. Conversely, food production was not an exclusively rural phenomenon; quite apart from the obvious feature of urban bakeries, towns like Pompeii had vineyards within the walls; market gardens clustered immediately around towns, and in parts of North Africa 'agrovilles' of the High

---

[69] Cf. Erdkamp (2005: 54).   [70] Horden and Purcell (2000: 271–4).
[71] Morel (2009).
[72] Peacock, Bejaoui, and Ben Lazreg (1990: 83); Mackensen (1993: 53; 1998: 355).

Empire had olive and wine presses within the walls.[73] This phenomenon became increasingly common in many cities throughout the southern and eastern Mediterranean in late antiquity.[74]

The links between agriculture and the market will be covered in more detail in the fourth volume of this series, on trade, but some brief remarks are in order here. In geographical terms, local markets were always important; costs of transport dictated that these were usually satisfied first unless political considerations (the supply of Rome, or later Constantinople, or some other regional capital) overrode them. Local urban centres naturally formed the main such markets, having the largest concentrations of demand; the distribution of villas concentrates around towns (very noticeable in south-east Britain and in Gaul). These were supplemented by periodic markets, both in rural areas and in some towns,[75] and would also attract merchants dealing in trade further afield—indeed, this may be a prime reason why Lucilius Africanus petitioned the Senate for permission to hold a periodic market on the Saltus Beguensis, to dispose of the oil or wine produced at his estate centre with its ten presses.[76]

Cities, and especially ports, served also as collecting centres for long-distance overseas trade in agricultural products. De Vos's analysis of the Dougga region shows how the intensive investment there in agriculture and pressing facilities was related not only to landholding patterns and institutional incentives encouraging long-term investment, but also to the development of a good communications infrastructure by road and river to transport agricultural surplus to Carthage and thence to overseas markets. The efforts by the Roman state to create a transport infrastructure, even if motivated to a considerable degree by military considerations, the need for swift communications, and the ability to extract tax revenue in kind, had profound implications for the ability to market an agricultural surplus, and thus helped stimulate production. The Roman sites with multiple olive presses in the Var *département* of southern France benefited from good road links to towns and coastal ports; but in exactly the same region in the eighteenth century the fruit rotted on the trees as the roads were so poor that it could not be transported to market.[77]

Long-distance trade in agricultural products appears from the surviving evidence to have been dominated by the Mediterranean triad: grain (especially but not only that destined for the *annona*), olive oil, and wine. That picture is doubtless influenced by the written sources' concern with the *annona*, and by

---

[73] e.g. Volubilis in Morocco (Akerraz and Lenoir 1981–2; 1987), Madauros in Algeria (Christoflé 1930), and Ksar el-Guellal (site KS 031 from the Kasserine Survey) in Tunisia (Hitchner 1988: 33–6).

[74] e.g. Wilson (2004) for Cyrenaica.   [75] MacMullen (1970); Shaw (1981).

[76] See n. 64.   [77] Hitchner (2012).

the nature of the amphora evidence for oil and wine containers; but it probably broadly reflects a reality: grain was a necessity, and there was large and widespread demand for olive oil and wine, but also niche markets for particular qualities. However, we should not overlook the evidence for the bulk long-distance transport of many other agricultural products too, often not transported in archaeologically durable, or easily identifiable, containers: the Murecine tablets show us the bulk transport of tonnes of lentils and chickpeas from Alexandria to Puteoli, while in the mid-second century BC Cato the Elder used the fact that fresh figs from Carthage could be bought at Rome to emphasize how near the enemy city was.[78] Long-distance trade in agricultural produce was not restricted to staples.

Agricultural produce might be brought to market by a variety of means. The producer might take goods to an urban market or to periodic *nundinae*, or specialist agents or traders might come to the landowner and buy the produce at the estate, even purchasing the crops on the tree or the vine, before the harvest.[79] Such an arrangement guaranteed a sale for the producer, usually at a lower price, since the merchants were assuming the risk of a bad harvest or speculating on future price movements. Landowners might also process the crops from their tenants' fields, either purchasing the crop from them and selling on the processed produce, or charging a pressing fee in either cash or kind; some of the estate centres with multiple presses may have served for such arrangements.

Even though state institutions such as the *annona*, and at times also the subsidized sale of olive oil and wine, clearly accounted for large long-distance movements of agricultural produce, the scale of private trade was, cumulatively, very large, as shown by the evidence of pressing installations for surplus production and of amphorae from both shipwrecks and terrestrial sites. De Vos's thought exercise on the possible value of the surplus olive oil that might be produced in a single press—she suggests a profit of *c*.92,000 *denarii* from the production of each press at the prices of Diocletian's Edict of AD 301 (but without accounting for the cost of the agricultural labour)—begins to show the value of investment in agricultural intensification in an economic system that could reach large and distant markets.

ECONOMIC POLICY

This brings us to the crucial issues that are discussed by Kehoe in his contribution to this volume and that are central also to the topics to be treated

---

[78] *TPSulp* 51; Plutarch, *Cat. Ma.* 27; Pliny, *NH* 15.20.
[79] e.g. Cato, *de Agr.* 147; Pliny, *Ep.* 8.2.1; Erdkamp (2005: 121–30).

in the next volume in the series, on trade. He seeks to identify the state institutions and actions that drive production in the agricultural economy and he plausibly argues that its legal institutions are the main constituents of what we might regard as 'economic policy'. Among the most important other factors are the methods and instruments by which the state encourages the uptake of technology and the increase of production by extension or intensification of land use, the effect of state landownership, and its withdrawal therefrom after the third century, its means of regulating the degree of central and local control of productive resources, methods of supporting productive activity by subsidy or loan, and the relationship between the state and private commercial institutions or individuals in realizing the value of the agricultural product. In effect this sets out the governmental and institutional infrastructure within which quantification of the agricultural economy needs to be contextualized. Kehoe's discussion concentrates heavily on the supply side. We will also want to consider the methods and instruments by which the state impacted on the demand side.[80] Taxation plays an obviously central role here, not least as a part, but only a part, of the way of meeting demands made by the army and the bureaucracy—institutions whose size and needs could be centrally regulated and modified (as the evidence of the law codes shows very clearly). The *annona* for Rome and military supply to the concentrations of troops on the frontiers are obvious instances, but the ways in which the state affected demand go beyond the mere handout of *annona* grain and other goods. Long before olive oil was included in the *annona*, the evidence of Monte Testaccio and inscriptions referring to officials responsible for oil supply suggest that the state was engaged in the bulk purchase of olive oil from Baetica and Africa, which it probably sold at either a subsidized price or an agreed stable price;[81] Aurelian is said to have designed a similar scheme for the state purchase and subsidized sale of Italian wine.[82] Urbanization is also a key factor, which can be to some extent consciously encouraged or discouraged, in that complex symbiotic relationship in which urban communities both absorb the resources of the agricultural economy and allow its value to be realized through institutions such as markets.

---

[80] More on this in Wilson and Bowman (forthcoming).
[81] Wilson (2008: 187–8). Officials: *CIL* II.1180 = *ILS* 1403; *CIL* XIV.20 = *ILS* 372 (AD 175); *CIL* VI.34001 = *ILS* 9022
[82] *HA, Aurelian* 48.

CONCLUSION

If the volume can offer neither a complete picture of the agricultural economy of the Roman empire, nor a macroeconomic model, what claims can it make for having 'quantified' the agricultural economy? A number of thematic issues are addressed through these regionally specific studies that have more general significance. As the comparison between Wadi Faynan and the Egyptian deserts shows, there are a number of potentially quantifiable ways in which the agricultural economy may respond to industrial development, while de Vos and Goodchild suggest possible responses to commercial and urban development. Patterns of control and tenure of land evolve at different paces and in different ways, but the configuration of dispersed landholding and exploitation through the villa system (in the west) or tenancy-based farming, with the admixture of free and slave labour, does make sense as a generaliza-tion, within which we can consider such issues as the balance of quantities of state and private land. Whether or not we accept the applicability of a 'taxes-and-trade model' for Egypt or anywhere else, we hope to have offered some material for analysis of levels of production, consumption, and surpluses, at least for a limited range of produce (almost exclusively the Mediterranean triad). As is now obvious, it makes sense to consider the agricultural economy in terms of capital investment and yield, and the underlying emphasis on the application of technology, particularly hydraulic and irrigation technology, is examined in detail in the contribution by Malouta and Wilson and recurs in several other chapters. As Marzano shows, we can also begin to trace trends in the investment of capital-intensive crop-processing facilities such as oil and wine presses, reflecting an agricultural system that commercialized large surpluses of cash crops; in several of the western Mediterranean provinces these trends peak in the second century AD, but the analysis also suggests variations in timing and scale between regions. Our approach is explicitly driven by the belief that it is only on the basis of a (large) number of such studies, many of which already exist, with a range of sound methodologies appropriate to the particular topic and body of data, that we can make progress towards a better understanding of the character of the agricultural economy of the Roman Mediterranean. Such an understanding will or should enable us to match the results of these studies against the existing and future macroeconomic models and test the goodness of fit. This will inevitably lead us to questions about level of performance over time and space, which cannot be isolated from the demographic issues, including the supposed Malthusian constraints addressed in an earlier volume[83] and discussed by Malouta and Wilson in this volume. Already it is clear, from the analysis of patterns of

---

[83] Bowman and Wilson (2011).

investment in large-scale production, that agricultural production was in some regions on a very different scale from anything known in pre-Roman times, or that was to be seen again after the fifth century until the early modern period. Looking forward, we will want to consider in greater detail the distribution of the wealth generated by the agricultural surpluses, implying (as we would surely want to do) that the value of the output at many or most times and places exceeded the basic subsistence needs of the empire's population. Here, as elsewhere, the tension generated by competition for control of the wealth and the resources between the state, civic community, and the private individual will be a key issue, and one in which one can undeniably identify changes in the balance over time.

It is perhaps otiose to repeat that the causes and effects of these processes have different manifestations in different times and places, and there is surely bound to be to some degree a smoothing effect that offsets decline in one place or sector by growth in another. There are many obvious individual instances of this phenomenon, as the balance of production, imports, and exports in wheat, oil and wine (to name only the staple foodstuffs) shifts between Italy, Spain, Gaul, North Africa, Egypt, and the eastern provinces. It is at this level, we believe, that the quantification of the performance of the agricultural economy is most usefully considered.

REFERENCES

Akerraz, A., and Lenoir, M. (1981–2). 'Les huileries de Volubilis', *BAM* 14: 69–120.

Akerraz, A., and Lenoir, M. (1987). 'Note sur les huileries du quartier nord-est de Volubilis', in A. Mastino (ed.), *L'Africa Romana 4. Atti del IV convegno di studio, Sassari, 12–14 dicembre 1986*, vol. 2. Sassari: 459–60.

Alcock, S. E. (2007). 'The Eastern Mediterranean', in Scheidel, Morris, and Saller (2007), 671–97.

Bagnall, R. S. (1992). 'Landholding in late Roman Egypt: The Distribution of Wealth', *JRS* 82: 128–49.

Banaji, J. (2002). *Agrarian Change in Late Antiquity: Gold, Labour, and Aristocratic Dominance.* Oxford.

Bang, P. F. (2006). 'Imperial Bazaar: Towards a Comparative Understanding of Markets in the Roman Empire', in P. F. Bang *et al.* (2006), 51–88.

Bang, P. F. (2008). *The Roman Bazaar.* Cambridge.

Bang, P. F., Ikeguchi, M., and Ziche, H. G. (2006) (eds). *Ancient Economies, Modern Methodologies: Archaeology, Comparative History, Models and Institutions.* Bari.

Beltrán Lloris, F. (2006). 'An Irrigation Decree from Roman Spain: The *Lex Rivi Hiberiensis*', *JRS* 96: 147–97.

Blouin, K. (forthcoming). *Triangular Landscape: Environment, Society, and the State in the Nile Delta under Roman Rule* (Oxford Studies on the Roman Economy). Oxford.

Bowman, A. K. (1985). 'Landholding in the Hermopolite Nome in the Fourth Century AD', *JRS* 75: 137–63.

Bowman, A. K., and Wilson, A. I. (2009) (eds). *Quantifying the Roman Economy: Methods and Problems* (Oxford Studies on the Roman Economy 1). Oxford.

Bowman, A. K., and Wilson, A. I. (2011) (eds). *Settlement, Urbanization, and Population* (Oxford Studies on the Roman Economy 2). Oxford.

Brun, J.-P. (2003a). 'Les pressoirs à vin d'Afrique et de Maurétanie à l'époque romaine', *Africa. Fouilles, monuments et collections archéologiques en Tunisie*, 1: 7–30.

Brun, J.-P. (2003b). *Le vin et l'huile dans la Méditerranée antique: Viticulture, oléiculture et procédés de fabrication*. Paris.

Brun, J.-P. (2004). *Archéologie du vin et de l'huile dans l'Empire romain*. Paris.

Christoflé, M. (1930). *Essai de restitution d'un moulin à huile de l'époque romaine à Madaure (Constantine)*. Algiers.

Cowper, H. S. (1897). *The Hill of the Graces: A Record of Investigation among the Trilithons and Megalithic Sites of Tripoli*. London.

Cuvigny, H. (2003) (ed.). *La route de Myos Hormos: L'armée romaine dans le désert oriental d'Égypte*. Le Caire.

De Sena, E. C. (2005). 'An Assessment of Wine and Oil Production in Rome's Hinterland: Ceramic, Literary, Art Historical and Modern Evidence', in B. Santillo Frizell and A. Klynne (eds). *Roman Villas around the* Urbs: *Interaction with Landscape and Environment. Proceedings of a Conference Held at the Swedish Institute in Rome, September 17–18 2004*. Rome, 135–49.

De Simone, G. F. (forthcoming). 'The Dark Side of Vesuvius: Landscape Changes and the Roman Economy', D.Phil. thesis, University of Oxford.

Du Coudray la Blanchère, R. M. (1895). *L'aménagement de l'eau et l'installation rurale dans l'Afrique ancienne* (= *Nouvelles archives des missions scientifiques*, 7, 1897: 1–109). Paris.

Dossey, L. (2010). *Peasant and Empire in Christian North Africa*. Berkeley and Los Angeles.

Duncan-Jones, R. P. (1994). *Money and Government in the Roman Empire*. Cambridge.

Durand, A., and Leveau, P. (2004). 'Farming in Mediterranean France and Rural Settlement in the Late Roman and Early Medieval Periods: The Contribution from Archaeology and Environmental Sciences in the Last Twenty Years (1980–2000)', in M. Barceló and F. Sigaut (eds), *The Making of Feudal Agricultures?* Leiden, 177–254.

Erdkamp, P. (2005). *The Grain Market in the Roman Empire: A Social Political and Economic Study*. Cambridge.

Foxhall, L. (1990). 'The Dependent Tenant: Land Leasing and Labour in Italy and Greece', *JRS* 80: 97–114

Frank, T. (1933–40). *Economic Survey of Ancient Rome*, I–V. Baltimore.

Frayn, J. M. (1979). *Subsistence Farming in Roman Italy*. Fontwell.

Glicksman, K. (2009). 'The Economy of Roman Dalmatia'. D.Phil. thesis, University of Oxford.

Goldsmith, R. W. (1984). 'An Estimate of the Size and Structure of the National Product of the Early Roman Empire', *Review of Income and Wealth*, 30: 263–88.

Hitchner, R. B. (1988). 'The Kasserine Archaeological Survey, 1982–1986', *AntAfr* 24: 7–41.

Hitchner, R. B. (1993). 'Olive Production and the Roman Economy: The Case for Intensive Growth in the Roman Empire', in M.-C. Amouretti and J.-P. Brun (eds), *La production du vin et de l'huile en Méditerranée* (Bulletin de Correspondance Hellénique, Suppl. 26). Athens, 499–508.

Hitchner, R. B. (1995). 'Historical Text and Archaeological Context in Roman North Africa: The Albertini Tablets and the Kasserine Survey', in D. B. Small (ed.), *Methods in the Mediterranean. Historical and Archaeological Views on Texts and Archaeology.* Leiden, 124–42.

Hitchner, R. B. (2012). 'Roads, Integration, Connectivity and Economic Performance in the Roman Empire', in S. E. Alcock, J. Bodel, and R. J. A. Talbert (eds), *Highways, Byways and Road Systems in the Pre-Modern World.* Malden, MA, and Oxford, 222–33.

Hobson, M. (2012). 'The African Boom? Evaluating Economic Growth in the Roman Province of Africa Proconsularis'. Ph.D. thesis, University of Leicester.

Hopkins, K. (1980). 'Taxes and Trade in the Roman Empire (200 BC–AD 400)', *JRS* 70: 101–25.

Hopkins, K. (1983). 'Models, Ships and Staples', in P. Garnsey and C. R. Whittaker (eds), *Trade and Famine in Classical Antiquity* (PCPS Suppl. 8). Cambridge, 84–109.

Hopkins, K. (2002). 'Rome, Taxes, Rents and Trade', in W. Scheidel and S. Von Reden (eds), *The Ancient Economy* (Edinburgh Readings on the Ancient World). Edinburgh, 190–230.

Horden, P., and Purcell, N. (2000). *The Corrupting Sea: A Study in Mediterranean History.* Oxford.

Jones, A. H. M. (1974). *The Roman Economy.* Oxford.

Jongman, W. (1988). *Economy and Society of Pompeii.* Amsterdam.

Kehoe, D. P. (1988). *The Economics of Agriculture on Imperial Estates in Roman North Africa* (Hypomnemata 89). Göttingen.

Kehoe, D. (2007). 'The Early Roman Empire: Production', in Scheidel, Morris, and Saller (2007), 543–69.

Kenrick, P. (2009). *Libya Archaeological Guides: Tripolitania.* London.

King, A. (1999). 'Diet in the Roman World: A Regional Inter-Site Comparison of the Mammal Bones', *JRA* 12: 168–202.

Kron, G. (2000). 'Roman Ley-Farming', *JRA* 13: 277–87.

Leveau, P. (2007). 'The Western Provinces', in Scheidel, Morris, and Saller (2007), 651–70.

Lo Cascio, E. (2007). 'The Early Roman Empire: The State and the Economy', in Scheidel, Morris, and Saller (2007), 619–47.

Mackensen, M. (1993). *Die spätantiken Sigillata- und Lamptöpfereien von El Mahrine (Nord Tunesien). Studien zur nordafrikanischen Feinkeramik des 4. bis 7. Jahrhunderts,* 1. Munich.

Mackensen, M. (1998). 'New Evidence for Central Tunisian Red Slip Ware with stamped Decoration (ARS, style D)', *JRA* 11: 355–70.

MacMullen, R. (1970). 'Market Days in the Roman Empire', *Phoenix* 24.4: 333–41.

Maddison, A. (2007). *Contours of the World Economy 1–2030: Essays in Macro-Economic History*. Oxford.

Manning, J. G., and Morris, I. (2005). *The Ancient Economy: Evidence and Models*. Stanford.

Marzano, A., and Brizzi, G. (2009). 'Costly Display or Economic Investment? A Quantitative Approach to the Study of Roman Marine Aquaculture', *JRA* 22: 215–30.

Mattingly, D. J. (1985). 'Olive Oil Production in Roman Tripolitania', in D. J. Buck and D. J. Mattingly (eds), *Town and Country in Roman Tripolitania: Papers in Honour of Olwen Hackett* (BAR International Series 274). Oxford, 27–46.

Mattingly, D. J. (1988a). 'Megalithic Madness and Measurement: Or how many Olives could an Olive Press Press?', *OJA* 7.2: 177–95.

Mattingly, D. J. (1988b). 'Oil for Export? A Comparison of Libyan, Spanish and Tunisian Olive Oil Production in the Roman Empire', *JRA* 1: 33–56.

Mattingly, D. J. (1988c). 'Olea Mediterranea?', *JRA* 1: 153–61.

Mattingly, D. J. (1988d), 'The Olive Boom. Oil Surpluses, Wealth and Power in Roman Tripolitania', *LibStud* 19: 21–41.

Mattingly, D. J. (1994). 'Regional Variation in Roman Oleoculture: Some Problems of Comparability', in J. Carlsen, P. Ørsted, and J. E. Skydsgaard (eds), *Landuse in the Roman Empire* (ARID Suppl. 22). Rome, 91–106.

Mattingly, D. J. (1996). 'Olive Presses in Roman Africa: Technical Evolution or Stagnation?', in M. Khanoussi, P. Ruggeri, and C. Vismara (eds), *L'Africa Romana: Atti del XI convegno di studio, Cartagine, 15–18 dicembre 1994* 2. Ozieri, 577–95.

Mattingly, D. J., and Hitchner, R. B. (1991). 'Ancient Agriculture. Fruits of Empire—The Production of Olive Oil in Roman Africa', *National Geographic Research and Exploration*, 7: 36–55.

Mattingly, D. J., and Hitchner, R. B. (1993). 'Technical Specifications for some North African Olive Presses of Roman Date', in M.-C. Amouretti and J.-P. Brun (eds), *La production du vin et de l'huile en Méditerranée* (Bulletin de Correspondance Hellénique, Suppl. 26). Athens and Paris, 439–62.

Merlin, A. (1906). 'Observations sur le texte du *senatus consultum Beguense*', *CRAI* 448–56.

Meunier, J. (1941). 'L'huilerie romaine de Kherbet-Agoub (Périgotville)', *Bulletin de la Société historique et géographique de Sétif*, 2: 35–55.

Moeller, W. O. (1976). *The Wool Trade of Ancient Pompeii*. Leiden.

Morel, J.-P. (2009). 'Entre agriculture et artisanat: Regards croisés sur l'économie de l'Italie tardo-républicaine', in J. Carlsen and E. Lo Cascio (eds), *Agricoltura e Scambi nell'Italia Tardo-repubblicana*. Bari, 63–90.

Moritz, L. A. (1958). *Grain Mills and Flour in Classical Antiquity*. Oxford.

Oates, D. (1953). 'The Tripolitanian Gebel: Settlement of the Roman Period around Gsar ed-Daun', *PBSR* 21: 81–117.

Panella, C., and Tchernia, A. (1994). 'Produits agricoles transportés en amphores: L'huile et surtout le vin', in *L'Italie d'Auguste à Dioclétien* (Collection de l'École française de Rome 198). Rome, 145–65.

Parker, A. J. (1992). *Ancient Shipwrecks of the Mediterranean and the Roman Provinces* (BAR International Series 580). Oxford.

Peacock, D. P. S. (1982). *Pottery in the Roman World: An Ethnoarchaeological Approach* (Longman Archaeology Series). London.

Peacock, D. P. S., Bejaoui, F., and Ben Lazreg, N. (1990). 'Roman Pottery Production in Central Tunisia', *JRA* 3: 59–84.

Pleket, H. W. (1993). 'Agriculture in the Roman Empire in Comparative Perspective', in H. Sancisi-Weerdenburg, R. J. Van der Spek, W. C. Teitler, and H. T. Wallinga (eds), *De agricultura: In memoriam Pieter Willem de Neeve (1945–1990)*. Amsterdam, 317–42.

Rathbone, D. W. (1991). *Economic Rationalism and Rural Society in Third-Century A.D. Egypt. The Heroninos Archive and the Appianus Estate*. Cambridge.

Rickman, G. (1971). *Roman Granaries and Store Buildings*. Cambridge.

Ruffing, K. (1999), *Weinbau im römischen Ägypten*. St Katharinen.

Sancisi-Weerdenburg, H., Van der Spek, R. J., Teitler, W. C., and Wallinga, H. T. (1993) (eds). *De agricultura: In memoriam Pieter Willem de Neeve (1945–1990)*. Amsterdam.

Scheidel (1994). 'Grain Cultivation in the Villa Economy', in J. Carlsen, P. Ørsted, and J. E. Skydsgaard (eds), *Landuse in the Roman Empire* (ARID Suppl. 22). Rome, 159–66.

Scheidel, W. (2007). 'A Model of Real Income Growth in Italy', *Historia* 56: 322–46.

Scheidel, W. (2009). 'In Search of Roman Economic Growth', *JRA* 22: 46–70.

Scheidel, W., and Friesen, S. J. (2009). 'The Size of the Economy and the Distribution of Income in the Roman Empire', *JRS* 99: 61–91.

Scheidel, W., Morris, I., and Saller, R. P. (2007) (eds). *The Cambridge Economic History of the Greco-Roman World*. Cambridge.

Schörle, K. (2008). 'The Roman Exploitation of the Eastern Desert of Egypt'. M.Phil. thesis, University of Oxford.

Schörle, K. (2011). 'From Harbour to Desert: An Integrated Interface on the Red Sea and its Impact on the Eastern Egyptian Desert', *Bolletino di Archeologia Online*, Special issue: *Roma 2008 – International Congress of Classical Archaeology: 'Meetings between Cultures in the Ancient Mediterranean'* <http://151.12.58.75/archeologia/bao_document/articoli/5_SCH%C3%96RLE.pdf> (accessed 23 Aug. 2012).

Shaw, B. D. (1981). 'Rural Markets in North Africa and the Political Economy of the Roman Empire', *AntAfr* 17: 37–83.

Shaw, B. D. (1982). 'Lamasba: An Ancient Irrigation Community', *AntAfr* 18: 61–103.

Spurr, M. S. (1986). *Arable Cultivation in Roman Italy* c. *200 B.C.–c. A.D. 100* (JRS Monograph 3). London.

Tchalenko, G. (1953–8). *Villages antiques de la Syrie du nord; le massif de Bélus à l'époque romaine*, 3 vols (Institut archéologique de Beyrouth, Bibliothèque archéologique et historique 1). Paris.

Tchernia, A. (1983). 'Italian Wine in Gaul at the End of the Republic', in P. Garnsey, K. Hopkins, and C. R. Whittaker (eds), *Trade in the Ancient Economy*. London, 87–104.

Tchernia, A. (1986). *Le vin de l'Italie romaine: Essai d'histoire économique d'après les amphores* (Bibliothèque de l'École française de Rome 261). Rome.

Tchernia, A. (2006). 'La crise de l'Italie impériale et la concurrence des provinces', *Cahiers du Centre de Recherches historiques*, 37: 137–56.

Temin, P. (2006). 'Estimating the GDP of the Early Roman Empire', in E. Lo Cascio (ed.), *Innovazione tecnica e progresso economico nel mondo romano* (Pragmateiai 10). Bari, 31–54.

Thonemann, P. (2007). 'Estates and the Land in Late Roman Asia Minor,' *Chiron* 37: 435–78.

Van Minnen, P. (2000). 'Agriculture and the "Taxes-and-Trade" Model in Roman Egypt', *ZPE* 133: 205–20.

Weber, M. (1924/1976). *The Agrarian Sociology of Ancient Civilisations*, trans. R. I. Frank (London), published in German as 'Agrärverhaltnisse im Altertum', in *Gesammelte Aufsätze zur Sozial- und Wirtschaftsgeschichte*. Tubingen.

White, K. D. (1970). *Roman Farming*. London.

Whittaker, C. R. (1980). 'Rural Labour in Three Roman Provinces', in P. Garnsey (ed.), *Non-Slave Labour in the Greco-Roman World* (PCPS, Suppl. 6). Cambridge, 73–92.

Wilson, A. I. (2002). 'Machines, Power and the Ancient Economy', *JRS* 92: 1–32.

Wilson, A. I. (2004). 'Cyrenaica and the Late Antique Economy', *AWE* 3.1: 143–54.

Wilson, A. I. (2006). 'Fishy Business: Roman Exploitation of Marine Resources', *JRA* 19.2: 525–37.

Wilson, A. I. (2008). 'Economy and Trade', in E. Bispham (ed.), *The Roman Era* (The Short Oxford History of Europe 2). Oxford, 170–202.

Wilson, A. I. (2009a). 'Approaches to Quantifying Roman Trade', in A. K. Bowman and A. I. Wilson (eds), *Quantifying the Roman Economy: Methods and Problems* (Oxford Studies on the Roman Economy 1). Oxford, 213–49.

Wilson, A. I. (2009b). 'Villas, Horticulture and Irrigation Infrastructure in the Tiber Valley', in F. Coarelli and H. Patterson (eds), *Mercator Placidissimus: The Tiber Valley in Antiquity. New Research in the Upper and Middle River Valley*. Rome, 731–68.

Wilson, A. I. (2011). 'Developments in Mediterranean Shipping and Maritime Trade from 200 BC to AD 1000', in D. Robinson and A. Wilson (eds), *Maritime Archaeology and Ancient Trade in the Mediterranean*. Oxford, 33–59.

Wilson, A. I., and Bowman, A. K. (forthcoming) (eds). *Trade, Commerce, and the State in the Roman World* (Oxford Studies on the Roman Economy). Oxford.

2

The State and Production in the Roman Agrarian Economy

Dennis Kehoe

INTRODUCTION

The possibilities for growth in the Roman economy depended on changes in productivity in agriculture, but these in turn were subject to the severe constraints imposed by population and technology.[1] But, if population and technology were the principal drivers of economic change, what importance should we ascribe to social, legal, and political institutions; should they be regarded as 'epiphenomenal'—that is, by-products of economic conditions shaped by larger forces?[2] In recent years, new theoretical models have provided a way to understand better the complex role in economic change played by institutions, including both formal institutions maintained by the state, such as property rights and courts, and informal ones, such as social values and even ideology.[3] From this perspective, institutions are evaluated for their efficiency, in the sense of facilitating economic exchange. To apply these considerations to the agricultural economy of the Roman empire, under the best of conditions, Roman institutions would have encouraged investment in irrigation technologies and more intensive ways of cultivating the land that would have raised productivity. In a second-best scenario, even without

---

[1] For general discussion of the link between economic growth and productivity in agriculture, see Johnson (2000). The importance of population and technology for economic growth is a major theme of the *Cambridge Economic History of the Greco-Roman World* (Scheidel, Morris, and Saller 2007); see especially Scheidel (2007).

[2] For this issue, see Field (1991).

[3] These methodologies include especially the New Institutional Economics, for an introduction to which see Mercuro and Medema (1997: 130–56); Klein (2000). For discussion on the application of NIE methodologies to the ancient world, see Frier and Kehoe (2007), and Kehoe (2007: ch. 1). For the role of ideology in shaping legal institutions, see Greif (2006: esp. 126, 190–1).

substantial technological change, legal institutions could affect the economy to the degree that they promoted property arrangements that made the best use possible of existing resources.

In this chapter, I would like to consider the Roman agrarian economy in the light of two areas of policy in which the state is likely to have had some significant effect. The first area is the role of the state as a landowner and economic actor, to use Elio Lo Cascio's formulation in his analysis of the state sector of the Roman economy in the *Cambridge Economic History of the Greco-Roman World*.[4] There can be no doubt that the state greatly affected the size and shape of the Roman economy. The state maintained direct control throughout the empire of a substantial network of lands and estates as well as other properties, including mines and quarries. These properties provided an important source of revenue, supplementing those achieved from direct taxes.[5] Imperial estates in Africa and various categories of state-owned land in Egypt furnished much of the grain distributed in Rome and later in Constantinople. In addition, the state's effort to supply the city of Rome and the armies played a significant role in the development of commerce in the Roman empire. Moreover, as Lo Cascio points out, the role of the state in the economy only increased over time, especially after the widespread confiscation of property following the victory of Septimius Severus over his rivals Clodius Albinus and Pescennius Niger.[6]

The second area I will examine is somewhat less clearly delineated, but it involves legal and administrative policies that the state adopted for various aspects of the rural economy, from the regulation of land tenure to the protection of small farmers against inroads by tax officials or even private creditors. The question here is whether the state developed its policies to accomplish any broad social agenda, and, if so, whether the policies accomplished their objectives in any meaningful way. One possibility is that Rome's legal institutions were developed with no greater purpose in mind other than to set as level a playing field as possible for all economic actors, without particular attention to the economic interests of any one group or any broader social policy. Even in this circumstance, the state's policies had consequences for the distribution of wealth, a crucial factor affecting the possibilities for economic growth, both in ancient Rome and today. Alternatively, if the state pursued particular goals, did they serve to promote the interests of the socially and privileged elite, even at the expense of the economy as a whole, or did they rather aim to protect the interests of the less advantaged?

---

[4] Lo Cascio (2007: esp. 642–6).
[5] On revenues from imperial estates, see Duncan-Jones (1994: 5–7); Lo Cascio (2007: 630–1, 642–6).
[6] Lo Cascio (2007: 645).

Admittedly, the study of the role of institutions does not always result in verifiable hypotheses, and this is particularly the case for ancient economies, given the problems with our evidence. Certainly it is difficult to prove that a particular disposition of property rights led to greater or less productivity in the economy, both today and in the ancient world. In spite of these shortcomings, the study of institutions is important because it allows us to analyse the incentives created by various property regimes and so to predict their likely significance for economic performance. At the very least, analysing the most important institutions affecting the agricultural productivity helps us to put studies of more specific aspects of the economy in a broader perspective. In what follows, I will argue that the Roman state's policies had complex and generally positive effects on the Roman economy. The policies it pursued in exploiting imperial properties were motivated by fiscal concerns, but they affected a substantial portion of the empire's agricultural resources, with consequences for how private agricultural property was exploited and its productivity as well. Rome's policies provided at least a modest check on the tendency towards an increasing stratification of wealth in the empire. At the same time, they created distortions in markets and diverted resources away from potentially productive uses. They also carried costs that resulted from the tendency of institutions to reinforce themselves, which made it prohibitively costly to change to more efficient property rights regimes.[7]

FISCAL POLICIES AND LAND TENURE

To begin, the fiscal policies of the state clearly had a notable effect on the agrarian economy. That the Roman economy expanded significantly during the Early Imperial period seems beyond dispute. The growth of the flourishing urban culture that was a hallmark of Roman rule would not have been possible without considerable expansion of agriculture and the transfer of wealth from the countryside to cities.[8] The expansion of urban markets promoted more intensive agriculture, which required substantial investment in irrigation and in an infrastructure to support the transport and marketing of agricultural products.[9] The fact that the major source of tax revenues for Rome came from agriculture is hardly surprising, since agriculture dominated the economy and land was a tangible form of wealth that could most readily be taxed.

---

[7] On this point, see Hodgson (1999: 119–219), and also Greif (2006: 124–52). For the concept of 'institutional path dependence', see also North (1990).

[8] For discussion of the concept of the 'consumer city', see especially Erdkamp (2001).

[9] Wilson (2002); Morley (2007).

The important question concerns the economic consequences for agriculture of the Roman government's tax policies.

One approach is to start from the premise that Rome exacted revenues from the provinces primarily to secure the privileges of a ruling elite at the expense of society at large. This would make Rome a 'predatory state', as discussed by Yoram Barzel.[10] With a short time horizon, the state would seek to exact as many resources as possible without much regard as to the consequences. But a more compelling model is that of a 'stationary' predator state, one that raises funds to benefit a privileged elite on a much longer time horizon, as discussed by the Princeton economist Avinash Dixit.[11] As Dixit suggests, the state faces the difficulty of finding economic assets that it can tax. The most talented and productive people will have a tendency to hide their assets, but the state will want to give them incentives not to do so, say by keeping their tax rates moderate and otherwise investing them in the system by offering them privileges. The result is that taxes are often collected at the expense of the less well-off, and Dixit suggests that predatory states tend to be very harsh towards the poor.

Dixit's description of the state as a 'stationary predator' corresponds to what many scholars have implicitly attributed to Rome, and to other ancient states as well, in that it had no long-term economic policy other than to safeguard its revenues and protect the interests of the politically and socially privileged elite on whom Rome relied to maintain order and loyalty throughout the provinces. Indeed, Peter Bang sees the Roman empire as a 'tributary' state that extracted revenues from the provinces to support an elite ruling class.[12] In a most radical view of this aspect of the Roman empire, Roman policies were largely political constructs that imposed taxes on the most vulnerable producers and increasingly shielded well-connected groups from paying them. From this standpoint, the state's policy of taxing of agricultural assets over other forms of wealth or income had potentially harmful consequences for agriculture. In late antique Egypt, to take an extreme example, Jairus Banaji describes how aristocratic houses controlled the collection of taxes to amass great stores of gold, which they then reinvested in agriculture, particularly viticulture, to serve flourishing urban markets in Alexandria and overseas.[13] Since these gold reserves were acquired at the expense of agricultural production, they removed assets from the agrarian economy, and the fact that the Apiones and other great houses reinvested some of them in agriculture only diminished somewhat the loss to agricultural production that late antique tax policies fostered. In the early empire, landowners also stored wealth in the form of gold, which

---

[10] See Barzel (1989, 2002).   [11] Dixit (2004: 13–43).
[12] Bang (2008).   [13] See Banaji (2001: esp. 134–89).

means that it was essentially lost to the economy.[14] The late-classical jurist Ulpian recognized the dangers of removing money from the economy, albeit from a quite different perspective, when he stated that guardians administering the property of wards were not to let their wards' money sit idle, but were to use it to purchase land when possible, or otherwise to invest in loans (Ulp. *dig.* 26.7.3.2; *dig.* 26.7.5 pr.; cf. *dig.* 27.4.3.4).[15] The state could compensate for this hypothetical transfer of wealth away from agriculture into other forms of investment that were largely immune from taxation, but only to a limited degree. It imposed a number of indirect taxes, in particular customs taxes and some taxes on trades, but the burden of taxation was distributed unevenly across the economy.

The notion of the predatory state, however, does not provide a satisfactory explanation for Rome's fiscal policies, even if its primary concern was to safeguard sources of stable revenues. The Roman administration was concerned to make the assessment of taxes reasonably consistent and to eliminate the worst abuses that had plagued tax collection under the Republic. The trend towards replacing tax farmers with local tax collectors performing compulsory public services surely offered greater protection for producers, and the establishment of a regular census schedule would have made the assessment of taxes within a given locality more consistent.[16] This is not to say that the Roman state ever achieved a uniform system of assessing taxes under the Principate; it attempted to create a theoretically more uniform system only in late antiquity with the system of assessing tax liability on the basis of *iuga* and *capita*.[17]

Although it is difficult to be certain on this point, tax rates on private agricultural land were probably modest in the early Roman empire, at least in comparison with other pre-industrial economies, generally in the range of about 10 per cent; at least they do not seem to have increased over time.[18] Much of our evidence for tax rates on agricultural land comes from Egypt, where the basic agricultural tax, the *artabia*, was assessed at one artab of wheat or a little bit more per aroura on private grain land, a figure that represents perhaps 10 per cent of an expected yield, and possibly substantially less.[19] There were additional taxes imposed on agricultural land, including the

---

[14] For the tendency of upper-class Romans to accumulate stores of wealth in gold, see Jongman (2003).

[15] For discussion of the tutor's obligations in investing the funds belonging to pupils, see Kehoe (1997: 22–76).

[16] See Lo Cascio (2007: 631–2).

[17] For the fundamentals of the late-antique tax system, see Jones (1964: i. 411–69), and Carrié (1993a, 1993b). For what *iuga* signified for the land tax, see Duncan-Jones (1990: 200–9).

[18] Cf. Duncan-Jones (1994: 57–9).

[19] For tax rates on Egyptian land, see Rathbone (2007: 716); Bowman, Chapter 7, this volume; see also Duncan-Jones (1994: 47–59), who sees taxes as somewhat higher.

naubion, to cover the costs of maintaining communal irrigation facilities. Lands devoted to viticulture or olive culture, which were more productive in terms of revenue for each unit of land, were taxed at a higher rate.

It also seems unlikely that the state ever collected anything close to what it was nominally owed. To cite one example, Aurelius Isidorus, a modest landowner and liturgist from Karanis in the Fayum in the late third and early fourth centuries, claimed to pay taxes at various times on 80 or 140 arouras of land, but to cultivate only a fraction of this land, 8 or 10 arouras (*P. Cair. Isid.* 68 (309–10), 69 (310), 78 (324), *P. Mert.* II. 92 (324)).[20] Admittedly, early fourth-century Karanis may not be the best example to illustrate normal conditions, since it was experiencing all sorts of difficulties because of the advancing desert. Still, no one seems to have tried to make Isidorus pay taxes for the land that he owned but did not cultivate, and he was free to supplement his income by renting in land from other landowners. The case of Aurelius Isidorus may represent an extreme of the discrepancy between the taxes that were nominally owed and actually collected, but it does show that the state's ability to collect taxes was limited. Throughout the period of the Principate, the Roman administration in Egypt had to confront the difficulty of compelling people to remain in their village of origin to perform their tax obligations.[21] One part of this solution was the occasional granting of amnesties to lure farmers back to their home villages. The worst effects of imperfect tax collection were mitigated to some extent by the practice of imposing the duty to collect taxes collectively, so that liturgists and, in the third century, town councils bore much of the financial responsibility for this obligation.[22]

To turn now to the economic consequences of the state's control over land, this provided some check to the accumulation of land in private hands and thereby fostered the continuing existence of a class of cultivators independent from the domination by large landowners. The effects of this policy can be readily seen in Egypt, where the state controlled a great deal of land in various classifications, at least until the third century. The portion of state-owned land, comprising public land in Egypt, or *ge demosia*, royal land, or *ge basilike*, and ousiac land, or *ge ousiake* (land that had once been assigned to close associates of the Julio-Claudian court but passed into direct control of the imperial government after the fall of the Julio-Claudian dynasty), varied considerably from one region to another, and it was probably highest in the Fayum, where the Ptolemies' efforts to drain marshland and create new farmland resulted in a substantial addition to the land under the direct control of the crown.[23] Much of this land became state land under Roman rule. The cultivators of this

[20] For discussion of Isidorus' situation, see Kehoe (1992: 158–65).
[21] On *anachoresis*, see Rupprecht (1994: 149); Jördens (2009: 313–15).
[22] On this point, see especially Goffart (1974).
[23] Manning (2007: 447–8); Monson (2012).

land enjoyed generally favourable conditions. Both under the Ptolemies and under the Romans the condition of being a state cultivator offered some status, as petitioners often refer to this to emphasize their important contribution to state revenues.[24] Moreover, tenure on public land in Egypt was secure, and could even be passed on from one generation to the next, as Jane Rowlandson has shown in her analysis of landowning in the Oxyrhynchite Nome.[25] The availability of public land in Egypt tended to promote a more egalitarian distribution of land than might have been the case in other parts of the Roman empire. For example, in his recent analysis of landownership in the Fayum during the second century, Michael Sharp shows that the village of Theadelphia had a large number of public tenants and small landowners, two groups that often overlapped.[26] The continuing importance of public land, however, did not completely keep external landowners away, and some of these developed vineyards in the village territory. In the second century there were private estate owners in Egypt who accumulated extensive properties, but it was mainly in the early third century that a class of elite landowners emerged comparable to the wealthiest classes in other urbanized areas of the empire. The development of such a class made possible the administrative reform that accorded municipal status to nome metropoleis.[27]

We can appreciate the distributional consequences of the state's role as an economic actor by considering land tenure on imperial estates in Africa, as documented in a series of famous inscriptions that record lease regulations as well as conflicts between the people involved in their cultivation.[28] To accomplish a broad goal of securing a stable source of revenues, the Roman administration established two groups of people with varying property rights to the land. The cultivators, or *coloni*, were sharecroppers. Their lease terms were based on a *lex Manciana*, in all likelihood an originally private lease arrangement that the Roman government adapted for its uses as the private land on which it applied passed into imperial control. Beginning at least by the reign of Trajan, the Roman government encouraged *coloni* to bring new lands under cultivation by extending the favourable terms of tenure associated with the *lex Manciana*. Under Hadrian, the Roman administration established a more systematic method of encouraging the cultivation of unused lands on imperial estates by offering these privileges in the *lex Hadriana de rudibus agris*, 'the Hadrianic law concerning unused lands'. This regulation, which almost certainly applied only to land on imperial estates, offered perpetual leaseholds to *coloni* who brought unused lands under cultivation, particularly with olives

---

[24] Manning (2007: 452–3).   [25] Rowlandson (1996: 70–101).   [26] Sharp (1999).
[27] Rathbone (1991; 2007: 703). For the administration of Egypt, see Bowman and Rathbone (1992).
[28] This discussion is based on Kehoe (1988; 2007: 53–91). See also de Vos, Chapter 6, this volume.

and vines. The revenues that the administration derived from the North African estates consisted of foodstuffs, primarily wheat, olive oil, wine, and figs, and, to enforce the obligation of the *coloni* to pay their rent in full, the administration set over them short-term lessees, or *conductores*. The *conductores* bid for the right to collect the rent from the *coloni*, and they also had the right to use the labour and draft animals of the *coloni* to cultivate certain lands within imperial estates.

The state's revenues depended on a dynamic tension between the *coloni* and the *conductores*. The *coloni* were offered incentives to invest in their land, and their production provided the revenues on which the administration depended, but the *conductores* had every incentive to focus on a short-term horizon and squeeze as much as they could out of the *coloni*. The administration's main role was to serve as a referee in this process, making sure that the efforts of the *conductores* to capture revenues from the *coloni* did not compromise the continued ability of that group to cultivate their land productively.

The most significant aspect of this system of land tenure for the distribution of wealth is the incentives that the imperial administration offered to *coloni* to invest in the long-term cultivation of their land. Cultivating vines and olives involved a commitment to the land, and to encourage *coloni* to make the necessary investment the Roman administration offered them perpetual leaseholds as well as rent-free seasons for the period in which newly planted vines, olive trees, and fruit trees would not produce much of a harvest. This method of promoting long-term investment came with some costs, since it provided little opportunity for cooperative bargaining between the *coloni* and the *conductores*—for example, over sharing the expenses involved in installing new plantations or maintaining or upgrading pressing installations. However, it apparently did accomplish reasonably well the goal of assuring the Fiscus stable revenues. At least the imperial administration did not abandon it, since it offered the incentives first formulated under the auspices of the *lex Hadriana de rudibus agris* in at least several locations and continued to do so at least until the reign of Septimius Severus.[29] Moreover, the perpetual sharecropping arrangement represented by the *lex Manciana* became widespread in North Africa. It is documented under the reign of Constantine (*CJ* 11.63, AD 319), and it even survived the collapse of Roman rule in North Africa, as is indicated by the sales of lands with *culturae Mancianae* in the Albertini Tablets during the Vandal period.[30]

The Roman administration's policies in managing imperial estates imposed significant costs on society. For one, a large portion of the crops comprising

---

[29] Three copies of the document from imperial copies applying the *lex Hadriana* are known: see de Vos (2001, and Chapter 6, this volume).

[30] Weßel (2003).

the rents was taken from the province to support the food distribution programmes in Rome. They supported a public good, but not one that benefited the producers of the food in any particular way. The revenues that the Fiscus collected represented a loss to the rural economy, even more so than wealth transferred from rural estates to North African cities by private land-owners, since, in the latter case at least, wealth produced in the cities did lead to some exchange with the surrounding countryside. Moreover, the Roman state captured a larger share of the surplus from imperial estates than it did from private land, where the tax rates were substantially lower than the one-third share of most crops that the *coloni* paid. But a larger issue is that, in protecting the tenure rights of imperial tenants against any challenge, the Roman government was reserving the resources of these farmers for its own uses, thereby depriving local towns of the benefits that might result from their production. The Roman government followed this policy consistently. For instance, in Asia Minor, a series of inscriptions from the early third century records conflicts between tenants on imperial properties and the authorities of nearby towns.[31] The conflicts centred around competition for the resources of the imperial tenants. Of course the imperial government valued such tenants because they provided revenues to the state, whereas towns saw the same tenants as forming part of the pool they could draw on for taxes and liturgical services.

The continuing attention of the Roman legal authorities suggests how contentious this issue was, since it affected the most important but conflicting interests of the imperial and local governments. The emperors Marcus Aurelius and Lucius Verus had ruled that imperial tenants would perform civic liturgies if they could do so without compromising their obligations to the Fiscus (*sine damno fisci*, Pap. Iust. *dig.* 50.1.38.1), whereas in the third century the jurist Callistratus argued that imperial tenants should be exempt from such obligations, since the Fiscus had a prior claim on their services (*dig.* 50.6.6.11). The conflict between towns and the imperial government for the services of farmers with resources continued into the later empire. Thus Constantine ruled that farmers registered for fiscal purposes on imperial property could not be required to perform civic liturgies (*CJ* 11.68.1, AD 325). The same emperor had somewhat earlier tried to prohibit imperial tenants from entering into private business arrangements (*CJ* 11.68.2, AD 319). In all probability, how-ever, it was impossible to enforce such rules strictly, because the lines between imperial tenants and landowners or tenants on private land were often blurred. Complicating the problem was the incentive for private landowners who otherwise might be tapped for liturgies to seek to avoid this service by claiming the status of imperial tenants. The emperor Constantius II tried to

---

[31] Hauken (1998); Kehoe (2007: 79–88).

achieve a workable compromise by ruling that imperial tenants who owned more than twenty-five *iugera* (*c.* six ha) of private land could be required to perform liturgies (*CTh* 12.1.33, AD 342). To return to the third-century petitions, the consistent response of the imperial administration was to uphold the tenure rights of imperial tenants. This meant, in effect, that the state claimed its rights to the services and revenues of these tenants at the expense of neighbouring towns.

The state's policy of using perpetual leaseholds to control the resources of *coloni* did have significant distributional consequences. For one, it supported the continued viability of an independent class of farmers who had considerable resources of their own. Even though the exaction of revenues by the imperial administration removed resources that otherwise might have been used in nearby towns, the terms of tenure accorded the *coloni* left some wealth in the countryside that otherwise would have been siphoned off to towns as rents. It seems likely that the *coloni* could typically expect to produce some surplus over and above the rent that they paid to the Fiscus, since their terms of tenure had to be attractive enough to induce them to invest continually in the productivity of their land. But the attractive terms of tenure that the state offered on imperial estates complicated matters for private landowners. There, landowners had to offer terms of tenure that would be, if not identical, at least competitive with what the imperial administration offered. Certainly some imperial tenants were aware of the possibility of competition for their services; in the third-century petition from Aga Bey in ancient Lydia, the imperial tenants complaining about the inroads against them made by imperial tax officials and representatives from a nearby town threatened to abandon their ancestral homes on the estate. The message that they wished to transmit to the Roman government was that, if it was unwilling to offer them protection, they would seek it with private landowners.[32]

The overall effect of the Fiscus' policy, then, would be to reduce the share of the surplus that private landowners controlled on their estates, and thereby to increase the share over which the actual cultivators disposed. It is plausible to see tenure systems on private estates comparable to the terms on imperial estates as a key factor in the development of a profitable olive culture in North Africa, as David Mattingly and Bruce Hitchner suggest.[33] If the spread of olive culture under these conditions represented an important source of wealth for the province's elite, it also produced some wealth for the tenants involved. The tenants could market some of the surplus they produced, and it seems likely that the wealth they gained from doing so contributed to the development of rural industries, most notably the ceramic industry.[34] These industries

[32] Hauken (1998: 35–57).
[33] Mattingly and Hitchner (1995: 195).
[34] Whittaker (1990).

provided a further source of revenue for the rural economy through exchange with urban markets. The same broad principle applies in Egypt, where villages provided the location for many small industries, such as weaving, which employed numerous people and provided a source of income to supplement agriculture.

ROMAN LEGAL POLICY AND PRIVATE LAND TENURE

Imperial estates did not operate independently from the private economy, and, in responding to legal disputes connected with the private economy, the Roman administration applied some of the principles that it saw as advantageous in promoting productivity on its own properties. Thus, if the Roman government encouraged investment by offering its *coloni* security of tenure, it also recognized the value of the continuing presence of productive tenants in private lease arrangements. This recognition led the Roman legal authorities to exercise some flexibility in interpreting lease arrangements as it responded to petitions involving farm tenancy. One important tendency of the office of the *a libellis*, which had the task to respond to petitions, was to interpret in terms of Roman law tenure arrangements that might in origin be based on local custom, and thus quite foreign to Roman law. The legal issues that the government confronted in these petitions, as I have discussed in other contexts, chiefly involved the tenant's security of tenure and allocating the costs of the very high degree of risk in Mediterranean agriculture.[35] The state's capacity to enact policies affecting private tenure arrangements was limited, but in responding to petitions the Roman legal authorities did their best to promote bargaining between landowners and tenants that would help to maintain productive tenure arrangements. The legal authorities did this by carefully defining the rights and obligations of both parties when landowners went beyond what was strictly required in a classical Roman lease in offering tenants security of tenure or in granting remissions for rent in the event of catastrophic harvests. The legal solution to the tenant's inability to pay the rent was not to terminate the lease (as it is in later civilian systems), but to define the rights and obligations of the two parties precisely so as to establish a legal basis for further negotiation.

To some extent, the Roman legal authorities were making an effort to have the law keep pace with social practice, since many private tenure arrangements involved tenants in open-ended leases that would not be recognizable in terms of classical Roman lease law. We can see the Roman government's concern

---

[35] Kehoe (1997: 221–34; 2007: 109–19).

with the legal complications from such arrangements in several imperial constitutions. In one, the emperors Valerian and Gallienus ruled that, in tacitly renewed leases, landowners were not allowed to raise the rent (*CJ* 4.65.16, AD 260). This constitution is of interest because the tacit renewal of the lease, which involved the tenant staying on the land and cultivating under the same terms as obtained previously as long as the landowner did not object, provided a legal principle to describe in conventional Roman terms long-term tenure arrangements that in origin were foreign to Roman law. Later, the emperor Constantine established that customary rents had the force of law, and he also provided tenants with a legal remedy against landowners who unlawfully raised their rents (*CJ* 11.50.1, AD 325).

This is not to say that the Roman government did not pursue policies that were detrimental to the interests of small farmers. One such policy was the series of currency reforms that emerged from the inflation of the late third century. As Andrea Giardina argues, the imperial government in the third century sought to protect the 'purchasing power' of the currency used across Roman society.[36] But the emperor Constantine gave up on this policy when he established the gold *solidus* as the basic unit of currency and allowed copper coinage to decline in value in relationship to it. This reform protected the wealth of people rich enough to hold stocks of gold, but it led to a rapid drop in the value of the coinage that the lower classes used to make their purchases. One long-term effect of the changeover to gold can be traced in Egypt, where, as we have seen, Jairus Banaji shows that wealthy landowners were able to use the gold they had accumulated to build up large estates.[37]

Certainly another policy that has to be considered in this light is the binding of *coloni* to their land, beginning in the fourth century. This policy was largely the product of fiscal concerns: the Roman state, in the face of military pressure on the frontiers, attached ever greater urgency to securing stable long-term revenues, and its twofold solution was to allow greater responsibility for collecting taxes to devolve upon large landowners, but at the same time making sure that such landowners would continue to have the capacity to pay taxes by binding their workforce to the land.[38] To maintain tax revenues, the imperial government had bound farmers to their *origo* or *idia*, their village of origin, where they were expected to remain and continue to cultivate the land. In the fourth century, the imperial government began to define the estate on which a farmer cultivated his land as the *origo* if the farmer was not already registered in the tax rolls as a landowner in his own right. This policy did not create a new class of farmers, but instead built upon existing land-tenure arrangements. However, as Giardina discusses, the legislation that the imperial

---

[36] Giardina (2007: 760).   [37] Banaji (2001).

[38] I discuss the process of binding of *coloni* in Kehoe (2007: 163–73, with further bibliography).

government issued over the course of the fourth century, which equated *coloni* with slaves, suggested that bound farmers were subject to new forms of oppression that surely diminished their economic power.[39] These develop-ments, however, do not mean that there was an inevitable accumulation of land by the very wealthiest of landowners at the expense of more modest landowners and tenants. Thus, in their analysis of census documents from fourth-century Magnesia in the Maeander valley in Asia Minor, both Peter Thonemann and Kyle Harper argue that several large landowners, including a senator and several prominent decurions, owned about half of the land, with the rest divided among a number of more modest landowners.[40] Indeed, in a recent paper, Harper argues against the common assumption that the fortunes of the largest landowners in late antiquity were on a scale different from that under the Principate.[41]

In other areas of the law, the Roman government's efforts to protect its interests in securing revenues created distortions that undermined incentives for investment. Take rural credit.[42] For example, in the fourth century, the government imposed restrictions on creditors providing loans to farmers, as documented in a constitution attributed to Constantine (*CTh* 2.30.1; *CJ* 8.16.7, AD 315).[43] In this circumstance, in the emperor's view, the possibility that the creditors might seize property, such as slaves and livestock, that the farmers used to cultivate their land caused economic peril for them and threatened imperial revenues. So the emperor imposed brutal sanctions, including capital punishment, on local officials who seized such property from farmers. In the fifth century, this policy of protecting the capacity of small farmers to cultivate their land was taken to its logical conclusion when the imperial government prohibited securing loans against equipment used for agriculture (*CJ* 8.16.8, AD 414). But the restrictions imposed on securing credit against the equipment that farmers needed to cultivate their land did not eliminate the need for rural credit. Instead, such restrictions would have tended to make credit harder to acquire and therefore more expensive. These measures should be seen against the background of a general policy pursued by the Roman government of asserting the authority of its legal institutions in the rural economy. This policy is particularly apparent in the government's efforts to bring the regula-tion of credit under state control. Self-help was always a component in the enforcement of Roman contracts, and the Roman government traditionally granted creditors some latitude in seizing the property of defaulting debtors.[44]

But, beginning at least by the reign of Marcus Aurelius, the government sought to curtail the free exercise of self-help by asserting that the seizure of

---

[39] Giardina (2007: 749–53).   [40] Thonemann (2007); Harper (2008).
[41] Harper (2011).   [42] This section draws on Kehoe (2007: 148–55).
[43] The author of this law may have been Licinius: see Corcoran (1996: 287, no. 5).
[44] Bürge (1980).

property of defaulting debtors could be carried out only when approved by a court. In a rescript quoted by the jurist Callistratus, Marcus insisted that creditors had to go through the courts if they wanted to proceed against debtors, and he defined as the use of force any means a creditor used to enforce a contract different from established legal remedies (Callistr. *dig.* 48.7.7). The policy that Marcus Aurelius articulated became fundamental to Roman legal ideology, as is indicated by the frequent practice of petitioners, including in the papyri, to allege that their opponents have acted with force, *vis*, or *bia*. In most cases what seems to be at issue is not physical violence as we would understand it, but what the petitioner interpreted as the unlawful exercise of self-help. A series of constitutions in the third century, especially from the reign of Diocletian, indicate that the Roman government was quite concerned to assert the sole authority of its courts to settle legal questions surrounding debt and disputes over property. Again, keeping seizures of property under the control of the courts would offer some protection to the economically less advantaged against the predatory actions of wealthier landowners.

But the restrictions on what could be used as security in agrarian loans could also potentially undermine the protections that the state sought to accord small farmers. The state was primarily interested in the revenues farmers would provide from their taxes, and not in protecting the investments of creditors or even in making much-needed credit more readily available in the rural economy. Whatever the interests of the imperial government, farmers would still need credit, and the restrictions on security would tend to drive the credit arrangements that small farmers entered into outside the control of the law. We might compare this type of restriction with the efforts of the late imperial government to restrict the movement of *coloni* registered for fiscal purposes on the estates of large landowners. In imposing these restrictions, the government was going directly against market forces, in that *coloni* with resources at their disposal were highly desirable to landowners in a period in which intermittent economic turmoil threatened profits from agriculture.[45] If restricting the movement of *coloni* helped to assure that landowners would have access to the labour and resources they needed to meet their fiscal obligations, not to mention to make a profit from their land, these restrictions also tended to drive outside the control of the law any tenure arrangements struck between mobile *coloni* and landowners who recruited them. The only solution to the problem of providing credit while also protecting farmers from potentially predatory creditors would be to establish a system of state seed loans, as existed on some royal lands in Ptolemaic and Roman Egypt, but in Egypt this was an age-old institution, and it is unlikely that any

---

[45] See Kehoe (2007: 163–91).

other province in the Roman empire had the institutional capacity to manage such a programme.[46] The restrictions on securing loans to farmers against their equipment and livestock certainly must have afforded small farmers greater security, but such an intervention in the market could also have unforeseen consequences.

STATE POLICY AND COMMERCE
IN AGRICULTURAL PRODUCTS

A final issue to be considered concerns the interventions by the state in the trade of agricultural products, and the likely effects that this intervention had on agricultural production. The main interest of the state, as stated earlier, was to secure access to vital foodstuffs to support the distributions at Rome and to feed armies. Assuring the food supply of Rome was a complex task. As Paul Erdkamp argues, the markets for grain and other foodstuffs in the Roman empire were highly imperfect.[47] The imperfections in the markets and the concomitant volatility of prices resulted from many factors, including the costs of information gathering and the slow response time from a region of surplus to a region of shortage. The expenses of shipping overland would tend to make it difficult to meet occasional shortages of food except from nearby sources. Moreover, because of the limitations of the sailing season, shortages of grain might be felt most keenly in the early spring, but this was too early in the sailing season for long-distance trade to react to the potential demand. The strategies that small farmers pursued to safeguard their own security could also reduce the supplies potentially available to meet sudden shortages.

To secure Rome's food supply, the state in the early empire tended to rely on providing private shippers with incentives to promote the importation of wheat into Rome. Under Claudius, contractors gained exemption from liabilities in Augustus' social legislation if they provided a ship of 10,000 *modii* (about 65 metric tonnes), and, in the second century, contractors who provided an individual ship of 50,000 *modii* or five ships of at least 10,000 *modii* were entitled to exemption from civic liturgies, apparently as long as they invested at least half their property in this type of shipping.[48] In the third century and later, what had been contracts freely entered into turned into liturgical obligations, as the state pursued a consistent programme of requiring people to remain in professions that were deemed essential to the public interest.[49] We must also add to these incentives significant investment in

---

[46] Rowlandson (1996: 95).   [47] Erdkamp (2005: esp. 143–205).
[48] Garnsey (1988: 234); Morley (2007: 585–6).
[49] Lo Cascio (2007: 641).

infrastructure, the most important of which were the construction and upkeep of the harbours at Ostia and Portus.

The intervention of the state in the market for foodstuffs created economic opportunities that promoted trade but also imposed some substantial costs on society. The state's intervention was designed to make sure that the city of Rome and the armies, a market of approximately 1.3 million consumers, could be supplied with basic foodstuffs and other commodities. Although some of the supplies used by the armies on the frontiers were produced locally, much had to be brought at long distance—for example, oil from Baetica.[50] As has been emphasized, most recently by Neville Morley, the same merchants who supplied Rome and the armies with foodstuffs and other necessities under contract with the state could also use their ships or other means of transport to bring other, potentially higher-value, goods to sell. So to some extent the state subsidized private commerce, but only in those areas where it had a direct interest, mainly Rome and the military frontiers. The state also developed harbour facilities and other infrastructure to support this type of trade as at Ostia and Alexandria, but this same infrastructure also supported commercial activity involving all sorts of commodities in which the state had no particular interest. The infrastructure that the Roman state subsidized, then, helped to create a greater interconnectivity in a world in which no particular area enjoyed a decisive advantage in producing foodstuffs and other basic commodities such as clothing.[51] Of course, an important factor contributing to this interconnectivity was the tendency for the Roman administration to enforce more uniform laws concerning trade, which, combined with the development by Roman merchants of governance structures to negotiate and enforce contracts, helped to reduce the costs of commerce.

At the same time, the role that the state played in encouraging commerce also carried some hidden costs. First, the incentives offered to shipowners serving the *annona*, which in the second century included immunity from liturgies, made unavailable to towns the resources of some of the wealthiest people, which would be sorely needed to assure the performance of vital functions. In this sense the state withdrew resources from the local economy, much as it did by its policy of maintaining direct control over imperial land and the resources of imperial tenants. But another, and perhaps serious, cost to society resulted from the *de facto* state subsidies for certain trade routes. If the state subsidized commerce between Alexandria or Carthage and Rome, or military zones on the frontiers, it did so at the expense of other potential trade routes, where resources might also have been directed. This is not to imply that commerce in the Roman empire was a zero-sum game, in the sense that provisioning Rome meant that other areas would be neglected, but the

---

[50] Morley (2007: 580–1).
[51] Horden and Purcell (2000: 123–72); Morley (2007: 579), based on Hopkins (1995/6).

resource pool to support commerce was finite. But, as Erdkamp emphasizes, the creation of infrastructure to support trade tended to be a self-perpetuating process, since merchants would be drawn to established trade routes, whereas more isolated routes would have less commerce, and much of that would be local.[52]

Markets for agricultural products remained highly imperfect, and cities had to develop their own strategies for maintaining food supplies, although they had far fewer means at their disposal to accomplish this goal than had the imperial government. One strategy that many cities followed, especially in the eastern part of the empire, was to establish permanent grain funds. The precise purposes of these funds is controversial, but the most likely explanation is that they were permanent accounts funded partly by taxes or other imposts collected by cities, and partly by benefactions from the wealthy, in particular those individuals who held the office of the *sitones*.[53] Ideally, the *sitonai* in charge of the funds could purchase and stockpile grain after abundant harvests. This strategy would provide some price support for local producers when low prices would otherwise threaten their incomes, and allow for the release of supplies on the market in times of shortages. Alternatively, the *sitonai* could use the funds to purchase grain when anticipated shortages threatened to raise prices substantially. Without such a permanent fund, cities faced with food shortages had to rely on the generosity of individual benefactors. On occasion, they had to seek both the permission of the emperor to import grain from Egypt as well as the generosity of local benefactors to be able to purchase it.[54] The subsidizing of trade with Rome, crucial as it was to provisioning the empire's capital, did not necessarily provide much benefit to cities not directly on trade routes with Rome or in inland locations.

CONCLUSION

This survey suggests the complexity of the role that the state played in the economy. One of the most important contributions that the Roman state made was to develop and maintain a stable currency system, one that endured for centuries, as Lo Cascio discusses in the *Cambridge Economic History*.[55] When we turn to the state's role as an economic actor, most of the measures that it adopted were to pursue specific fiscal or political goals, rather than to define a coherent economic policy. But the state's intervention in the economy

---

[52] Erdkamp (2005: 177–96).
[53] See Erdkamp (2005: 258–316, esp. 268–83); Zuiderhoek (2008).
[54] Pleket (1984); Garnsey (1988: 69–86, 244–68).
[55] Lo Cascio (2007: 627–30).

to secure revenues, especially critical supplies for the city of Rome and the army, had broader significance for the economy as a whole, affecting the organization of commerce and the distribution of wealth between city and countryside. From this perspective alone, the political unification of the Mediterranean world under Rome brought important institutional changes that shaped the economy. In my view, one of the most significant institutional changes that Roman rule produced was to develop more responsive legal institutions that provided protection not just to the very wealthy or well connected, but also to the economically less advantaged. It is in the operation of these legal institutions that we can trace an economic policy. As I have tried to show, in responding to disputes involving land tenure or credit, areas of the law crucial to the rural economy, the Roman government sought, within the constraints allowed it by responding to petitions, to apply the same principles that guided its fiscal policies, especially the protection of the tenure rights of small farmers. In spite of the overwhelming social and political power of elite landowners, the Roman government consistently pursued policies to protect small farmers, even when doing so tended to undermine the authority of the very institutions that were supposed to accomplish this goal. The results of the Roman government's policies can perhaps best be seen in the late antique Oxyrhynchite Nome, a region of the empire dominated by landowners who were members of the empire's elite. Even here, there were still independent landowners and tenants who could freely bargain with the powerful land-owners. The institutions of the Roman state made a critical difference in the Roman economy, and, as they fostered an urban culture, they also mitigated to some extent at least the worst effects of the transfer of wealth from countryside to city.

REFERENCES

Banaji, J. (2001). *Agrarian Change in Late Antiquity: Gold, Labour and Aristocratic Dominance*. Oxford.

Bang, P. F. (2008). *The Roman Bazaar*. Cambridge.

Barzel, Y. (1989). *Economic Analysis of Property Rights*. Cambridge.

Barzel, Y. (2002). *A Theory of the State: Economic Rights, Legal Rights, and the Scope of the State*. Cambridge.

Bowman, A. K., and Rathbone, D. (1992). 'Cities and Administration in Roman Egypt', *JRS* 82: 107–27.

Bürge, A. (1980). 'Vertrag und personale Abhängigkeiten im Rom der späten Republik und der frühen Kaiserzeit', *ZRG* 97: 105–56.

Carrié, J.-M. (1993a). 'Le riforme economiche da Aureliano a Constantino', in A. Schiavone (ed.), *Storia di Roma*. III, pt 1. Turin, 283–322.

Carrié, J.-M. (1993b). 'L'economie e le finanze', in A. Schiavone (ed.), *Storia di Roma*. III, pt 1. Turin, 751–87.

Corcoran, S. (1996). *The Empire of the Tetrarchs: Imperial Pronouncements and Government A.D. 284–324*. Oxford.

De Vos, M. (2001) (ed.). *Rus Africum: Terra acqua olio nell'Africa settentrionale. Scavo e recognizione nei dintorini di Dougga (Alto Tell tunisino)*. Trento.

Dixit, A. K. (2004). *Lawlessness and Economics: Alternative Modes of Governance*. Princeton.

Duncan-Jones, R. P. (1990). *Structure and Scale in the Roman Economy*. Cambridge.

Duncan-Jones, R. P. (1994). *Money and Government in the Roman Empire*. Cambridge.

Erdkamp. P. (2001). 'Beyond the Limits of the "Consumer City": A Model of the Urban and Rural Economy in the Roman World', *Historia* 50.3: 332–56.

Erdkamp. P. (2005). *The Grain Market in the Roman Empire: A Social, Political, and Economic Study*. Cambridge.

Field, A. J. (1991). 'Do Legal Systems Matter?', *Explorations in Economic History* 28: 1–35.

Frier, B. W., and Kehoe, D. P. (2007). 'Law and Economic Institutions', in W. Scheidel, I. Morris, and R. Saller (eds), *The Cambridge Economic History of the Greco-Roman World*. Cambridge, 113–43.

Garnsey, P. (1988). *Famine and Food Supply in the Greco-Roman World: Responses to Risk and Crisis*. Cambridge.

Giardina, A. (2007). 'The Transition to Late Antiquity', in W. Scheidel, I. Morris, and R. Saller (eds), *The Cambridge Economic History of the Greco-Roman World*. Cambridge, 743–68.

Goffart, W. (1974). *Caput and Colonate: Towards a History of Late Roman Taxation* (Phoenix Suppl. 12). Toronto.

Greif, A. (2006). *Institutions and the Path to the Modern Economy: Lessons from Medieval Trade* (Political Economy of Institutions and Decisions). Cambridge.

Harper, K. (2008). 'The Greek Census Inscriptions of Late Antiquity', *JRS* 98: 83–119.

Harper, K. (2011). 'Patterns of Landed Wealth in the Long Term', paper presented at conference on *Land and Natural Resources in the Roman World*, Brussels, 27 May.

Hauken, T. (1998). *Petition and Response: An Epigraphic Study of Petitions to Roman Emperors 181–249* (Monographs from the Norwegian Institute at Athens 2). Bergen.

Hodgson, G. M. (1999). *Evolution and Institutions: On Evolutionary Economics and the Evolution of Economics*. Cheltenham and Northampton, MA.

Hopkins, K. (1995/6). 'Rome, Taxes, Rents and Trade', *Kodai* 6.7: 41–75; repr. in W. Scheidel and S. von Reden (2002) (eds). *The Roman Economy*. New York, 2002, 190–230.

Horden, P., and Purcell, N. (2000). *The Corrupting Sea: A Study of Mediterranean History*. Oxford and Malden, MA.

Johnson, D. G. (2000). 'Population, Food, and Knowledge', *American Economic Review* 90.1: 1–14.

Jones, A. H. M. (1964). *The Later Roman Empire, 284–602: A Social, Economic, and Administrative Survey*. Oxford.

Jongman W. (2003). 'A Golden Age: Death, Money Supply and Social Succession in the Roman Empire', in E. Lo Cascio (ed.), *Credito e moneta nel mondo romano*. Bari, 181–96.

Jördens, A. (2009). *Statthalterliche Verwaltung in der römischen Kaiserzeit. Studien zum praefectus Aegypti* (Historia Einzelschriften 175). Stuttgart.

Kehoe, D. P. (1988). *The Economics of Agriculture on Roman Imperial Estates in North Africa*. Göttingen.

Kehoe, D. P. (1992). *Management and Investment in Estates in Roman Egypt during the Early Empire* (Papyrologische Texte und Abhandlungen 40). Bonn.

Kehoe, D. P. (1997). *Investment, Profits, and Tenancy: The Jurists and the Roman Agrarian Economy*. Ann Arbor.

Kehoe, D. P. (2007). *Law and the Rural Economy in the Roman Empire*. Ann Arbor.

Klein, P. G. (2000). 'New Institutional Economics', in B. Bouckaert and G. De Geest (eds), *Encyclopedia of Law and Economics*, I. Cheltenham and Northampton, MA, 456–89. Online edition (1999): <http://users.ugent.be/~gdegeest/>.

Lo Cascio, E. (2007). 'The Early Roman Empire: The State and the Economy', in W. Scheidel, I. Morris, and R. Saller (eds), *The Cambridge Economic History of the Greco-Roman World*. Cambridge, 619–47.

Manning, J. S. (2007). 'Hellenistic Egypt', in W. Scheidel, I. Morris, and R. Saller (eds), *The Cambridge Economic History of the Greco-Roman World*. Cambridge, 434–59.

Mattingly, D. J., and Hitchner, R. B. (1995). 'Roman Africa: An Archaeological Review', *JRS* 85: 165–213.

Mercuro, N., and Medema, S. G. (1997). *Economics and the Law: From Posner to Post-Modernism*. Princeton.

Monson, A. (2012). *From the Ptolemies to the Romans: Political and Economic Change in Egypt*. Cambridge.

Morley, N. (2007). 'The Early Roman Empire: Distribution', in W. Scheidel, I. Morris, and R. Saller (eds), *The Cambridge Economic History of the Greco-Roman World*. Cambridge, 570–91.

North, D. C. (1990*). Institutions, Institutional Change and Economic Performance*. Cambridge; repr. 2002.

Pleket, H. W. (1984). 'Urban Elites and the Economy in the Greek Cities of the Roman Empire', *MBAH* 3.1: 3–35.

Rathbone, D. (1991). *Economic Rationalism and Rural Society in Third-Century A.D. Egypt: The Heroninos Archive and the Appianus Estate*. Cambridge.

Rathbone, D. (2007). 'Roman Egypt', in W. Scheidel, I. Morris, and R. Saller (eds), *The Cambridge Economic History of the Greco-Roman World*. Cambridge, 698–719.

Rowlandson, J. (1996). *Landowners and Tenants in Roman Egypt: The Social Relations of Agriculture in the Oxyrhynchite Nome* (Oxford Classical Monographs). Oxford.

Rupprecht, H.-A. (1994). *Kleine Einführung in die Papyruskunde*. Darmstadt.

Scheidel, W. (2007). 'Demography', in Scheidel, Morris, and Saller (2007), 38–86.

Scheidel, W., Morris, I., and Saller, R. (2007) (eds). *The Cambridge Economic History of the Greco-Roman World*. Cambridge.

Sharp, M. (1999). 'The Village of Theadelphia in the Fayyum: Land and Population in the Second Century', in A. K. Bowman and E. Rogan (eds), *Agriculture in Egypt from Pharaonic to Modern Times* (Proceedings of the British Academy 96). Oxford, 159–92.

Thonemann, P. (2007). 'Estates and the Land in Late Roman Asia Minor', *Chiron* 37: 435–78.

Weßel, H. (2003). *Das Recht der Tablettes Albertini*. Berlin.

Whittaker, C. R. (1990). 'The Consumer City Revisited: The Vicus and the City', *JRA* 3: 110–18; repr. in C. R. Whittaker, *Land, City and Trade in the Roman Empire*. Aldershot, 1993.

Wilson, A. (2002). 'Machines, Power and the Ancient Economy', *JRS* 92: 1–32.

Zuiderhoek, A. (2008). 'Feeding the Citizens: Municipal Grain Funds and Civic Benefactions in the Greek East', in R. Alston and O. M. van Nijf (eds), *Feeding the Ancient Greek City*. Leuven, 159–80.

3

GIS Models of Roman Agricultural Production

Helen Goodchild

1. INTRODUCTION

The use of models in historical discourse is by no means a new approach. Numerous theoretical models of various aspects of Roman society have been put forward over the years, and many of these have been explicitly quantitative in nature, particularly since the seminal discussion of formal models in archaeology by Clarke.[1] With the increasing use of Geographical Information Systems (GIS) within archaeology, such models have become the norm, yet we still run the risk of accepting compelling models at face value, without consideration of their construction or intent.

We must first define what a model is:

> Models are usually idealized representation of observations, they are structures, they are selective, they simplify, they specify a field of interest and they offer a partially accurate predictive framework.[2]

It is all too easy to forget this when confronted by reams of tables and statistics that purport to explain the various mechanisms and institutions of the Roman empire. Models are designed to test hypotheses, but we forget that they often cannot provide us with the real 'answer'. Whether this actually matters, however, is subject to debate: 'all models are wrong; the practical question is how wrong do they have to be to not be useful?'[3] So, if we cannot reconstruct real life, then why use models at all? Clarke offered five reasons, which ultimately demonstrated that, if we are to be objective and try to see past our cultural preconceptions and utilize a more rigorous scientific framework,

---

[1] Clarke (1972).   [2] Clarke (1972: 2).
[3] Box and Draper (1987: 74).

making explicit our assumptions about the past, then models are our best hope.[4]

As archaeologists we will always be dealing with incomplete datasets, and we must attempt to fill these gaps by putting forward potential models in order to explain the systems under study. However, just because one model may offer a plausible result does not mean it is correct, and many competing models can coexist for a specific system. This variety is essential if we are fully to explore the possibilities and potentials of ancient societies, and there is a range of approaches that may be used, each offering its own advantages and drawbacks. This chapter will, therefore, discuss research into the use of computer models for the quantification of agricultural production, and demonstrate how such models can augment established debates. Recent work in the Tiber valley is presented as an example of the contribution computer-generated models can bring to conventional views of antiquity.

2. MODELLING ANCIENT SYSTEMS

In modelling Roman agriculture and land use we touch on a number of different systems: agricultural production directly affects settlement distribution, demography, urbanization, and economy, each of which has its own long-standing background in historical theoretical models.[5] One thing that most of these models have in common is their generic (and therefore idealized) nature. Many operate on a national or even international scale, and are often divorced from the realities on the ground: in the case of settlement patterning, for example, they can often be completely abstract.[6] They attempt to explain systems such as food supply or market economics, but, as models, they are inherently simplifications of what *may* be happening in the real world.

There is a large amount of literature available on the agricultural regimes and economic structure of different societies within the Roman world,[7] but as yet there have been few attempts to place these types of theoretical agricultural models into a real environment.[8] Such a process would enable the original

---

[4] Clarke (1972: 3).

[5] e.g. Christaller (1966) and von Thünen (1966) for settlement patterns in general; Hopkins (1978) and Lo Cascio (1999) for economics and demography, etc.

[6] e.g. von Thünen (1966).

[7] For example, for Greece, see Foxhall and Forbes (1982); Foxhall (1990); Sallares (1991; for Egypt, see Bowman, Chapter 7, this volume; for Italy, see Rosenstein (2004); Erdkamp (2005).

[8] Exceptions are primarily for prehistoric agricultural landscapes: see, e.g., Robb and van Hove (2003), which attempts to reconstruct a southern Italian Neolithic landscape using a rich faunal record and evidence for foraging. The landscape is reconstructed using iterative models to determine the likely economic strategy.

model builders to determine which of their arguments hold up in a range of scenarios and which do not, and this has great implications for a broader understanding of the systems under discussion.

While the models under discussion here are, by necessity, simplifications, an attempt has been made to locate them spatially in the 'real world'. In doing this, they move from generic statistics applied wholesale to large systems, to more regional, localized patterns. We cannot report the actual production of a particular area in a given period, but we can offer models to demonstrate the effects of ranges of production and investigate the implications. In the specific case of modelling agricultural systems, the available evidence can go only so far. There are inevitably gaps that cannot be filled by a single truth. Instead, we can explore the possibilities via a combination of archaeological evidence, comparative data, and random sampling. This process and having to quantify the range of criteria used mean that we have an opportunity really to get into the detail of the evidence available to us.

This advantage can also be dangerous, however. By actively quantifying the ranges of production potential, it is all too easy to translate possibilities into certainties in order to support a particular side of a debate,[9] and, as Fentress argues, archaeologists are willing to accept such modelled figures purely on the grounds of their apparent plausibility.[10] It could, therefore, be argued that such modelling simply tells us what we already know. However, such a process forces us to recognize and give quantitative weight, or even simply just logical form, to our assumptions, and allows us to explore how far our preconceptions are shaped by historical texts, or even personal experience. Van de Leeuw goes on to argue that such models are 'sufficiently abstract not to be confounded with reality, and sufficiently detailed, rigorous, and...."realistic" to force people with different backgrounds to focus on the same relational and behavioural issues'.[11]

To avoid the uncritical use of models to explain phenomena, and their possible misuse in order to support a particular theory, the model itself should state clearly its function, explore potential possibilities, and outline its underlying assumptions and methodology.[12] Being able to formalize hypotheses can create a dialogue between the model and the (in this case) historian, confronting them with possible flaws in their way of reasoning. As Verhagen goes on to argue: 'realism is not what is aimed for, but rather the isolation of the parameters of interest, and the extrapolation of (assumed) causal relationships, that can then be tested by using the available evidence.'

To shift his argument into this particular context, we might use models to argue that, for example: if yields of a particular crop were as stated by the Roman agricultural writers Cato, Varro, or Columella, and cultivated in farms

---

[9] For example, the high–low demography debate: Scheidel (2001).
[10] Fentress (2009: 138).   [11] Van de Leeuw (2004).   [12] Verhagen (2007: 191).

or villas of sizes as suggested by the texts, does this mean that this area could produce enough to support a local non-agriculturally productive population? What scales of production would have been necessary under different agricultural regimes? What might have been the difference in output between slave-based agriculture and free labour? Indeed, this type of model has been approached by a number of scholars in recent years, at least in the abstract, in order to investigate the productivity of small farmers, and to look at aspects such as the robustness of farms in the face of military recruitment.[13]

3. MODELLING LANDSCAPES

What must also be considered is why certain modelling techniques have been used in some areas but not in others. It is not possible to discuss all approaches fully here, but there are a number of different methods of modelling and reconstruction being used within different projects. The choice of which techniques are utilized is highly dependent on both the research aims and datasets available.

The modelling of ancient agricultural systems often relies on palaeo-environmental analysis in order to reconstruct landscapes and productivity.[14] Indirect techniques include calculation using methods such as estimating the amount of land under cultivation from produce (as mentioned in texts, for example), or annual peak production from grain storage capacity,[15] or even experimental archaeology, such as the Butser Ancient Farm experiments, where ancient cultivation methods are tested on the ground.[16] The original key technique for assessing resources and potential production, however, is site catchment analysis, which was first used by Vita-Finzi and Higgs in 1970 to investigate resource potential in a delimited area, and which revived in popularity with the advent of GIS.[17] Settlement and territorial modelling has become more sophisticated with advances in spatial analysis,[18] but we still need to remember that, despite their compelling nature, these are *theoretical* models and not accurate reconstructions.

Many examples of landscape analysis have concentrated on the technique of predictive modelling in order to identify areas of archaeological interest. There is a significant corpus dedicated to this expanding field, and it is an area that seems to polarize archaeological opinion.[19] Predictive modelling has been

---

[13] Rosenstein (2004); Erdkamp (2005).   [14] e.g. Leveau *et al.* (1999).
[15] e.g. Duncan-Jones (1982); Berqvist (1992).   [16] Reynolds (1981).
[17] See, e.g., Saile (1997); Stančič *et al.* (1997).
[18] See Posluschny *et al.* (2008) for examples of current techniques in use.
[19] See, e.g., Kvamme (1990, 2005); Verhagen *et al.* (1999); Verhagen (2007) for support of the method.

strongly criticized on a number of levels, including environmental determinism and its uncritical use in cultural resource management.[20] The methods
used, whether or not one agrees with their application, are nevertheless very
useful tools for investigating landscape suitability (see Section 4.1, 'Creating
production maps using multi-criteria analysis').

High-resolution satellite data may also be used in a similar way—for
example, by using Maximum Likelihood Classifiers in order to identify areas
most likely to be used for a particular crop[21]—but this often requires significant financial outlay to acquire data of sufficient resolution, and is strongly
affected by modern environmental conditions.

Landscape reconstruction and land evaluation are potentially more appropriate methods. Land evaluation techniques have been in existence since the
1970s, but have only relatively recently been applied to archaeological landscapes, with applications in places such as Iran,[22] Spain,[23] and Italy.[24] The
Food and Agriculture Organization (FAO) of the United Nations outlined the
methodology, which is typically applied to modern landscapes, in order to
ascertain land performance and suitability for different types of agriculture.[25]
The central analysis compares the requirements of different types of land use
with the resources available. Essentially, this is performing a suitability classification based around similar precepts as multi-criteria evaluation (a tool used
for predictive modelling), but with the incorporation of palaeo-ecological
factors such as climate, soils, and vegetation, along with economic and social
analysis.[26] Such data are not often available to regional landscape projects,
meaning that this approach, though desirable, is not always feasible to carry
out.

A recent technique being applied to the reconstruction of systems is simu-
lation or agent-based modelling.[27] While there have been a few published
archaeological agent-based models,[28] the most applicable use of the method
thus far is the work done to investigate agricultural sustainability in Mesopotamia.[29] Altaweel has used a combination of geographical, historical, and
comparative data, similar to those used in the Tiber valley examples (see
below), to construct models in which individual autonomous 'agents' (in
this case Mesopotamian farmers) are programmed to abide by certain behavioural rules in order to gauge which strategies were sustainable given the
environment and climate. Archaeological and historical records govern the

---

[20] Gaffney and van Leusen (1995); Wheatley (2004).   [21] Schowengerdt (1983).
[22] Farshad (2002).   [23] Verhagen *et al.* (1999).
[24] See Finke *et al.*(1994); Verhagen (2002); van Joolen (2003); Kamermans (2004).
[25] FAO (1976).
[26] FAO (1976: 1.1).
[27] Christiansen and Altaweel (2006); Wilkinson *et al.* (2007).
[28] For examples, see Graham (2006); Kohler and van der Leeuw (2007).
[29] Altaweel (2008).

model in terms of composition of families, age of marriage, number of
offspring, and so on, and would shape a community over a few generations;
while systems of agriculture (length of fallow, manuring, irrigation, and so on)
are also tested to gauge their effect on potential food production. By altering
such parameters, the effects may be seen over a long time period (in this case
over a period of 100 years), thereby allowing us to view the long-term effects of
different strategies, with each individual agent's actions and interactions
combining to build a larger, 'bottom-up', system.

The main advantages of agent-based models were defined by De Smith *et al.*
as (1) the ability to capture emergent phenomena; (2) the provision of a
natural environment in which to study systems; and (3) their flexibility,
particularly in terms of the development of spatial models.[30] The primary
limitation of this type of modelling is one common to all models discussed
here: that 'a model is only as useful as the purpose for which it was constructed', and is dependent on the quality of data input, and how the data are
applied. As well as this, agents are human beings, and as such can demonstrate
irrational behaviour, which can be difficult—or even impossible—to quantify.[31] The ability to explore complex systems, however, outweighs such issues.
Many regional landscape projects have appropriate source data for agent-
based modelling, and this approach, while a significant undertaking, is an
extremely useful tool, and one from which the study of Roman Italy would
benefit greatly.

4. MODELLING THE TIBER VALLEY

To illustrate the potential of agricultural modelling, two studies are briefly
discussed. The first was originally undertaken as part of my doctoral thesis,[32]
and the second built on this original work further to develop the models.[33] The
methods developed were entirely dependent on the data available (as is often
the case with landscape studies). Using a combination of geographical and
textual data, I was able to construct a model to investigate potential levels of
production and the resulting demographic effects. Theoretically this study
could be argued to resemble a more sophisticated form of site catchment
analysis, using the territories of farms and villas in order to determine whether
the resources available could adequately supply its inhabitants or create a
surplus.

---

[30] De Smith *et al.* (2006: 8.2.5).   [31] De Smith *et al.* (2006: 8.2.6).
[32] Goodchild (2007).
[33] See Section 5, 'Further Modelling'; also Goodchild and Witcher (2009).

For the initial study, the area under investigation was a region of approximately 2,600 km^2 located to the north of Rome and straddling two historically important areas: south Etruria and Sabina (Fig. 3.1). These areas (particularly south Etruria) were the focus of intensive and extensive fieldwork during the twentieth century,[34] and the British School at Rome's Tiber Valley Project has created a vast database of multi-period settlement information derived from these legacy data.[35]

The complete settlement dataset for the whole study area is very large, comprising in the Early Imperial Roman period 535 farms and 653 villas. These are point data (that is, stored by coordinate) and classified by period and site type, interpreted on the basis of the material culture found at each site (this reliance on material culture is likely to be a good explanation for the high proportion of elite villa sites to smaller farms). Geographical datasets were also available (the elevation, geology, modern river system, and modern land use), which were combined with comparative evidence for farming practice from later periods, as well as a substantial corpus of textual material on agriculture dating from the Roman period.[36] The use of textual material is not without problems,[37] and these sources must be approached with caution, particularly regarding the promotion of certain types of economic strategy (particularly viticulture). Nevertheless, they provide an invaluable, if biased, picture of farming, with agricultural strategies that were presumably within the realms of credibility for their contemporary audience. As such, these figures provide a base for quantitative modelling of different agricultural scenarios.

Such a large database provides a great opportunity for theoretical landscape modelling. Use of these data enables investigation of a number of aspects. First, there is locational modelling in order to investigate why settlement sites appear where they do: which areas were used preferentially and what types of land were settled?[38] Further to this is the modelling of potential agricultural production: which crops were grown and where? What were yields likely to have been? What other sources of food may rural Romans have had access to?

The questions of site location and agricultural production are related and have the potential to shed light on larger issues, such as the effects on demography that different levels of production may have had—not only on a local site scale, but also in wider economic terms. For example, how would a

---

[34] See, e.g., Potter (1979); Muzzioli (1980).

[35] Patterson (2004); Coarelli and Patterson (2009).

[36] The main sources for ancient agriculture are Cato, *de Agr.*, Varro, *Rust.*, Columella, *Rust.*, Pliny, *NH*, Palladius, *de Re Rust.*, and the Byzantine *Geoponika*.

[37] Dyson (1992: 22), for example, has described these texts as 'weapons' used in contemporary discussions regarding the optimum use and improvement of agricultural resources and how to strengthen the economic base of the Roman elite.

[38] This was carried out on a basic level as part of previous work on the area (Goodchild 2007) but requires further analysis to create a more robust model.

Helen Goodchild

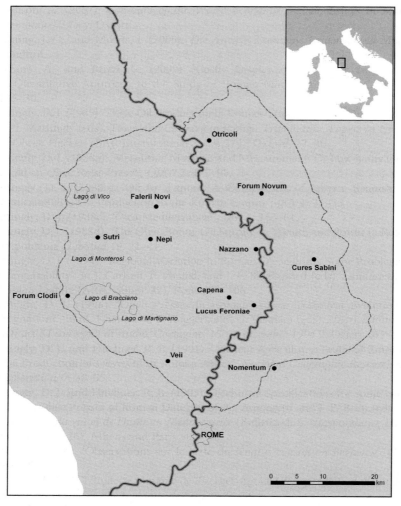

Fig. 3.1. Map of the study area showing major towns, lakes, and the course of the Tiber (base data from the British School at Rome)

rural surplus (or lack thereof) affect the non-agricultural population and consequently the urbanization of the region? Conversely, how might changes in demography affect agricultural practice, for example, in terms of surplus production or size and quality of exploited areas? By modelling ranges of potential production, it is also possible to explore how individual sites may have integrated into larger agricultural systems, and how this may have been affected by social institutions such as tenancy. What might be the impact of different scales of production or crop specialization on both the individuals involved in production and the system at large?

The models discussed here relate to a theoretical reconstruction of production potential during the Late Republican and Early Imperial Roman periods. They are intended to determine the amount of food that the area could potentially produce, with the aim of analysing what effects this could have on a supported population. The basic methodology is as follows:

1. Create a production map (yield per hectare) for different crops.
2. Overlay farm and villa estates.
3. Extract total production statistics, subtracting seed corn and waste.
4. Convert into calories and determine the range of a hypothetical supported population.

This is a highly simplified description of the methodology and in reality there are many steps in the process and decisions that have to be made at various stages. Each of these steps allows the model maker to outline what assumptions are being made at each stage, and really explore the detail of the agricultural system.

The geographical factors available were used in conjunction with comparative data and Roman textual evidence to create the production map of Step 1. The locations of farms and villas in the rural landscape for Step 2 were derived from the South Etruria Survey site database.[39] Issues associated with these data are discussed below. The remainder of the stages were carried out using GIS modules (particularly multi-criteria analysis) and basic statistical analysis.[40]

4.1. Creating production maps using multi-criteria analysis

The primary method for creating production maps in these examples is a decision-making technique known as multi-criteria analysis (MCA) or multi-criteria decision analysis (MCDA). This method works by scaling data from least to most suitable for a certain task and combining different factors together to assign an overall suitability to an area. This process assists in decision-making in a variety of disciplines—anywhere where choices must be made between conflicting interests.[41] Applications can be as broad as deciding who is best qualified in a job application[42] to forest management.[43] Within

---

[39] Potter (1979); Patterson (2004).

[40] As with all models, the techniques used are being continually developed and refined. As such there are other versions in print that demonstrate the variability of results that can be obtained from such an exercise: Goodchild (2006, 2008); Goodchild and Witcher (2009).

[41] Eastman (2001).   [42] Anestis *et al.* (2006).

[43] Henig and Weintraub (2006).

archaeology the technique is ordinarily associated with predictive modelling.[44] The output of such an analysis is a map showing suitability for a particular task on a relative scale; in this instance, the objective is to determine the areas most suitable for certain economies in the Roman period. To do this, it is necessary to know both what the requirements of ancient crops were, and what was considered to be good practice at this time. This is a difficult task, but such information can be gleaned to a certain extent from comparative evidence or the literary evidence of the agronomists, though not without problems. By modelling, it would theoretically enable us to see which sites were located on potentially 'better' land (that is, more suitable for a particular purpose) regardless of actual yield.

Details are available from the ancient texts that outline the best locations for certain crop types (for example, steepness of slope, slope direction, soil texture, and so on), and these descriptive sources can be converted into quantitative factors for each geographical data type and combined within a multi-criteria analysis model. Here it must be highlighted that, although the maps created are quantitative (that is, on a numerical scale), the sources on which these were based were not. Cato might say that south-facing slopes were beneficial for crop growth, but actually converting this into a scale from worst to best slope direction is not a straightforward matter. It is necessary to remember that practices change over time, and perceptions of appropriate and inappropriate areas for cultivation are not set in stone.[45] However, comparative data can still be an important element: for example, later agronomic practices, or scientific studies of the effects of solar radiation/sunshine hours on crop growth.[46] Regarding steepness of slope, Columella (*Rust.* 1.2.4) argues that cultivating steep slopes is not practical, and hence we look to how well a plough might function at different gradients, or the differences in location between animal-drawn ploughing and human manual labour.[47] Even with these useful additions, the factor maps created are still essentially qualitative, based on subjective human decision. However, this is a good example of where the practicalities of creating the model lead us to enquire further about farming techniques that may previously have been assumed to have been straightforward.

To illustrate how such a model could be constructed in practice, some factors that may affect crop production, according to the agronomists, were preferences for: strong, rich soil, plains or gentle slopes, and south- or east-facing slopes (e.g. Cato *de Agr.* 1.2–4). As different crops have different

---

[44] Exceptions include Howey (2007) and Haggis (2008).

[45] For example, Favory *et al.* (1995) have shown that what was recommended by the agronomists does not necessarily equate with modern practice.

[46] e.g. Groenman-van Waateringe and van Wijngaarden-Bakker (1987); Fu and Rich (2002).

[47] See van Joolen (2003: 28, 108) for one assessment of likely slope divisions.

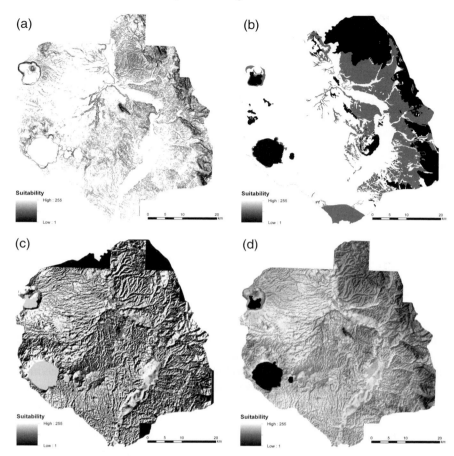

Fig. 3.2. (a) Slope map coded from 1 to 255 (worst to best); (b) fertility based on underlying geology, coded as 1 = unsuitable, 127 = medium suitability, 255 = most suitable; (c) aspect maps showing south- and east-facing slopes as most suitable (255); (d) output of analysis incorporating all three factors into a single 'suitability' image

requirements, this example demonstrates suitability for wheat production (Fig. 3.2). In order to realize the agronomists' descriptions in a quantitative way, a series of factor maps was created, all of them on a common scale of 1–255 (worst to best). First, a slope map (derived from elevation) was divided into categories to indicate the agronomists' recommendation for plains or gentle slopes. Plains were considered to be those slopes of 0–2 per cent, while gentle slopes were 2–8 per cent. These two categories were given the highest rating of 255, and all others given progressively lower ratings. It must be remembered also that modern definitions of what constitutes a gentle or moderate slope may not necessarily be the same as ancient conceptions. The evidence for aspect had shown south-facing slopes to be preferred (Cato *de*

Agr. 1.2) but eastern-facing slopes were also recommended by Columella (*Rust.* 1.2.3). The aspect map was, therefore, classified to show south-, south-eastern-, and eastern-facing slopes as highly suitable, and all other slopes as less suitable.

As there was no useable soil information available, the potential fertility was determined from the underlying geology. As the agronomists specified heavy, rich soils, the volcanic geology types and alluvial areas were classified as being suitable. As chalky soils were considered acceptable for use, calcareous geology types were given a medium rating. Types of geology completely unsuitable for agriculture included areas of rubble and scree. Those types deemed suitable were given a high classification of 255, while those considered unsuitable were classified as 1. Areas of uncertainty or of medium suitability were given a classification of 127. These included the urban areas for which we have no information, as well as areas of sandy deposits that contained concretions, which may have been an obstacle for farming.

This is a very simple example of a model, and methods of classification can range from this basic end of the scale up to far more complex factors involving fuzzy datasets and more robust statistical methods based on a variety of evidence. The way that the factors are amalgamated can also vary, as it is up to the modeller to decide the relative weighting and importance of each in the final output. In other words, which of the factors used (such as soil fertility or sunshine hours) will have had the biggest impact on production? There are also a number of different agricultural strategies to take into consideration. The Mediterranean landscape has been characterized since at least the seventh century BC in many areas by the use of intercultivation (the growing of multiple crops in the same area, such as wheat between vine rows),[48] which needs to be taken into consideration when creating models, particularly as it impacts heavily on agricultural output. As well as this are a number of fallowing and rotation practices, plus animal rearing, which can significantly alter overall production levels.[49] A variety of configurations for crops is therefore necessary, in order fully to test the outputs of possible strategies used in the area.

4.2. Creating site territories

The aspect with the greatest potential impact on production is site size. The site database used as the basis for early imperial settlement distribution is compiled from the results of field survey, and so it is not a straightforward matter to reconstruct the territories of each site using traditional means. The

---

[48] Spivey and Stoddart (1990: 62); Barker and Rasmussen (1998: 193).

[49] See Kron (2002) and Mackinnon (2004) for assessments of the productivity of livestock farming.

(a) (b)

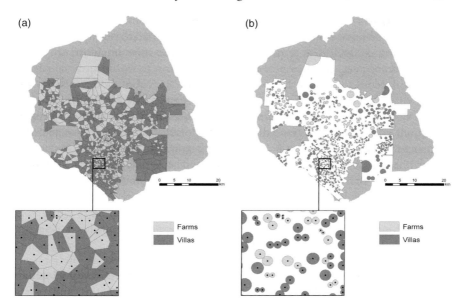

Fig. 3.3. (a) Thiessen polygons showing farm and villa territories; (b) buffers created by graphing distances between sites and their nearest neighbours. The lack of site hierarchy can be seen, as farms and villas appear to have similar-sized territories

use of field survey data is problematic, and there is a large corpus of work devoted to the interpretation of such data.[50] Examples of problems include biased collection strategies, incomplete datasets, and the generalized interpretation of sites as villas or farms, with no intermediate distinctions.

Typical methods of territory construction include the use of Thiessen polygons to carve up the available land by associating each area with its nearest site, but, with an unknown recovery rate of sites, this can create significant problems, as site territories can be artificially enlarged because of missing sites (Fig. 3.3a).[51] It also cannot account for site hierarchies (that is, whether villas would have had larger estates than farms, or whether farms operated within villa estates as tenants). However, what this *can* do is to provide a *maximum* size for sites that can then be whittled down according to other evidence.

Other techniques used to investigate potential site size included graphing average distances between known sites. In order to reduce the problems of missing sites that so badly affected the Thiessen polygons in this example, each site's nearest two neighbours were measured to ascertain potential estate radii

[50] For discussion, see Francovich *et al.* (2000); Witcher (2006, 2011).
[51] See Witcher (2011).

(Fig. 3.3b). While there is still a margin of error because of unrecovered sites, this is an improvement on simple tessellation. These results were then transformed into circular buffers, and the areas compared to written evidence concerning the size of rural Roman sites (both farms and villas), thereby determining a range of potential site sizes for further modelling. This is a simplistic method, though (not least with the assumption of circular territories), and leaves scope for more sophisticated modelling of potential site sizes using alternative geographical models (for example, the weighted XTENT model, or weighted Thiessen polygons, which derive territories based on physical factors as well as incorporating site hierarchy[52]), or incorporating other types of archaeological evidence (for example, land divisions).[53]

4.3. Total production figures

Once crop production maps have been created, and the area exploited determined, the next stage is to estimate total production for the area. It is at this point that we must consider the variety of agricultural strategies likely to have been in use: whether intercultivation was used, how much of a rotation was given over to fallow, and how much seed was retained for the next year's crop. The practice of monoculture (cultivation of a single crop) is extremely unlikely given what we know from both the Roman writers and comparative evidence. It is very risky, as well as making for a dull diet, and so farmers are more likely to have produced a variety of crops, whether for their own, or for market consumption.[54] Fortunately, the nature of the model allows us to consider different crop configurations using the Mediterranean triad of wheat, olives, and vines, each with its own production suitability map. These suitability maps, scaled 1–255, can therefore be reclassified to represent kilograms per hectare of yield, based on the crop, or different yields to model bad years, or different sowing amounts, for example. This therefore allows us to model variable yields based on land quality rather than the uniform yields put forward in previous models.

Fallowing and crop rotation schemes aid the fertility of the soil, guarding against soil exhaustion, and can dramatically affect the number of crops grown on a landholding. The Roman period seems to have had great diversity in the methods used, and no common system seems to have been followed.[55] Several

---

[52] Ducke and Kroefges (2008).
[53] e.g. Pelgrom (2008).
[54] Halstead and O'Shea (1989); Gallant (1991); Erdkamp (2005); see also Kron (2008) for an optimistic view of peasant production capability.
[55] White (1970a: ch. 4; 1970b); Spurr (1986: 117–25). Kron (2000) argues that rotations were incorporated within a system similar to modern ley-farming (intensive mixed farming).

different rotation schemes are known from the ancient writers (see especially Pliny, *NH* 18.91, and Columella, *Rust* 2.17.4). Reasons for choosing a particular rotation system rested on a number of factors: these included the amount of labour available, the amount of land owned, the location of the agricultural units, whether livestock was kept, and, if the cultivator was a tenant or slave, whether the landlord allowed it.[56] The fallow and rotation systems mentioned in the ancient literature range from a simple two-field fallow to three-field rotations involving legumes or other field crops (see Pliny, *NH* 18.91). The systems used in these analyses therefore range from a continual cropping model to an extensive three-quarter fallow regime.

Establishing an appropriate sowing rate is an integral part of the production map, as the original amount sown must be known in order to gauge total production (that is, if a yield is fivefold, one might sow 100 kg of seed and reap 500 kg of wheat). It also indicates how much of the total crop needs to be retained for the next year's sowing (that is, keep aside 100 kg, leaving a useable crop of 400 kg). The agronomists suggested five *modii* per *iugerum* (135 kg/ha) as a typical rate for a reasonable crop return (Varro, *Rust.* 1.44.1; Columella, *Rust.* 2.9.2), though there are other documented rates (6 *modii* /*iugerum*: Cicero, *Verr.* 2.3.112; 8–10 *modii* /*iugerum*: Columella, *Rust.* 2.9.1–2). Both Columella (*Rust.* 2.9.2–6) and Varro (*Rust.* 1.44.1), however, suggest that the amount sown really depends on local variables, such as soil, topography, and intensity of cultivation. In practice, these aspects are modelled outside the GIS. In this instance, once production was established, the statistics were extracted to a spreadsheet to allow deductions based on these factors.

4.4. Estimating supported population

Using the statistics created thus far, it is possible to calculate the potential population that could be supported in an area. As each production map provides the amount of crop, this can easily be converted into calories per unit area, and it is then a matter of determining the likely daily intake of a family group. This process has been discussed fully elsewhere, and a range of likely intake from slightly malnourished to well fed was used to determine population figures.[57]

A number of different models were created, but here are shown only the results for small farms in order to demonstrate the effect of different regimes.[58] The first two models use one-quarter fallow on 12-*iugera* farms using a range of different yields from 4:1 up to 15:1 and two different sowing

---

[56] Gallant (1991: 53).   [57] Goodchild (2007).
[58] For more detailed discussion of model results, see Goodchild (2006, 2007); Goodchild and Witcher (2009).

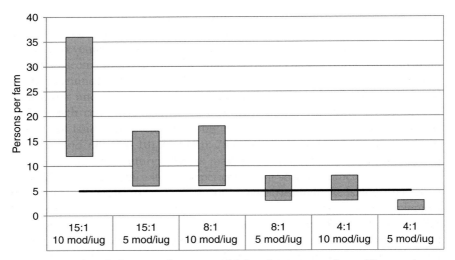

Fig. 3.4. Results of a basic production model for wheat monoculture. The grey boxes show the range in number of hypothetical people supported per farm and are based on consumption from malnourished to a healthy body mass index (i.e. more people can be supported if malnourished). The heavy line shows the assumed family of five people per farm

rates (5 and 10 *mod/iug*). The first iteration of the model is the result of modelling wheat as a single crop (monoculture, see Fig. 3.4).

The results shown in Fig. 3.5 are from an intercultivation model of half olives, half vines, with wheat between the rows. This is a high proportion of commodity goods compared with staples, and other configurations have been modelled elsewhere. The same basic parameters (yield, area cultivated, fallow) demonstrate that, although the 15:1 yields in both models appear to provide ample surplus beyond the mere subsistence of the five-person household, for the lower yields (especially 4:1) monoculture can leave the household short, while intercultivation is a less risky strategy. The overall highest-yielding model might be from wheat monoculture, but it also has the potential to yield the lowest. A bad year could therefore be potentially devastating. Lower overall yields in a mixed cultivation strategy are a safer bet. For the small farmer, it is better to have a variety than to go all out for a marketable surplus of a single crop.

4.5. Discussion

As is evident from the example shown here, this type of modelling can assist in highlighting which agricultural strategies were the most robust option in a

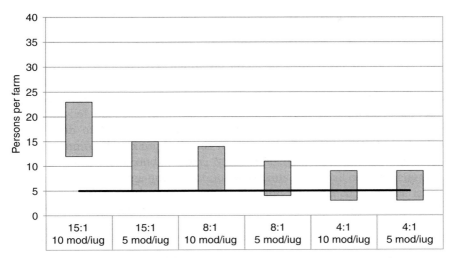

Fig. 3.5. Results of a basic production model for intercultivation (wheat, vines, and olives). The grey boxes show the range in number of hypothetical people per farm and are based on consumption from malnourished to a healthy body mass index. The heavy line shows the assumed family of five people per farm

particular area *according to the data provided in the ancient sources and the model variables used.* It highlights which might have been prone to failure and which would have meant the difference between profit and famine. Nevertheless, this type of modelling assumes that each farmer uses his land in the most logical and productive way. It is, however, unlikely that this would have happened in the 'real world'. Even if the model were perfect, lack of knowledge about the fertility or appropriate positioning of crops, or other social factors are likely to have resulted in land not being used to its full potential, thereby lowering the likely output of a farming unit. Also, we cannot assume that every farm and villa followed the same agricultural regime. It is highly likely, for instance, that subsistence farmers would use their land very differently from villa owners producing for the market, and might change their strategy annually in response to environmental or market conditions. Similarly, not all villa owners would have operated in the same way, depending on whether agriculture was their main source of income and whether their villa was a simple country retreat or a full-scale market-oriented operation.

The farming of crops is not the only means of obtaining food. Many other food sources would have been available to the rural Roman. In terms of self-sufficiency there is pastoral farming, foraging, dairy and eggs, or meat from domestic animals, vegetables from kitchen gardens, and fruit trees. Goods (either food or non-food items) may be traded for foodstuffs such as garum, which may provide much-needed dietary variety. It would be impossible to gauge the quantities of non-food products produced at a site—for example, textiles or pottery—thus highlighting one of the major issues with such models. It would be simply impossible to know a site's full income (either in produce or in monetary terms), but, by taking such aspects into consideration, we may, for example, be able to suggest potential economies for sites that may seem to be located in agriculturally unproductive areas.

With these problems in mind, we can appreciate clearly the advantage of models. By their very nature, models are iterative. It is possible to evaluate different combinations to see their effects. Parameters such as site size, the crops grown (and their configuration), yield, farm/villa population, and consumption levels may all be altered either because of the discovery of new data, or by testing hypothetical scenarios. This is not straightforward, however. In terms of the modelling process, we have the decision on how to weight factors (tied in with the problem of the Roman perception of suitability, discussed briefly above). How yields are applied to the maps can be problematic owing to lack of scientific data, in particular in relation to intercropping. Plot size, as discussed, was highly variable, and the wide variety of farming strategies leads unavoidably to generalization and assumptions. The greatest issue, however, was the sheer size of the study area. The size and variety of the area meant any regional patterning was completely obscured. It was therefore decided to focus on a small area in order to look at local production and individual units in more depth, also enabling an inter-regional comparison of the results in future work.

5. FURTHER MODELLING

This section summarizes recent work in the area that has attempted to address some of these issues.[59] A far smaller area of 11 km^2 was used to test a new model of agricultural production (Fig. 3.6).

The original approach was combined with an enhanced model to produce a preliminary model for the area, incorporating a variety of crops plus animal products, and using our own estimate of consumption based on slave workloads from Columella combined with skeletal data for stature (Table 3.1). The results shown in Figs 3.7 and 3.8 are, as before, for farm models only. Here two different farm sizes were used, and data were analysed from four periods dating from the Middle Republic to the Early Imperial. As this analysis was based on field survey data, the rise in site numbers (and therefore presumed population) is reflected in the results. As opposed to the previous figures

---

[59] Goodchild and Witcher (2009).

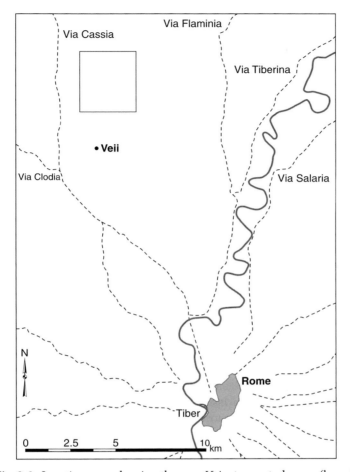

Fig. 3.6. Location map showing the *ager Veientanus* study area (boxed)

(Figs 3.4 and 3.5), which demonstrated individual farm populations, these results are aggregate numbers from the total site numbers from each of the four periods (the previous models concentrated only on the Early Imperial period). As such, the growing number of archaeologically visible sites is reflected in the assumed population (bold line in Figs 3.7 and 3.8).

The variables such as farm size, yield, and so on were used in order to test models put forward by Erdkamp and Rosenstein.[60] Two farm sizes were used (9 and 22 *iugera*) as alternative models with a yield of 8:1, and both sizes achieved production fully capable of supporting the farms' hypothetical five

---

[60] Rosenstein (2004); Erdkamp (2005).

Table 3.1. Variables used in Goodchild and Witcher (2009)

Yield rate (cereal)	Farm (9 and 22 *iugera*)	Villa (100 *iugera*)
Sowing rate (*modii per iugerum*)	8:1	8:1
Fallow	5	5
Intercultivation	1/4 wheat fallow	1/4 wheat fallow
Crops	50% wheat	50% wheat
	25% vines with wheat	25% vines with wheat
	25% olives with wheat	25% olives with wheat
Animal population/ composition	1 × 2-year-old undernourished scrap-fed pig slaughtered per annum	42 × sheep 2 × goats 3 × pigs slaughtered per annum (cf. farm model)
Human population/ composition	Adult male; Adult female; 18-year-old son; 15-year-old son; 10-year-old daughter	15 x slaves (equivalent of 3 families)
Mean daily consumption in calories	2,199–2,434	2,199–2,434

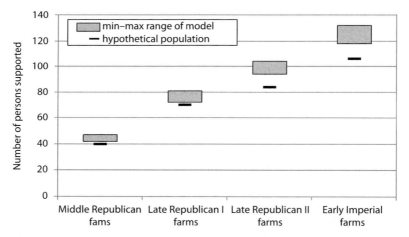

Fig. 3.7. Results of the local production model for 9-*iugera* farms from the Middle Republic to the Early Imperial period. The grey boxes show the range in total number of people supported in the area and is based on consumption from malnourished to a healthy body mass index. The heavy line shows the assumed family of five people per 9-*iugera* farm

inhabitants with some surplus. It is important to note that this model achieved a higher supported population using an 8:1 yield in this small area than was achieved in the previous example using the higher yield of 15:1 across the larger region (see Figs 3.4 and 3.5). This result therefore identifies important

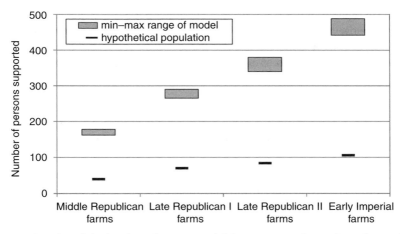

Fig. 3.8. Results of the local production model for 22-*iugera* farms from the Middle Republic to the Early Imperial period. The grey boxes show the range in total number of people supported in the area and are based on consumption from malnourished to a healthy body mass index. The heavy line shows the assumed family of five people per 22-*iugera* farm

regional variation, as it shows an area of high potential fertility able to generate substantial produce with a medium yield.

This produce would not all have been consumed locally. There are no towns directly within the study area, but there was a dense urban network in the middle Tiber valley (see Fig. 3.1), as well as the market in Rome to provide an outlet for surplus (and stimulus for production). This region is known historically as being a productive area, and it is not unlikely that farmers would have aimed to produce a marketable surplus.

Modelling such a variety of strategies and production levels has allowed us to see which methods were viable in the study areas (according to the written evidence). As I have stressed, these models are not an accurate portrayal of actual production, but being able to compare methods on a relative scale allows us to gauge what impact aspects such as the inclusion or exclusion of certain foodstuffs, or the size of the plot farmed (and how intensively), might have.

An example of how these models might be taken forward is in the potential yields of different periods, and to consider how farm and villa production compared. All rural sites were therefore analysed for mean potential production per hectare based on their modelled site territory. Table 3.2 shows that—according to this model—villas in continual occupation from the Late Republic to the Early Imperial period have the highest mean wheat production potential per hectare (1,087 kg/ha), while farms of the same period have lower potential output (1,015 kg/ha)—as we might expect from our assumptions about the elite having priority access to the best land. However, looking

Table 3.2. Comparison of mean productivity for farm sites in continual occupation and new Early Imperial foundations

	No. of farms	Mean kg/ha	No. of villas	*Mean kg/ha*
Continued occupation Late Republican II to Early Imperial period	5	1,015	9	1,087
New Early Imperial foundation	15	1,086	6	1,061

Source: Goodchild and Witcher (2009: 215, table 8).

at new foundations in the Early Imperial period, we see that farms appear to be sited on 'better' land than the new villas—in other words, on that land with a higher potential for wheat production according to the model. Farmers potentially produced an average of 1,086 kg/ha, while newly founded villas produced 1,061 kg/ha on average. This is at odds with our expectations, and appears to show that smaller farms have the priority on more productive land.

One possible explanation could be that land previously owned by the aristocracy was being opened up for use through tenant farming. In an early study of this area, De Neeve divided sites discovered through field survey into 'capitalist' villas and 'peasant' farms,[61] labels that have connotations of particular productivity and subsistence strategies. His interpretation assumed that villa culture had precedence in terms of access to good-quality land over the smaller farms, and therefore that their locations may be used to identify areas of cultural phenomena such as tenancy, and that freehold farms were restricted in their choice of location. Using this type of modelling, we can reassess De Neeve's arguments for Veii, testing whether the pattern holds up under more rigorous study. While initial results appear to support De Neeve's assertion, tenant farming is but one attractive possibility, and further modelling is required in other areas to assess whether the pattern is an artefact of the modelling process (that is, if different parameters are used, will the same pattern occur?), and, if not, whether it is a localized pattern confined to this area, or a more widespread phenomenon throughout the region.

6. CONCLUSION

The tenancy interpretation demonstrates that models are not just about quantifying the past (in terms of production or population), but also about understanding its qualitative character (for example, socio-economic relationships). This is just one direction that this type of modelling can take, but there

---

[61] De Neeve (1984: 26).

are many possibilities. Models are being continually refined as new evidence is unearthed, or improved modelling techniques come into being. A new focus on the excavation of smaller sites rather than villas will, one hopes, also redress the balance of knowledge, and initial discoveries have already demonstrated small farmers' ability to produce a surplus and their engagement with the market,[62] which ties in well with the models presented here. This is the most useful aspect of the process—the ability to incorporate a wide variety of evidence, and continually refine and improve. By modelling one particular aspect—agricultural production—it also allows us to study the effects on closely related areas such as demography and the economy. While we can never recreate these systems, approaching them from alternative perspectives allows hypotheses to be tested rigorously.

As such, constraining such models to one single area should also be avoided. Regional landscape projects primarily based on the results of field survey and other non-invasive techniques are becoming increasingly common,[63] and the generation of such datasets may be used to apply similar techniques to other regions of the empire. We cannot know the implications of comparing such models in provinces such as Greece or North Africa, or even between different regions of Italy herself, but such an undertaking would broaden our understanding of the larger economic systems. In this sense it is interesting to look at the 'less productive' areas. Could they support themselves or would they be reliant on larger local or global mechanisms such as trade?

In terms of improved modelling of geographic factors, since the original study was completed,[64] techniques have improved, with the incorporation of fuzzy datasets as well as as improved GIS modules to simplify the process.[65] As soil warmth is crucial to plant development, this is one aspect that can already be improved upon, and doubtless other factors will be addressed in the future. Along similar lines, modern agronomic modelling is a very advanced discipline, with specialist systems such as CropSyst, CERES, and DSSAT (among others) capable of analysing modern landscapes. Whether or not such systems may be used with a fragmentary Roman dataset is one area that would be interesting to pursue and, if possible, see how results compare from different modelling methods. Breaking down the study to the household level would also be a potential area, and agent-based-modelling approaches (as discussed above) would seem the ideal tool for exploring the effects of, for example, good and bad years in crop production, or changes in family numbers through

---

[62] Ghisleni *et al.* (2011).
[63] e.g. Dietz *et al.* (1995); Attema *et al.* (2002); Fentress (2009).
[64] Goodchild (2007).
[65] Fu and Rich (2002), for example, discuss GIS modules that enable the calculation of sunshine hours to determine which areas of a landscape will have received the most warmth.

aspects such as death, marriage, or absence on military service, and how this change in manpower could affect output. It would also allow the re-aggregation of these household-level actions in order to study their effects as larger systems.

Eisenhower famously stated: 'Farming looks mighty easy when your plow is a pencil and you're a thousand miles from the corn field.'[66] While he was referring to the tight state control of crops sown and market prices in the USA, his statement holds true when dealing with any agricultural modelling that is removed from actual experience. We cannot hope to reconstruct exactly what was happening in the fields of Roman Italy, but what we can do is offer a dialogue between the ancient evidence as gleaned from the agronomic texts, and the archaeological evidence—offering an opportunity explicitly to outline our assumptions. His statement therefore sums up the lack of reality we face when we create theoretical models of production. We are far removed, not only temporally but also in our understanding of the countryside, from Roman farmers, yet we can use ranges of production and orders of magnitude to decide whether certain historical models were possible in a real-life environment.

These models are merely the beginning. While computer models seem extremely remote from the real experience of Roman farmers, this is not to say that they cannot contribute to the debate. Just as the increased use of viewsheds (computer-generated models of visibility)[67] has coincided with much more critical thinking about visual perception, so we should expect that approaches to past land use such as these will lead to greater theoretical sophistication, and a deeper and more critical approach to how we interpret the archaeological and historical evidence for ancient farming.

ACKNOWLEDGEMENTS

I am very grateful to Vince Gaffney and Niall McKeown for their supervision and direction during my Ph.D., as well as to Helen Patterson and Andrew Wallace-Hadrill for use of the Tiber Valley Project data. Many thanks also go to Rob Witcher, Hannah Friedman, and Ulla Rajala for providing valuable feedback on earlier versions of this chapter. Finally, thanks go to the organizers of the Oxford Roman Economy Project for their invitation to present at the conference on 'The Agricultural Economy'.

---

[66] Eisenhower (1956).   [67] Lake (2003); Llobera (2003).

REFERENCES

Altaweel, M. (2008). 'Investigating Agricultural Sustainability and Strategies in Northern Mesopotamia: Results Produced Using a Socio-Ecological Modeling Approach', *Journal of Archaeological Science* 35: 821–35.

Anestis, G., Grigoroudis, E., Krassadaki, E., Matsatsinis, N. F., and Siskos, Y. (2006). 'Skills Evaluator: A Multicriteria Decision Support System for the Evaluation of Qualifications and Skills in Information and Communication Technologies', *Journal of Multi-Criteria Decision Analysis* 14.1–3: 21–34.

Attema, P., Burgers, G.-J., van Joolen, E., van Leusen, M., and Mater, B. (2002) (eds). *New Developments in Italian Landscape Archaeology: Theory and Methodology of Field Survey, Land Evaluation and Landscape Perception, Pottery Production and Distribution. Proceedings of a Three-Day Conference Held at the University of Groningen, April 13–15, 2000* (BAR International Series 1091). Oxford.

Barker, G., and Rasmussen, T. (1998). *The Etruscans*. Oxford.

Berqvist, S. (1992). 'Consideration on Yields, the Distribution of Crops and the Size of Estates: Three Roman Agricultural Units', *Classica et mediaevalia* 43: 111–39.

Box, G. E. P., and Draper, N. R. (1987). *Empirical Model-Building and Response Surfaces* (Wiley Series in Probability and Mathematical Statistics). New York.

Christaller, W. (1966). *Central Places in Southern Germany*, trans. C. W. Baskin. Englewood Cliffs, NJ.

Clarke, D. L. (1972) (ed.). *Models in Archaeology*. London.

Christiansen, J. H., and Altaweel, M. R. (2006). 'Understanding Ancient Societies: A New Approach Using Agent-Based Holistic Modeling', *Structure and Dynamics: eJournal of Anthropological and Related Sciences* 1.2: Article 7 <http://repositories.cdlib.org/imbs/socdyn/sdeas/vol1/iss2/art7/> (accessed 13 Aug. 2012).

Coarelli, F., and Patterson, H. (2009) (eds). *Mercator Placidissimus: The Tiber Valley in Antiquity (Proceedings of the Conference held at the British School at Rome, 27–28 Feb. 2004)*. Rome.

De Neeve, P. W. (1984). *Peasants in Peril. Location and Economy in Italy in the Second Century BC*. Amsterdam.

De Smith, M. J., Goodchild, M. F., and Longley, P. A. (2007). *Geospatial Analysis: A Comprehensive Guide to Principles, Techniques and Software Tools*. 3rd edn <http://www.spatialanalysisonline.com> (accessed January 2009).

Dietz, S., Ladjimi Sebaï, L. and Ben Hassen, H. (1995). *Africa Proconsularis: Regional Studies in the Segermes Valley of Northern Tunisia 1–2. Archaeological Fieldwork*. Aarhus.

Ducke, B., and Kroefges, P. C. (2008). 'From Points to Areas: Constructing Territories from Archaeological Site Patterns Using An Enhanced Xtent Model', in A. Posluschny, K. Lambers, and I. Herzog (eds), *Layers of Perception: Proceedings of the 35th International Conference on Computer Applications and Quantitative Methods in Archaeology (CAA). Berlin, Germany, April 2–6, 2007*. Bonn, 245–51.

Duncan-Jones, R. P. (1982). *The Economy of the Roman Empire: Quantitative Studies*. Cambridge.

Dyson, S. L. (1992). *Community and Society in Roman Italy*. London.

Eastman, J. R. (2001). *Guide to GIS and Image Processing*, II. Worcester, MA.

Eisenhower, D. D. (1956). 'Address at Bradley University, Peoria, Illinois September 25, 1956' <http://www.eisenhowermemorial.org/speeches/19560925%20Address%20at%20Bradley%20University%20Peoria%20Illinois.htm> (accessed January 2009).

Erdkamp, P. (2005). *The Grain Market in the Roman Empire: A Social, Political, and Economic Study*. Cambridge.

FAO (1976). *A Framework for Land Evaluation*. Rome.

Farshad, A. (2002). 'Land Evaluation in Archaeology, a Way to Enrich the Reconstruction of Past Agrarian Landscape: A Case Study of Iran', in P. Attema, G.-J. Burgers, E. van Joolen, M. van Leusen, and B. Mater (eds), *New Developments in Italian Landscape Archaeology: Theory and Methodology of Field Survey, Land Evaluation and Landscape Perception, Pottery Production and Distribution. Proceedings of a Three-Day Conference Held at the University Of Groningen, April 13–15, 2000* (BAR International Series 1091). Oxford, 189–95.

Favory, F., Girardot, J.-J. and Zannier, M.-P. (1995). 'La Perception des sols et des plantes chez les agronomes romains', in S. E. van der Leeuw (ed.), *The Archaeomedes Project: Understanding the Natural and Anthropogenic Causes of Soil Degradation and Desertification in the Mediterranean Basin*, III. *Dégradation et impact humain dans la moyenne et basse vallée du Rhône dans l'Antiquité (part II)*. Cambridge, 73–114.

Fentress, E. (2009). 'Peopling the Countryside: Roman Demography in the Albegna Valley and Jerba', in A. Bowman and A. Wilson (eds), *Quantifying the Roman Economy. Methods and Problems* (Oxford Studies in the Roman Economy 1). Oxford, 127–61.

Finke, P., Harding, J., Sevink, J., Sewuster, R., and Stoddart, S. (1994). 'The Dissection of a Bronze and Early Iron Age landscape', in C. Malone and S. Stoddart (eds), *Territory, Time and State: The Archaeological Development of the Gubbio Basin*. Cambridge, 81–93.

Foxhall, L. (1990). 'The Dependent Tenant: Land Leasing and Labour in Italy and Greece', *JRS* 80: 97–114.

Foxhall, L., and Forbes, H. (1982). 'Sitometreia: The Role of Grain as a Staple Food in Classical Antiquity', *Chiron* 12: 41–90.

Francovich, R., Patterson, H., and Barker, G. (2000) (eds). *The Archaeology of Mediterranean Landscapes 5: Extracting Meaning from Ploughsoil Assemblages*. Oxford, 16–26.

· Fu, P., and Rich, P. M. (2002). 'A Geometric Solar Radiation Model with Applications in Agriculture and Forestry', *Proceedings of the Second International Conference on Geospatial Information in Agriculture and Forestry*. I: 357–64 <http://www.creeksidescience.com/files/fu_rich_2000_giaf.pdf> (accessed September 2008).

Gaffney, V., and M. van Leusen (1995). 'Postscript—GIS, Environmental Determinism and Archaeology: A Parallel Text', in G. Lock and Z. Stančič (eds), *Archaeology and Geographical Information Systems: A European Perspective*. London, 367–81.

Gallant, T. (1991). *Risk and Survival in Ancient Greece: Reconstructing the Rural Domestic Economy*. Cambridge.

Ghisleni, M., Vaccaro, E., and Bowes, K. (2011). 'Excavating the Roman Peasant I: Excavations at Pievina (GR)', *PBSR* 79: 95–145.

Goodchild, H. (2006). 'Modelling Roman Demography and Urban Dependency in Central Italy', in B. Croxford, H. Goodchild, J. Lucas, and N. Ray (eds), *TRAC 2005: Proceedings of the 15th Theoretical Roman Archaeology Conference*. Oxford, 42–56.

Goodchild, H. (2007). 'Modelling Roman agricultural production in the Middle Tiber Valley, Central Italy'. Ph.D. thesis, University of Birmingham. http://etheses.bham. ac.uk/175/.

Goodchild, H. (2008). 'Modelling the Productive Landscape of the Middle Tiber Valley', in F. Coarelli and H. Patterson (eds), *Mercator Placidissimus: The Tiber Valley in Antiquity*. Rome, 769–96.

Goodchild, H., and Witcher, R. (2009). 'Field Survey and the Agricultural Landscape of Late Republican Italy', in J. Carlsen and E. Lo Cascio (eds), *Agricoltura e Scambi nell'Italia tardo repubblicana*. Bari, 187–220.

Graham, S. (2006). 'Networks, Agent-Based Models and the Antonine Itineraries: Implications for Roman Archaeology', *JMA* 19.1: 45–64.

Groenman-van Waateringe, W., and van Wijngaarden-Bakker, L. H. (1987) (eds). *Farm Life in a Carolingian Village: A Model Based on Botanical and Zoological Data from an Excavated Site*. Maastricht.

Haggis, D. (2008). 'Public Archaeology and the Analytic Hierarchy Process: Listening to the Crowd', *International Journal of the Humanities* 6.4: 153–62.

Halstead, P., and O'Shea, J. (1989) (eds). *Bad Year Economics: Cultural Responses to Risk and Uncertainty*. Cambridge.

Henig, M. I., and Weintraub, A. (2006). 'A Dynamic Objective–Subjective Structure for Forest Management Focusing on Environmental Issues', *Journal of Multi-Criteria Decision Analysis* 14.1–3: 55–65.

Hopkins, K. (1978). *Conquerors and Slaves* (Sociological Studies in Roman History 1). Cambridge.

Howey, M. C. L. (2007). 'Using Multi-Criteria Cost Surface Analysis to Explore Past Regional Landscapes: A Case Study of Ritual Activity and Social Interaction in Michigan, AD 1200–1600', *Journal of Archaeological Science* 34.11: 1830–46.

Kamermans, H. (2004). 'Archaeology and Land Evaluation in the Agro Pontino (Lazio, Italy)', in S. Holstrom, A. Voorrips, and H. Kamermans (eds), *The Agro Pontino Archaeological Survey* (Archaeological Studies, Leiden University 11). Leiden.

Kohler, T. A., and van der Leeuw, S. E. (2007) (eds). *The Model-Based Archaeology of Socionatural Systems*. Santa Fe, New Mexico.

Kron, G. (2000). 'Roman Ley-Farming', *Journal of Roman Archaeology* 13.1: 277–87.

Kron, G. (2002). 'Archaeozoological Evidence for the Productivity of Roman Livestock Farming', *Münstersche Beiträge zur Antiken Handelsgeschichte* 21.2: 53–73.

Kron, G. (2008). 'The Much-Maligned Peasant: Comparative Perspectives on the Productivity of the Small Farmer in Classical Antiquity', in L. De Ligt and S. Northwood (eds), *People, Land, and Politics: Demographic Developments and the Transformation of Roman Italy 300 BC–AD 14*. Leiden, 71–119.

Kvamme, K. L. (1990). 'The Fundamental Principles and Practice of Predictive Archaeological Modeling', in A. Voorrips (ed.), *Mathematics and Information Science in Archaeology: A Flexible Framework* (Studies in Modern Archaeology 3). Bonn, 257–95.

Kvamme, K. L. (2005). 'Archaeological Modeling with GIS at Scales Large and Small', in *Reading Historical Spatial Information from Around the World: Studies of Culture and Civilization Based on Geographic Information Systems Data* (International Symposium 24, International Research Center for Japanese Studies). Kyoto, 75–91.

Lake, M. (2003). 'Visibility Studies in Archaeology: A Review and Case Study', *Environment and Planning B: Planning and Design*, 30: 689–707.

Leveau, P., Walsh, K., Trément, F., and Barker, G. (1999) (eds). *The Archaeology of Mediterranean Landscapes 2: Environmental Reconstruction in Mediterranean Landscape Archaeology.* Oxford.

Llobera, M. (2003). 'Extending GIS-Based Visual Analysis: The Concept of Visualscapes', *International Journal of Geographical Information Science* 17.1: 25–48.

Lo Cascio, E. (1999). 'The Population of Roman Italy in Town and Country', in J. Bintliff and K. Sbonias (eds), *The Archaeology of Mediterranean Landscapes 1: Reconstructing Past Population Trends in Mediterranean Europe (3000 BC–AD 1800).* Oxford, 161–71.

Mackinnon, M. (2004). *Production and Consumption of Animals in Roman Italy: Integrating the Zooarchaeological and Textual Evidence* (Journal of Roman Archaeology Supplementary Series 54). Portsmouth, RI.

Muzzioli, M. P. (1980). *Forma Italia Regio 4.2. Cures Sabini.* Florence.

Patterson, H. (2004) (ed.). *Bridging the Tiber: Approaches to Regional Archaeology in the Middle Tiber Valley* (Archaeological Monographs of the British School at Rome 13). London.

Pelgrom, J. (2008). 'Settlement Organization and Land Distribution in Latin Colonies before the Second Punic War', in L. De Ligt and S. Northwood (eds), *People, Land, and Politics: Demographic Developments and the Transformation of Roman Italy 300 BC–AD 14.* Leiden, 333–72.

Posluschny, A., Lambers, K., and Herzog, I. (2008) (eds). *Layers of Perception: Proceedings of the 35th International Conference on Computer Applications and Quantitative Methods in Archaeology (CAA). Berlin, Germany, April 2–6, 2007.* Bonn.

Potter, T. W. (1979). *The Changing Landscape of South Etruria.* London.

Reynolds, P. J. (1981). 'Deadstock and Livestock', in R. Mercer (ed.), *Farming Practice in British Prehistory.* Edinburgh, 97–122.

Robb, J., and van Hove, D. (2003). 'Gardening, Foraging and Herding: Neolithic Land Use and Social Territories in Southern Italy', *Antiquity* 77.296: 241–54.

Rosenstein, N. (2004). *Rome at War: Farms, Families, and Death in the Middle Republic.* London.

Saile, T. (1997). 'Landscape Archaeology in Central Germany: Site Catchment Analysis Using GIS', in I. Johnson and M. North (eds), *Archaeological Applications of GIS: Proceedings of Colloquium II, UISPP XIIIth Congress, Forli, Italy, September 1996* (CD-ROM). Sydney.

Sallares, R. (1991). *The Ecology of the Ancient Greek World.* London.

Scheidel, W. (2001) (ed.). *Debating Roman Demography* (Mnemosyne, Bibliotheca Classica Batava 211). Leiden.

Schowengerdt, R. A. (1983). *Techniques for Image Processing and Classification in Remote Sensing.* New York.

Shiel, R. S. (1999). 'Reconstructing Past Soil Environments in the Mediterranean Region', in P. Leveau, K. Walsh, F. Trément, and G. Barker (eds), *The Archaeology of Mediterranean Landscapes 2: Environmental Reconstruction in Mediterranean Landscape Archaeology.* Oxford, 67–79.

Spivey, N., and Stoddart, S. (1990). *Etruscan Italy.* London.

Spurr, M. S. (1986). *Arable Cultivation in Roman Italy c.200 BC–c. AD 100* (Journal of Roman Studies Monographs 3). London.

Stančič, Z., Gaffney, V., Ostir-Sedej, K., and Podobnikar, T. (1997). 'GIS Analysis of Land-Use, Settlement Patterns and Territories on the Island of Brač', in I. Johnson and M. North (eds), *Archaeological Applications of GIS: Proceedings of Colloquium II, UISPP XIIIth Congress, Forli, Italy, September 1996* (CD-ROM). Sydney.

Van de Leeuw, S. (2004). 'Why Model?', *Cybernetics and Systems* 35.2: 117–28.

Van Joolen, E. (2003). 'Archaeological Land Evaluation: A Reconstruction of the Suitability of Ancient Landscapes for Various Land Uses in Italy Focused on the First Millennium BC.' Ph.D. Thesis, University of Groningen <http://www.ub.rug. nl/eldoc/dis/arts/e.van.joolen/> (accessed February 2004).

Verhagen, P. (2002). 'Some Considerations on the Use of Archaeological Land Evaluation', in P. Attema, G.-J. Burgers, E. van Joolen, M. van Leusen, and B. Mater (eds), *New Developments in Italian Landscape Archaeology: Theory and Methodology of Field Survey, Land Evaluation and Landscape Perception, Pottery Production and Distribution. Proceedings of a Three-Day Conference Held at the University of Groningen, April 13–15, 2000* (BAR International Series 1091). Oxford, 200–4.

Verhagen, P. (2007). *Case Studies in Archaeological Predictive Modelling*. Leiden.

Verhagen, P., Gili, S., Micó, R., and Risch, R. (1999). 'Modelling Prehistoric Land Use Distribution in the Rio Aguas Valley (Province of Almería, S.E. Spain)', in L. Dingwall, S. Exon, V. Gaffney, S. Laflin, and M. van Leusen (eds), *Archaeology in the Age of the Internet. CAA97. Computer Applications and Quantitative Methods in Archaeology 25th Anniversary Conference, University of Birmingham* (BAR International Series 750). Oxford.

Vita-Finzi, C., and Higgs, E. S. (1970). 'Prehistoric Economy in the Mount Carmel Area of Palestine: Site Catchment Analysis', *Proceedings of the Prehistoric Society* 36: 1–37.

Von Thünen, J. H. (1966). *Von Thünen's 'Isolated State': An English Edition*, trans. C. M. Wartenberg. Oxford.

Wheatley, D. (2004). 'Making Space for an Archaeology of Place', Internet Archaeology 15 <http://intarch.ac.uk/journal/issue15/wheatley_index.html> (accessed July 2007).

White, K. D. (1970a). *Roman Farming*. London.

White, K. D. (1970b). 'Fallowing, Crop Rotation, and Crop Yields in Roman Times', *Agricultural History* 44.3: 281–90.

Wilkinson, T. J., Gibson, M., Christiansen, J. H., Widell, M., Schloen, D., Kouchoukos, N., Altaweel, M., Ur, J., and Hritz, C. (2007). 'Modeling Settlement Systems in a Dynamic Environment: Case Studies from Mesopotamia', in T. A. Kohler and S. E. Van Der Leeuw (eds), *Model-Based Archaeology of Socionatural Systems*. Santa Fe, 175–208.

Witcher, R. E. (2006). 'Broken Pots and Meaningless Dots? Surveying the Rural Landscapes of Roman Italy', *PBSR* 74: 39–72.

Witcher, R. E. (2011). 'Missing Persons? Models of Mediterranean Regional Survey and Ancient Populations', in A. Bowman and A. Wilson (eds), *Settlement, Urbanization, and Population* (Oxford Studies in the Roman Economy 2). Oxford, 36–75.

4

Agricultural Production in the Hinterland of Rome: Wine and Olive Oil

Annalisa Marzano

INTRODUCTION

The Roman period was marked by unprecedented agricultural exploitation in many of the areas of the empire. In various provinces, such as the Three Gauls, the presence of farms and villas in the territory reached concentrations achieved again only in later historical periods, while in other regions, such as North Africa, marginal lands were brought under cultivation.[1] The case of olive oil production in North Africa and Baetica, or of wine in Tarraconensis and Gallia Narbonensis, represented an unsurpassed scale of production and specialization for the ancient world. Rome, with its estimated one million inhabitants, was the receiver of much of this surplus produced in the provinces, as Monte Testaccio, the artificial hill made entirely of discarded empty amphorae, attests in the case of olive oil. Rome, however, relied on Italian agricultural production as well as imports.

Understanding the production capacity of the Roman hinterland is important in many respects. Not only can this help in assessing the degree of Rome's needs, which ultimately stimulated the development of intensive agricultural exploitation in the provinces, but it also sheds light on the type of land exploitation, settlement patterns, and degree of capital investment in production facilities, and on whether there was a crisis in Italian agricultural production in the Imperial period; all these elements are connected to the question of the degree of economic growth and/or contraction in the Imperial period. This chapter focuses on Italy, in particular on the hinterland of Rome,[2]

---

[1] Brun (2005: 178).

[2] This area, larger than the traditional extension of the *suburbium* proper (on differences in defining the ancient *suburbium*, see De Franceschini 2005 and Mayer 2005), has been defined by previous studies on the basis of geographical features and travel times, and supplied Rome and

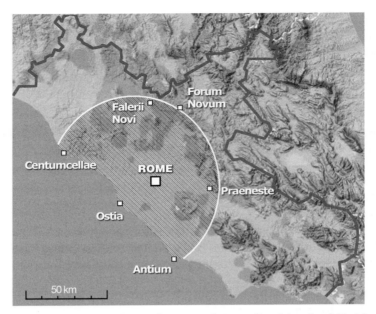

Fig. 4.1. Area considered in this study as Rome's immediate hinterland (A. Marzano)

in order to analyse its potential production capacity in wine and olive oil. The area under examination encompasses the territory that stretches from Centumcellae (Civitavecchia), on the coast north of Rome, to Falerii Novi, Forum Novum, Praeneste, and Antium, covering an area of *c*.5,500 km² (Fig. 4.1).

THE HINTERLAND AND ITS
AGRICULTURAL PRODUCTION

The territory surrounding Rome was densely occupied by modest farms and luxurious villas;[3] both types of settlement were engaged in some form of agricultural production, even if not always of wine and oil. *Pastio villatica*, or the production of luxury foods for the urban market, was considered by the Latin agronomists part of agriculture proper.[4] It ranged widely from the

---

Ostia with many fresh products. It is the same area considered by De Sena (2005), on which see my discussion below.

[3] De Franceschini (2005); Di Giuseppe (2005); Marzano (2007).

[4] See Pliny, *HN* 9.168, Varro, *Rust.* 3, *de villatica pastione*, for discussion of different forms of *pastio villatica*, and 3.2.15–16 about the profit made by his aunt by breeding thrushes; Martin (1971) for analysis of the works of the agronomists.

breeding of poultry and fish to the production of honey, and is well attested in the region around Rome both in the archaeological finds and in the references in the literary sources.[5] The production of these quality products, stimulated by the demand of the large Roman market, went alongside the limited production of staple foods needed to feed the inhabitants of the metropolis, which had to be topped up by massive imports.[6] However, although the agricultural production in this area was very varied and devoted to the fresh products required by the city that could not be transported over long distances—fresh vegetables, fruit, flowers—the production of olive oil, and above all wine, attested as early as the sixth and fifth centuries BC,[7] appears to have remained substantial also in the Imperial period. An example of very successful intensive grape cultivation only 16 km from Rome referred to in the written sources is the estate of Acilius Sthenelus and the *fundus* developed with his help by the grammarian Remnius Polemon. Columella (*Rust.* 3.3.3) reports that this vineyard produced the equivalent of 40 hectolitres of wine/*iugerum*, and we are told that the property was later purchased by Seneca for its productivity.[8] From an archaeological point of view, even though we have literary evidence about vegetable production in the *suburbium* and many elements of hydraulic infrastructure such as cisterns can plausibly be related to irrigation of gardens and orchards,[9] the best evidence in trying to assess the agricultural productivity of the area around Rome and the level of capital investment reached in this sector relates to wine and oil production because of the presence of the pressing facilities to process grape and olives, which are very visible archaeologically.

In an important article on olive oil production in the Roman empire published twenty years ago, David Mattingly offered some considerations on Italian agriculture and discussed how it differed from the developments observed in the provincial areas where the most intensive olive cultivation took place.[10] Without denying the existence of a surplus production of oil in Roman Italy, Mattingly pointed out that it must have been, overall, rather small. Despite the frequent praise for Italian olive oils found in the literary sources, in his view the absence of sites that could be described as oileries (facilities comprising multiple presses), the prevalence of winemaking as the preferred form of investment for the elite,[11] and, in the immediate environs of

---

[5] Soprintendenza Archeologica di Roma (1986); Marzano (2007: 85–100).

[6] Morley (1996). On the grain market to feed the capital, see Erdkamp (2005).

[7] see Volpe (2000) for discussion of trenches for vineyards identified in the *suburbium* near Centocelle (sixth–fifth century BC); Carandini *et al.* (1997) for the olive press in the Auditorium villa, dated to the fifth-century-BC phase.

[8] Plin., *HN* 14.5.48–51; Suet., *Gram.* 23. See also Kolendo (1994: 61–2).

[9] Thomas and Wilson (1994); Wilson (1999, 2009b).

[10] Mattingly (1988b).

[11] Purcell (1985).

Rome, the possibility of exploiting commercially other types of production—fresh fruit, vegetables, *pastio villatica*—were all indications of the limited oil production possible in Italy. Over twenty years later, it is worth asking whether anything more can be added to this reconstruction.

THE DATA

Part of the problem in assessing the potential production in wine and oil of the area around Rome is that we are dealing not only with a ravaged archaeological record,[12] but also with containers used for the local distribution of these commodities that were perishable, and therefore remain invisible to modern research. In stark contrast with what one can observe in, say, Gaul, no amphora kilns are known for the areas around Rome where evidence of wine and oil presses exists.[13] Unlike the transmarine imports or the wine coming to Rome from Umbria and the Adriatic regions via the Tiber, oil and wine produced in the hinterland and distributed locally and in Rome were transported in perishable containers and/or in reused amphorae, thus escaping detection.[14] Therefore, inevitably, one relies on the evidence offered by the processing facilities themselves.

Looking at known elite villas, meaning by this designation the establishments presenting a well-appointed *pars urbana* and indications of a productive sector, of the 384 villas recorded for Latium,[15] as many as 338 were located in the area under consideration in this study. Only forty-four of these sites, however, presented secure evidence for the presence of presses, for the production of either wine or olive oil. To these occurrences, attestations of presses at sites that did not fall into the category of elite villas have been added.[16] Thus,

---

[12] See the (unheeded) appeals launched by Ashby in 1903 and 1908 to the Direzione Generale alle Antichità e Belle Arti to proceed with the systematic excavation and recording of villas and farms in the territory around Rome before development in the area destroyed the record: Quilici (1979).

[13] Amphora production (Spello type) destined for a very local market was identified in Sabina in the territory of ancient Eretrum (Marzolano): Bousquet *et al.* (2003).

[14] Tchernia (1986: 285–92); Panella (1989: 162–3); De Sena (2005: 140); Wilson (2009a: 216). Barrels and skins (Lat. *cupae, cullei, utres*) started to be widespread earlier than previously thought (Marlière 2002; Brun 2005: 10–11). In Gaul, products that were not destined for transmarine shipment were distributed in barrels, as attested by finds of large barrels dating to the Augustan period in the military forts along the Rhine. In some cases barrels were simply preferred to amphorae: this seems to have been the case for Portugal: Brun (2004: 47–8, 284–94). For the likelihood that some wine was shipped overseas in barrels, see Wilson (2009a).

[15] Marzano (2007).

[16] A number of farms equipped with presses were derived from Bastianelli (1939), De Sena (2005), De Franceschini (2005), Allegrezza (2007), and from the *Forma Italiae* volumes on Tibur (Giuliani 1970, 1976; Mari 1983, 1991) and Tusculum (Valenti 2003).

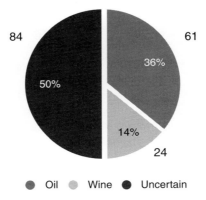

Fig. 4.2. Numbers and types of presses attested archaeologically in the study area (n = 169)

if the available data on presses at both villas and farms are combined, in the area under consideration there are 140 sites that display secure evidence for the presence of pressing equipment, and a total of 169 attested presses.

Only sites with *secure* evidence of the presence of presses have been taken into consideration: the recovery of press beds, counterweights, blocks to fix the *arbores*, the layout of vats faced with hydraulic mortar according to a typology that can be associated with presses with a degree of confidence, or the presence of olive mills. Unlike wine, oil cannot be extracted in any significant quantity without a press, even if rudimentary; the presence of an olive mill, used to crush the olives into a paste before pressing, is therefore a secure indication that there was a press for oil. There are many more sites in the area under examination where the presence of vats lined with hydraulic mortar may point to oil or wine making,[17] but they have been excluded unless other elements indicated the presence of a press on site, even if in some cases sizeable wine production was achieved apparently by only treading the grapes. Taking only the secure press sites into account also allows us a meaningful sense of comparison with the research work carried out in North Africa and Spain.[18] Of the 169 attested presses, 61 can be attributed securely to olive oil production, while 24 relate to wine; for the remaining 84 presses it remains unclear whether they were used for oil or wine production (Fig. 4.2). Considering that the data largely derive from chance finds in field survey in a densely inhabited and urbanized area, these figures represent only the minimum number of presses that were present in the region. In addition to this, a certain degree of processing of oil must also have taken place in the towns of Italy, as inferred

[17] For example, at Veio villa Campetti: De Franceschini (2005: 4–9), with other examples.
[18] Ponsich (1974, 1979, 1987, 1991); Mattingly (1988b, 1995); Hitchner (1990);. de Vos (2000).

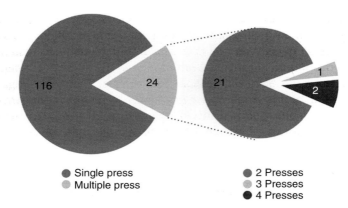

Fig. 4.3. Number of sites equipped with single or multiple presses (left) and breakdown of number of presses attested at various sites (right)

from epigraphic evidence, although to my knowledge, with the exception of the presses for perfume making discovered at Pompeii and Paestum, we do not know yet of any olive presses in urban contexts in Italy.[19]

Only 24 out of 140 sites equipped with presses had multiple pressing facilities. Normally two presses are attested in these cases, but in two instances we find four presses (at the villa of Val Melaina, in the *suburbium*, and at Granaraccio, near Tivoli), and in one case three presses (the villa of Via Togliatti, also located in the *suburbium*) (Fig. 4.3).[20] It is apparent that one does not find in this area large industrial production centres with multiple presses, as in the case of the large oileries of North Africa or Istria.[21] Even in the case of wine production, which boomed in the Republican period, to judge on the basis of the available evidence, sites with more than two presses are rare in Italy: we know only of the famous villa at Settefinestre, which was equipped with three wine presses, and of the nearby, but unfortunately little known, site of Via della Fattoria, which had four.[22] When multiple presses are attested, in most cases they belong to sites producing both olive oil and wine and using one press for each production. This is also a common trend in Italian villas outside this region, as, for instance, in the villas of Campania, which were often devoted to both wine and oil production.[23]

[19] Brun (2004: 8), referring to the attestation of *collegia capulatorum/caplatorum* (those who refined and bottled olive oil, e.g., *ILS* 1909: Anagnia; *ILS* 6244: Tibur; *ILS* 7298: Allifae); for the perfume press at Paestum: Brun (2000); at Pompeii, in Via degli Augustali: Mattingly (1990).

[20] Marzano (2007: 559, 561, 574).

[21] For instance, the villa of Barbariga (Istria) equipped with at least ten presses (Brun 2004: 56–7) or the production centre at Senam Semana (Tripolitania) with seventeen presses (Mattingly 1995: 142; Brun 2004: 190–1).

[22] Carandini (1985); Carandini and Cambi (2002: 150, 156).

[23] For example, the villa Pisanella at Boscoreale, with two wine presses and one oil press: Brun (2004: 14–18).

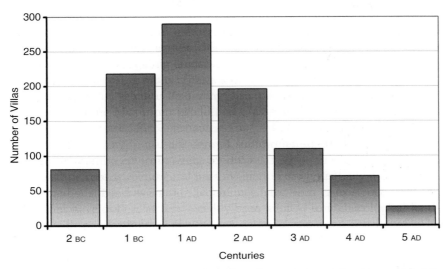

Fig. 4.4. Chronological phases attested at elite villas in Latium (after Marzano 2007)

Unlike the case of Gaul, where it seems that to a certain degree in the second century AD various small winemaking sites were abandoned while some multi-press sites appeared, the trend to centralize production facilities in large villas is not apparent in this region for the Imperial period.[24] Of course not all of the presses listed here would have been in use at the same time, but the data on their chronology are too fragmentary and scanty to allow for a detailed temporal analysis. In those few cases when chronological data are available, the installation of the presses can be dated to the late Republican or Julio-Claudian period. This is also the period when we see the peak in attested phases in elite villas of Latium, both in constructions *ex novo* and in beautification projects occurring at existing sites (Fig. 4.4).[25]

In the area under consideration, measuring *c.*5,500 km², there is therefore a density of one press every *c.*32.5 km². This figure is not impressive when compared to the situation known for the North African oil-producing regions. In Libya, the hinterland of Lepcis Magna and Oea, in particular the Fergian area and the Tarhuna Plateau, shows a great concentration of presses; the sites include both farms with a single press and larger oileries with more than three presses. In total there are 262 presses recorded for this area, but, as pointed out by Mattingly, this is only a minimum figure.[26] The Fergian area alone has 138 presses over 300 km²; this means that, allowing for some loss in the recovery rate, there was an average of one press every 2 km². From this density value,

---

[24] Brun (2005: 25, 39–41); Marzano, Chapter 5, this volume.
[25] Marzano (2007: 771–8).   [26] Mattingly (1988b: 35).

Mattingly estimated that the whole territory of Lepcis Magna alone may have had *c.*1,500 presses, theoretically able to produce 15 million litres of oil; adding to this the possible production of the regions surrounding Oea and Sabratha, one arrives at a total maximum production capacity for the region of 30 million litres of oil. For Tunisia, the data available, especially for the Kasserine, Sbeïtla, and Thelepte areas, show a minimum number of 350 presses over 1,500 km^2,[27] meaning that, on average, there was one press every *c.*4 km^2.

However, the archaeological attestations of press sites in the third major oil-producing region of the empire are, in comparison, rather scant. For the Guadalquivir valley in Spain, from where the massive oil imports attested by Monte Testaccio originated,[28] in spite of the field survey work carried out by Ponsich, we do not have a detailed knowledge of the production centres. Assessing the presence of presses, whether single or multiple, depended on the chance recovery of part of presses or olive mills. Ponsich recorded *c.*1,500 sites in this region; of these, only 111 are certain press sites and 50 are possible press sites.[29] The total surveyed area measured *c.*2,500 km^2; although the precise extent of this territory devoted to olive cultivation is not known, the securely attested presses equal a concentration of only one press every *c.*23 km^2.

If we move from the degree of production to other issues such as type of ownership and capital investment, a few considerations can be advanced. There are two cases of a press attested in a villa belonging to the emperor, but generally speaking, although some of the sites considered in this chapter, especially those in Tusculum and Tibur, became with time the property of the imperial *fiscus*, that was not the case when the presses were installed. Thus, the attestation of investment of capital in production facilities relates to both villas and farms, with a considerable number of presses appearing in farms. It is generally agreed that the installation of a press required considerable capital.[30] It is an open question how one should interpret the many medium-sized farms that were equipped with a *torcular*, whether as properties owned by small farmers who were still able to afford the investment and be competitive on the market,[31] or as part of larger estates. A small farm does not automatically mean that the proprietor was a person of limited means; farms could be part of the large estates owned by the wealthy, which encompassed villas and smaller settlements. Not much can be said, therefore, about the type of ownership of these properties, but, if one agrees that the installation of a press required

---

[27] Mattingly (1988b: 47); Hitchner (1993).

[28] It is estimated that *c.*320,000 Baetican amphorae reached Rome annually: Rodríguez Almeida (1984: 116–17).

[29] Ponsich (1974, 1979, 1987); Mattingly (1988b: 38 n. 32).

[30] See, e.g., the various contributions in Amouretti and Brun (1993).

[31] For a re-evaluation of the productivity of Roman agricultural practices, arguing in favour of the competitiveness on the market of small farmers, see Kron (2008).

substantial capital, it seems plausible to infer that the sites equipped with these presses were owned by proprietors with sufficient financial resources and land to want to make such a capital investment in production facilities.[32] The fact that in the Italian peninsula we have rare attestations of sites with more than two presses, and that these double-press sites were producing both wine and oil, is a direct indicator of the size of the estates devoted to the cultivation of vines and olive trees. It means that, particularly in central Italy, the large estates of the Roman wealthy were not one contiguous property, but several scattered properties in different geographical locations. Such fragmented landowning patterns, emerging also from epigraphic documents such as the *Tabulae Alimentariae* of Veleia and Ligures Baebiani,[33] did not allow the concentration of production at fewer, larger production facilities.[34]

QUANTIFYING OIL AND WINE PRODUCTION

In a recent article Eric De Sena put forward a possible model for assessing the production of the hinterland of Rome. Considering amphora capacity, he starts by assessing the maximum volume/year of imported wine and oil as reflected by ceramic assemblages of the DAI/AAR excavations at Ostia and Rome. Then, looking at the total projected needs of ancient Rome and Ostia in terms of wine and oil,[35] and combining modern data on oil and wine production in the area around Rome, the scant archaeological evidence, and indications in Cato's work, he suggests that as much as 33 per cent of the wine and 25 per cent of the oil consumed in Rome may have derived from its hinterland. De Sena's model takes as its starting point the portion of territory nowadays devoted to vine and olive cultivation in Latium. In modern-day Latium, an average of 340 million litres of wine is produced annually from 45,000 hectares

---

[32] Rosenstein (2008: 11) writes that, considering the price for an oil press given by Cato, *Agr.* 22, proprietors able to afford ownership of several slaves could also easily buy a press; however, Cato's passage refers to the *trapetum* or oil mill, not the press proper, the price of which is not given (see *Agr.* 18).

[33] Pliny the Elder (*HN* 18.35) famously stated that *latifundia* had ruined Italy and that the same was happening in the provinces, but, except for some geographic areas such as Apulia, the Italian evidence points to the fact that these *latifundia* were not contiguous property. For the property listed in the alimentary tables (*ILS* 6509, 6675; Criniti 1991), see Kron (2008: 94–5) for a synthetic presentation of the data.

[34] As stated above, this picture is very different from the case of the large Roman villas known in Istria, which were equipped with many presses for one type of production: Brun (2004: 50–8).

[35] De Sena (2005). The needs of Rome and Ostia are calculated considering a population of 1 million in Rome and *c.*50,000 in Ostia, consuming *per capita*, on average, 20 litres of olive oil/year and 100 litres of wine/year. Estimates for ancient wine consumption vary widely: Kehoe (2007: 556) posits 100 litres, Tchernia (1986: 26) between 146 and 182 litres, Purcell (1985: 13) 250 litres. Cf. also Jongman (2007: 602–3).

of vines. Considering that the immediate hinterland of ancient Rome corresponds to *c.*65 per cent of the land at present used for vineyards, De Sena takes the figure of an expected production of 221 million litres from 29,000 hectares. To counterbalance the higher modern productivity because of advanced viticultural techniques, he then considers the production figures given by Cato of 800 *cullei* = 413,600 litres for a 100-*iugera* vineyard (*Agr.* 11), and applies this figure for productivity to the 29,000 hectares of possible land devoted to vine cultivation, thus suggesting a potential production of 96 million litres/year. On the basis of a rough estimate, De Sena takes 250,000 as the number of inhabitants of the hinterland, and thus, having subtracted their wine consumption, proposes *c.*54 million litres of surplus wine available for consumption in the metropolis.

If we turn to olive cultivation, modern-day Latium has 86,000 hectares of olive groves, producing an average of 24 million litres of virgin oil/year (the variation in yield is due to the two-year cycle of the olive trees, to variations in rainfall, and so on). The area that in antiquity was in the immediate hinterland of Rome and is now cultivated with olives would have been equal to 56,000 hectares of olive groves.[36] Bearing in mind that recent technology employing hydraulic presses, in comparison to the efficiency of ancient presses, reduces the time needed to press a given amount of olive paste, but does not increase production,[37] and assuming that ancient and modern yields were essentially the same, De Sena proposes an average possible annual oil yield of 15 million litres. When considering a more conservative figure of an average yield of 9.7 million litres, based on Brun's research on ancient oil production in Provence,[38] De Sena suggests that 4.7 million litres were the available surplus for Rome. Finally, he combines this projection with the ceramic data, calculating the rough volume of imports in litres from the various parts of the empire. The conclusions he reaches on the origins of the wine and oil consumed in Rome/Ostia annually in *c.* AD 100–150 are illustrated in Figs 4.5 and 4.6.

In this hypothetical reconstruction, the contribution of the hinterland of Rome, in terms of both wine and oil, is considerable. It is also worth noting that the percentage of wine supplied from Etruria and Umbria, as inferred from the ceramics, is also notably more than the imports from Narbonensis, so that more than 50 per cent of the wine for Rome would have come from Italy alone. This may offer an insightful contribution to the debate over the agricultural crisis encountered, especially by Italian wine producers, in the late first and early second century AD in the wake of strong competition from those provinces (Gallia, Tarraconensis) that had turned them from importers

---

[36] According to Cato, *Agr.* 6.1, and Plin., *HN* 17.93–4, agricultural practices in Italy envisaged *c.*180 olive trees/ha; see Mattingly (1994: 93).
[37] Mattingly (1988a).   [38] Brun (1986).

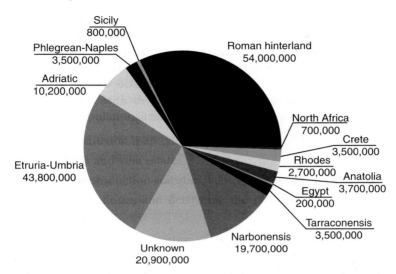

Fig. 4.5. Origins of the wine (in litres) consumed annually in Rome on the basis of ceramic evidence and estimates of local produce, AD 100–150 (after De Sena 2005: fig. 3)

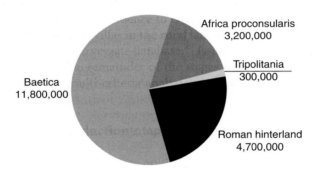

Fig. 4.6. Origins of the olive oil (in litres) consumed annually in Rome on the basis of ceramic evidence and estimates of local produce, AD 100–150 (after De Sena 2005: fig. 4)

of Italian wine into producers and exporters. As pointed out by some scholars, it seems exaggerated to posit a total crisis of Italian agriculture and, consequently, a collapse of the villa system, when, more likely, the cessation of exports meant a reorganization of distribution at regional level;[39] the ceramic assemblage studies by De Sena appear to confirm this.

[39] Marzano (2005; 2007: 199–222); Tchernia (2006). Ancient evidence quoted in support of a crisis of Italian agriculture is: Suet., *Dom.* 7, referring to an edict that prohibited the planting of new vineyards in Italy and prescribed the destruction of vineyards in the provinces, and Trajan's alimentary scheme, by some seen as a measure to stimulate investment in agriculture. On the *alimenta* see Jongman (2002), with previous bibliography.

There is obviously a series of assumptions and hypotheses upon which De Sena relies in his reasoning—for instance, that the patterns of land use in antiquity and in modern times were similar, which, of course, is not necessarily true. There is one case when this tenet is particularly questionable and that is the area of modern Tivoli, ancient Tibur. Nowadays the territory is completely devoted to olive cultivation; however, literary texts for antiquity mention the production of various wines in this area.[40] Even in the case of the whole of Sabina, the oil of which was renowned in antiquity, the land was not devoted exclusively to oleoculture. Strabo gives as chief cultivars of Sabina olive groves and vineyards, and Sabine wine was still widely produced and appreciated in the fourth and sixth centuries AD, as we can infer from its inclusion in Diocletian's Price Edict and the mention of it by Cassiodorus.[41] As regards the archaeological evidence, of the thirty-three presses identified from field survey data in this territory, only seven can securely be attributed to oil production.

One part of the territory here considered that might have played a considerable role in supplying Rome with oil and wine is the Caere/Centumcellae area. The territory around Caere constitutes an excellent example of the intensity of occupation and agricultural exploitation practised throughout the Republican and Imperial periods, with some secure evidence for the production of wine and olive oil, and possible indicators in the modern landscape of the types of cultivars characterizing the territory in Roman times. Field survey carried out in this territory identified *c.*500 sites dated to the Roman era; occupation was intense, and only at the higher elevations (400–600 metres above sea level) were no traces of Roman villas or farms found.[42] The survey ascertained that the number of settlements increased, expanding towards more marginal lands, between the first century BC and the early first century AD. For the Imperial period, the same number of sites was recorded between the first century and the Antonine period. Many medium-sized sites continued to exist well into the Imperial period, connected by a capillary network of roads, with a decline in

---

[40] Pliny, *HN* 14.38; Ath., *Deipn.* 1.26; Galen, *de Sanitate Tuenda* 5.5; Hor., *Carm* 1.9.5-6, 1.20.1, for the mention of Sabine wine possibly produced at his villa near Tibur, if the attribution of the Licenza villa to the poet is correct. Tibur was renowned also for mulberries, apples, figs, and flowers: Plin., *HN* 15.97; 15.70; Columella, *Rust.* 5.10.11; Hor., *Sat.* 2.4.70; Mart., 9.60.

[41] Pliny, *HN* 15.4.3, for a type of olive used in Sabina called *sergia* or *regia*. In Diocletian's edict *de pretiis* (AD 301) wine from Tibur is among the more expensive ones. Alvino and Leggio (1995: 204).

[42] Maffei (1990: 169, 177); Maffei and Nastasi (1990). The sites surveyed were divided into eight categories according to their area (presumably of the surface scatter); these are (1) 300–400 m², (2) 600–750 m², (3) 900 m², (4) 1,200 m², (5) 1,500–2,000 m², (6) 2,500–3,000 m², (7) 5,000–7,000 m², (8) 10,000 m²; the large coastal villas were not included. However, since the research was still ongoing at the time (the full publication has not appeared), percentages of sites for each category are not given. Categories from 1 to 5 are considered to refer to farms run by one family only.

the number of settlements in the third century AD and not in the second century, as was the case in other areas of Italy, such as the *ager Cosanus*.[43] As regards agricultural production, literary sources mention olive oil and mediocre wine.[44] Large quantities of Graeco-Italic, Dressel 1, and Dressel 2–4 amphorae have indeed been recovered at some of the villa sites. The precise place of production for a large proportion of the amphorae has not been identified, but it was suggested that some of these wine amphorae might have been produced locally.[45] Not only does Pliny refer to wine produced at Caere and Gravisca, but at Gravisca deposits of wasters related to kilns producing Dressel 1 are known, while another kiln was identified inland from Pyrgi.[46] However, judging from the presence in the modern landscape of many wild olive trees (oleaster), it seems that at some point in the past a good portion of the territory was under olive cultivation. It has been suggested that these oleasters are remnants of olive trees planted in the Roman period, since documentary evidence does not attest olive cultivation in the area in the Middle Ages or in later historical periods.[47]

Some sites yielded evidence for the presence of presses. Twenty-seven of the sites included in this study, with a total of thirty-four presses, are located in this area.[48] Although only three oil mills have been recovered, most of the presses are attributed to oil production on the basis of the hypothesis that the oleasters attest olive cultivation in the Roman period. In one case at least, it seems that the press base displays signs of corrosion from oleic acid.[49]

Other cultivars that appear to be the result of human impact on the landscape are pear trees, present along the whole seaside strip of territory together with the oleasters, and wild chestnut trees attested in the northern portion of the territory. In this case, too, it is suggested that the plants are indicative of the type of cultivation practised in the Roman period.[50] Maffei suggests that the pear trees are relics of orchards planted in the Late Republican/Early Imperial period, in part replacing earlier olive trees, and that, with the construction of the new harbour at Centumcellae under Trajan, the

---

[43] Enei (1992: 80); Carandini and Cambi (2002).

[44] Plin., *HN* 14.67; Mart., 13.124; Columella, *Rust.* 3.3.3; 3.9.6: the productivity of vineyards in the area of Caere was notable.

[45] Twenty-seven of thirty-one Late Republican sites examined yielded Greco-Italic amphorae and Dressel 1; 27% presented fabrics typical of the Vesuvian region, while the origin of the remainder was not identified.

[46] On the basis of amphora wasters (either Greco-Italic or Dressel 1) in an area significantly known as 'Cava di Caolino'.

[47] Maffei (1990: 177–9).

[48] Data drawn from information in Bastianelli (1939); Maffei and Nastasi (1990, 2007); Allegrezza (2007).

[49] I base this observation on photo 5 published in Allegrezza (2007).

[50] Maffei (1990: 179); Allegrezza (2007) stresses also the presence of wild pigs in the territory, the breeding of which is likely to have occurred in the woods in the Roman period.

cultivation of fruit boomed because of the ease with which Rome could be reached by sea. The density of rural settlements in this area throughout the Early Imperial period is certainly explained by the important role that the agricultural production of the region had for Rome. In addition, the impact of Trajan's new harbour at Centumcellae was not limited to allowing for quicker and bulkier shipments of goods to Ostia and Rome by sea, but it created a new urban centre around the harbour, which also needed feeding.[51] It is tempting to connect the new shipment opportunities offered by the infrastructure of the harbour with the possible shift, detected in some of the coastal plains, from the cultivation of olive trees to pear trees. If pear cultivation was indeed practised in this area in Roman times and in part replaced the olive trees, it might be worth considering whether it would be more appropriate to posit such a shift for a later date. I would be inclined to place this occurrence, not in the early first century AD as proposed by Maffei, but right after the completion of the harbour by Trajan. It is worth remembering that it was from the time of Trajan onwards that Spanish oil prevailed in supplying Rome; the conversion of part of the coastal land around Centumcellae from olive to fruit cultivation might have been prompted also by the competition from the provincial oil arriving in the capital that the oil producers were facing.

POTENTIAL PRODUCTION OF THE PRESSES

Notwithstanding some of the objections one might have to De Sena's assumptions discussed above, his approach is a useful attempt at assessing the magnitude of oil and wine production in the region, and I would like to push his working hypothesis further. I am focusing in particular on olive oil, for which earlier studies on the productivity of ancient oleoculture and the processing capacity of Roman presses offer a good basis for our analysis,[52] whereas the production capacity of wine presses is more difficult to quantify if one lacks the information relating to the storage capacity of the *dolia* in which the must fermented.[53]

In wanting to test further the hypothesis of the ancient Roman hinterland having 56,000 hectares of olive groves, equal to the higher estimate of an annual production of 15 million litres, we should consider how many presses were needed for such a production. Brun, in his study of the olive presses in

[51] Correnti (1990).

[52] Mattingly (1988a) with previous bibliography.

[53] See the disagreement on the annual production of wine for the villa of Settefinestre: 800 hectolitres for Brun, 1,000 hectolitres for Carandini: Brun (2004: 41). For an attempt at quantifying the wine production of a Byzantine pressing complex: Seligman (1999: 164).

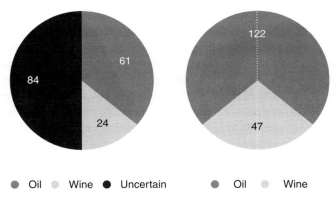

● Oil ● Wine ● Uncertain   ● Oil ● Wine

Fig. 4.7. Attested presses (left) and suggested attribution to wine and oil production for the uncertain cases (right)

France in the region of Var, had estimated as possible production capacity for each press 1,500–2,000 litres of oil/year.[54] Mattingly revised this suggestion, proposing, on the basis of a press load of 470–650 kg, similar to figures found in the writings of Varro and Pliny, 8,500–12,000 kg instead.[55] For the large Tripolitanian presses he estimated a possible output of 6,300–12,600 kg (depending on two different heights for the stack of baskets with olive pulp placed on the press bed). If we take an average of 10,000 litres[56] as the amount of oil a press could produce in the ninety-day period of the olive harvest, which went from November to January,[57] we would need 1,500 presses in order to be able to process the 15 million litres of oil postulated by De Sena. This is for oil production alone, without considering wine. It is true that theoretically the same press could be used for both productions, since the two harvest periods do not coincide, but this does not seem to have been common practice in antiquity.

As we have seen, there is a total of 169 presses for the area under examination, of which only 61 are securely identifiable as oil presses. If we assign the unattributed presses to oil in the same proportion as observed for the attributed ones, we would have a total of 122 presses devoted to oil production (Fig. 4.7). Although this figure is higher than the data available twenty years ago when Mattingly wrote his article, it still is only a small fraction of the presses needed to process the hypothetical 15 million litres of oil. Can this lack

---

[54] Brun (1986: 279–81).   [55] Mattingly (1988a: 185).
[56] The accurate volume/weight ratio is actually 1 litre of olive oil = 0.92 kg.
[57] Note, however, that Pliny, *HN* 15.4.13, mentions several varieties of olives that were not harvested before March: the Licinia, Cominia, Contia, and Sergia. The latter did not ripen before early February.

of an abundant number of presses from the archaeological record of the hinterland of Rome be plausibly defended?

If we consider the Guadalquivir valley, of the *c.*1,500 sites recorded by Ponsich in his field survey, we have seen that only 111 are certain press sites. Ponsich proposed that 10 per cent of the territory surveyed was devoted to olive cultivation, equalling 250 km^2 of olive groves over a region measuring 2,500 km^2. This percentage, in fact, might have been much higher, and likewise the total number of sites with oil presses is considered to have been vastly higher than what was visible on the surface, 'well in excess of 1000' according to Mattingly.[58] This example shows unequivocally that the recovery rate of press elements from field survey in areas densely inhabited since antiquity is very low. According to projections of the maximum volume of oil imports from Baetica in the early second century AD on the basis of ceramic assemblages, 14.5 million litres of olive oil reached Rome, and this is just the surplus exported to the capital, without considering local needs. Such a scale of production means that a minimum of *c.*1,450 presses was needed to produce the oil and that the 111 press sites known are but a fraction of the original total.

It is undoubtedly true that there is 'considerable bias'[59] in the manner in which sites were identified and published in the hinterland of Rome: in most cases the discoveries were the result of emergency excavation in relation to building activity in the suburbs of Rome, and the records of finds show a varying degree of accuracy. However, it is also true that the density of rural settlements in the area was very high: in the region north of Rome that was studied by the South Etruria Survey and more recently by the Tiber Valley Project, about 995 villas and 1,127 farms were identified over a surface of *c.*1,000 km^2, giving a density of 1.12 sites per km^2.[60] It is *possible* that many of these sites were equipped with presses, but obviously there is no way of knowing this with certainty. It seems relevant to note, however, that, in spite of this vacuum in the record, in the region here investigated the number of *known* olive presses is the same as that available in the case of the intensively exploited Guadalquivir valley, the oil production of which is well attested from the amphorae rather than from the press sites alone. I would argue, therefore, that in the hinterland of Rome we are missing quite a large number of press sites and that the recorded oil presses are a small percentage of the original total that existed in the region. The same considerations about a low recovery rate can be applied to the wine presses.

---

[58] Mattingly (1988b: 41).   [59] De Sena (2005: 139).
[60] Di Giuseppe (2005: 8); see also De Sena (2005: 140).

CONCLUSIONS

In the case of the large provincial oil-producing regions, it was above all the evidence of the millions of amphorae that indicated the massive production capacities reached by these areas. For the hinterland of Rome the lack of similar evidence has somehow put in the background the production capacity of this territory in terms of oil and wine in the Imperial period. No doubt this area was Rome's primary supplier of fresh fruit, vegetables, and various fresh products, including luxury foods, that could not be transported long distances.[61] But, if we consider carefully the archaeological record pertaining to pressing installations and compare it with areas well known for intensive oleoculture, such as Spain, then the scenario proposed by De Sena for the contribution in terms of wine and oil production of the hinterland of Rome appears more convincing.

Basing his comments on the data collected on presses and the proportion of modern land under olive and vine cultivation, he argued that the extension of land devoted to olive cultivation in ancient Latium must have been higher than that under viticulture. However, as mentioned earlier, besides the literary references to intensive viticulture, there are numerous sites, not included in this study, that produced wine by treading alone. In addition to this, the discovery of evidence for ancient vine trenches, especially in the immediate *suburbium*, is becoming more frequent. The proportion of land devoted to viticulture in antiquity was therefore probably higher than De Sena's model, based on modern practices, suggests. The attested number of press sites (140) and presses in this region (167), albeit small in comparison with the production capacity of the hinterland hypothesized by De Sena (96 million litres of wine; 15 million litres or 9.6 million using a lower estimate in the case of oil), is nonetheless comparable in size to the 111 secure press sites known for the Guadalquivir valley, the annual production capacity of which, just in terms of the product shipped to Rome, was in the range of 14–15 million litres of oil. It is therefore apparent that the recovery rate of press sites from field survey and from areas densely inhabited from antiquity is rather low. The visibility of the great oil production achieved by Baetica rests mainly on the amphora record, while the use of containers in perishable materials instead of amphorae for the distribution of the wine and oil produced around Rome has made this production much less visible, with the result that its extent has not been fully appreciated. Although we are unable to quantify with precision the wine- and oil-production capacity of the hinterland, there is sufficient evidence to infer that it was a sizeable production, definitely higher than has hitherto been assumed.

---

[61] Morley (1996); Wilson (2009b).

Further consideration of the precise chronology of the pressing installations and of the type of ownership, and therefore of those involved in investing capital in agricultural production facilities, is necessarily limited. Only in a few cases is the installation of a press datable, and it is very rarely possible to ascertain for how long the installation was in use. The dated cases point to the early first century AD, a period when intensification in building activities is observable in Italy at both rural and urban sites. Most of the known presses are attested at farms rather than elite villas, although it ought to be borne in mind that in many cases investigations at elite villas have concentrated on the residential part, ignoring the production quarters. Farms could have been part of larger estates owned by the wealthy, and this is how the many rural settlements recorded in this region for the Late Republican and Imperial periods have generally been understood. Recently, it has been argued that small farmers were competitive on the commercial market and that thus they continued to exist alongside *latifundia*.[62] If this scenario were correct, small and medium farmers as well would have been able to invest in production facilities. The presence of a press at a farm cannot therefore be taken as incontrovertible proof that the property was part of a large estate. Finally, if one considers the provenance of the wine as reflected by the proportions of the ceramic assemblages dated to the second century AD, it does not appear that Italian viticulture as a whole was experiencing a crisis caused by the successful viticulture practised in the provinces: Rome, the large metropolis, which grew from an estimated 500,000 inhabitants around 100 BC to one million under Augustus,[63] was able to absorb a good amount of what was earlier destined for export.[64]

REFERENCES

Allegrezza, V. (2007). 'Le proto-ville nella campagna presso il fiume Mignone. *Fas, mos e locatio* tra fattorie e *villae* catoniane nella repubblica romana', *L'Approdo: Periodico di informazione storico-culturale dell'Etruria meridionale* 9 <http://www.lap-prodo.info/archivi/archivi.htm> (accessed 10 Sept. 2009).
Alvino, G., and Leggio, T. (1995). 'Evoluzione dell'insediamento e dell'economia nella Sabina in età romana', in N. Christie (ed.), *Settlement and Economy in Italy*.

---

[62] Kron (2008).   [63] Morley (1996: 39).
[64] Although between the Republican and the Imperial periods there was a clear shift in the producing areas dominating the market: some areas earlier in a privileged position for the transmarine market (*Ager Cosanus*) declined, while regions favoured by a connection to Rome via the Tiber (Umbria, Adriatic) became more dominant: Panella (1989); Panella and Tchernia (1994).

1500 B.C.–A.D. 1500. Papers of the Fifth Conference of Italian Archaeology (Oxbow Monograph 41). Oxford, 201–7.

Amouretti, M.-C., and Brun, J.-P. (1993) (eds). *La production du vin et de l'huile en Méditerranée: Actes du symposium international organisé par le Centre Camille Jullian (Université de Provence-C.N.R.S.) et le Centre archéologique du Var (Ministère de la culture et Conseil général du Var), (Aix-en-Provence et Toulon, 20–22 novembre 1991)* (Bulletin de correspondance hellénique, Suppl. 26). Athens and Paris.

Bastianelli, S. (1939). 'Gli antichi avanzi nel territorio di Civitavecchia', *StEtr* 13: 385–402.

Bousquet, A., Di Giuseppe, H., Felici, F., Patterson, H., Witcher, R., and Zampini, S. (2003). 'Le produzioni ceramiche nella media valle del Tevere tra l'età repubblicana e tardoantica', in *Rei Cretariae Romanae Fautorum Acta 38*: 161–70.

Brun, J.-P. (1986). *L'oléiculture antique en Provence: Les huileries du département du Var.* Paris.

Brun, J.-P. (2000). 'The Production of Perfumes in Antiquity: The Cases of Delos and Paestum', *AJA* 104.2: 277–308.

Brun, J.-P. (2004). *Archéologie du vin et de l'huile dans l'Empire romain.* Paris.

Brun, J.-P. (2005). *Archéologie du vin et de l'huile en Gaule romaine.* Paris.

Carandini, A. (1985) (ed.). *Settefinestre: una villa schiavistica nell'Etruria romana.* Modena.

Carandini, A., and Cambi, F. (2002) (eds), with M. Celuzza and E. Fentress. *Paesaggi d'Etruria: Valle dell'Albegna, Valle d'Oro, Valle del Chiarone, Valle del Tafone: Progetto di ricerca italo-britannico seguito allo scavo di Settefinestre.* Rome.

Carandini, A., *et al.* (1997). 'La Villa dell'Auditorium dall'età arcaica all'età imperiale', *MDAI(R)* 104: 117–48.

Carandini, A. (2006) (ed.), with T. D'Alessio and H. Di Giuseppe. *La fattoria e la villa dell'Auditorium nel quartiere Flaminio di Roma.* Rome.

Correnti, F. (1990). 'Centumcellae: La villa, il porto e la città', in Maffei and Nastasi (1990), 209–14.

Criniti, N. (1991). *La tabula alimentaria di Veleia.* Parma.

De Franceschini, M. (2005). *Ville dell'Agro Romano.* Rome.

De Sena, E. C. (2005). 'An Assessment of Wine and Oil Production in Rome's Hinterland: Ceramic, Literary, Art Historical and Modern Evidence', in B. Santillo Frizell and A. Klynne (eds), *Roman villas around the* Urbs: *Interaction with Landscape and Environment. Proceedings of a Conference Held at the Swedish Institute in Rome, September 17–18 2004.* Rome, 135–49.

De Vos, M. (2000). Rus Africum. *Terra acqua olio nell'Africa settentrionale. Scavo e ricognizione nei dintorni di Dougga.* Trento.

Di Giuseppe, H. (2005). '*Villae, villulae* e fattorie nella Media Valle del Tevere', in B. Santillo Frizell and A. Klynne (eds), *Roman Villas around the* Urbs: *Interaction with Landscape and Environment. Proceedings of a Conference Held at the Swedish Institute in Rome, September 17–18 2004.* Rome, 7–25.

Enei, F. (1992). 'Ricognizioni archeologiche nell'*Ager Caeretanus*: Rapporto preliminare', in E. Herring, R. Whitehouse, and J. Wilkins (eds), *Papers of the Fourth Conference of Italian Archaeology*, vol. 3.1. London, 71–90.

Erdkamp, P. (2005). *The Grain Market in the Roman Empire*. Cambridge.

Galletti, M. (2007). 'Valle del Marangone: Censimento delle ville romane. Risultati preliminari', *L'Approdo: Periodico di informaizone storico-culturale dell'Etruria meridionale*, vol. 4 <http://www.lapprodo.info/archivi/archivi.htm> (accessed 10 Sept. 2009).

Giuliani, C. F. (1970). *Forma Italiae. Regio I: Tibur, pars prima*. Rome.

Giuliani, C. F. (1976). *Forma Italiae. Regio I: Tibur, pars altera*. Rome.

Hitchner, R. B. (1990), with contributions by S. Ellis, A. Graham, D. Mattingly, and L. Neuru. 'The Kasserine Archaeological Survey—1987', *AntAfr* 26: 231–59.

Hitchner, R. B. (1993). 'Olive Production and the Roman Economy: The Case for Intensive Growth in the Roman Empire,' in Amouretti and Brun (1993), 499–508.

Jongman, W. M. (2002). 'Beneficial Symbols, *Alimenta* and the Infantilization of the Roman citizen', in W. Jongman and M. Kleijwegt (eds), *After the Past: Essays in Ancient History in Honour of H. W. Pleket* (Mnemosyne Suppl. 233). Leiden, 47–80.

Jongman, W. M. (2007). 'The Early Roman Empire: Consumption', in W. Scheidel, I. Morris, and R. Saller (eds), *The Cambridge Economic History of the Greco-Roman World*. Cambridge, 592–618.

Kehoe, D. P. (2007). 'The Early Roman Empire: Production', in W. Scheidel, I. Morris, and R. Saller (eds.), *The Cambridge Economic History of the Greco-Roman World*. Cambridge, 543–69.

Kolendo, J. (1994). '*Praedia suburbana* e loro redditività', in J. Carlsen, P. Ørsted, and J. E. Skydsgaard (eds), *Landuse in the Roman Empire* (ARID Suppl. 22). Rome, 59–71.

Kron, J. G. (2008). 'The Much Maligned Peasant. Comparative Perspectives on the Productivity of the Small Farmer in Classical Antiquity', in L. de Light and S. J. Northwood (eds), *People, Land and Politics: Demographic Development and the Transformation of Roman Italy, 300 BC–AD 14*. Leiden, 71–119.

Maffei, A. (1990) 'La romanizzazione della fascia costiera tirrenica', in Maffei and Nastasi (1990), 163–81.

Maffei, A., and Nastasi, F. (1990) (eds). *Caere e il suo territorio: Da Agylla a Centumcellae*. Rome.

Maffei, A., and Nastasi F. (2007). 'Comprensorio di Civitavecchia-Centumcellae', *L'Approdo. Periodico di informazione storico-culturale dell'Etruria meridionale* 7 <http://www.lapprodo.info/archivi/archivi.htm> (accessed 10 Sept. 2009).

Mari, Z. (1983). *Forma Italiae. Regio I: Tibur, pars tertia*. Florence.

Mari, Z. (1991). *Forma Italiae. Regio I: Tibur, pars quarta*. Florence.

Marlière, E. (2002). *L'outre et le tonneau dans l'Occident romain*. Montagnac.

Martin, R. (1971). *Recherches sur les agronomes latins et leurs conceptions économiques et sociales*. Paris.

Marzano, A. (2005). 'Country Villas in Roman Central Italy: Reassessing the Evidence', in J. J. Aubert and Z. Várhelyi (eds), *A Tall Order: Writing the Social History of the Ancient World. Essays in Honor of William V. Harris* (Beiträge zur Altertumskunde 216). Munich, 241–62.

Marzano, A. (2007). *Roman Villas in Central Italy: A Social and Economic History*. Leiden.

Mattingly, D. J. (1988a). 'Megalithic Madness and Measurement: Or how Many Olives could an Olive Press Press?', *OJA* 7.2: 177–95.

Mattingly, D. J. (1988b). 'Oil for Export? A Comparison of Libyan, Spanish and Tunisian Olive Oil Production in the Roman Empire', *JRA* 1: 49–56.

Mattingly, D. J. (1990). 'Painting, Presses, and Perfume Production at Pompeii', *OJA* 9.1: 33–56.

Mattingly, D. J. (1994). 'Regional Variation in Roman Oleoculture: Some Problems of Comparability', in J. Carlsen, P. Ørsted, and J. E. Skydsgaard (eds), *Landuse in the Roman Empire* (ARID Suppl. 22). Rome, 91–106.

Mattingly, D. J. (1995). *Tripolitania*. London.

Mayer, J. W. (2005). Imus ad villam. *Studien zur Villeggiatur im stadrömischen Suburbium in der späten Republik und frühen Kaisezeit.* Stuttgart.

Morley, N. (1996). *Metropolis and Hinterland.* Cambridge.

Morley, N. (2007). 'The Early Roman Empire: Distribution', in W. Scheidel, I. Morris, and R. Saller (eds), *The Cambridge Economic History of the Greco-Roman World.* Cambridge, 570–91.

Panella, C. (1989). 'Le anfore italiche del II secolo d.C.', in M. Lenoir, D. Manacorda, and C. Panella (eds), *Amphores romaines et histoire économique: Dix ans de recherches* (Collection de l'École française de Rome 114). Rome, 139–78.

Panella, C., and Tchernia, A. (1994). 'Produits agricoles transportés en amphores', in *L'Italie d'Auguste à Dioclétien: Actes du Colloque International (Rome, 25–28 mars 1992).* Rome, 145–65.

Ponsich, M. (1974). *Implantation rurale antique sur le Bas Guadalquivir: Séville-Alcalá del Río-Lora del Río-Carmona.* Paris.

Ponsich, M. (1979). *Implantation rurale antique sur le Bas Guadalquivir: La Campana-Palma del Río-Posadas.* Paris.

Ponsich, M. (1987). *Implantation rurale antique sur le Bas Guadalquivir: Bujalance, Montoro, Andújar.* Madrid.

Ponsich, M. (1991). *Implantation rurale antique sur le Bas Guadalquivir: Écija, Dos Hermanas, Los Palacios y Villafranca, Lebrija, Sanlúcar de Barrameda.* Madrid.

Purcell, N. (1985). 'Wine and Wealth in Ancient Italy', *JRS* 75: 1–19.

Quilici, L. (1979). 'La villa nel suburbio romano: Problemi di studio e di inquadramento storico-topografico', *ArchCl* 31: 309–17.

Rodríguez Almeida, E. (1984). *Il Monte Testaccio: Ambiente, storia, materiali.* Rome.

Rosenstein, N. (2008). 'Aristocrats and Agriculture in the Middle and Late Republic', *JRS* 98: 1–26.

Seligman, J. (1999). 'Agricultural Complexes at Ras Abu Ma'Aruf (Pisgat Ze'Ev east A), North of Jerusalem', *'Atiqot* 38: 137–70.

Soprintendenza Archeologica di Roma (1986). *Misurare la terra: Centuriazione e coloni nel mondo romano. Città agricoltura commercio: materiali da Roma e dal suburbio.* Modena.

Tchernia, A. (1986). *Le vin de l'Italie romaine : Essai d'histoire économique d'après les amphores* (BEFAR 261). Rome.

Tchernia, A. (2006). 'La crise de l'Italie impériale et la concurrence des provinces', *Cahiers du centre de recherches historique* 37 (April), 137–56.

Thomas, R., and Wilson, A. I. (1994). 'Water Supply for Roman Farms in Latium and South Etruria', *PBSR* 62: 139–96.

Torelli, M. (1969). 'Senatori etruschi della tarda repubblica e dell'impero', *DArch*, 3: 285–363.

Valenti, M. (2003). *Forma Italiae 4.1. Ager Tusculanus.* Florence.

Volpe, R. (2000). 'Il Suburbio', in A. Giardina (ed.) *Roma antica.* Roma and Bari, 183–210.

Wilson, A. I. (1999). 'Deliveries *extra urbem*: Aqueducts and the Countryside', *JRA* 12.1: 314–31.

Wilson, A. I. (2009a). 'Approaches to Quantifying Roman Trade', in A. I. Wilson and A. K. Bowman (eds.), *Quantifying the Roman Economy: Methods and Problems* (Oxford Studies on the Roman Economy 1). Oxford, 213–49.

Wilson, A. I. (2009b). 'Villas, Horticulture and Irrigation Infrastructure in the Tiber Valley', in F. Coarelli and H. Patterson (eds), *Mercator Placidissimus: The Tiber Valley in Antiquity. New Research in the Upper and Middle River Valley. (Proceedings of the Conference Held at the British School at Rome, 27–28 Feb. 2004).* Rome, 731–68.

5

Capital Investment and Agriculture: Multi-Press Facilities from Gaul, the Iberian Peninsula, and the Black Sea Region

Annalisa Marzano

INTRODUCTION

Wine and olive oil, besides wheat, were the major agricultural products of the Roman world. While in the case of cereals, shipment usually occurred in sacks and perhaps in skins, and is therefore invisible archaeologically, the transfer of wine and oil from place of production to place of consumption is more easily traceable in the archaeological record, at least in the case of transmarine shipping, through their containers: the amphorae. However, amphorae were not the only containers used, and the extent of the distribution of these products in archaeologically invisible containers such as barrels and skins has in recent years become much clearer than it was in the past.[1] Therefore, as in the previous chapter on the hinterland of Rome, rather than attempting a study of agricultural production through the containers for foodstuffs, this investigation focuses on the presses, the machinery for the processing of grapes and olives. More specifically, this chapter discusses the analysis of data pertaining to capital investment in large-scale processing facilities related to wine and oil and is concerned only with sites showing evidence for multi-press facilities (that is, two or more wine/oil presses).

In many provinces of the empire one can find notable evidence for Roman wine and oil presses; certainly, in order to address the questions of the proportion of agricultural production and agrarian exploitation of a given region, knowing the number of presses present per square kilometre is a crucial factor.[2] However, investigating multi-press sites only in a given region,

---

[1] Tchernia (1986: 285–92); Panella (1989: 162–3); Marlière (2002); Brun (2005: 10–11).
[2] See Mattingly (1988); Hitchner (1990); de Vos (2000).

rather than considering the totality of presses attested in a region, aims at assessing the degree of capital accumulation. In addition, tracing this form of high investment both geographically and chronologically is not only indicative of the status of the economy in terms of productivity, capital availability, and effectiveness of market distribution, but may also shed some light on the forms of landownership and management. It is true that we do not know the exact cost of installing a press, and this would have varied depending on the type of press. The central-screw press, with all its elements made of wood, which therefore remains largely archaeologically invisible, was much smaller and probably much cheaper than the large lever press or the lever and screw press, which required heavy monolithic elements such as counterweights and press-beds, and a long, solid wood beam. These kinds of presses were very large and occupied a dedicated space within the farm/villa, one or two rooms,[3] without counting the space needed to store the produce. It is generally accepted that the presence of a press at a site, particularly of a wine press,[4] indicates a level of production above self-sufficiency and a market-oriented distribution. It is also generally accepted that the choice to invest in a press, which meant not simply the initial cost of installation but also the commitment (in some cases the construction *ex novo*) of dedicated rooms and regular upkeep of the machinery, was a commitment that not everyone could afford.[5] However, whereas a single press could theoretically be built as a joint investment by several owners of farms located close to each other, installation of a second press (or more) at one site is more indicative of general trends of demand and supply in the markets. The extra produce to be processed, which justified the need for additional pressing machinery, also meant an investment in land, plants (olive trees or vines), and labour. For these reasons, the presence of two or more presses at a given site in a given time period is here taken to be indicative of considerable capital investment in the amelioration of production facilities

---

[3] A dedicated space to allow the lowering of the counterweight in the case of the lever press was also needed.

[4] In the case of grapes it is easy to produce wine simply by treading; this is possible in the case of olives (see the use of special wooden clogs to tread olives in a vat, the *solea et canalis* of Columella, *Rust.* 12.52.6–7, a method attested as far back as the site of Ugarit in *c.*1500 BC and known also through modern ethnographic examples from Corsica and Turkey (White 1975: 226–7; Amouretti 1996; Mataix and Barbancho 2006: 50), but this method is much more laborious and wasteful than the treading of grapes. Another method, attested widely in the Levant in antiquity, for extracting oil from olives without the use of a press reduced the olives into a paste by using a mortar and pestle. The paste was then placed in a container and hot water poured on it; the oil coming to the surface was skimmed off and collected in a second container (Amouretti 1996).

[5] This is the general opinion expressed in the various contributions in Amouretti and Brun (1993). Recently Rosenstein (2008: 11) argued, on the basis of the price given by Cato for an oil press, that those able to afford several slaves could also buy a press, but Cato's passage (*Agr.* 22) refers to the olive mill (*trapetum* or rotary olive crusher) used to crush the olives into a paste before pressing, not to the press itself, whose price is not given by Cato (see *Agr.* 18).

for products destined for external markets, whether a free commercial market or, in the case of olive oil from Baetica and the *annona*, a market in which the state intervened directly as regards prices and transport costs.[6]

While it would certainly be very useful and desirable to contrast trends emerging from the study of the multi-press sites against the base of known single-press sites in a region, such a comparison, which would require the collection and analysis of an enormous amount of data scattered through a myriad publications or in grey literature pertaining to rescue excavations, is beyond the scope of this chapter.[7]

This study initially considered 295 multi-press sites (with a total of 999 presses) attested across the Roman empire. From this corpus the three regional samples examined here, the Iberian peninsula, Gaul, and the Black Sea region, were chosen. There are various reasons behind this choice. First, particularly in the case of the Iberian peninsula and Gaul, the production of oil and wine was substantial and the products were widely distributed in various areas of the empire. It is well known how the great Republican boom in Italian wine exports had, by the first century AD, subsided, to be replaced by an opposite flow of products shipped from the provinces into Italy. Imperial legislation, such as the famous edict by Domitian prohibiting the planting of new vineyards in the provinces,[8] has been seen by some as a protectionist measure taken by the imperial authority in favour of Italian wine production in response to the threat of predominance of provincial wines on the Italian market.[9]

The second important reason is that, at least in the case of Gaul and of some of the Spanish sites, several sites have been excavated, and therefore we have a corpus of multi-press sites for which chronological data are available.[10] The availability of data on the chronology of the installations and the periods of use of the presses is obviously very important. In order to extract meaningful conclusions from the material evidence and place them in a wider context, one needs to answer as a priority the questions of *when* high levels of investment started and *when* they stopped. It is for this reason—the lack of detailed

---

[6] Chic García (2005) for some considerations on the three systems of distribution of agricultural produce from the Iberian peninsula: redistribution on the part of the elite, for instance through euergetism; free market; and state-controlled distribution.

[7] A recent Ph.D. thesis by Matthew Hobson (2012) does attempt a study along these lines for Africa Proconsularis.

[8] Suet., *Dom.* 7.2.15. There might have been more than one edict, the prohibition then being extended to the planting of vines within city boundaries: Garnsey and Saller (1987: 60). It has sometimes been stated that there was also a Republican ban on vine and olive cultivation in the provinces in order to favour Italian products, on the basis of Cic., *Rep.* 3.16, but this is not a satisfying interpretation of Cicero's enigmatic reference and does not appear to be correct. see Paterson (1978) for the analysis of these issues.

[9] See discussion in Tchernia (1986: 221–53).

[10] Brun (1986, 1999, 2004, 2005); Peña Cervantes (2010).

Table 5.1. Distribution of multi-press sites in Gaul, Iberia, and the Black Sea according to production type

Region	Oil	Wine	Both	Uncertain	TOTAL
Gaul	6	7	2		15
Iberia	23	14	2	8	47
Black Sea		18			18
TOTAL	29	39	4	8	80

Table 5.2. Distribution of presses at multi-press sites in Gaul, Iberia, and the Black Sea according to production type

Region	Oil	Wine	Uncertain	TOTAL
Gaul	19	26		45
Iberia	71	39	30	140
Black Sea		53		53
TOTAL	90	118	30	238

chronological data—that North Africa was left out of this analysis. North Africa is the area with the highest number of Roman multi-press sites known, and yet, although it is undeniable that the scale of the phenomenon of capital investment in processing facilities in this region in Roman times was unsurpassed,[11] and that in this period there was a completely different scale of production in wine and oil compared to earlier and later epochs, we do not have detailed data on the date of installation and demise of these facilities.

Finally, all three geographic areas here examined, despite the variations in the overall number of sites and presses attested, present similar figures for the average number of presses attested at multi-press sites, making them comparable in this kind of analysis (Tables 5.1 and 5.2).[12]

SOUTHERN GAUL

The great production of wine and oil in this region is an early imperial phenomenon connected with the Caesarean and Augustan colonization and the settlement in the region of veterans from Italy. In the case of wine

---

[11]   See, e.g., the case of the Kasserine area in Tunisia: Hitchner (1990); Tripolitania: Mattingly (1995). Algeria: de Vos (2000); and de Vos, Chapter 6, this volume, for new data collected in recent fieldwork.

[12]   Average number of presses at multi-press sites: Iberian peninsula: 2.98; Gaul: 3; Black Sea: 2.94, whereas regions such as Mauretania Caesariensis have on average 10.38 presses/site.

production, the Early Imperial period does not represent the absolute start of production in the region. The area around the Greek colony of Massilia was already producing wine, which had local distribution, in the Classical and early Hellenistic period. This production retained a monopoly of distribution in southern Gaul until the third century BC, when Italian wines started to appear in the region.[13] During the second and first centuries BC imports of Italian wines, especially from Latium and Etruria, completely dominated in the area. The picture of dominance of Italian wine imports started to change in the Late Republic. After the capitulation of Massilia in 49 BC, Caesar, and later Augustus, founded various new towns/*coloniae*. Settlers came especially from central Italy, and the increase of viticulture in connection with the colonization phenomenon is clear from the archaeological record. Trenches for vineyards in the context of land centuriation have been identified in different areas (for example, the cadasters of Orange, Lapalud, Girardes) and dated to the first century AD. Also in this period various amphora production centres started to operate. The workshops of the area of Orange were imitating Italian amphorae such as Dressel 1 and Dressel 2–4, and also producing Pascual 1 (originally a Spanish type) and Gauloise 2. The wine producers of the area were evidently aiming at entering the same markets in which Italian products were distributed. The typical flat-bottomed Gallic wine amphorae, suitable for transport on riverine barges, were also an innovation of this period; the kilns to the west of Port d'Aix produced the Gauloise 2, the Gauloise 1, and later the 4 and 5 types, which became the standard wine amphorae for the whole province during the second and third centuries AD. However, the commercialization of wine in barrels along river routes was already an important phenomenon in the Augustan period; large barrels of wine coming from production centres in the central Rhône valley have been found in military camps of the Rhine in Augustan contexts. As noted by Brun, there is a distinct regional differentiation in the use of amphorae versus barrels: to the south of an imaginary line that goes from the river Iser to the sea one finds amphorae; to the north barrels.[14] The wines produced in Narbonensis were common wines destined especially for Rome, as was the case with the Tarraconensis production.[15]

As regards production centres with multiple presses, a total of fifteen sites, many located in the province of Gallia Narbonensis, are currently known in Gaul. Seven sites were engaged in wine production, six in olive oil, and two had presses for both wine and oil; in total, twenty-six of the presses identified at these sites were for wine and nineteen for oil (see Tables 5.1 and 5.2). Most

---

[13] Brun (2005), on which the following account relies.

[14] Brun (2005: 10–11, 66–9).

[15] Low vines were cultivated, requiring less labour than the kind trailing on posts: Brun (2005: 59).

sites had two presses, but four, five, or six presses are attested (Fig. 5.1). The common press type in use in this region was the lever press.[16]

These production centres started as modest farms and villas, but, since in most cases the earlier installations have been obliterated by later phases, data on the earlier production facilities are not available, and it is impossible to say whether the first-phase farms were equipped with presses and in what number. The cumulative chronology of all multiple presses indicates that the peak in their usage occurred in the second century AD (Fig. 5.2), while the boom in their installation can be placed in the first century and in the first half of the second century AD, with no known installation of multiple presses for the period after the second century (Fig. 5.3).

In Languedoc, Provence, and Rhône valley, the excavated wine production centres (some of which were equipped with multiple presses) feature production facilities and the addition of a nicely appointed *pars urbana* during the Flavian period.[17] It appears that the owners were in this period in a position to invest more capital in the improvement of their production facilities and in the beautification of their residences. It is therefore a logical inference, although it cannot be incontrovertibly proved, that this capital came from the successful wine production which began in the Late Republican/Augustan period. As an example of this development one can cite the site Pardigon 2 in the Bay of Cavalaire. Built in the Augustan period (only a kiln of Dressel 2–4 amphorae remained from this phase), it was razed to the ground in the reign of Nero in order to build a luxury villa provided with a *pars urbana* and a *pars rustica*. The wine-producing area, completed with *cella vinaria*, was located in the northern sector of the villa. The site was occupied until the fifth century AD.[18]

Improvements and increased production in the Flavian period, and therefore, presumably, enlargement of the portion of land under cultivation,[19] are phenomena not limited to large sites, but occur also in small and medium-sized farms, such as those at Pignans, La Quintarie, and Baresse.[20] In general, viticulture appears to have been a very dynamic element in the agrarian economy of Narbonensis between the first and third centuries AD.

Most of the wine production installations known archaeologically in Gaul date to the second half of the first century AD or the first half of the second century AD; many installations appear to have been abandoned between the

---

[16] Brun (1986) on press typologies.

[17] Brun (2005: 25).

[18] Brun (2005: 37–9).

[19] Brun (2005: 68–70); Revilla (2008: esp. 122) for methodological considerations about arbitrarily relating production capacity and size of an estate.

[20] Brun (2005: 71); he also wondered whether one could see in this the effect of the *lex Manciana* known in the context of North Africa that stimulated the cultivation of unoccupied land (cf. Kehoe, Chapter 2, and de Vos, Chapter 6, this volume).

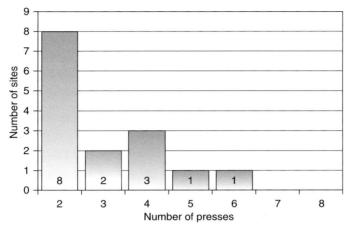

Fig. 5.1. Gaul: number of presses per site (n = 45)

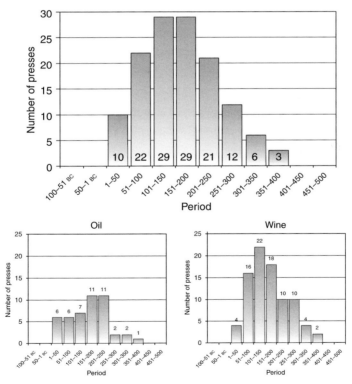

Fig. 5.2. Gaul: chronology of periods of operation of all presses at multi-press sites, and according to type of production (n_{total} = 39 [6 undated]; n_{oil} = 17; n_{wine} = 22)

Annalisa Marzano

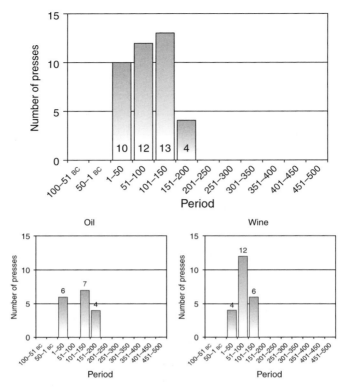

Fig. 5.3. Gaul: installation date of all presses at multi-press sites, and according to type of production (n = 39; n_{oil} = 17; n_{wine} = 22)

end of the second and the end of the third century AD.[21] This chronological trend is only partially reflected in the attested chronology for the multi-press sites: the highest number of wine presses was in use in the second century AD, with only a minor contraction occurring in the second half of this century; a few of these presses continued to operate into the fourth and fifth centuries AD. A similar pattern emerges in the case of multi-press installations for oil, although only a small number of sites is known in this case. The peak in installation of multi-press sites for wine clearly occurred in the second half of the first century AD (Fig. 5.3). As in the case of the Iberian peninsula, the sites that continued to be occupied into late antiquity were some of the larger villas.[22] As an example, one can cite the largest wine villa of the Bay of

---

[21] Brun (2005: 25). See also the export of wine amphorae from Narbonensis and their production, which stops in the third century AD; for instance, at Sallèles d'Aude the kilns, after reducing production in the course of the third century AD, were abandoned completely *c.* AD 300.

[22] Such as Les Toulois, La Rue du Port, Portissolò, La Ramiere, Les Prés Bas, Les Farguettes à Nissan: Brun (2005: 71).

Cavalaire, the so-called villa of Cavalaire-Rue du Port, which had four lever presses and was in use from the late first century AD down to the Constantinian period.[23] The case of the maritime villas of the Bay of Cavalaire is interesting, because the sites combine residential luxury with production (wine, amphora kilns) and good shipping facilities (ports).

The chronological data for abandonment of wine production at many sites in Gaul during the second century AD are not limited to the production facilities (Fig. 5.4); for instance, in the Tricastin region (near the Rhône; the corridor along this river developed intensive viticulture in the Roman period), where in a villa four wine presses went out of use in the second century AD, archaeologists also observed that the drainage channels associated with vine cultivation were filled in the same period.[24] In addition to this, pollen analysis indicated a move from vineyards to meadows in the late second century AD, which might point to cattle and horse breeding replacing viticulture.[25]

For other parts of Gaul, the evidence for pressing installations is not as abundant and clear as for Narbonensis, because of the type of press that was most commonly in use. In Aquitania, the lever-type press, so widespread in Narbonensis, is rare. Instead, it was the central screw press, with all components made of wood, that was usually employed, and it is therefore difficult to identify it archaeologically, except in the presence of specific conditions that allow preservation of the organic material.[26] Instead, it is the ceramic evidence and remains of vine trenches that offer information about wine production in the region. Aquitania in the first century AD was importing wine from Italy, but during the second half of this century Italian imports were replaced by wine from Tarraconensis, perhaps because of the influence and connections of some important personalities from this province.[27] In this region, locally produced wine amphorae, imitating Italian types, Gauloise 5, and Dressel 28, appeared in the second half of the first century AD. The amphora production stopped in the second century AD, not because wine production came to an end, but rather because of the replacement of amphorae by barrels.[28]

Around Lutetia, trenches for vineyards dating to the Roman period were discovered in the Oise and Aisne. More than 5,000 land drainage trenches were found near a villa occupied from the first to the fourth century AD; the trenches have been dated to the mid-first/early second century AD.[29] Overall, it

---

[23] Brun (2005: 39–40).

[24] Brun (2005: 46–7): villa at Le Molard, Donzère, Drôme.

[25] Brun (2005: 72–3).

[26] Brun (2005: 116).

[27] Étienne and Mayet (2000: 236); Brun (2005: 174).

[28] Brun (2005: 105); Marlière (2002: 187–96) for general remarks on geographic distribution of barrels and their role in the transport of oil and wine in the Roman West.

[29] Brun (2005: 126–7); various workshops producing wine amphorae are also known in the valleys of the Oise and Seine.

has been noted that the density of rural settlements reached in Gaul in the second century had no equal in history until the early fourteenth century.[30] Nevertheless, right after such a production boom there are signs of downsizing of wine production in the region; the interpretation of this 'downsizing' is a matter open to debate. As rightly pointed out by Brun,[31] in order to assess the cessation of winemaking at many sites one needs to start by listing the conditions that allowed the great production boom in the first place: (1) high demand; (2) good transport; (3) organization of sales; and (4) abundant manpower.

Some of these conditions must have changed during the second century; Brun finds it unlikely that the change was due to a contraction in demand or to disorganization in the structure of trade in the Antonine and Severan periods. He rather emphasizes the need for abundant qualified manpower on the large estates engaged in viticulture; a significant lowering of population might, in his opinion, explain the abandonment of an exploitation that had become too large.[32] This scenario would also fit well with the conversion of vineyards into pastures mentioned above. However, a lowering of population levels because of the Antonine plague may have caused a decline in demand as well as in qualified labour. The larger estates, which were probably those whose owners had both reserve capital and extremely good social and commercial networks, were the ones that could continue production in the face of the new conditions. The continuation of wine production at large villas might also indicate the concentration of land in the hands of fewer and larger landlords, but the evidence is not conclusive in this direction.[33] Leaving aside the thorny question about sources of slavery and agricultural manpower in the Imperial period, the chronology of the abandonment of large-scale wine production is temptingly close to the years affected by the Antonine plague, and therefore the explanation of a decline in population, affecting labour and also demand, appears rather attractive.[34] Similarly, the abandonment of estates at the end of the third century AD seems to indicate a profound crisis owing to demographic factors.[35]

This picture, however, does not pertain to the whole of Gaul: it applies mostly to the valleys of the Rhône and Biterrois, whereas in Languedoc,

---

[30] Brun (2005: 178).   [31] Brun (2005: 73).   [32] Brun (2005: 73).

[33] A possible example of incorporation of smaller properties into a larger estate, with consequent centralization of production, is the villa of Saint Martin at Taradeau, where in the second century four treading vats and other structures related to wine production were built (and also a watermill attesting cereal cultivation), while production of wine at two nearby farms is also attested during the same period (Brun 2005: 42–5).

[34] The Antonine plague may have been preceded by a series of bad harvests owing to drought/ unusual climate conditions, as indicated by tree rings from Central Europe and also by current studies relating to the Near East: Jongman (2012).

[35] Brun (2005: 73).

especially around Nîmes, viticulture continued. Even if by the end of the third century Gallia Narbonensis was no longer involved in the Mediterranean wine trade, the local production was consumed in the region.[36] It is therefore difficult to evaluate the general trends in this region in terms of capital investment and agricultural production, and the economic situation as a whole when the picture is so diverse between one region and another, and only partial data are available.

When it comes to oleoculture, there is a clear geographic limitation in the spread of olive trees because of climatic conditions: Narbonensis is the northern limit for olive cultivation in Gaul. Compared to viticulture, oil production had a minor role, but it was still commercialized, although apparently not for overseas markets, since the majority of the amphorae known for Narbonensis are for wine, a few for salted fish, but none for oil.[37]

A total of eight oil-producing sites with multiple presses is known in this area (see Table 5.1). Of these, two are sites with one olive press and multiple wine presses, three had two oil presses, one was equipped with three presses, and the last site, with six presses, was truly a large production centre. The sample available is extremely small and does not allow the meaningful extrapolation of trends about massive capital investment in this type of production. However, one can observe, for what it is worth, that the installation dates available in the case of oil-producing centres with multiple presses (one site with two oil presses is unfortunately undated) indicate two chronological periods for development of multi-press installations: the first half of the first century AD and the second century AD (see Fig. 5.3). The sites dated to the first century AD (three in number) have just two presses, whereas the larger oileries date from the second to the third centuries AD.

Brun has suggested that in Gaul regional distribution of olive oil towards the interior was important, in addition to the urban demand, because of the population growth during the first and early second centuries AD.[38] Data on oil production for the third century and later are scarce, but for this cultivation also it seems that a recession occurred during the third century, especially at the end of the century, when various oileries were abandoned, even in the case of villa sites that continued to be occupied into the fourth century (Fig. 4).

---

[36] Brun (2005: 76).

[37] Oleoculture in the area is referred to in literary sources, such as Sid. Apoll., *Carm.* 22.47, celebrating Narbonne and her *trapeta*. See Brun (2005: 100, 102).

[38] Brun (2005: 100).

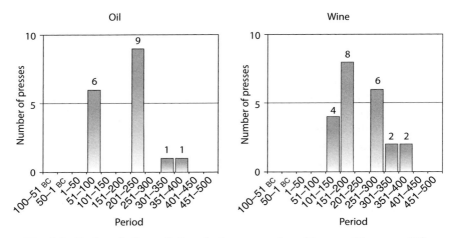

Fig. 5.4. Gaul: end of use of oil and wine presses (n = 39; n_{oil} = 17; n_{wine} = 22)

IBERIAN PENINSULA

The bulk of the Italian colonization in the Iberian peninsula occurred after the Sertorian war, when colonies were settled in coastal areas and in the valley of the Baetis. As noted by Strabo (3.2.8–9), the mines were the main resource attracting people to the area, but the region soon also acquired a reputation for abundant agricultural production in wheat, wine, and oil.[39] Indeed, the Haltern 70 amphorae from Baetica, transporting, as we learn from the *tituli picti*, *defrutum*[40] and olives preserved in *defrutum*, appear on shipwrecks around the middle of the first century BC.[41] Initially, the wine from Baetica was commercialized in amphorae imitating the Italian Dressel 1, and probably also in the flat-bottomed Dressel 28. While in Tarraconensis the rural settlements connected to wine production dating to the first century BC are generally medium-sized farms, it is in this period that one can see the appearance of dedicated spaces for the installations of presses and the adoption of fermentation techniques typical of Italy (the *dolia defossa*).[42] The importance of wine production in the region is reflected also in the coin

---

[39] Strabo 3.2.6, dependent on the account of Posidonius of Apamea. The distribution of wild olive trees in the region is attested by place names recorded in some literary sources: e.g. Oleastrum (Pompon., 3.4; Plin., *HN* 3.3.15); Kotinai (Strabo, 3.2.3); see Lagóstena Barrios (2009: 294). Peña Cervantes (2010: 158–62) for an outline of available archaeological data on wine production in Tarraconensis in the second century BC.

[40] *Tituli picti* give *defrutum* also as the content of the Dressel 28 amphorae on the wreck of Port-Vendres, dated to the reign of Claudius: Colls *et al.* (1977).

[41] e.g. on the Madrague de Giens shipwreck of 60–50 BC: Tchernia *et al.* (1978); Brun (2003: 144–5).

[42] Peña Cervantes (2010: 161–2).

types referring to grapes and vines used by the mints of various cities in the first century BC, such as Orippo, Baesippo, and Iulia Traducta.[43] In particular, the wine production of modern Catalonia, the Laietanian wine, was heavily exported to Aquitania and Narbonensis in the Augustan period.[44] In this period an intensification and reorganization of production in the region, with the construction of several new wine-producing sites, took place.[45] The amphorae also indicate an interesting shift in the market that the wine producers of Baetica sought to conquer: towards the end of the first century AD, Haltern 70 and Dressel 28 amphorae were substituted by imitations of the Gallic Gauloise 4 produced in various ateliers of Baetica.[46] The chronology of this shift coincides with the peak of investments in infrastructure for winemaking observed in Gaul in the Flavian period, and a link between the two phenomena is possible.

The great wine production of Tarraconensis rested on three main factors: high yields, lower production costs compared to other wines, and a favourable geographical position in terms of distribution (vineyards located in coastal zones allowing direct export by sea).[47] The choice of low vines, without any supporting posts as was common in Italy, reduced the manpower and the workdays needed; furthermore, instead of the variety *aminaea*, commonly used in Italy, *coccolobis* was used, a kind of grape apparently originating from Epirus that gave higher yields and was suitable for the production of cheap and abundant wine marketed among the army and the urban *plebs*.[48] The region, however, also produced good-quality wine; praise for Laietanian and Lauro-nensian wines is found in Pliny, while Martial ranked some wines from the region of Tarraco higher than Campanian wines.[49] Possibly the containers Oberaden 74 and Gauloise 4, which seemed to have been manufactured in lesser quantities in comparison to the Pascual 1 and Dressel 2–4 amphorae, were the containers used for the transmarine shipments of this better-quality wine.[50]

---

[43] On Iberian and early Roman coinage: Chaves Tristán (1998); Étienne and Mayet (2000: 61–6).

[44] Étienne and Mayet (2000: 236).

[45] According to Peña Cervantes (2010: 163), twenty-two out of the thirty-eight sites she catalogued for Tarraconensis were built in the Augustan period.

[46] Brun (2005: 280) notes the possible use of barrels in addition to amphorae. Barrels appear to have been widely used in Roman Portugal, where funerary markers in the shape of a barrel are attested: Étienne and Mayet (2000: 56–7); Marlière (2002: 120, 154–7); Brun (2004: 286).

[47] Tchernia (1986: 179–88); Brun (2004: 264).

[48] On this varietal of grape: Pliny, *HN* 14.29–30; Columella, *Rust.* 3.2.19; Saez Fernandez (1987: 24–5) (discussing it in the context of Baetica). However, in general *aminaea* was cultivated in Hispania as well. Pliny, *HN* 14.41, mentions a type of *aminaea* called 'hispania'; see Saez Fernandez (1987: 22–3).

[49] Plin., *HN* 14.71; Mart. 7.56; 13.118.

[50] Peña Cervantes (2010: 160 n. 233).

As regards oil production in the Late Republican period, no evidence referring either to production centres or specific containers is known; it is only with Augustus that the Dressel 20, the typical oil amphora from Spain, is found both in Italy and along the Rhine; the Haltern 70 becomes widely common during the first century AD. Many production centres that specialized in the manufacture of Dressel 20 amphorae have been archaeologically identified in the territories of Seville and Cordoba.[51]

The boom in oil production in Baetica is indissolubly linked with the supply of the army along the German *limes* and the *annona urbis*. Probably it was Vespasian who increased the control exercised by the *fiscus* over the Baetican olive oil trade.[52] As is well known, starting with Hadrian, the *annona* administration took charge of the collection and transport of oil from Baetica, and later from Africa; the exact reasons behind this are not clear—whether it was in response to increased urban demand or difficulties in the available supply. Hadrian offered fiscal incentives to the *navicularii* and *mercatores olearii*, and the policy of fiscal benefits for those trading for the *annona* continued also under Antoninus Pius.[53] The development of the organization of the *annona* in relation to oil continued under Marcus Aurelius, when we find attested a *praefectus annonae ad oleum afrum et hispanum recensendum*.[54] While the evidence from Monte Testaccio indicates a cessation of Baetican oil imports into Rome and the total substitution by African oil in the reign of Gallienus, oil production in Baetica continued and was still exported to areas of the western Mediterranean during the fourth and fifth centuries AD.[55]

However, for all the information available from ceramics, literary, and epigraphic sources in regard to wine and oil production in the Iberian peninsula, the overall archaeological data about processing installations are somewhat disappointing. Despite the great agricultural production of this region and the density of rural settlements, not many sites have been excavated; when excavations have occurred, they have largely been in the context of rescue excavations in connection with development.[56] When field survey was carried

---

[51] Chic García and García Vargas (2004: 282–307): in the province of Seville a total of 117 pottery production centres are known; 44 were certainly producing oil amphorae; in the territory of Cordoba 45 amphora kilns are known.

[52] Blázquez (1992: 177). The army and the city of Rome absorbed the majority of the oil production, but Baetican oil was exported also to other regions, such as Tingitana: see Pons Pujol (2006).

[53] *Dig.* L 4.5: *naviculari et mercatores olearii qui magnam partem patrimonii ei rei contulerunt intra quinquennium muneris publici vacationem habent*; Chic García (1995).

[54] Ulpius Saturninus Possessor, *CIL* II.1180 from Hispalis.

[55] Revilla (2008: 123). All explicit attestations of *collegia* involved with the *annona* date before the early third century AD (Kulikowski 2004: 55). On the role of *collegia* in the shipment and distribution of Baetican olive oil, see also Lagóstena Barrios (2009: 304–5).

[56] Revilla (2008: 121) for considerations on the uneven quality of the archaeological data for Spain.

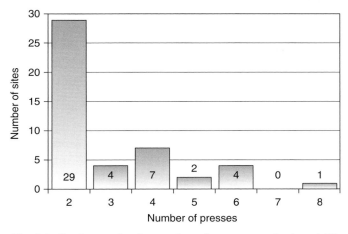

Fig. 5.5. Iberian peninsula: number of presses per site (n = 140)

out,[57] we have data on only a portion of what must have been the totality of multi-press sites;[58] needless to say, in this scenario precise data on chronology are scant.

For the Iberian peninsula as a whole there are 47 known sites showing evidence for multiple-press installations, with a total of 140 presses (see Tables 5.1 and 5.2). The majority of the sites were equipped with two presses (Fig. 5.5). Of these sites, those devoted to wine production (fourteen) included one with six presses, two sites with double presses, whereas for eight sites, equipped with two presses each, the type of production remains undetermined.

We are thus left with twenty-four sites devoted to oil production (this count includes one site with five oil presses and one wine press, and one site with a total attestation of four presses, but not in use at the same time, which apparently switched from oil to wine production in the mid-third century AD). Most of the presses in this corpus were for oil, although a considerable number remains unattributed. Out of 140 presses 53 are unfortunately undated, their identification coming from the recovery of elements of presses or of oil mills in field survey. The attested chronology of use for the production facilities and/or general occupation of the sites shows a steady occupation spanning from the first to the fourth centuries AD, with a slight increase in the second half of the

[57] Ponsich (1974, 1979, 1987, 1991).
[58] See Mattingly (1988: 38–41) and Marzano, Chapter 4, this volume. On press types and press rooms in use in the Iberian peninsula, Peña Cervantes (2010); it is worth noting, in regard to the chronology and diffusion of the lever and screw press, that this author concludes (p. 214) that, contrary to the current theory saying that this kind of press did not spread to Hispania before the late second/early third centuries AD, recent data indicate that Baetica was the birthplace of this technology.

Annalisa Marzano

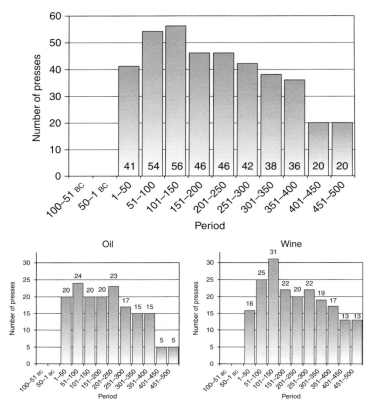

Fig. 5.6. Iberian peninsula: chronology of all presses, and according to type of production (n = 87 [53 undated]; n_{oil} = 42; n_{wine} = 37 [8 uncertain])

first century and the first half of the second century AD, the beginning of a contraction in the second half of the second century, which becomes more pronounced in the fifth. If we separate the presses according to type of production, we see that the number of oil presses remains relatively stable from the first to the mid-third century AD, while the peak for the largest number of wine presses in use occurred in the first half of the second century AD (Fig. 5.6).

This is still a relatively small corpus of sites considering the volume of olive oil and wine production otherwise known from amphora evidence and the density of rural settlement, particularly in Tarraconensis and Baetica. Nonetheless, despite the high number of undated presses, some trends in the type of capital investment practised in the region can be extrapolated. The available data for these multi-press sites show a clear peak in installations in the Julio-Claudian period (forty-one presses), followed by the second half of the first century (fifteen presses), with new installations still appearing in the fourth

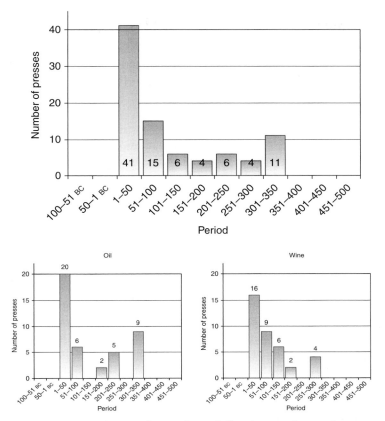

Fig. 5.7. Iberian peninsula: installation date of all presses and according to type of production (n = 87; n_{oil} = 42; n_{wine} = 37)

century AD.[59] In the case of both wine and oil, the installation of multi-presses is concentrated in the first century AD; a small number of new installations appears in subsequent periods, but it is only at the end of the third century and in the fourth that a notable increase in this kind of investment is seen again in the case of multi-press sites (Fig. 5.7).

The following considerations about the agricultural production of the region rest on ceramic and epigraphic evidence, on field survey, and on excavation of farms and villas.[60]

---

[59] In a few cases a *possible* third-century date has been taken as secure for the purposes of the graph, and an unknown starting date has been given as the first century AD on the basis of comparisons with other sites.

[60] The following account mainly relies on Brun (2004); Olesti Vila and Carreras (2008); Clavel-Lévêque and Olesti Vila (2009); Peña Cervantes (2010).

Production boom and contraction

It has been suggested that the increase in the production of wine and oil that we can observe in various parts of the Roman empire during the first century and for most of the second is a sign of the effects of population increase, while the occupation of marginal lands was the result of small proprietors being pushed to the margins because the best land was in the hands of the big landlords.[61] This picture is attested not only in the well-known case of the marginal lands of North Africa. Recent data from the Spanish Pyrenees (Cerdanya) indicate important transformations in the early empire. While in the plains we see the establishment of towns, centuriated fields, and *villae*, on the lower parts of the uplands pig breeding and vines appeared, alongside an increased production of cereals.[62]

In the area around Barcino (Barcelona), in the Maresme region, and in the region of Tarraco (Tarragona), we can observe during the second half of the second century AD the abandonment of many rural settlements that dated to the early first century AD. It is a phenomenon that especially affected farms and productive installations, such as kilns and *cellae vinariae*, but not the *pars urbana* of villas.[63] In fact, a significant proportion of villas was enhanced by the addition of baths and new decorative programmes during the Severan period.[64] Possibly, in some cases these refurbishments were the result of new ownership after the Severan confiscations of properties affecting the partisans of Clodius Albinus. Peña Cervantes observes that those sites established in the early first century AD that can be classified as villas (comprising also residential quarters in addition to production facilities) generally continued to produce wine in the second century, in some cases increasing production capacity; production at these sites continues until at least the third century AD.[65] In addition, while several wine-producing sites were abandoned in the course of the second century, others were established (in the group of multi-press sites examined here only three sites installed wine presses in the second century,

---

[61] Brun (2005: 175).

[62] Olesti Vila, pers. comm. The data on the cultivars come from pollen analysis.

[63] For example, see recent excavations at Mas d'en Corts (Reus), revealing that the wine amphora kiln was abandoned in the second half of the second century AD; Peña Cervantes (2010: 167).

[64] For instance, in Maresme region, Torre Llauder, Cal Ros Cabres, Can Ferrerons, Can Sentromà. For the El Vallés region, some local studies show a similar trend: Egara area: wine production centres, like Can Jofresa or Can Feu, ceased to function at the end of the second century AD. Many *villae* (Aiguacuit, Can Bosch de Basea, Can Fonollet, Can Cabassa-St Cugat) survived until the fourth or fifth century AD: Olesti Vila, pers. comm.; see also Chavarría Arnau (2007).

[65] Peña Cervantes (2010: 167).

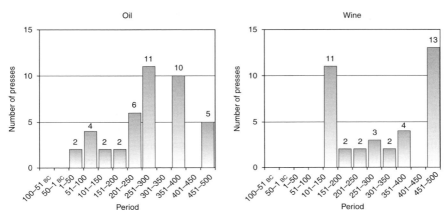

Fig. 5.8. Iberian peninsula: end of use of oil and wine presses (n_{oil} = 42; n_{wine} = 37)

but in one case, the villa of Vallmora, the new presses replaced two older ones).[66]

The end of the intensive Laietanian wine production can be placed in the last quarter of the first century AD, when various wine production centres had already been abandoned, and there was a sharp decline in wine exports. Even in the case of sites that continued to be occupied, a reduction in the volume of wine production has been noted (for example, near Tarraco, at Torrent de les Voltes or Mafumet: the *cella vinaria*, in use from the first to the fifth century AD, was downsized in the late second century). Eleven wine presses in our multi-press corpus went out of use during the first half of the second century AD (Fig. 5.8). Overall in the *ager Tarraconensis* the most recent survey work has identified that in the third century AD 58 per cent of the settlements were abandoned.[67] The trend is similar to what was observed earlier for Gaul, where, in Narbonensis alone, between AD 150 and 200, there was a decrease in rural settlements of *c*.40–50 per cent.

These changes are documented not only in the rural context, but also in the cities, where already in the mid-second century AD one can observe signs of demise and/or abandonment of some public buildings/structures, such as in the capital Tarraco, in the hinterland (Llivia), and in the coastal areas (Iluro, Baetulo, Emporiae).[68] The crisis in rural settlements seems to have occurred again in the second half of the third century AD, and one needs to wait for the

---

[66] See the site of Tiana, Can Sent-Romà, where in the second century a grain silo was obliterated by the installation of *dolia defossa*: Peña Cervantes (2010: 423–7) (Catalogue BAR 40); on Vallmora: Martín i Oliveras *et al.* (2007).

[67] Data courtesy of Olesti Vila.

[68] A similar picture emerges for Baetica: Keay (1998).

fourth century to see the end of it. Indeed several wine-producing sites, with single or multiple installations, were in use in the fourth century.

The wine production of the upper part of the Ebro valley, in the areas of Navarra and La Rioja, also needs to be noted here. Several wine-producing villas appeared in this region in the late first century AD (only one of the known sites has multiple installations: four wine presses), but interestingly at these sites no associated amphorae were found. Peña Cervantes objects to Brun's hypothesis that the wine was transported in skins and/or barrels to the Catalan coast, where it was bottled in amphorae for overseas shipping, observing that all but one site start producing towards the end of the first century AD, when the great boom in Laietanian wine export had subsided. Instead, she suggests that the produce was destined for provincial consumption and was distributed along land routes towards the north-west of the country and to the north of the Meseta.[69]

Considering what was also observed in Gaul, it is tempting to connect these data on rural abandonments in the second century with a demographic decrease resulting from the effects of the Antonine plague, although there were probably also other factors affecting the economy of the region before this date.[70] Hadrian spent the winter of AD 122–3 in Tarraco, promoting a *Concilium Hispaniae*, and we know that the *concilium provinciae Hispaniae Citerior* sent several missions to Rome during the second century AD, although their purpose is unknown.[71] In addition to this, there were the uprisings of the governor of Citerior Cornelius Priscus in AD 145, and of Maternus in AD 187: what consequences these events might have had for agricultural production and distribution are unclear.[72] The demographic explanation is by no means secure. Scholars have put forward different suggestions to explain the apparent contraction in wine production, such as a change in landowning patterns caused by the obligation for provincial senators to invest one-third of their wealth in Italian properties,[73] or environmental changes on the basis of the tree-ring data from central Europe.

The intensive olive oil production to supply Rome and the army occurred in the Guadalquivir valley;[74] it has been estimated that more than 1,000 presses

---

[69] Brun (2004: 277) and Peña Cervantes (2010: 169).

[70] Revilla (2008: 123) seems to express some scepticism about the idea of crisis of viticulture and population, stressing instead that the 'wine-based economy had a different intensity and evolutionary rhythm in the regions associated with wine production'. Also note that the available chronology for the multi-presses indicates that the majority of the wine presses went out of use in the first half of the second century, so before the Antonine plague.

[71] *RIT* 331–332, *CIL* II.4.055; 4.057.

[72] But see discussion in Grünewald (2004: 124–32) about Maternus' 'revolt'.

[73] Alföldi (1998); a decision by Trajan, as we learn from Pliny, *Ep.* 6.19. According to *SHA*, *M. Aurelius* 11.8, Marcus Aurelius reiterated the provision, reducing the amount to one-quarter.

[74] The most impressive attestation of the volume of oil production is Monte Testaccio in Rome, an entire hill made of discarded oil amphorae; the excavations carried out here and the

must have been in use in the region in order to produce the amount of oil that reached Rome every year.[75] Unfortunately, only six oil-producing centres have been excavated in the Guadalquivir valley; none of these sites continued to be occupied after the third century AD.[76] The *annona* was reorganized under Septimius Severus, and with the reign of Gallienus Baetican amphorae were no longer dumped on Monte Testaccio. By the fourth century AD North Africa was the major source of state oil for the population of Rome,[77] but obviously the occupation chronology of only six sites out of the hundreds and hundreds that existed in the region cannot securely be seen as a consequence of these changes. It has been stressed years ago that the changes in the commercialization and transport of oil from Baetica, which have been seen as having important consequences for the economy of the province, were based on weak data that made it hard to assess their real consequences.[78] Although the amount of data has grown in recent years, we still face an incomplete picture. Furthermore, the major role the *annona* played in the distribution of Baetican oil obscures the extent to which this product was also distributed according to normal commercial channels; the role Baetican oil played on the commercial markets of Rome remains difficult to define.[79] The corpus of multi-press sites producing oil in the whole of the Iberian peninsula indicates that eleven presses went out of use in the second half of the third century, and ten in the second half of the fourth century AD (see Fig. 5.8). None of the currently known multiple-press sites for olive oil was created in the third or fourth centuries (see Fig. 5.7), and this scenario may indicate that the cessation of state involvement in the purchase of Baetican oil, with the need to reorganize distribution according to privately controlled channels, had an effect on landlords' decisions, and ability, on whether or not to invest capital in production facilities.

The production of oil in the Iberian peninsula was not limited to Baetica; in Tarraconensis, the area of modern Murcia in particular appears to have been devoted to oil production, possibly not for export but intended for Carthago Nova and environs, since no oil amphorae, well attested elsewhere, are known here.[80] The area around Malaga also produced oil, this time for export, since

study of the *tituli picti* on the amphorae have shed light on the complex organization and control mechanisms; see Blázquez Martínez and Remesal Rodríguez (1999–2010); Peña (1998); Remesal Rodríguez (2002).

[75] Mattingly (1988).
[76] Peña Cervantes (2010: 177).
[77] Blázquez (1992); Peña (1998); Broekaert (2011) suggesting that Septimius Severus, who according to the *SHA* introduced regular oil distributions in Rome, did not intensify the imports, but levelled out the structural differences between grain and oil traffic, since the peak in imports as shown by the *tituli* occurred in the Antonine period.
[78] Rodà (1997: 217).
[79] Lagóstena Barrios (2009: 301).
[80] Peña Cervantes (2010: 170).

various workshops producing Dressel 20 have been identified. But the sites here are small and medium farms, with no clear residential quarters and equipped with one press only, not the large oileries that have emerged in some areas in recent years.[81] The very high density of these small and medium farms and the amphora kilns nonetheless indicate the ability to produce a surplus.[82] The fact that in this area we do not see any tendency to concentrate production might indicate that well-to-do landlords had fragmented land-holdings that were not conducive to centrally organized production, or that there were several free farmers with medium-sized holdings able to participate in the wider commercial network; or it may simply indicate a mode of production that preferred to leave the initiative in processing the produce to tenants rather than having an estate manager closely supervising the activity on the main estate.[83]

Lusitania, which also shows a high level of oil and wine production from the first century AD onwards, has a few instances of villas with multi-press facilities, such as the large complex of São Cucufate. This site started its life in the mid-first century; to this phase belongs a *cella vinaria* featuring *dolia defossa*. In the second century a larger and richer villa was built, equipped with two presses and, interestingly, no longer using sunken *dolia* for the vinification process, but barrels.[84] It has been suggested that the agricultural production of Lusitania was aimed at the internal needs of the province.[85] Such a scenario, in which agricultural surplus remained in the province rather than being exported, can also find support in the urban growth and city sizes achieved in this province in comparison to Baetica and Tarraconensis.[86]

BLACK SEA REGION

Finally, I would like to bring into the picture a region from the eastern part of the empire, the Black Sea area. There is a possible correlation between the emergence of a higher number of sites provided with multiple presses and devoted to wine production in this region and the situation described for

---

[81] As, for instance, the villa with six oil presses installed in the Augustan period at Marroquíes Bajos, near Jaén: Peña Cervantes (2010: 590–3) (Catalogue JAE 5). Discoveries such as this one indicate that in Baetica the area of intensive olive cultivation included the territory of modern Jaén as well.

[82] Peña Cervantes (2010: 178).

[83] This is a less likely scenario, especially in the case of rent paid in kind/share-cropping, when close supervision on behalf of the landlord was necessary; see considerations in Pliny, *Ep.* 9.37. Cf. Olesti Vila and Carreras (2008) for interesting considerations on the social background of landlords of the area of Barcino.

[84] Brun (2004: 288–90).

[85] Peña Cervantes (2010: 184).   [86] Marzano (2011).

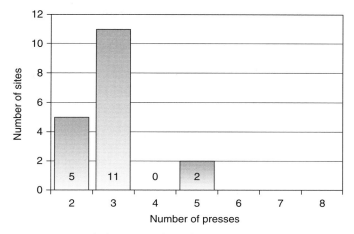

Fig. 5.9. Black Sea: number of presses per site (n = 53)

Spain. It has to be pointed out, however, that the chronological data for the Black Sea installations are not extremely accurate, since in most cases they are based not on excavation data, but on the typology of the presses.

Wine production in this region was not an innovation of the Roman period, but dates back to at least the fifth century BC, when local wild species of vine were cross-bred with a cultivated type introduced from Greece, although the main export of the region at the time was grain and processed fish.[87] There are nineteen sites showing evidence for multi-press installations, with a total of fifty-three presses concentrated in the area of the Kimmerian Bosporus.[88] Most multi-press sites have three wine presses (Fig. 5.9).

Of these sites, one, equipped with two lever and screw presses, is dated between 100 BC and AD 100; six sites (with a total of seventeen presses, all but two classified as lever and screw presses) date from between the very beginning of the first century AD to AD 200; nine sites with twenty-six presses may have started to operate around AD 100 (the date range is AD 100–300) and two sites with eight presses in total may have started around AD 200 (AD 200–400). The overall chronology of use of these installations displays an apparent increase in the second century AD (Fig. 5.10). Although the chronological range indicated for these wine-producing installations is rather long and,

---

[87] Savvonidi (1993: 227); Bekker-Nielsen (2005).

[88] Data derived from Savvonidi (1993); at the time of his study seventy wineries were known along the northern coast of the Black Sea, spanning the fifth century BC to the end of the third century AD (p. 230). One of the sites in his tabulation (Chersonesos 15) did not have evidence for press beds, but three vats and other elements led the author to believe in the original presence of a lever or lever and screw press; for the purpose of this study, considering the presence of three tanks (which sometimes occurs with three press beds, e.g. Mirmekeion 2, Tyritake 4), a minimum of two presses has been assumed.

Annalisa Marzano

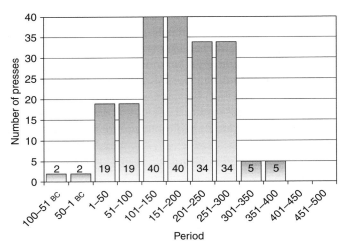

Fig. 5.10. Black Sea: chronology of all presses (n = 53)

because of the lack of excavation at all the sites, we cannot pinpoint with absolute certainty the installation and demise date of the complexes, it is worth noting that it is in the Roman Imperial period that one observes a clear intensification in capital investment in multi-press facilities (Fig. 5.11). Wineries with presses identified in the area and dated to the Hellenistic period feature, with the exception of four cases out of twenty-three, one press only.

The location of these multiple-press sites (Mirmekeion, Tyritake, Chersonesos, Olbia, and so on) coincides with the location of facilities for another product for which the region was known since before the Roman period:

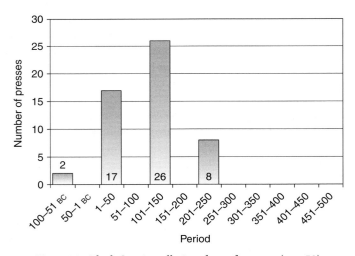

Fig. 5.11. Black Sea: installation date of presses (n = 53)

processed fish.[89] Although much is known from literary sources about the salted fish produced here, only five salting factories with concrete vats dating to the Roman period are known archaeologically in the region.[90] The date of construction appears to coincide, in broad terms, with the general chronology given for the wine presses. At Tyritake, it appears that all the vats were built in the first century AD and were used until after the third century.[91] At Chersonesos the construction of all the vats dates, on the basis of ceramic evidence, to the first to second centuries AD, whereas those at Mirmekeion were built in the second/third centuries AD and were used until the late third century. Finally, for Zolotoe, judging from ceramic finds, the construction of the salting vats should date to the second and third centuries AD.[92]

Certainly these data are incomplete, and subject to change with the advancement of research, but it is suggestive that the known cases of capital investment in the improvement of the fish-salting production coincide, in location and general chronology, with the cases of capital investment in multi-press sites. Furthermore, the boom of capital investment in presses for winemaking appears to have occurred in the first half of the second century, when the number of presses doubled, going from nineteen to forty, around the same time as the construction of salting vats at Myrmekeion and Zolotoe started. There is a possible correlation between the two phenomena. I would like to suggest that the surge in capital investment in multi-press sites in this period was essentially triggered by the desire to increase or render more efficient wine production because of the opportunities created by the existence of regular shipments of salted fish occurring between this region and the Eastern Mediterranean. In the same way as oleoculture in modern times emerged in the Ermionid district in southern Greece when there was a local merchant fleet regularly importing wheat from the Black Sea, and thus being able to carry on their outward voyage goods for which there was a demand at the destination,[93] so wine producers may have seized the opportunities of exploiting a larger market by sending their products in mixed cargoes of wine and salted fish (and also the other products for which this region had been known since Greek times: grain, timber, and slaves). However, until transport amphorae for Pontic fish products and wine are securely identified, any

---

[89] Højte (2005).

[90] Other preservation methods not to be underestimated, but that leave scant archaeological traces, are drying and smoking; see Højte (2005: 141–2).

[91] Højte (2005: 144).

[92] Fish product amphorae for this region have not yet been securely identified; see Opait (2007) for a working hypothesis regarding the so-called Zeest 75, 83, 85, 89 attested in the Black Sea region (but, except for a kiln site at Demirci in the area of Sinope, no other kiln is known: Lund 2007: 186); some of these amphorae are pitched and other scholars believe they carried wine: e.g. Kassab Tezgör (2006). For remarks on scholarly disagreement about the geographical origins of some amphorae, see Lund (2007: 184).

[93] Forbes (1993).

remarks about distribution of these products remain hypothetical and provisional. At the moment, amphorae that have been identified as produced in the Black Sea region seem to have a predominantly Eastern Mediterranean distribution in the Roman period, with a few examples appearing in Ostia (see below). However, the correlation of wine and salted fish in terms of production area and distribution channels is not new: the port of Cosa in Italy had in the Republican period exported, mainly to Gaul, large quantities of salted fish and wine produced nearby.[94]

The problem of Pontic amphorae

Notwithstanding the uncertainty over the attribution of the origin of certain types of transport amphorae in the Roman period to the Black Sea region or other places in the Eastern Aegean, several types of amphorae probably manufactured in the Black Sea area have recently been identified on the basis of petrological analysis.[95] These amphorae, together with Pontic sigillata, had a wider geographical distribution in comparison to the Classical and Hellenistic period, when Pontic vessels appear to have been limited to the Aegean area. As observed by Lund, in the Roman period transport amphorae and fineware from the Black Sea are attested in Athens, Asia Minor, Cyprus, and Knossos, and also in Libya (Berenike/Benghazi), Malta, Ostia, and Rome, albeit in very small quantities, thus suggesting that the volume of trade in these classes of material was low and that the majority of commercial transport between the Black Sea and the Mediterranean related to archaeologically invisible commodities: grain, timber, and slaves.[96] Besides amphora shapes typical of the eastern Aegean, it appears that after the Roman conquest shapes widespread in the Roman Mediterranean (so-called pan-Roman amphorae) also started to be produced in the Black Sea area, such as Dressel 2–4 and Mau XXIX.[97] Panella, in a study of the amphora finds from the Terme del Nuotatore in Ostia, observed that for many of the Aegean amphorae the place of manufacture is still unknown and that the label 'Aegean' is generic and hypothetical. It is, therefore, interesting that the quantities of these 'Aegean' amphorae increase in the second and third centuries AD, and that, at least for the third century, they are in second place, following African amphorae, which

---

[94] McCann (1987).   [95] Erten *et al.* (2004); Lund (2007: 186–7).

[96] For example, the Pontic sigillata found at Berenike constituted only 1.7% of the fine ware datable to the second century AD: see Panella (1986: 628, 631) and Lund (2007: 189–90) for considerations about generally weak commercial connections between the Black Sea and the western Mediterranean in the second century AD.

[97] Vnukov (2004).

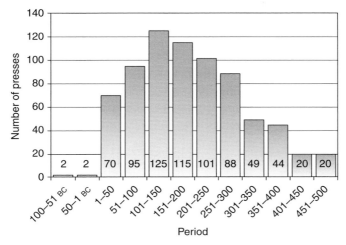

Fig. 5.12. Cumulative total, chronology of all multiple presses (n = 179)

are the most common, and, among imports of wine, closely competing with Gallic and Mauretanian wine.[98]

CONCLUSIONS

This examination of sites equipped with multi-press facilities and of general trends in the wine and olive oil production in Gaul, the Iberian peninsula, and the Black Sea region has revealed different investment patterns in the three areas. In the case of Gaul, a different investment pattern between commodities (wine and oil) was also identified. In the case of both Iberia and Gaul a similar hiatus between the start of the Roman colonization process and the beginning of investment in large production facilities can be observed. If one looks at the chronology of multiple-press installations in the three regions here examined, it is evident that the second century is the period when the highest number of presses was in operation (Fig. 5.12). In all regions the decline in the fourth century is steep. But, if we look at the cumulative known installation dates for the press facilities, the peak in investment in the creation of multiple-press sites occurred in the first two centuries of the empire, but with the first half of the first century AD clearly standing out for number of installations (Fig. 5.13).

[98] Panella (1986: 632); the quantity of Aegean amphorae decreases again in the fourth century, with fewer common types also present, basically only the Kapitän I and the Agora K113, shapes already produced in the earlier centuries and with a long history of use.

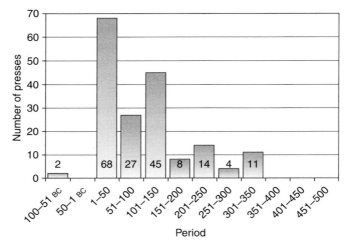

Fig. 5.13. Cumulative total, installation dates of all multiple presses (n = 179)

The picture of economic growth during these centuries that emerges from these samples (admittedly at times too small to have statistical relevance, as in the case of olive oil production in Gaul) is in line with the available evidence relating to other types of production and activities in the Roman empire, from mining to building, and, consequently, with the idea that on average inhabitants of the empire experienced improved standards of living in the first two centuries AD, up to the Antonine plague.[99]

It has to be mentioned that recently some scholars have started to doubt the idea of drastically reduced wine production in the Iberian peninsula starting in the late first century AD.[100] The strongest element pointing to such a reduction is the disappearance of the typical wine amphorae in archaeological contexts around the empire. But some believe that there was instead a shift to barrels and skins,[101] and point to the cases when the volume of wine production increased or stayed constant in the second century. One such case is the villa of Vallmora, where excavations uncovered remains of three press rooms, each equipped with two wine presses, and various *cellae vinariae*. Only four presses were simultaneously in use at any given time, but, when around AD 150 one press room went out of use because it collapsed, another large press room was immediately built to replace it.[102] Even for Gaul, where more data about sites—both farms and villas—are available than for the Iberian peninsula, we do not find a homogeneous picture: if wine production ceased at many sites,

[99] Jongman (2007).
[100] Martin i Oliveras *et al.* (2007).   [101] e.g. Peña Cervantes (2010: 167).
[102] I thank Toni Martin i Oliveras for sending me information about this site and for providing data for the Oxford Roman Economy Project presses database.

replaced by meadows, presumably for pasture, it continued in other regions. Nonetheless, at the moment in the light of the available data, which especially for the Iberian peninsula indicate the demise of many structures in both urban and rural contexts, the idea of demographic contraction in connection with the Antonine plague seems the best working hypothesis.

Peña Cervantes sees a clear correlation between the changes in trade routes and the decreased strategic importance that Baetican olive oil had in supplying the empire in the third century, and changes in the production system. She believes that the reduction in the amount of oil traded ultimately caused the abandonment of many production centres before the end of the third century.[103] While one would suspect that the modifications in the origin of oil supply provided by the *annona*, bringing North Africa to the forefront, had a negative impact on the Iberian peninsula,[104] I believe we should treat the claim that the majority of oil-producing centres had been abandoned by the end of the third century with some caution. Indeed, the oil-producing sites with secure chronology that Peña Cervantes could collect in her study are only eleven, out of the possibly 1,000 that existed in the Guadalquivir valley alone.

Moving to the Black Sea region, I suspect that the wider distribution of wine and fish products from this area in the second and third centuries might be related also to what was happening in the west, especially in Spain, in relation to fish salting and wine production. The capital investment in production facilities in the Black Sea very interestingly occurs when we see a decrease in wine production, as discussed above; furthermore, in the third century AD the fish-salting production capacity of the west Mediterranean contracts (Fig. 5.14). For instance, the various workshops of Baelo Claudia ceased to operate around AD 200, and at the same time we see a reduction in the aggregate production capacity at another important fish-salting site, Troia. Other industrial and commercial zones, such as Emporiae and Munigua, were also abandoned by the third century AD.[105]

---

[103] Peña Cervantes (2010: 219); changes in the volume of traded goods would be reflected also by the switch from Dressel 20 amphorae to the smaller Dressel 23 that were in use in southern Spain from the third century.

[104] Even if the state purchased at imposed prices that were below market price, the fact that purchase of a predictable and steady amount of oil every year was guaranteed must have had a positive effect in stimulating growth; however, it is difficult to model the effect that the end of this state-controlled trade had on producing centres when so few oil-producing centres have been excavated. Exact chronology is crucial here.

[105] Rodà (1997: 215); the late second–third century is also the period when in urban centres many houses are abandoned (see discussion above), although coin and ceramic circulation attest to some economic prosperity. Whether, and how, these data correlate to the dramatic events that affected the peninsula in the period is debated and not clear: for instance, the effects of the invasion of the Mauri, who crossed from Africa during the reign of Marcus Aurelius, of the Antonine plague, the third-century barbarian invasions, the effects of which have recently been considered less devastating than in the past (Kulikowski 2004), the formation of the Imperium Galliarum in the Spanish provinces, and the monetary crisis of the AD 260s.

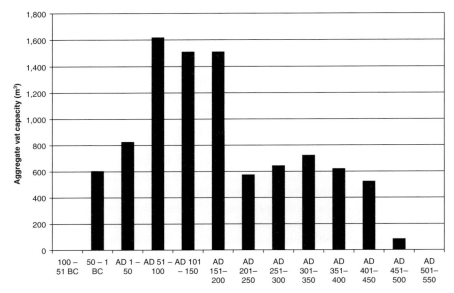

Fig. 5.14. Aggregated capacities of salting factories in Lusitania, Baetica, and Mauretania Tingitana (26 factories at 13 different sites) (Wilson 2006: fig. 3)

As we have seen, this is a period when signs of demise are visible in rural (for smaller sites) and urban contexts: the elites were no longer interested in social advancement through civic magistracies and tended to invest much less in euergetism, while moving from urban centres to their large villas in the countryside. Overall, the Iberian production of salted fish and *garum* fluctuated greatly during the third century, with a resurgence in the fourth, especially in relation to workshops in the north-east of the peninsula, such as Barcino, which, at this time, had privileged relationships with Burdigala (Bordeaux).[106] Perhaps Black Sea products replaced Spanish products in some markets in the third century, but, in view of the lack of sufficient amphora studies for the Pontic production, this remains only a working hypothesis.[107]

What is clear, however, from the sites in the Black Sea region is that the boom in investing in the improvement of production facilities for both fish products and wine occurred in the Roman Imperial period, and this confirms developments observed in other regions of the empire. As evidenced also by recent studies of oil production in Greece in the Classical and Hellenistic

---

[106] Rodà (1997: 217).

[107] For the fourth century one should remember that the foundation of Constantinople created new needs and patterns of trade, although it would take some time for the population of this city to grow to a considerable size.

period,[108] political unity across the Mediterranean and the relative peace achieved in the Early Imperial period played a crucial role in allowing certain economic developments in terms of both production and distribution.

REFERENCES

Abad Casal, L., Keay, S., and Ramallo Asensio S. (2006). *Early Roman Towns in Hispania Tarraconensis* (JRA Suppl. 62). Portsmouth, RI.

Alföldi, G. (1998). 'Hispania bajo los Flavios y los Antoninos: Consideraciones históricas sobre una época', in M. Mayer, J. M. Nolla, and J. Pardo (eds), *De les estructures indígenes a l'organització provincial romana de la Hispània Citerior*. Barcelona, 11–32.

Amouretti, M.-C. (1996). 'La fabricación del aceite de oliva: Una historia técnica original', in Consejo Oleícola Internacional del Olivo, *Enciclopedia Mundial del Olivo*. Barcelona, 26–9.

Amouretti, M.-C., and Brun, J.-P. (1993) (eds). *La Production du vin et de l'huile en Méditerranée: Actes du symposium international organisé par le Centre Camille Jullian (Université de Provence-C.N.R.S.) et le Centre archéologique du Var (Ministère de la culture et Conseil général du Var), (Aix-en-Provence et Toulon, 20–22 novembre 1991)* (Bulletin de correspondance hellénique, Suppl. 26). Athens and Paris.

Aranegui Gascó, C. (1999). 'El commercio del vino en la costa mediterranea española en epoca romana', in S. C. Pérez (ed.), *El vino en la antigüedad romana (Jerez 2, 3, y 4 de Octubre 1996)*. Madrid, 79–96.

Bekker-Nielsen, T. (2005) (ed.). *Ancient Fishing and Fish Processing in the Black Sea Region*. Aarhus.

Blázquez, J. M. (1992). 'The Latest Work on the Export of Baetican Olive Oil to Rome and the Army', *Greece & Rome*, 39/2: 173–88.

Blázquez Martínez, J. M., and Remesal Rodríguez, J. (1999–2010) (eds). *Estudios sobre el Monte Testaccio (Roma)*. Barcelona.

Broekaert, W. (2011). 'Oil for Rome during the Second and Third Century AD: A Confrontation of Archaeological Records and the *Historia Augusta*', *Mnemosyne* 64.4: 591–623.

Brun, J.-P. (1986). *L'oléiculture antique en Provence: Les huileries du département du Var* (Revue archéologique de Narbonnaise, Suppl. 15). Paris.

Brun, J.-P. (1993). 'L'oléiculture et la viticulture antiques en Gaule d'après les vestiges d'installations de production', in Amouretti and Brun (1993), 307–41.

Brun, J.-P. (1999). *Carte archéologique de la Gaule, 83 Var*. Paris.

Brun, J.-P. (2003). *Le vin et l'huile dans la Méditerranée antique: Viticulture, oléiculture et procédés de fabrication*. Paris.

Brun, J.-P. (2004). *Archéologie du vin et de l'huile dans l'Empire romain*. Paris.

---

[108] Foxhall (2007: ch. 8).

Brun, J.-P. (2005). *Archéologie du vin et de l'huile en Gaule romaine*. Paris.

Chavarría Arnau, A. (2007). *El final de las 'villae' en 'Hispania' (siglos IV–VII D.C.)*. Turnhout.

Chaves Tristán, F. (1998). 'Iberian and Early Roman Coinage of Hispania Ulterior Baetica', in Keay (1998), 147–70.

Chic García, G. (1995). 'Un factor importante en la economía de la Bética: El aceite', *Hispania Antiqua*, 19: 95–128.

Chic García, G. (2005). 'El comercio de la Bética altoimperial', *Habis* 36: 313–32.

Chic García, G., and García Vargas, E. (2004). 'Alfares y producciones cerámicas en la provincia de Sevilla: Balance y perspectivas', in D. Bernal and L. Lagóstena (eds), *Figlinae Baeticae. Talleres alfareros y producciones cerámicos en la Bética romana (ss. II a.C. – VII d.C.). Actas del Congreso Internacional (Cádiz, 12–14 de noviembre de 2003)* (BAR International Series 1266). Oxford, 279–348.

Clavel-Lévêque, M., and Olesti Vila, O. (2009). 'Regards croisés sur la viticulture en Catalogne et en Languedoc romains', in A. Orejas, D. Mattingly, and M. Clavel-Lévêque (eds), *From Present to Past through Landscape*. Madrid, 85–116.

Colls, D., Étienne, R., Lequément, R., Liou, B., and Mayet F. (1977). 'L'épave Port Vendres II et le commerce de la Bétique a l'époque de Claude', *Archeonautica* 1: 1–144.

De Vos, M. (2000). Rus Africum. *Terra acqua olio nell'Africa settentrionale: Scavo e ricognizione nei dintorni di Dougga*. Trento.

Drachmann, A. G. (1932). *Ancient Oil Mills and Presses* (Archaeologisk-kunsthistoriske Meddelelser I.1). Copenhagen.

Edmondson, J. C. (2001). 'Les Fondements économiques de la puissance des élites hispano-romaines', in M. Navarro Caballero and S. Demougin (eds), *Élites hispaniques*. Bordeaux, 63–8.

Erten, H. N., Kassab Tezgör, D., Türkmen, I. R., Zarasiz, A. (2004). 'The Typology and Trade of the Amphorae of Sinope: Archaeological Study and Scientific Analyses', in J. Eiring and J. Lund (eds), *Transport Amphorae and Trade in the Eastern Mediterranean: Acts of the International Colloquium at the Danish Institute at Athens, September 26–29, 2002*. Athens, 103–116.

Étienne, R., and Mayet, F. (2000). *Le vin hispanique*. Paris.

Forbes, H. (1993). 'Ethnoarchaeology and the Place of the Olive in the Economy of the Southern Argolid, Greece', in Amouretti and Brun (1993), 213–26.

Foxhall, L. (2007). *Olive Cultivation in Ancient Greece: Seeking the Ancient Economy*. Oxford and New York.

Garnsey, P., and Saller, R. (1987). *The Roman Empire: Economy, Society and Culture*. Berkeley and Los Angeles.

Gonzàles Blanco, A. (1993). 'Pressoirs à huile d'époque romaine dans la Péninsule ibérique', in Amouretti and Brun (1993), 397–412.

Gorges, J.-G. (1979). *Les villas hispano-romaines: Inventaire et problématique archéologiques*. Paris.

Grünewald, T. (2004). *Bandits in the Roman Empire: Myth and Reality*, trans. J. Drinkwater. London.

Hitchner, R. B. (1990), with contributions by S. Ellis, A. Graham, D. Mattingly, and L. Neuru. 'The Kasserine Archaeological Survey—1987', *AntAfr* 26: 231–59.

Hitchner, R. B. (1993). 'Olive Production and the Roman Economy: The Case for Intensive Growth in the Roman Empire', in Amouretti and Brun (1993), 499–508.

Hobson, M. (2012). *The African Boom? Evaluating Economic Growth in the Roman Province of Africa Proconsularis*, Ph.D. thesis, University of Leicester.

Højte, J. M. (2005). 'The Archaeological Evidence for Fish Processing in the Black Sea Region', in Bekker-Nielsen (2005), 133–60.

Jongman, W. M. (2007). 'The Early Roman Empire: Consumption', in W. Scheidel, I. Morris, and R. Saller (eds), *The Cambridge Economic History of the Greco-Roman World*. Cambridge, 592–618.

Jongman, W. M. (2012). 'Roman Economic Change and the Antonine Plague: Endogenous, Exogenous or What?', in E. Lo Cascio (ed.), *L'impatto della "Peste Antonina"*. Bari, 253–63.

Kassab Tezgör, D. (2006). 'The Trade Roads of the Amphorae Produced in Sinope from the 2nd or 3rd to the 6th c. AD'. Abstract for conference 'Production and Trade Amphorae in the Black Sea. Round-table, Batumi and Trabzon, April 2006' <http://www.patabs.org/?p=show&id=14> (accessed 22 December 2009).

Keay, S. (1998) (ed.). *The Archaeology of Early Roman Baetica* (JRA Suppl. 29). Portsmouth, RI.

Kulikowski, M. (2004). *Late Roman Spain and its Cities*. Baltimore and London.

Lagóstena Barrios, L. G. (2009). 'Productos Hispanos en los mercados de Roma: En torno al consume de aceite y salazones de *Baetica* en el alto imperio', in J. Andreu Pintado, J. Cabrero Piquero, and I. Rodà de Llanza (eds), Hispaniae. *Las provincias hispanas en el mundo romano* (Documenta 11). Tarragona, 292–307.

Lund, J. (2007). 'The Circulation of Ceramic Fine Wares and Transport Amphorae from the Black Sea Region in the Mediterranean, c.400 BC–AD 200', in V. Gabrielsen and J. Lund (eds), *The Black Sea in Antiquity: Regional and Interregional Economic Exchanges*. Aarhus, 183–94.

McCann, A. M. (1987) (ed.). *The Roman Port and Fishery of Cosa: A Center of Ancient Trade*. Princeton.

Mataix, J., and Barbancho, F. J. (2006). 'Olive Oil in Mediterranean Food', in J. L. Quiles, M. C. Ramirez-Tortosa, and P. Yaqoob (eds), *Olive Oil and Health*. Wallingford and Cambridge, MA, 1–44.

Marlière, E. (2002). *L'Outre et le tonneau dans l'Occident romain* (Monographies Instrumentum 22). Montagnac.

Martín i Oliveras, A., Rodà de Llanza, I., and Velasco i Felipe, C. (2007). 'Cella vinaria de Vallmora (Teià, Barcelona) un modelo de explotación vitivinícola intensiva en la Layetania, Hispania Citerior (s. I a.C. – s. V d.C.)', *Histria Antiqua*, 15: 195–212.

Mattingly, D. J. (1988). 'Oil for Export? A Comparison of Libyan, Spanish and Tunisian Olive Oil Production in the Roman Empire', *JRA* 1: 49–56.

Mattingly, D. J. (1995). *Tripolitania*. London.

Marzano, A. (2011). 'Rank-Size Analysis and the Roman Cities of the Iberian Peninsula and Britain', in A. K. Bowman and A. I. Wilson (eds), *Settlement, Urbanization, and Population* (Oxford Studies in the Roman Economy 2). Oxford, 196–228.

Olesti Vila, O., and Carreras, C. (2008). 'New Methods for the Study of the Social Landscape from Laietania Wine Production Region (NE Spain)', in P. P. A. Funari,

R. S. Garraffoni, and B. Letalien (eds), *New Perspectives on the Ancient World: Modern Perceptions, Ancient Representations.* Oxford, 131–44.

Opait, A. (2007). 'A Weighty Matter: Pontic Fish Amphorae', in V. Gabrielsen and J. Lund (eds), *The Black Sea in Antiquity: Regional and Interregional Economic Exchanges.* Aarhus, 101–21.

Panella, C. (1986). 'Oriente ed Occidente: Considerazioni su alcune anfore "egee" di età imperiale ad Ostia', in J. Y. Empereur and Y. Garlan (eds), *Recherches sur les amphores grecques: Actes du Colloque International organisé par le Centre National de la Recherche Scientifique, l'Université de Rennes II et l'École Française d'Athènes (Athènes, 10–12 Septembre 1984)* (Bulletin de correspondance hellénique, Suppl. 13). Athens and Paris, 609–36.

Panella, C. (1989). 'Le anfore italiche del II secolo d.C.', in M. Lenoir, D. Manacorda, and C. Panella (eds), *Amphores romaines et histoire économique: Dix ans de recherches* (Collection de l'École française de Rome 114). Rome, 139–78.

Paterson, J. (1978). '*Transalpinae Gentes*: Cicero, De Re Publica 3.16', *CQ* 28.2: 452–8.

Peña, J. T. (1998). 'The Mobilization of State Olive Oil in Roman Africa: The Evidence of Late 4th-c. Ostraca from Carthage', in J. T. Peña *et al.*, *Carthage Papers: The Early Colony's Economy, Water Supply, a Public Bath, and the Mobilization of State Olive Oil.* (JRA Suppl. 28). Portsmouth, RI, 116–238.

Peña Cervantes, Y. (2010). Torcularia: *La producción de vino y aceite en Hispania* (Documenta 14). Tarragona.

Pons Pujol, L. (2006). 'L'importation de l'huile de Bétique en Tingitane et l'exportation des salaisons de Tingitane (i^{er}–iiie siècle après J.-C.)', *Cahiers Glotz* 17: 61–77.

Ponsich, M. (1974). *Implantation rurale antique sur le Bas Guadalquivir: Séville-Alcalá del Río-Lora del Río-Carmona.* Paris.

Ponsich, M. (1979). *Implantation rurale antique sur le Bas Guadalquivir: La Campana-Palma del Río-Posadas.* Paris.

Ponsich, M. (1987). *Implantation rurale antique sur le Bas Guadalquivir. Bujalance, Montoro, Andújar.* Madrid.

Ponsich, M. (1988). *Aceite de oliva y salazones de pescados: Factores geo-económicos de Bética y Tingitana.* Madrid.

Ponsich, M. (1991). *Implantation rurale antique sur le Bas Guadalquivir: Écija, Dos Hermanas, Los Palacios y Villafranca, Lebrija, Sanlúcar de Barrameda.* Madrid.

Remesal Rodríguez, J. (2002). 'Baetica and Germania: Notes on the Concept of 'Provincial Interdependence' in the Roman Empire', in P. Erdkamp (ed.), *The Roman Army and the Economy.* Amsterdam, 293–308.

Revilla, V. (1995). *Producción cerámica, viticultura y propiedad rural en Hispania Tarraconensis.* Barcelona.

Revilla, V. (2008). 'Agrarian Systems in Roman Spain: Archaeological Approaches', in P. P. A. Funari, R. S. Garraffoni, and B. Letalien (eds), *New Perspectives on the Ancient World: Modern Perceptions, Ancient Representations.* Oxford, 117–29.

Rodà, I. (1997). 'Hispania: From the Second Century AD to Late Antiquity', in M. Diaz-Andreu and S. Keay (eds), *The Archaeology of Iberia: The Dynamics of Change.* London, 211–34.

Rosenstein, N. (2008). 'Aristocrats and Agriculture', *JRS* 98: 1–26.

Saez Fernandez, P. (1987). *Agricultura romana de la Bética.* Sevilla.

Savvonidi, N. (1993). 'Wine-Making on the Coast of the Black Sea', in Amouretti and Brun (1993), 227–35.

Tchernia, A. (1986). *Le vin de l'Italie romaine: Essai d'histoire économique d'après les amphores* (BEFAR 261). Rome.

Tchernia, A., *et al.* (1978). *L'épave romaine de la Madrague de Giens (Var), campagnes 1972–1975: Fouilles de l'Institut d'archéologie méditerranéenne* (Gallia Suppl. 34). Paris.

Teichner, F. (2008). *Zwischen Land und Meer—Entre tierra y mar: Studien zur Architektur und Wirtschaftsweise ländlicher Siedlungen im Süden der römischen Provinz Lusitanien* (Studia Lusitana 3). Merida.

Vnukov, S. Yu. (2004). 'Pan-Roman Amphora Types Produced in the Black Sea Region', in J. Eiring and J. Lund (eds), *Transport Amphorae and Trade in the Eastern Mediterranean: Acts of the International Colloquium at the Danish Institute at Athens, September 26–29, 2002*. Athens, 407–15.

Warnock, P. (2007). *Identification of Ancient Olive Oil Processing Methods Based on Olive Remains* (BAR International Series 1635). Oxford.

White, K. D. (1975). *Farm Equipment of the Roman World*. Cambridge.

Wilson, A. I. (2006). 'Fishy Business: Roman Exploitation of Marine Resources', *JRA* 19.2: 525–37.

6

The Rural Landscape of Thugga: Farms, Presses, Mills, and Transport

Mariette de Vos

INTRODUCTION

This chapter discusses the most relevant results of a collaborative project in the extraordinarily well-preserved North African landscape of the middle Medjerda valley in the High Tell of Tunisia, and draws some comparisons with recent survey work in north-eastern Algeria. The fieldwork in Tunisia was conducted with an interdisciplinary research team of twenty members over six years, 1994–2000 (150 km²), with a second series of field seasons in 2007–8 (221 km²), totalling an area of 371 km².[1] A transect of 2 km oriented east–west of 69 km² in the first 150 km² around Thugga and Aïn Wassel was covered with intensive fieldwalking by surveyors who collected all surface pottery and documented the many extant remains clearly visible in the arable fields of the region (Fig. 6.1). The remaining area was investigated by extensive survey concentrated on the many conspicuous extant settlements on hilltops and slopes; here also all surface scatters were collected during mapping activities with total stations and GPS. The transect contains all the different landscape types of the mountainous region between Djebel Gorraa in the west and Djebel Cheidi in the east. The overall average density of pottery sherds in

[1] For preliminary publications of the 1994–2000 work, see de Vos (2000, 2004, 2005, 2007, 2008); Attoui (2004); Ciotola (2004); Maurina (2004, 2010, 2011); Polla (2004–5, 2006, 2011); de Vos and Polla (2005); de Vos and Attoui (2011); de Vos et al. (2011); Maurina and Fermo (2011). The results achieved by the survey were due to the hard-working collaboration of the team members during long and busy seasons and in weather that was at times uncomfortably warm, cold, or wet, and I record my thanks to them all. The data collection presented here is due to the collaboration of: Mustapha Khanoussi (co-director INP), Redha Attoui (survey and GIS), Silvia Polla (pottery), Barbara Maurina (Aïn Wassel excavation, amphorae), Caterina Ognibeni (bronze finds), Romano Lanfranchi (oil presses), Annamaria Marras (inscriptions), Paola Fermo (archaeometrical analyses), Stefano Marconi (animal bones), Michela Cottini, Daniela Moser (archaeobotanical analyses), and Alessandro Battisti (virtual archaeology).

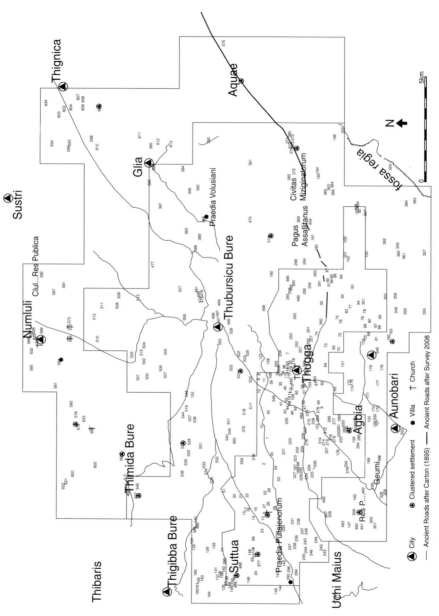

Fig. 6.1. Map of the sites discovered around Thugga in Tunisia (R. Attoui, M. de Vos)

Note: Inner polygon: 69 km² intensive survey. Intermediate polygon: 81 km² extensive survey (1994–2000). Outer polygon: 221 km² extensive survey (2007–8)

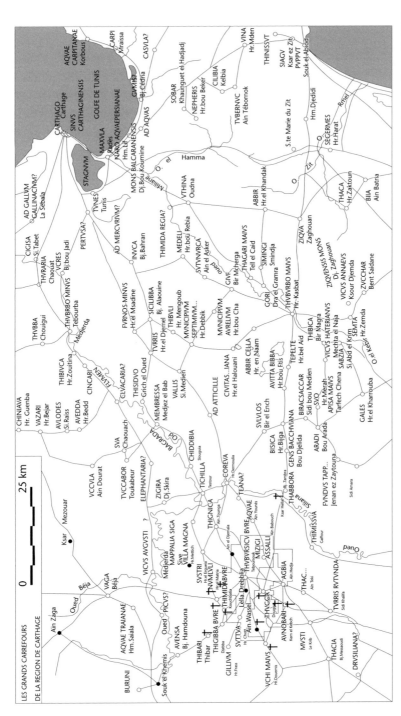

Fig. 6.2. Map of the road system, based on Salama (1951), with black dots showing the findspots of the 'great inscriptions' of the Bagradas Valley (R. Attoui)

the intensive survey was 0.76 fragment/m², in the extensive survey 0.2 frag-ment/m². Each settlement was geo-referenced, and its structures, even when partially *in situ*, were mapped.² The survey revealed a landscape that had been intensively exploited in the Roman and still more in the Late Roman periods and in late antiquity, with numerous farms with presses for oil or wine, and mills for grain (see the section on 'Chronology'). This evidence can be linked with inscriptions that shed light on land tenure arrangements and property extents to suggest that the region produced a surplus that was exported further afield, either commercially or as sharecropping rents on imperial estates, via the region's road network and the river Medjerda (Fig. 6.2).

One of the key aims of the survey was to investigate the working and living conditions of the *coloni* who in the Severan period had asked the emperor to ensure they received the benefits of the *lex Hadriana de rudibus agris*. In 1891 Carton had found a copy of this request *in situ* in the ancient farm of Aïn Wassel, 12 km to the west of Thugga.³ A small part of the farm (252 m²) excavated in 1994–6 turned out to have been totally rebuilt in the Byzantine period on older (probably middle-imperial) wall foundations, reflecting a common pattern in the region. The discovery during the survey of another copy of the *lex Hadriana de rudibus agris*,⁴ at Lella Drebblia, 7 km to the east of Aïn Wassel, and in the *pagus Suttuensis* of the boundary marker of T. Statilius Taurus, Octavian's general (Fig. 6.3), 1 km to the north of Aïn Wassel, enabled us to establish the dimensions of the imperial estate, and to locate the *saltus Neronianus*, the name of the estate after its transfer from the Statilii to Agrippina or Nero (Fig. 6.4). The intention of the emperors was to promote the intensification of agriculture by attractive sharecropping regula-tions described in the 'great inscriptions' of the Bagradas valley, a key grain-producing region for the *annona* of Rome. The historical and legal questions implied in these inscriptions have been studied and discussed since the first of a series of seven was discovered 130 years ago, beginning with Theodor Mommsen;⁵ but so far there has been no investigation on the ground of the production systems in the many senatorial and imperial *saltus* of the Bagradas region (the seven find spots of the 'great inscriptions' are indicated by black dots on Fig. 6.2) since the early reconnaissance by the pioneering army doctor Louis Carton, who published his discoveries in an exemplary way in 1895. Our survey is the first that has applied systematic mapping and collecting to this territory; it revealed an unexpected density and variety of settlement, with important and well-exploited potential that was exploited on an even greater

² De Vos (2000: map 1).
³ Carton (1895: 247–8, pls VIII–X); de Vos (2000: 36, figs 58.1–3; 2004: 34–8).
⁴ De Vos (2000: 35, figs 57.1–6; 2004: 42–45); *AE* 2001, 2083; Sanz Palomera (2007).
⁵ Mommsen (1880); comprehensive recent studies about the great inscriptions: Flach (1978, 1982, 1990); Kehoe (1988; the present chapter takes much advantage of Kehoe's many acute observations and analysis of rural life); Sanz Palomera (2007).

Fig. 6.3. Oued Arkou, *pagus Suttuensis*, site 66: boundary marker of *T. Statilius |*
Taurus | Imp(erator) iter(um) (M. de Vos)

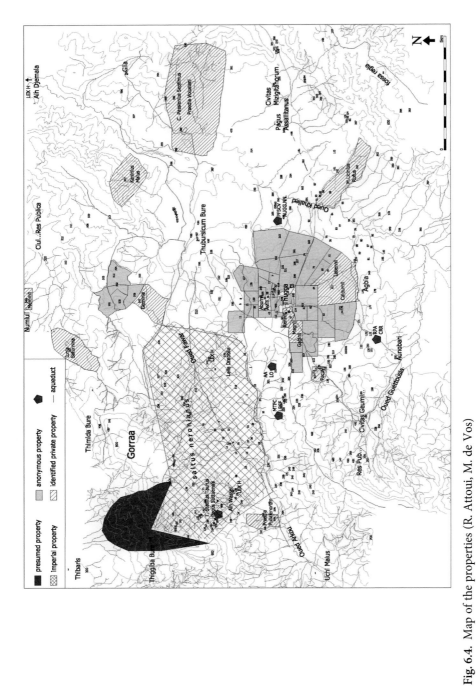

Fig. 6.4. Map of the properties (R. Attoui, M. de Vos)

Note: 'Lex H' indicates findspots of the *lex Hadriana de rudibus agris* at Aïn Wassel (*saltus Neronianus* – west), Lella Drebblia (*saltus Neronianus* – east), and Aïn Djemala (top right). Names of cities, *pagi*, and *civitates* in roman type; the numbers indicate rural settlements.

scale from the moment the area was no longer subject to the restrictions imposed by the Roman *annona*: in the Vandal and Byzantine periods the export possibilities increased enormously and the benefits could be reinvested in the development of the region itself. The dynamic North African export trade around the Mediterranean sea and its coasts, partially sustained by the Church and described in Paul Reynolds's recent important in-depth study of these periods, corresponds very well with the reality of the inland area that is the subject of this chapter.[6]

The survey was a comprehensive investigation, providing a complete geographic coverage, not proceeding by sample areas; and consequently the results are based not on extrapolated estimates but on real values. The excellent preservation of the ancient North African landscape encouraged this approach.[7]

CLIMATE, ECOLOGY, LAND USE

The region surveyed lies in the middle Medjerda valley in Tunisia, on the southern side of the river (the ancient *Bagradas*) around Dougga, Teboursouk (Numidian and Roman Thugga and Thubursicu Bure respectively) and Aïn Wassel at 400–960 m above sea level. The area is characterized by a semi-arid Mediterranean climate with hot summers and an average rainfall of 400–500 mm per year, sufficient for non-irrigated crops. The soil consists of clay and marl on limestone, and the porous soil retains water during the dry season. The stony slopes of the hilly landscape are suitable for olive culture, less so for grain growth, but intercultivation was probably practised in antiquity, as many olive groves with barley crops and other cultivation between the trees are to be seen nowadays. In the case of intercultivation Columella (5.9.7) and Palladius (18) recommended maintaining a greater distance between the olive trees: 40–60 feet instead of 25 feet. Fallow crops of barley, chick pea, fodder, and sunflower today predominate in the landscape around Dougga and Teboursouk (Fig. 6.5);[8] many new olive groves have been planted in recent years in the Arkou and Guetoussia valleys especially, as world olive oil consumption and consequently the olive oil market price have increased.[9] The different valleys in the area surveyed are distinguished by different micro-climates.

---

[6] Reynolds (2010).
[7] Stone (2004) offers a useful overview of different North African surveys.
[8] Kassab and Sethom (1980: 240–1); de Vos (2000: 22, figs 66–7).
[9] De Vos (2000: 23, figs 35, 68–70).

Fig. 6.5. Oued Khalled near Teboursouk: *cultura promiscua* in an olive grove (M. de Vos.)

NATURAL RESOURCES: STONE, SOIL, WATER, WOOD

The region has a rich base of natural resources, and was inhabited from prehistoric times onwards, as indicated by the concentration of sites immediately around Dougga and Teboursouk.[10] Two burials dating back to the first half of the second millennium BC have recently been excavated at the foot of the northern slope of Kef Dougga,[11] attesting the earliest known human activity in the area later occupied by the city of Thugga.

The many outcrops of limestone bedrock supplied material in prehistoric times for stone (flint) tools and for the building of megalithic tombs, and later for cities, roads, monumental farms, and for mills, crushers, and presses for grain, olive, and grape processing. The quarries of Agbia, Teboursouk, and Bir Tersas are active again today, and around Dougga there exist several ancient quarries; the circus of Thugga is located in a former quarry. Traces of stone cutting in limestone outcrops near many settlements (Fig. 6.6) indicate that the transport costs of high-quality building material were minimal. The frequent marl lenses in

[10] See Gradgueb *et al.* (1987).
[11] Ritter and Khanoussi (2004–5: 49–51).

Fig. 6.6. Glia, site 396: limestone quarry (M. de Vos)

the permeable limestone bedrock of area form an effective barrier to water percolation and force groundwater to many spring outlets, providing excellent drinking water and permitting a dispersed settlement pattern.

In ancient times the region was more heavily wooded, contributing to a rich faunal and floral biodiversity and providing fuel and building material. Carbonized remains of olive, ash, stone pine (*pinus pinea*), and juniper have been excavated in the Byzantine farm of Aïn Wassel: trees, except for the olive, that today have vanished completely from the local landscape. Ash trees are now planted as street trees in Teboursouk and many other North African towns. Their habitat is along streams, so one may imagine that the torrent and the abundant Aïn Wassel spring 40 m below the farm were bordered by ashes.[12]

---

[12] De Vos (2000: map 5; the thick black line indicates Oued Aïn Wassel, the double line the trackway to the spring).

Its hardwood is ideal for tool handles and farming implements, especially ploughs, today still on sale at Teboursouk. The potential for hunting and fishing (in the river Khalled), silvo-pastoral activities, agriculture, and arbori-culture shaped the early settlement and development of the region. The Medjerda valley has been throughout history a very productive and valuable landscape for agriculture and pasturing.

SETTLEMENT HIERARCHY AND DISTRIBUTION

The region around Thugga was densely urbanized in antiquity; it is a textbook example of dense urban concentration of medium-sized towns, which must reflect intensified agricultural production. Thugga itself, a town of 25 ha, is estimated to have had *c.*5,000 inhabitants, its territory a further 5,000. Its theatre has 3,500 seats.[13] Besides Thugga there were a further seven smaller towns in the surveyed area: Thimida Bure, Numluli, Thubursicu Bure, Glia (the ancient toponym is unknown), Aquae, Agbia (12 ha), Aunobari (see Figs 6.1 and 6.2);[14] and four bigger towns on the periphery of the zone (but outside the surveyed area), which of course influenced the settlement pattern of their surroundings: Uchi Maius (6 ha),[15] Thignica (30 ha),[16] Sustri, Thibaris. The lesser nucleated settlements of the survey region include two *pagi* (*Suttuensis, Assallitanorum*), two *civitates* (*Mizigitanorum, Geum*[. . .]), two respublicae (*res pub*[. . .], and *Clul res publica*), and eleven smaller rural agglomerations. Apart from Uchi Maius, Thignica, and Numluli, the smaller towns are not excavated. Most of them developed from *pagi* assigned to the *pertica* of Carthage by Augustus in 27 BC to *municipia* under Septimius Severus.[17] These *pagi* were often associated with a *civitas* of local population with which they reached a fusion after two centuries of integration. The information about this process is based on epigraphic evidence. Thugga, although not the most important town of the region, is the one about which we know most, because it has been very extensively excavated, producing more than 2,000 inscriptions and a large number of well-preserved monuments: *forum, macellum,* theatre, circus, three baths (two public, one private), twenty-eight temples, three honorific arches, and spacious houses provided with cisterns and mosaics. Many of the public buildings and temples were financed by rich local families, for example, the Gabinii (see the section on 'Investment'). Thubursicu Bure, later partly

---

[13] Poinssot (1983: 18, 22).
[14] Lepelley (1981: 194 (Thigibba Bure), 197 (Thimida Bure), 206–9 (Thubursicu Bure), 62–3 (Agbia), 76 (Aunobaris)).
[15] Balut (1903: 61); Lepelley (1981: 233–5).
[16] Lepelley (1981: 194–7); Ben Hassen (2006: 39).
[17] Mastino and Porcheddu (2006: 139–45); Reynolds (2010: 69 and n. 271); Aounallah (2010).

enclosed within a Byzantine fortress, like Agbia, is buried under the modern city of Teboursouk.

Updating the survey data published in 2000,[18] we can make a comparison between the survey around Thugga and another survey conducted in north-eastern Algeria in 2003–9.[19] The settlements are better preserved in the Algerian survey than in Tunisia, as a result of the more wooded landscape and minimal occupation in modern times (the frontier zone was off limits during the colonial period, and was thus not disturbed by modern roads and settlements), in contrast with the more arable and urbanized countryside in the region surveyed in Tunisia.

The area surveyed in Algeria was less urbanized, with only two cities: Thullio (Cheffia), Onellaba (Senhedja), and a *castellum Ma[. . .]rensium* (5 km to the south of R'mel Souk, just across the border, in Tunisia).[20] Next to nothing is known about these centres. The veteran and *flamen perpetuus* C. Iulius Getulus called Thullio his *civitas* (*CIL* 8.5209), and by the time of Augustine the *civitas* was promoted to *municipium*.[21] Thullio was destroyed and is now covered by a cork oak forest; its different and widespread *necropoleis* contained many Libyan, Latin, and Libyco–Latin epitaphs.[22] Onellaba, mentioned in the *Itinerarium Antonini*, is hypothetically located at Sanhedja, where we found farms, many rock-cut wine presses and sarcophagi, but no urban structures.

A large number of sites in both surveys were farms with evidence for the processing of agricultural crops, principally the remains of olive oil or wine presses, olive-crushing mills, and grain mills (Tables 6.1–6.2). In the Tunisian survey between Thugga and Thubursicu Bure we found 636 sites in 371 km², in which were 274 farms in the countryside containing 335 presses composed of 605 stone press elements, and 7 cities, 2 *pagi*, and 2 *res pub*[. . .] containing 48 presses composed of 83 stone elements, totalling 371 presses (Table 6.2).[23] In the Algerian survey we found 341 sites in 1,338 km², of which 338 were farms with a total of 523 presses composed of 1,200 stone elements. More than

---

[18] De Vos (2000: 20, 81–4).

[19] For some concise preliminary information, see de Vos (2005: 76–80); <http://periodicounitn. unitn.it/110/lantico-paesaggio-rurale-nordafricano-ricostruito> (accessed 3 Sept. 2012).

[20] For Ma(. . .)rensium we have only tetrarchic epigraphic evidence: *CIL* 8.17327. Interpretation as *castellum* instead of *pagus*: Lepelley (1979: 133; 1981: 139–40); Ben Abdallah (1986: 65, 167); *AAT* 18, 7 (Aïn Tella): *pagus*. The *universi seniores* restored a temple to Mercury; Shaw (1991: 36) compares this terminology to that used in Roman municipal assemblies, in imitation of municipal senates of Roman towns.

[21] Augustine, *De cura pro mortuis gerenda* 12 (15), *CSEL* 41: p. 44, l. 8–9; Lancel (1984: 1089, 1092).

[22] Lepelley (1981: 224–5).

[23] The larger quantity of sites in Tunisia is due to the presence of 8 cities; moreover, the 129 shafts and 7 bridges of the aqueduct from Aïn Hammam to Thugga are mapped as 136 sites.

Table 6.1. Comparison between agricultural processing elements found in surveys around Thugga and in north-eastern Algeria

Elements	Thugga	Algeria
Surveyed area (km^2)	371	1,338
Sites	636	341
Farms (with and without presses)	274	338
Presses	335	523
Olive-grinding mill basin	0	167
Olive crusher or wheel rotating in the grinder	0	54
Ashlar block with mortise for the lower end of a vertical lever press beam	200	210
Lintel with recess for the upper end of the vertical lever press beam	55	26
Press bed stone	88	387
Press counterweight	262	260
Basin	15	105
Cylinder	15	26
Flour collectors	4	1
Meta (conical lower stone of a mill)	19	11
Catillus (upper stone of a mill)	23	3
Mola manualis (hand quern)	27	27
Total number of stone elements used for pressing and grinding	708	1,277

Table 6.2. Thugga survey, rural and urban presses

Elements	Rural (farms)	Urban (cities, *pagi, res pub*[. . .] etc.)
Surveyed area (km^2)	371	—
Sites	629	9
Farms (with and without presses)	183	—
Presses	323	48
Ashlar block with mortise for the lower end of a vertical lever press beam	183	17
Lintel with recess for the upper end of the vertical lever press beam	50	5
Press bed stone	79	9
Press counterweight	214	48
Basin	14	1
Cylinder	12	3
Flour collectors	4	0
Meta (conical lower stone of a mill)	19	0
Catillus (upper stone of a mill)	23	0
Mola manualis (hand quern);	25	2
Total number of stone elements used for pressing and grinding	623	83

Fig. 6.7. Oued Arkou, Aïn Wassel, site 25, partially excavated Byzantine farm: reused counterweight, rotated 90° (M. de Vos)

40 of these 523 presses are rock-cut and mostly designed to process grapes into wine.

In Tunisia 48 elements were reused as orthostats in more recent (probably Byzantine) rural buildings, of which 33 are counterweights,[24] 8 mortise blocks,[25] 6 press beds, and 1 lintel; in addition, 20 other elements were reused in the Byzantine fortresses of Agbia (7 counterweights) and Thubursicu Bure (2 *arbores*) and within the cities of Aunobari (3 counterweights, 1 mortise block), Numluli (1 bed, 1 counterweight), Thimida Bure (1 *arbor*, 1 mortise block, 1 counterweight), and Glia (1 counterweight), *Res Pub*[. . .] (1 counterweight). On the contrary, in late antiquity twenty-three presses were reconstructed reusing monolithic sarcophagi as collecting vats, and thresholds, bossed ashlar blocks, funerary altars, and even the dedicatory inscription of a temple to Iuno Lucina (*CIL* 8.27357), transformed into counterweights or mortise blocks; or reusing a counterweight transformed into a mortise block and a counterweight rotated 90° with its dovetail wedges recut (Fig. 6.7).

In north-eastern Algeria olive grinders (*molae oleariae*) abound: 167 examples were recorded, but none in Tunisia, where 14 farms are equipped with a cylinder with a socket in both short sides (Fig. 6.8);[26] 9 other similar cylinders are collected in the factory of the White Fathers at Thibar. These cylinders were probably used as crushing rollers to compact olives or grapes[27] on a resistant flat surface. In Tunisia we found four 'flour collectors', but none

---

[24] De Vos (2000: fig. 72, site 161), counterweight reused as orthostat.

[25] Three in the church of site 5 (de Vos 2008: 277, fig. 24) and one in the church of site 282 (de Vos 2000: fig. 29.1–2.)

[26] Type Ben Baaziz (1991: pl. 1, broyeur 1). In the farms there is no evidence of the Catonian *trapetum* equipped with two hemispherical *orbes*, but in the city of Thugga there are three *orbes* scattered in three different places.

[27] Cf. Amit and Baruch (2009).

Fig. 6.8. *Pagus Suttuensis*, site 66, cylinder (M. de Vos)

Table 6.3. Distribution pattern of presses in the Thugga and Algerian surveys

Presses	Thugga rural (farms)	Thugga urban (cities, *pagi*, *res pub*[. . .] etc.)	Algeria rural (farms)
None	72	0	25
Single	82	0	128
Double	24	1	6
Triple	5	1	1
2 single presses	43	1	59
3 single presses	17	3	13
4 single presses	5	0	10
5 single presses	3	2	7
6 single presses	1	1	0
7 single presses	0	1	4
8 single presses	0	0	7
9 single presses	0	1	1
10 single presses	0	0	2
11 single presses	0	0	2
12 single presses	0	0	0
13 single presses	0	0	1

in north-eastern Algeria, although there are many in the south and west of Numidia (see below). There were, therefore, differences on a micro-regional scale between the crop-processing machinery and technologies used by rural communities.[28]

---

[28] Ben Baaziz (1991) underlines the different regional characteristics of the presses in Tunisia and offers a typology of grinders and crushers.

In Table 6.3 the multiple presses (sets of two and three presses planned and built side-by-side in the same phase) are distinguished from the single presses in the farms, which range from two to six examples arranged in different places in or around isolated or clustered farms without any overall planning. In Tunisia we recorded twenty-five double presses (Fig. 6.9a–b) and six triple presses (Fig. 6.10); in Algeria only six double presses and one triple press. All the other presses are either single or arranged in different places within single or clustered farms probably built in different phases with different orientations (Fig. 6.11), following economic and or demographic growth. They might have been amalgamated by intermarriage, or expanded to cope with the growth of the olive yield (an olive tree needs on average 25–60 years before reaching its maximum yield of fruit) or enlarged by acquisition of additional fields over the course of time, through investment of the profits from earlier production or pledges of the leased lands. This kind of growth in the relatively short period of two or three generations had already been noticed by the *coloni* of the *saltus* of Aïn Djemala, who mentioned an *[i]ncrementum habit[atorum]* in the neighbouring *fundus Neronianus* since the application of the *lex Manciana* (*CIL* 8.25943, I.11), which had enabled the tenants there to plant olive trees and vines in marshes and forests. Given this rapid economic and demographic progress, the farmers of Aïn Djemala requested the same conditions for themselves (*CIL* 8.25943, I.4–8): *dare no{s} | b[is eos agros] qui sunt in paludibus | et silvestribus instituendos olivetis | et vineis lege Manciana, condicione | [s]altus Neroniani vicini nobis*. This *incrementum* took place in the last quarter of the first and the first quarter of the second century AD. The *lex Manciana* was probably proposed by T. Curtilius Mancia, suffect consul in AD 56, and probably introduced under Vespasian. Kehoe considers the law as part of a general reorganization of North African agriculture,[29] arguing that Vespasian re-established the frontiers in the whole empire, also of the *fossa regia* (see Fig. 6.1), and that, before him, Nero had confiscated the properties of six landlords who owned half of Africa, as we know from the famous comment of Pliny (*NH* 18, 35): *latifundia perdidere Italiam, iam vero et provincias: sex domini semissem Africae possidebant, cum interfecit eos Nero princeps* ('the large domains have been the ruin of Italy, and the same evil is doomed to affect the provinces: six landlords owned half of Africa at the time emperor Nero killed them'—and confiscated their properties, of course). This sentence is wonderfully applicable to the *saltus Neronianus* and the observations of the *coloni* contained in the inscription from Aïn Djemala, who say that initially the *saltus Neronianus* contained woods (probably on Djebel Gorraa) and swamps (in the Arkou and Fawar valleys). It means also that in the eighty years of its management the Statilii family did not succeed in or was not interested in

---

[29] Kehoe (1988: 48–55).

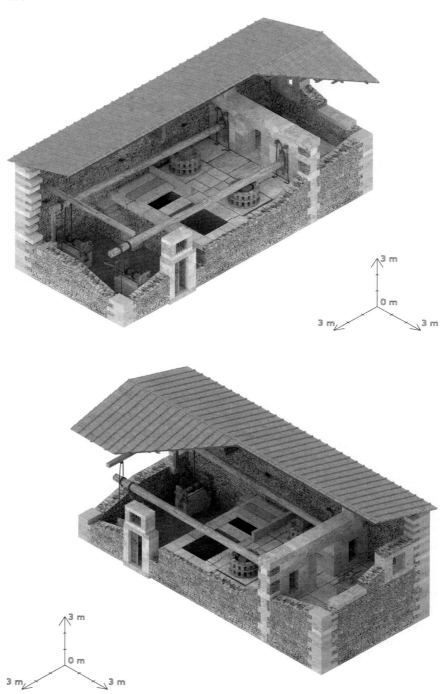

Fig. 6.9. Oil farm, site 205; 3D reconstruction of double press (R. Attoui, A. Battisti)

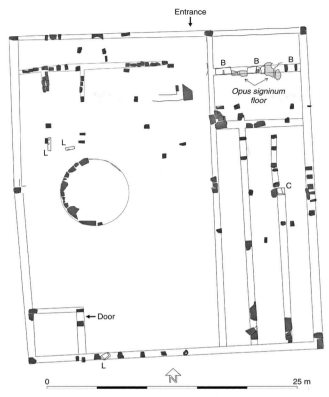

Fig. 6.10. Plan of farm site 207 with triple press (P. Tedesco, R. Attoui, M. Andreoli, M. de Vos)

Note: B = mortise block, C = counterweight reused as orthostat, L = lintel with two mortises for lifting the lever.

intensive clearing and cultivation of its African estate, but after the application of the *lex Manciana*, which permitted the plantation of olive groves and vineyards in swamps and woodland, the population in the *fundus Neronianus* increased. The development of these rural clusters may be compared with that of the hamlets of modern times that contain up to fifty inhabitants.[30]

Sometimes the press blocks have been moved for some metres on the same site, so we cannot be sure they were arranged side-by-side even if the architectural setting would suggest so. It is therefore very probable that double or triple press installations were originally more numerous, but recent disturbance hinders a correct interpretation of the original layout. In Table 6.3 those presses are highlighted that were planned from the beginning in a set of two or three, placed side-by-side in an organic setting and intended to process large

[30] Sethom and Kassab (1981: 99).

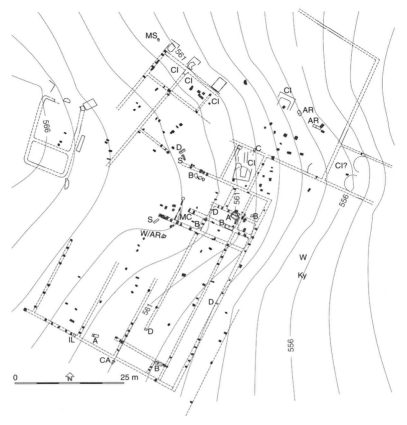

Fig. 6.11. Plan of farm site 49 with four single presses (R. Attoui, M. Andreoli, M. de Vos)

Note: A = press bed, AR = architrave, B = mortise block, C = counterweight, CA = capital, CI = cistern with buttress, D = doorpost, IL = Libyan inscription, Ky = kyma, MC = mosaic, MS = milestone, S = threshold, W = window post).

harvests: they reveal a planned and organized investment.[31] In the two regions investigated, this type of arrangement is relatively rare: in the Tunisian rural survey area there are twenty-four double presses in twenty-three farms and six triple presses in six farms: six of these thirty multiple presses are in the imperial property of the *saltus Neronianus*. One double press in a surprisingly small farm belonged to the Gabinii (site 47).[32] One might think that the multiple presses were built in the farms run by well-to-do *conductores*

---

[31] Cf. Marzano, Chapter 5, this volume.

[32] De Vos (2004: 47–8): the farm includes two buildings: one containing the *torcularium* (18.3 × 7.7 m), one containing the living quarter or stockroom (15.4 × 15.4 m), located either side of the tomb of M. Gabinius Aequus.

(middlemen—and lessees as well—between the emperor and the *coloni*) who could in addition rely on six days per year of *operae* or labour services, which the *coloni* were obliged to provide according to the *lex Hadriana*. But the *conductores*, short-term tenants (for five years) of the estates, are thought to have been less interested in intensive cultivations than in crops that could be harvested immediately.[33] The multiple presses in the *pagus Suttuensis* and in the AA area (*Agri Accepti* or *Attributi*) around sites 203, 205, 207 (see below and Fig. 6.4) might have been public property; the multiple presses of Uchi Maius were built in public spaces, that could, however, have been invaded by private people, as occurred not infrequently in late antiquity. The other multiple presses outside the imperial estate might have belonged to the farms of rich landowners, but, except for the Gabinii farm, there is no epigraphic evidence that sustains this hypothesis.

The total number of presses around Thugga and Teboursouk is 323 in the countryside and 49 in the 7 cities, 2 *Pagi* and 2 *Res Pub*[. . .]. In the Algerian survey region the multiple presses are even fewer: six double presses and only one triple press. Only in the villa of Ksar Laatach, the most southerly site in the surveyed area (60 km from the coast), 22 km north of Thagaste (Souk Ahras), did we find a monumental winery with a set of eight wine-treading floors and presses. The plant is similar to that of the winery at Kherbet Agoub in the Sétif region.[34]

Uchi Maius, the city in the south-west of the area surveyed in Tunisia, whose territory included the *praedia Pullaienorum*, was provided in the Vandal and Byzantine period with one unit of seven presses, three units of three, and two units of two and five single presses, all installed in public spaces, often recycling stone blocks and inscriptions of the former Middle and Late Imperial period.[35] Multiple presses may thus also be an urban phenomenon. In the other cities of the region the press elements are all *ex situ*, so they cannot permit a reconstruction of the original layout. At Dougga a press was installed in the eastern end of the *porticus* of the temple of Mercurius Silvius,[36] and the presence of a large counterweight in the entrance hall of the Licinian Baths may indicate that the space was reused as a press in late antiquity. In late antiquity presses were also built in public spaces in other cities of northern and central Tunisia, as in the Capitolium of Thuburbo Maius[37] and in a street of Sufetula (Sbeïtla).

The centre of the *saltus Neronianus* contains a triple press in the *pagus Suttuensis*, and two double presses near each other in the Aïn Wassel settlement, which is provided also with six single presses.[38] The double presses are

---

[33] Kehoe (1988: 142).   [34] Brun (2004: 233–5).   [35] Vismara (2007).
[36] Poinssot (1983: 33); the sarcophagi placed in late antiquity in the eastern cella were probably reused to collect oil, a rural practice frequently observed in the survey areas in Tunisia and Algeria.
[37] Maurin (1967).   [38] De Vos (2000: map 6).

near the entrance of the settlement and might have been run by the *conductor*. In both urban and rural habitations the *vilicus* had his living quarters near the entrance where he could check the mobility of persons, tools, and commodities. The triple press of farm site 207 (see Fig. 6.10) has preserved two mortise blocks (M); the eastern mortise block has vanished, but its two supporting blocks are still *in situ*. Maybe the plant was symmetrical with three more presses opposite in the southern part, which may have been dismantled when the north-eastern part was rebuilt with *spolia* in the Byzantine period. These late antique walls are double faced; they consist of large blocks placed side-by-side and not at regular distances like the *orthostats* of *opus africanum*, visible in the north-eastern part and the south wall of the farm. The two lintels with recesses for the consoles sustaining the rope that lifted the lever are also reused in the Byzantine north-western part, in a horizontal position. Many farms exhibit these two building phases. Farm site 207 presents a modular plan of 29.42 × 33.83 m (100 × 115 Severan–Diocletianic feet) divided into 10 × 16 m, the portion 10 m wide is divided into three equal parts for the presses, each 12 feet wide.[39] This modularity—very rare in the surveyed farms, as far as one may see on the surface—the almost perfect orientation of the farm, and its multiple press layout, all suppose a large and well-planned initial investment; these qualities make the farm outstanding. The same is to be said of its nearest neighbour (site 205), 1 km away. The boundary marker inscribed *AA//LO* of the nearby farm site 203, *Agri Accepti* or *Agri Attributi* of Thugga (?),[40] may contain the key to the question, but unfortunately the initials are rather enigmatic (see Fig. 6.4).

It is striking to note the same distribution of presses in the single farms (see Table 6.2): in the landscapes of both Tunisia and Algeria relatively small- to medium-scale farming prevailed, though still oriented towards surplus production. Almost half of the farm buildings had only one press, a quarter had two single presses, 13 per cent in Tunisia and 9.3 per cent in Algeria had 3–4 single presses; 14 per cent in Tunisia are provided with a double press and 3 per cent with a triple press; some farms have both multiple and single presses. One press, however, could process more than 10,000 litres per year, leaving a market surplus after the deduction of one-third due as rent in kind to the emperor or a private landlord. The clustered settlements possessed 6–12 presses, but here also the presses were arranged individually, without any overall concentration. In Tunisia twenty-nine settlements and in Algeria eleven settlements with oil/wine presses are also equipped with an hourglass-shaped mill, apparently used also for olive compacting. Five poorly preserved settlements in Tunisia without presses have an hourglass-shaped mill. The eleven settlements in Algeria contain twenty-seven *molae oleariae*.

---

[39] De Vos (2008: 281–2, fig. 31, plan with grid of Severan–Diocletianic feet (29.42 cm)).
[40] Cf. similar *termini* at Cirta: *CIL* 8.7090, 10821, 19104, 19329, and at Milev: *CIL* 8.8211 (Cuomo 2007: 126).

Table 6.4. Chronology of the sites in the Thugga survey based on the surface pottery

Period	% sites occupied	Total sites	New	Continuing	Reoccupied	Abandoned
Pre-Roman	20	36				
Early Roman	25	46	24	22	0	14
Middle Roman	30	55	19	33	7	13
Late Roman	50	91	31	44	8	11
Vandal	70	126	37	78	11	13
Byzantine	67	121	13	101	7	25
Islamic	3	6	0	5	1	116

Chronology

Hitherto, the density of the settlements, the vitality of the region, and the dynamic developments documented by the survey in the hinterland of Provincia Africa Proconsularis/Zeugitana were unknown. The gradual increase in the rural population can be summarized as follows using the data from diagnostic ceramics collected from 179 sites (Table 6.4 and Fig. 6.12a–g): 20% of the sites (36 sites) go back to the pre-Roman period, 25% (46 sites, 24 of which are new, 22 continued from the previous period, while 14 sites are abandoned) to the Early Imperial period, 30% (55 sites, of which 19 are new, 33 continued from the previous period, and 7 reoccupied; 13 abandoned) go back to the Middle Imperial period, 50% (91 sites, of which 31 are new, 44 continued from the previous period, 8 reoccupied; 11 abandoned) to the Late Imperial period, 70% (126 sites, of which 37 are new, 78 continued from the previous period, 11 reoccupied, and 13 abandoned) to the Vandal rule, and 67% (121 sites, of which 13 are new, 101 continued from the previous period, 7 reoccupied, and 25 abandoned) to the Byzantine period, and 3% (6 sites, of which 5 are continued from the previous period, 1 reoccupied, and 116 abandoned) to the Islamic period.[41]

AGRICULTURAL INVESTMENT

The ancient agricultural technology everywhere evident in the North African landscape was applied in all kinds of farms; the ancient principle of pressing

---

[41] Preliminary data in Polla (2004–5, 2006, 2011); de Vos (2007: 43). The ceramic survey conducted from 1994–2000 covers sites in a region of 150 km². The Islamic period is under-represented because of the paucity of Early Medieval pottery studies.

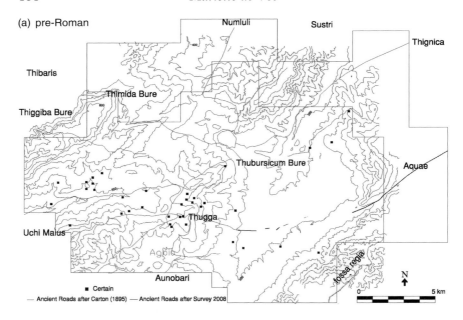

(a) pre-Roman

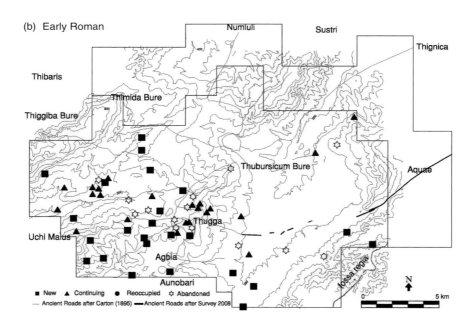

(b) Early Roman

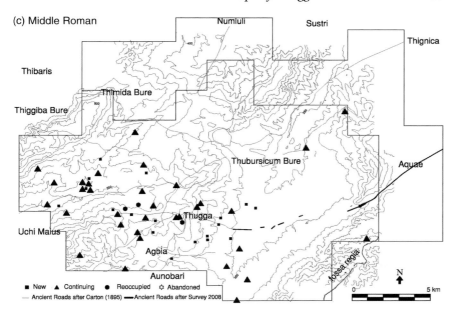

(c) Middle Roman

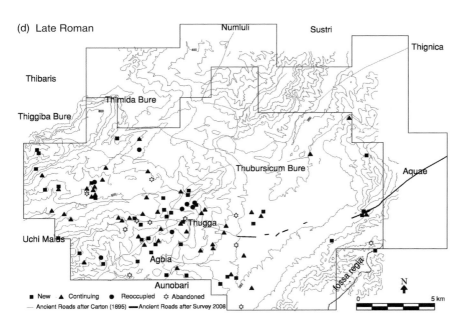

(d) Late Roman

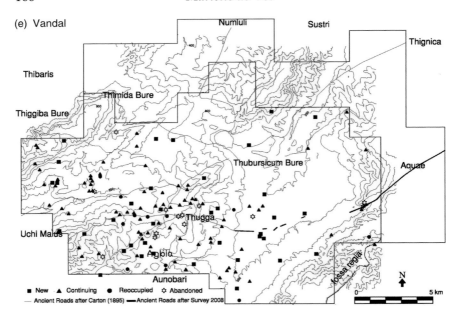

(e) Vandal

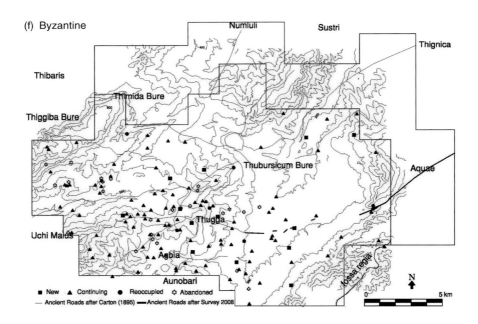

(f) Byzantine

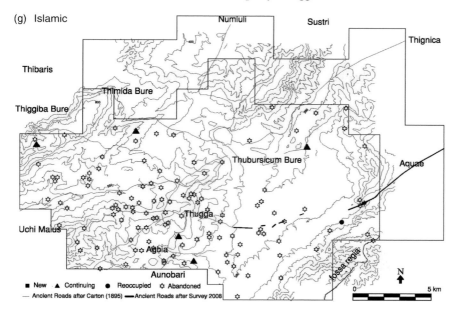

Fig. 6.12. Chronological maps of pottery distribution: (a) pre-Roman; (b) Early Roman; (c) Middle Roman; (d) Late Roman; (e) Vandal; (f) Byzantine; (g) Islamic (R. Attoui, S. Polla)

olives and wine, of crushing olives and of milling grain, did not change until very recent years and was used also in modern mechanized plant. The ubiquitous bedrock was used as building material in monumental solid farms built in *opus africanum* (a framework of rusticated ashlar blocks filled with courses of regular brick-like stones: Fig. 6.13a–b) and *opus vittatum*, and for presses, crushers, and mills. These devices are present everywhere, in small, medium, and large farms. For special requirements volcanic rocks were imported from Sardinia or Italy, used for hand and donkey mills, but only in Tunisia, not in north-eastern Algeria. Normally the landlord had to equip the farm with processing plant and tools, while the tenants had to pay for the seed and cuttings for exhausted vines and probably also for new plantations (in the case of olives, either by planting them in holes or by grafting them onto wild olives: *in scrobibus posuerit aut oleastris inseverit*); they also had to maintain livestock for ploughing and transport; in the *fundus Villae Magnae aut Mappalia Siga* they even had to pay a fee of four *asses* for the pasture of each animal and one *sextarius* for each beehive, starting from the sixth—the first five hives were free.[42] In the *saltus Burunitanus* the coloni protested

---

[42] *CIL* 8.25902 III.16–20; I.29–30; Kehoe (1988: 40–1).

(a)

(b)

Fig. 6.13. Aïn Zillig, site 570, farm with double press: (a) exterior of west and south walls *in opus africanum*; (b) interior face of west wall with two mortise blocks and window; lower right: the rim of the masonry basin (M. de Vos)

against the *procuratores* and the *conductor,* who increased their claims for the use of draft animals (*praebitio iugorum*).[43] The landlord was required to supply *villa,* stables, and pens, but no legal source indicates who had to supply livestock; probably the tenant had to invest in livestock and husbandry.[44] The faunal remains found in the Byzantine farm of Aïn Wassel include the bones of (MNI) one ass, three cattle, one aurochs, six pigs, two dromedaries, twelve goat/sheep, six domestic fowl, a barbary partridge,[45] a hare, and a rat. This sample is small and of late antique date, but, as farm life is rather conservative and has few alternatives, it may also give an idea of husbandry in earlier periods.

Presses

Both surveys, in Tunisia and Algeria, recorded numerous examples of presses, either for olive oil or for wine. To build a press (*torcularium*) was a considerable investment: monoliths had to be quarried and afterwards dressed on the spot by experienced stonecutters. We found some quarries in limestone outcrops in the immediate surroundings of the farms, which would have avoided expensive transport costs.[46] The extractive technology, cutting a very shallow trench with wedge holes inside for splitting the rock by hammering in iron wedges introduced into the holes (see Fig. 6.6), dates back to the archaic Greek period and was probably applied also in North Africa: as the many pre-Roman megalithic and rock-cut tombs show, the practice of stone cutting had a long tradition here.[47]

The typology of oil and wine presses in the Mediterranean area shows endless local variety. In northern Tunisia the horizontal anchor block for the end of the press beam prevails, an ashlar block of 1.30–2.00 m with a dovetail wedge cut at or near the centre of the long side facing the press bed (see Figs. 6.9 and 6.13).[48] The horizontal press beam was fixed in a hole in a vertical beam, which had a tenon at its base inserted in a mortise in a stone block, which prevented the upward movement of the beam during pressing as the horizontal lever beam was lowered. The vertical beam was arranged in a niche

---

[43] *CIL* 8.10570, 14464, III 8–9; Kehoe (1988: 70, 89, 93–6).

[44] Ulp. *Dig.* 19.2.15.1; Frier (1979: 217).

[45] *Alectoris barbara,* an autochthonous African species, still nowadays so common in the area that it is represented in the stem of the place name Teboursouk.

[46] De Vos (2008: 270–1, fig. 1).

[47] For the Greek world: Waelkens, *et al.* (1988: 104–6, figs 15–6); North Africa: Stone (2007); de Vos (2008: 270–1, fig. 1).

[48] De Vos (2000: fig. 78).

of the outer wall of the pressing room. The press bed is a square or circular slab (1.10–2.00 m on a side) with a circular channel, which collected the juice of the fruits compacted in round baskets placed inside the inner circumference of the channel. The inner circle of the channel indicates the diameter of the baskets. The channel has a mouth, sometimes but not necessarily cut in a protruding part of the slab, which conducted the juice into a vat. The size of the vat may be a marker of the kind of fruits processed by the press: for wine the vat had to be large, for oil it was much smaller. The vat may be provided with a decantation and cleaning depression in the centre of the bottom (Fig. 6.14). The moving end of the horizontal lever beam was pulled down by the rope of a wooden windlass fixed on top of a rectangular counterweight block by two tenons socketed into dovetail mortises in the two short sides of the block. The pulley fixed in a beam of the ceiling might be made of stone (items at Tébessa, diameter 34 cm, height 8 cm; in a farm to the south of Madauros, diameter 21 cm, height 8 cm; and in the Byrsa Museum garden). Normally, the long side of the counterweight block is parallel to the vat and the anchor stone; the many exceptions to this rule may be explained by its upward movement during the pressing and its subsequent imperfect landing.

R. Frankel supposes a Punic origin for the ashlar block counterweight type, because of its distribution area limited to North Africa and the areas around

Fig. 6.14. Oued Khalled, farm site 633: basin with overflow, and decantation and cleaning depression (M. de Vos)

the western Mediterranean basin in contact with Carthage.[49] Another possibly Punic legacy is the absence of *dolia* as storage vessels; in the Dougga survey only one *dolium* rim was found (site 31, near the city), contrasted with the many thousands of amphora sherds. In North Africa *dolia* are not frequently attested: to store oil, wine, and cereals, amphorae were probably used. In the silo excavated in the Byzantine farm of Aïn Wassel we indeed found four large cylindrical amphorae stored in compact order, each having a capacity of 150 litres.[50] The available space in the silo is exactly enough for seven amphorae. The 1,050 litres thus potentially contained might correspond with the annual oil storage for a group or *familia* of fifty-two persons, consuming 20 litres each.[51] The many different fabrics of late antique amphorae and jars found in the excavation and in many of the other sites surveyed are not attested elsewhere outside Tunisia; they were produced in northern Tunisia and circulated only there, and are to be considered instances of intraprovincial diffusion. They arrived at Aïn Wassel containing and transporting commodities not produced in the farm—for example, wine or fish sauce.[52] They were recycled, if possible, as water or oil containers.

Monolithic press elements had to be dressed and refined once they were placed in the pressroom. Some unfinished dovetail wedges tell us that the stonecutter optimized his work by doing it only after the blocks had been set in the wall.[53] A precise fit between the fixed press elements was necessary for the press to function properly. The dovetail mortise of the horizontal ashlar block had to be placed exactly on the axis of the press bed, otherwise the baskets filled with olives would slip away under the pressure of the lever beam or would not be equally pressed. Investment costs are evident also in the reuse of the monolithic press elements. Different blocks have been remodelled—for example, counterweight blocks could be adapted as anchor stones by cutting a mortise in one of their long sides (site 282), a counterweight block might receive a second dovetail wedge cut at 90° to the original one (site 25; Fig. 6.7), or the wedge could be deepened to the base of the block, or enlarged, creating a larger trapezoid at the lower part of the dovetail.[54] Some press elements are cut out of former bossed ashlar building blocks, obviously when the original elements had to be replaced and means were lacking to finance the cutting of a new block in the quarry. The boss was not removed in order to avoid reducing its weight. A threshold has been remodelled into a counterweight block in the outdoor press added in the late antique period at the north-eastern corner of

---

[49] Frankel (1999: 102–5, T55121).

[50] De Vos (2000: 36, fig. 58.5, pl. 7 'silo'); Maurina (2000; 2004; 2004–5; 2010; 2011: 110–4).

[51] The estimate of 20 litres per person per *annum* is proposed by Amouretti (1986: 181–3), *pace* Mattingly (1988c: 159, 161).

[52] Maurina (2004, 2005, 2010, 2011).

[53] De Vos (2008: 279, fig. 22 (the outline of the dovetail is to the left of the mortise)).

[54] De Vos (2007: 54, figs 11–12).

farm site 31. The circular channels of pressing beds sometimes received corrections or were doubled or provided with more outlets in order to improve the flow or to replace obsolete old channels. Many elements fell out of use because the dovetail wedge was widened by the frequent use and pressure exercised on it, and no longer held firm the wooden tenon of the windlass or of the vertical lever beam. Many such redundant counterweight blocks and mortise stones were reused as orthostats in *opus africanum* walls or as doorposts during the late antique period.

The pressing rooms were carefully coated with waterproof *opus signinum* for hygienic reasons and to avoid the seepage of compacted and pressed fruits and juice (oil and probably wine). Parsimony is evident from recycling tile and amphora sherds for the construction of *opus signinum* wall, floor, and vat coatings, and of *opus figlinum* made from rectangular amphora and tile fragments set in a mortar bed in a herringbone pattern or in pairs coupled top to base. Some press rooms have a mosaic pavement of white tesserae (2 × 2 cm) (sites 329 and 349).[55] No luxury markers have been found such as architectural decoration, marble, or baths.

In the inscriptions of Lella Drebblia and Aïn Wassel wine growing is not mentioned, probably because the microclimate of the area did not easily permit cultivation of grapes—nor does it today. Nowadays there exists one vineyard irrigated by water transported on trucks in the Maatria valley and another one near Agbia. On the north slope of Djebel Gorraa in the more humid Thibaris valley, the vineyards set up by the French Pères Blancs yield so much that a pressing plant is needed. The Henchir Mettich inscription (*CIL* 8.25902) permits sharecroppers (*coloni*) to plant and cultivate grapevines *expressis verbis* only in abandoned vineyards. As an incentive to planting new vines or grafting them onto old stock, the sharecroppers enjoyed a rent-free period of five years for wine in the Aïn Djemala estate and of ten years for oil in the areas of Aïn Djemala, Lella Drebblia, and Aïn Wassel. As noted above, the *coloni* of the Aïn Djemala estate do indeed mention the planting of vines in the *saltus Neronianus*.

Processing capacity and productivity

Estimates of production capacity are necessarily very rough, but some figures are offered here to give an idea of the possible output of the region. The maximum annual processing capacity of the 371 oil presses in the Thugga survey region of 371 km², working twenty-four hours a day during the ninety days of the olive-pressing season with a 20 per cent return oil/fruit, may be

[55] De Vos (2000: 21, fig. 32.4; 2008: 275–7, figs 15–17b).

estimated as yielding 43,778 kg of olive oil, taking in account the biennial cycle of the olive tree and that one press could press 590 kg of olives, producing 118 kg of oil a day or 10,620 litres per year. The annual yield of 371 presses amounts to 3,940 tonnes of oil.[56] The estimate is based on the size of the press elements and the estimated capacity of the presses. The dimensions and weight of the individual press elements employed in this calculation include the average length of the lever (*prelum*) of 9.85m and the average inner diameter of the pressing bed of 1.31m.[57] The inner diameter marks the dimension of the baskets (*fisci* or *fiscinae*) containing the olives. The processing capacity of the press is estimated assuming that the presses were constructed in order to process bumper crops. Varro (*Rust.* 2.1) recommends that farms should not be built too big in order to avoid an excessive investment, nor too small in order to avoid the loss of a part of the crops through inability to process it. Calculating the weight of olives (supposing 20 per cent return oil/fruit, even if 25–33 per cent is confirmed today by many local producers) and the numbers of trees (supposing an average of 100 kg of fruit per tree, also confirmed by local information[58]) needed to produce 19,700 tonnes of olives a year for the potential of 371 presses, the area of olive orchard needed for the estimated yield is 39.4 km² (or 10 per cent of the total surface) with a planting density of 50 olives/ha, recommended by Mago quoted by Pliny (*NH* 17.93–94), the only author who takes Africa into consideration. The distance between the trees recommended by Mago of 20 m is in contrast with the practice of 7–10 m of today and supposes intensive intercultivation. Of course the amount of 3,940 tonnes of olive oil is a theoretical but reasonable, rather minimal quantity. Twenty per cent of the surface area was covered with cities, farms, roads and tracks, torrents, aqueduct, pottery, and ashlar block scatters. Besides the 10 per cent of olive groves estimated here, 70 per cent remains for pasture, fields of crops, and unuseable areas such as ravines, and so on. Not all presses were working contemporaneously and continuously over five centuries; surface pottery finds do not permit the dating of the construction, use, and abandonment of the presses; not all antique farms and presses are visible; there had to be more.

The hypothetical annual yield of 3,940 tonnes of olive oil was sufficient to provide a third (*tertias partes*) tax in kind of 1,313 tonnes. The population of the seven towns is estimated at 20,000 in total, and that of the 374 farms (assuming households of 10–15) at 3,740 to 7,480, so the regional population may be estimated at 25,000 (totalling and rounding off). The estimated annual

---

[56] Mattingly (1988d: 184, 192) estimates 150–200 kg oil a day and 6,300–12,600 kg a year with a 15–20% return oil/fruit. The quantity of 118 kg of oil is based on Lanfranchi (2004).

[57] Surprisingly close to Cato's *canalem rutundam* (*Agr.* 18): 4¾ feet = 1,405 m, probably including the width of the canal.

[58] Abu Zahra (1982: 10): according to the villagers of Sidi Ameur near Monastir, an olive tree may produce in a bumper year up to 42.8 litres of oil or 140–60 kg.

consumption by 25,000 persons consuming each 20 litres per year would amount to 500,000 litres or 450 tonnes, just 2.2 per cent of the region's olive oil production. This means that a large surplus remained that might be exported: 2,177 tonnes. If dromedaries, which can transport 200–450 kg, were used, 4,837 trips to the *horrea* were needed, or 97 caravan journeys a year of 50 maximally burdened animals; this number would rise if (as is probable) donkeys were used for some or most of these journeys. These journeys might have taken two days' round trip, if the load was to be carried to the Bagradas river 17 miles north of the Thugga area, or 4/5 days to Carthage, 71–87 miles from the area surveyed. Draft animals were probably the property of the *coloni*[59] and were also used for carts (see Figs 6.20 and 6.21).

Hand querns and donkey or hourglass-shaped mills

No granaries were found in the rural areas investigated, nor in the towns. Instead, the evidence for grain production is indirect, consisting of the tools used to process the grain into flour and bread, activities that typically occurred closer to the point of consumption than production. In contrast to the oil and wine presses, rotary hand querns and donkey mills processed grain, probably barley, into flour destined for local consumption. Any surplus would have been exported unground in sacks. Milling was carried out when the cereals reached their final destination in the bakeries, which contained mills or *pistrina*, as at Ostia and Pompeii. Indeed, *pistrinum* ('mill') became synonymous with bakery.

In the farms of Africa Proconsularis rotary hand querns are preserved in 9 per cent of the Tunisian sites and in 7 per cent of the Algerian sites, and donkey mills in 13 per cent of the productive sites in Tunisia and in 5 per cent of the settlements in Algeria.[60] Their smaller dimensions and less robust structure contribute to their lesser visibility and preservation in comparison to the oil/wine presses. It is impossible to know the quantities of grain grown and exported. The transport costs for the Thugga region, 100 km from the Mediterranean coast, would have been considerable if grain was conveyed by road, but less so if floated down the river on boats or rafts. We may presume that it was more profitable to transport oil than cereals, as the same weight of oil has a higher economic and nutritional value than that of barley. In the region surveyed around Thugga 60 per cent of the hand and donkey mills were imported from volcanic zones in Sardinia (Mulargia), Sicily, or the Italian mainland. In the zone surveyed in north-eastern Algeria only 3 per cent of the mills are imported. The other mills found in Algeria are made of

[59] Kehoe (1988: 93–4).
[60] De Vos *et al.* (2011: 132, table 1; distribution maps 146–7, figs 29 and 30).

Fig. 6.15. Djebel Gorraa, site 131: unfinished nummulitic *catillus* (M. de Vos)

local sandstone (quartz conglomerate), and in Tunisia of local limestone (nummuliths from Djebel Gorraa, compact white limestone or conglomerate) (Fig. 6.15).

The distribution in Tunisia of mills imported from the Italian peninsula and islands has been explained by the movement of the many grain-collecting ships sailing from Carthage to Italy, which on their return journey carried millstones as tradable ballast.[61] Carthage played an important role as importer and distributor of Italian millstones. Thugga lies in the *pertica Carthaginiensis*, a zone of tax-free cities whose territory belonged to Carthage. Thugga was dependent on Carthage until the reign of Septimius Severus, when the city became a *municipium*. Evidently the trade circuit did not change in the following centuries, when the African rural settlements continued to develop and increase, especially during the Vandal and Byzantine periods, when Sardinia was under the control of Carthage.[62] The circuit did not stop at Thugga: at Mustis, 7 km south of Thugga, outside the *pertica*, four out of eleven hand and donkey mills were imported from the Mulargia region of Sardinia.

[61] Williams-Thorpe (1988: 286); Williams-Thorpe and Thorpe (1989: 108–9).
[62] Peacock (1980: 50).

The hand and donkey mills, so-called 'flour collectors' and a dough-mixer attested in 16 per cent of the oil- and/or wine-producing farms are markers of grain cultivation, probably wheat (*triticum*) and barley (*hordeum*), both mentioned in the Henchir Mettich inscription (*CIL* 8.25902 I.25–6): barley is the only grain type grown locally today. The palaeo-botanical remains in the excavated Byzantine farm of Aïn Wassel do not include cereals, even though the farm was provided with a stone 'flour collector'. Either the seeds are not preserved or the collector was used for collecting oil.

Indeed, it is not excluded that donkey mills were used also or exclusively to pulp olives instead of for grinding grain. Eight out of twenty-three oil press rooms in the city houses of Volubilis in Morocco are provided with two grinding tools considered by Akerraz and Lenoir to have had different functions: a *meta* and collared *catillus* for crushing the olives at the start of the process, while a cylindrical flat basin with a crushing wheel (similar to the 167 examples found in the north-eastern Algerian survey: see above) was for mixing the olive pulp between the different pressings (*factus*): a practice still extant in the region of Volubilis (now Zerhoun).[63] The collar *catillus* is short, and its inside grinding surface is dressed in a herringbone pattern of grooves, two features present in some of the *catilli* of the north-east Algerian survey. The olive crushers at Aphrodisias (Asia Minor) are also grooved.[64] A Byzantine oil press at Ashqelon was provided with both *mola olearia* and *meta/catillus*; the last one is considered to be for crushing small amounts of olives.[65]

The so-called 'flour collectors'

If some donkey mills were used for pulping olives, then the so-called 'flour collectors' at their base were used to collect olive paste or *sampsa*, and not flour. The 'flour collector' found broken into two pieces in two different rooms near the press room of the Byzantine farm excavated at Aïn Wassel (12 km west of Dougga) has circular traces of the rotating *catillus* (Fig. 6.16):[66] the stratigraphic excavation of the farm confirms the continued use of 'flour collectors' in Byzantine times. The 'flour collectors' of sites 355 and 494 show the same circular signs of wear through use. The 'flour collector' of site 494 is not perforated. The tronconical hole is 11 cm deep, and the diameter of 46 cm corresponds with the average diameter of the local *metae*. A similar

---

[63] Akerraz and Lenoir (1982: 70–4, pls VI–VIII): the oil *metae* and *catilli* are made of local shelly sandstone and their internal grinding surface is grooved, the grain mills are made of lava and are not grooved.

[64] Ahmet (2001: 161, fig. 5).

[65] Israel (2009).

[66] De Vos (2000: 36, fig. 58.10–11). A typological scheme in de Vos *et al.* (2011: 143, fig. 25).

Fig. 6.16. Oued Arkou, Aïn Wassel, site 25: flour (or oil?) collector; threshold reused as orthostat (M. de Vos)

unperforated receptacle is present at Mustis and in the press room of a farm in north-east Algeria, site OH-005 (Safhe 1). According to Ben Baaziz, the 'flour collector' of site 068.296, Ksar Tlili in central Tunisia, was also used for olives, as the soil and climate conditions of this region do not permit grain cultivation.[67] At Madauros two sets of *meta-catillus* 'flour collectors' are present in one oil press and three *metae* in another oil press. The other thirty-one oil presses at Madauros lack these elements because: (1) they have been dismantled for the building of the Byzantine fortress and other constructions; (2) the site was used until recently as a quarry providing ready-made building material; and (3) during and after the French excavations of 1900–30 smaller and fragmentary finds were removed from the site, without record.

The distribution map of 'flour collectors' published by Olwen Williams-Thorpe in 1988 showing three sites with 'flour collectors' (Naples, Adrano, and St Charles (Ramdan Jamel) near the Algerian coast) has to be corrected, as the example at Naples concerns a *meta* and collector made of a single block of lava,[68] and the example in Adrano, a city situated on a lava hill on the western slope of Mount Etna, is a *trapetum*. The map can be updated with seventeen other sites in Tunisia and Algeria.[69] At Pompeii, the flour was caught in lead

---

[67] Ben Baaziz (1991: 196).   [68] Moritz (1958: 76–7, 94).

[69] Williams-Thorpe (1988: 259, fig. 3b), now updated by de Vos *et al.* (2011: 144, fig. 26 with Tiddis (3 items), Timgad (1), Hippo Regius (1), Madauros (6), Theveste (7), Thala (1), Ksar Tlili (2), Thubursicu Bure (2), Thignica (2), Uchi Maius (3), Thugga (3), Mustis (5), Rohia (3), Carthage (2), Thuburbo Maius (1), Sidi Daoud (1), and Sidi Ali Bou Kachabia (1)). For Uchi Maius, see Vismara (2007: 200, 284–5, figs 6.7, 10.17–9). The terracotta collector discovered in 1893 at Vetulonia is no longer in Grosseto's Museo Civico: Falchi (1894: 357–8, fig. 27).

collectors resting around the *meta* on a masonry base.[70] Few examples are preserved, owing to the post-eruption recuperation of precious and recyclable material.[71] The absence of such stone equipment in Ostia is due to the gradual abandonment of the city and the removal of materials that could be used in the several medieval lime kilns. The cost of volcanic hand and donkey mills of course encouraged their removal for reuse elsewhere.

Williams-Thorpe noticed a preponderance of donkey mills in North Africa, and a preponderance of hand mills in Spain.[72] The statistical proportions are probably influenced by the patterns of data collection. Our survey is systematic, concentrated, and limited to small specific areas, and includes also small fragments collected from the surface during the intensive and the extensive survey; the results may reflect more closely the original distribution pattern.

We can also update the distribution map of mills from Mulargia on Sardinia published in 1989 by Olwen Williams-Thorpe and Richard Thorpe, adding four sites as a confirmation of red Mulargia lava as the preferred grinding rock in northern Tunisia and north-eastern Algeria: ten items at Hippo Regius (Annaba), one at Thabraca (Tabarka), two at Thuburbo Maius (El Fahs), and four at Mustis (Le Krib).[73] The preference for red Mulargia rhyolite results from the hard quality of this type of lava. The bulk production of mills at Mulargia is attributable to its location in former Punic Sardinia and to the invention of the animal-driven rotary mill—a Punic, not a Sicilian, invention.[74]

Dough-kneading machine

One kneading machine or dough-mixer was found in the ruins of the farm at site 369 (Fig. 6.17). The position of the farm in the area where the important road from Carthage to Theveste enters the Khalled valley near the *Pagus Assallitanus* explains the presence of a bakery, situated in a village near arable fields and with a potentially large amount of passing traffic. Cereal culture dominates the Khalled valley nowadays, while the slopes are occupied by olive groves. There is also a kneading machine in the city of Thugga near the Byzantine fortress, in a square room of a small late antique building. In Mustis there are six such dough-mixers, and one each at Hippo Regius (of white limestone), Theveste, Timgad, and Thibilis (Announa). At Pompeii and Ostia

---

[70] Fiorelli (1873: 29).   [71] Ling (1997: 10–11).
[72] Williams-Thorpe (1988: 259).   [73] De Vos *et al.* (2011: 134, fig. 7).
[74] Curtis (2001: 343): the two oldest datable Mulargia millstones, a *catillus* and *meta*, were found in the wreck (375–350 BC) of El Sec near Mallorca.

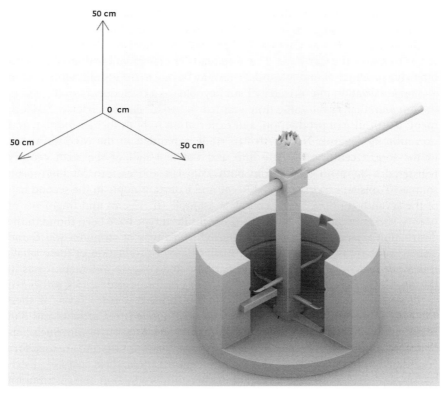

Fig. 6.17. Oued Khalled, Fadden Souk, *Pagus Assallitanus*, farm site 369: reconstruction model of kneading machine (A. Battisti, A. Andreoli, M. de Vos)

the dough-mixers are made from black or grey lava, in North Africa usually from limestone.

Pottery

No amphora kiln was discovered in the survey area; the new types of amphora Aïn Wassel I and II and Sidi Jdidi 14.9 (frequently found at different sites) and the local ceramic table-and kitchenware—an intermediate class between African Red Slip and coarse ware—produced during the Byzantine period circulated apparently on local or intraregional circuits, but not further afield.[75] The local table-and kitchenwares (whose production site is so far unknown)

---

[75] Maurina (2000, 2004, 2005, 2010, 2011); de Vos and Polla (2005: 483–5, figs 4–5, 8.1–6).

have been found at Uchi Maius,[76] Althiburos,[77] and Haïdra,[78] but not in our extensive north-eastern Algerian surveys along the Tunisian frontier from the Mediterranean coast to Ouenza, 70 km north of Theveste, so the circulation seems to follow the Carthage–Theveste road. The surprisingly flourishing and intensive production under Vandal rule may be due to trends of fragmentation and regionalization interpreted by Paul Reynolds as a consequence of the end of the *annona*, that in the same time granted the possibility of regional development, continuity of production, and exportation to both former *annona* and non-*annona* regions. North African trade expanded in the Mediterranean in the fourth century; the late fifth and the first half of the sixth century registered a boom in trade, from both Tunisian and eastern Mediterranean sources; Tunisian exports reached Rome and Constantinople in the second half of the seventh century.[79] One complete example (h. 32 cm) and fragments of twenty-two amphorae similar to the Castrum Perti type have been found in the destruction layers of the Aïn Wassel farm.[80] This type of amphora was found also at some twenty other sites. The main phase of production of these small, thin-walled, globular amphorae with flat base and concave indentation was in the later seventh century. They present a range of forms and fabrics, attributed to different and so far unidentified North Tunisian centres (even if their Tunisian find spots outside our survey area are limited to Carthage and Sidi Jdidi), and were exported everywhere in the western Mediterranean. Such flat-bottomed amphorae are easier to handle in small boats or rafts and are therefore considered to have been used also for intraregional trade; their creation, distribution, and success are also a marker of changing production and distribution processes. They may have contained oil or wine. At Aïn Wassel they appear together with large cylindrical amphorae.

WATER SUPPLY

Nearly every farm found by the survey shows evidence that it was built on top of a cistern: vaults emerge at the surface and/or ceramic vaulting tubes are

[76] M. Biagini in Vismara (2007: 375–6). The forms found at Uchi are dated to the end of the fifth century, earlier than the ones in the Byzantine farm of Aïn Wassel.

[77] I thank Victor Revilla for the information about the Spanish–Tunisian excavations in Althiburos: Ben Moussa *et al.* (2011: 282–3 nn. 217–29; 295 n. 140; 308 n. 62; 329 n. 20; 349 nn. 63–5; 351 nn. 41, 44).

[78] Jacquest (2009: 185–7, figs 141.22–3, 194–5).

[79] Reynolds (2010: 76, 100–5, 124, 126–8, 130, 146–8).

[80] Maurina (2005).

scattered around.[81] Roofs were covered with tiles and *imbrices* in order to collect the maximum amount of rainwater,[82] which was stored in cisterns where possible. The annual average rainfall in the region is currently 400–500 mm, but it falls chiefly during the north-western storms in the autumn. Water channels carved from long ashlar limestone blocks transported water from springs to some farms, as at site 31, situated below Aïn ben Nsira (Fig. 6.18), and sites 25, 107,[83] 214, 526, and 540. The blocks are jointed with male–female sockets. Another example of a private water channel is the one built on the limestone pavement of the Ras Gaça plateau.[84] Two low side walls enclose the canal; its inside is coated with *opus signinum*. Probably it was not covered and irrigated the lower-lying fields in the property of the Passieni (see below). The *praedia Pullaienorum* are also provided with an aqueduct, which needed a bridge to conduct the water over a small wadi.[85] The cistern (site 255) built on the west bank of the wadi Nsira has been broken by a landslide into three pieces, although its ashlar blocks were embedded in a concrete foundation and jointed with dovetail cramps (Fig. 6.19). There are no other constructions in the area, so the cistern might have been built to take and store water from the wadi to irrigate the fields.

Fig. 6.18. Oued Khalled, farm site 31, limestone water channel (M. de Vos)

---

[81] De Vos (2000: figs 11.1, 11.2, and map 1 for distribution of cisterns; 2007); for a comparison of water supply in rural landscapes of central Italy, see Thomas and Wilson (1994) and Wilson (1999); for Northern Africa, see Hitchner (1995).

[82] De Vos (2008: 267–73, figs 3–12).

[83] Carton (1895: pl. I).   [84] De Vos (2004: 28).

[85] Site 143: de Vos (2000: 33, fig. 51). For the inscription above the entrance of the *praedia* (site 296): de Vos (2000: 34, fig. 56).

Fig. 6.19. Oued Khalled, Oued Nsira, tributary of Khalled, cistern (M. de Vos)

The city of Thugga was supplied by two aqueducts, one conducting water from a local spring, Aïn Mizeb, the other one from the source at Aïn Hammam, a distance as the crow flies of 8.27 km from the city. This aqueduct is 10.94 km long because it has to traverse a hilly landscape, maintaining a shallow gradient over a fall of only 8 m between the spring basin at 578 m above mean sea level and the cisterns of Thugga at 570 m. One hundred and twenty-nine inspection shafts are still visible on the surface. It was built in AD 184/187 by the local community (*civitas Aurelia Thugga*)[86] to supply the baths of Aïn Doura

---

[86] *CIL* 8.1480 = 26534; Chouchane and Maurin (2000: 102–9); de Vos (2000: 29–34, figs 40–50, 81–93, pls 2–3; 2004: 16–26).

and also the lower quarters of the city. The distribution tank (*castellum divisorium*) of the *specus* to the city, to the east of the annexe of the Temple of Caelestis, now invaded by a fig tree, needs further investigation. The farm at site 214, attributed to the Pacuvii (see Table 6.3 and Fig. 6.4), took water from a source near the aqueduct, as it has a monumental cistern 250 m in length, roofed with monolithic slabs,[87] and a fountain house with elegantly moulded limestone basins that might have been used both for irrigation and as a drinking place for animals.[88]

ORGANIZATION AND MANAGEMENT OF THE RURAL LANDSCAPE

Large private estates

The boundary marker of the estate of Statilius Taurus (see p. 193 and Fig. 6.3) suggests that also the other *saltus—Blandianus, Udensis, Lamianus, Domitianus, Tuzritanus*, all mentioned in the copies of the *lex Hadriana*— and the estate of Passienus Rufus and perhaps Caninius Gallus, proconsul of Africa in AD 5/6,[89] had a similar Early Imperial origin. All the supposed original landlords of estates just to the west of the *fossa regia* and to the south of Bagradas are from equestrian families (except Caninius Gallus) elevated by Augustus to senatorial status to swell the ranks of his aristocratic supporters. The descendants of these original proprietors were disgraced under Nero, who terminated them in order to inherit their estates. Syme attributes the *saltus Blandianus* and *Lamianus* to the late Republican equestrian families mentioned in Cicero's letters, both founders of senatorial families in the next generation: Rubellius Blandus, a member of an equestrian family from Tibur, and Aelius Lamia from Formiae, close friend of Tiberius.[90] Maybe it was his grandson of the same name, Rubellius Blandus, husband of Tiberius' granddaughter Julia from AD 33,[91] proconsul of Africa in 35/6 (attested by inscriptions at Lepcis Magna), who became the first proprietor of the *saltus Blandianus*, which contained *centuriae elocatae*, divisions of surveyed land comprising 200 *iugera*, c.50 ha.[92] His son Rubellius Plautus

---

[87] Carton (1895: 226–8, figs 72–5); de Vos (2004: 24–5).
[88] Carton (1895: 229, fig. 76); de Vos (2004: 26), now destroyed by road building.
[89] *AE* 1938.2 (Lepcis Magna): *L(ucius) Caninius L(uci) f(ilius) Gallus XVvir sacris fac(iundis)* | *co(n)s(ul) proco(n)s(ul) patron(us) dedic(avit)*.
[90] Syme (1982: 65).
[91] Syme (1982).
[92] Kehoe (1988: 87).

was peer and equal to Nero[93] and terminated for this reason in 62.[94] Octavia Claudia received the estates of Plautus (the *saltus Blandianus* included)[95] as an ominous gift on the moment Nero removed her under colour of civil divorce,[96] but she too was executed in her exile at Pandateria on a false charge of adultery. Then the *saltus Blandianus* probably returned to being an imperial estate, maintaining its original toponym.

Lucius Aelius Lamia jr, *cos.* AD 3, was appointed by Tiberius as personal legate to Africa in AD 19. His gardens on the Esquiline in Rome, the *Horti Lamiani* near those of Maecenas just outside the limits of the Servian walls (Phil. Iud., *de leg. ad Gaium* 2.597), became imperial property[97] and Caligula's ashes were deposited there before being carried to the mausoleum of Augustus.[98] It is quite probable that the *horti* (and so also the African *saltus*) were left by him to Tiberius, as he died in AD 33 without offspring.

Imperial estates

The abundant epigraphic evidence of the Mancian and Hadrianic laws in the Bagradas valley allows us to suppose an intensification of tilling, field clearing, and cropping activities of numerous *coloni* stimulated by the advantages of the *lex Hadriana de rudibus agris*. Three copies of the *lex Hadriana de rudibus agris* have been found in imperial estates of the region surveyed in Tunisia (see Figs 6.1 and 6.2): two are Hadrianic copies, one previously known, at Aïn Djemala, the other newly discovered during our survey in 1999 at site 539 (Lella Drebblia); the third, discovered in 1891 at site 25 (Aïn Wassel), bears a dedication to the Severan family (AD 198–211).[99] The law granted perpetual leases (*usus proprius*) to the *coloni* who tilled and brought into cultivation vacant lands and those that had not been cultivated for ten consecutive years. One-third of the harvest was due to the owner, but, in the case of a new plantation of olives, only after the first ten years, and, for dry crops, only after five years. As sharecropper, the *colonus* had to deliver this rent in kind already threshed or pressed: *tritici ex a | [r]ea{m} partem tertiam, hordei ex area{m} | (p)artem tertiam, fab(a)e ex area{m} | [pa]rtem qu | (ar)tam, vin<i> de lac<u> partem tertiam, ol[e] | [i co]acti partem tertiam*: CIL 8.25902, I.26–9. In this way the emperor incentivized the intensification of land use and the increase

---

[93] *per maternam originem pari ac Nero gradu a divo Augusto*: Tac., *Ann.* 13.19.3.
[94] Tac., *Ann.* 14.57–9.
[95] *PIR* 7.1, 1999, 85–6, C. Rubellius Blandus 111.
[96] *movetur tamen primo civilis discidii specie domumque Burri, praedia Plauti infausta dona accipit*, Tac., *Ann.* 14.60.
[97] *CIL* 6.8668.   [98] Suet., *Cal.* 59.
[99] See text editions and analysis of Flach (1978, 1982, 1990) and Kehoe (1988); de Vos (2000: 35, figs 57.1–58.8).

in the area of cultivated land, involving all difficult lands such as marshes and woods. *Coloni* lost their rights if they neglected to cultivate the fields for two consecutive years. In that case the *conductores* would confiscate the land. The *colonus* had the right (*usus proprius*) to bequeath the new land brought under cultivation and its improvements to his legal sons (*CIL* 8.25902, IV.5: *qui ex legitim[is matrimoniis nati sunt eruntve]*).[100]

Sharecropping is often the most profitable method for landlords and tenants: comparative studies in less-developed regions of the modern world suggest that the productivity is higher than that of wage labourers or even owner-occupiers.[101] Slaves and other contracted labourers might not have the same levels of motivation as tenants who benefit from larger harvests. Tenants will therefore work harder than a hired labour force and invest more in the land, for example, in higher-yielding vine and olive cultivation. Risks were shared by both owner and tenant; tenants were not obliged to compensate the *frugalitas* of one year with the *ubertas* of following years. In case of loss or damage of the harvest, the lease was not cancelled.[102] The emperor as absentee landlord of many estates distributed all over the empire evidently preferred sharecropping arrangements, controlled by a series of imperial *procuratores* (structured according to a hierarchy: Rome–*tractus*–*regio*) and *conductores* (*saltus*).[103] In disputes between *coloni* and *conductores*, arising from contrasting long- and short-term interests, the emperor intervened in favour of the first, obviously while 'the long-term goals were best served by protecting the rights of the coloni'.[104] As we have seen above (see the section on 'Processing capacity and productivity'), the 371 presses of the region might have produced an average market surplus of *c.* 2,200 tonnes oil, net of rent and local consumption. So sharecroppers would have earned 5.9 tonnes of oil per press to be sold in big cities further afield, like Carthage, or overseas. We can attempt somewhat hypothetically to put some value on this figure using the prices in Diocletian's Edict of AD 301. The surplus probably consisted of 50 per cent first-quality oil with a maximum price of 40 *denarii* per *sextarius* (0.546 l), and 50 per cent oil from the second pressing, priced at 24 *denarii* per *sextarius*.[105] If we deduct land, river, and sea transport costs, the surplus amounts to respectively 232,067 and 136,847 *denarii*. The transport cost of 2.2 *denarii*/litre is calculated as follows: 5,000 *denarii* for thirty dromedaries loaded with 200 kg going 17 miles from Thugga to Tichilla (at 8 *denarii*/mile), driven by a *camellarius* (25 *denarii*/day); 5,000 *denarii* for barges conveyed 100 miles

---

[100]   Kehoe (1988: 37, 39).
[101]   Foxhall (1990: 101–2); Kehoe (1996); cf. Kehoe (1988: 71–3) and Kolendo (1991: 122).
[102]   Kehoe (1996).
[103]   Kolendo (1968).
[104]   De Ligt (2008: 208).
[105]   2,200 tonnes/371 presses = 5.9 tonnes per press. At a density of 0.9 kg/litre, this = 6.588 litres = 12067.4 *sextarii*.

downstream along the meandering river Bagradas for four days by a lighter-man or *caudicarius* (ratio river:land = 1:5); 4,425 *denarii* for sea transport from Africa to Rome. The total net return to the producer of 368,914 *denarii* has to be spread over two years (184,456 *denarii* per year), as the olive tree normally alternates heavy and light crops. It has to be divided again more or less in two, if the producer sells the crops to a *negotiator* for marketing. On these assump-tions, the producer would keep on average 92,228 *denarii* per year from the production of each press, the equivalent of 10.2 years' wage for an unskilled labourer (25 *denarii* per day). If this calculation is correct, we can better understand why the archaeological record shows a constantly increasing dens-ity of oil-pressing plants in the long run.

The *usus proprius* benefits were perpetual, so legal sons and grandsons could profit from the clearing, tilling, and cropping activities of the *colonus* who first brought marginal, unused, or abandoned land under cultivation. One of the causes of the success of the application of the *lex Hadriana* to imperial estates was this perpetual guarantee that private landlords could not supply. In this way the imperial management favoured 'long-term investment in intensive agriculture'.[106] The categories of uncultivated land (*rudes agri*) include woodland (*silvestres*), marshes (*palustres*), and leased-out *centuriae* or divisions of surveyed land comprising 200 *iugera* or 50 ha (*centuriae elocatae*) not being worked by the lessees or middlemen (*conductores*). The Severan Aïn Wassel inscription adds as a new category to the *lex Hadriana* those lands of the nearby *saltus* that had not been cultivated for ten consecutive years (*CIL* 8.26416, II.12–13: *qui per X an<n>os conti | nuos inculti sunt*). It means that in the second century there was a shortage of farmers and that the imperial administration was steadily looking for methods to promote intensive cultiva-tion and to increase the production in its estates.[107] The *colonus* owed a third of the crop as rent and had to deliver it as pressed olive oil or wine, not as olives or grapes, and therefore every farmer needed his own individual press (or access to one). The presses were presumably located near the olive groves and vineyards, reducing transport costs. The weight of the olives is reduced to a quarter after pressing, as 100 kg of olives produce on average 25 litres of oil, but in the Tunisian survey area this reduction is less, to a third (33 litres) according to local information. To find oil-pressing facilities during the harvest period is problematic even nowadays: notwithstanding modern tech-nology and transport, even today during the harvest period Mediterranean pressing and conserving industries have difficulties accepting and processing all the fruit crops that need to be processed without delay. The Lella Drebblia inscription enables us to correct the incorrect restoration *quae **dari** solent partes tertias* ('the one-third share that normally is given') proposed by its

---

[106] Kehoe (1988: 106).   [107] Kehoe (1988: 87–9).

discoverer at Aïn Djemala[108] with the interesting word *rigari: ea loca neglecta ab [con] | ductoribus, quae **rigari** solent, partes terti | as partes fructum dabit*[109] 'the one-third share of the crops from those fields that are neglected by the lessees and that normally are *irrigated*, will be given [*sc.* to the landlord]'. So the sharecroppers also had to supply one-third of the produce from irrigated fields, including kitchen gardens and fruit trees, which have a high yield, but which also need more labour: digging/maintaining and/or building canals and cisterns (see Fig. 6.19). (For irrigation systems in the survey area, see the section on 'Water supply'.) Further new information supplied by the same inscription is the diversity of rent pressure between the different imperial *saltus*: from the farmers of the *saltus Blandianus* and *Udensis* the rent demanded is not more than a quarter, probably because of the poor quality of the soil:[110] *nec ex Blandiano et | [Uden]si saltu maiores parte<s>| [fr]uctu(u) m exigentur a posse | <s> soribus quam quartas.*

Farm structures

The farms identified in the survey consist of compact square or rectangular buildings with long and narrow rooms, whose form was determined by the length of the lever beam used for oil (and wine) processing (see Figs 6.9–6.11). A horizontal monolithic rectangular block with a dovetail wedge for the vertical wooden beam was very often embedded in the bottom of the outer wall of the farm, near the corner of the pressing room, leaving little space for the lever beam and the counterweight block (see Fig. 6.13a–b). In this way the press takes advantage of the *opus africanum* technique with a framework of ashlar blocks.[111] The pressing room or *torcularium* is often installed in one of the corners of the building, rarely in the hottest one, as recommended by the agronomists. Presumably the rest of the farm was occupied by habitation, storage, and productive facilities; but geophysical survey and excavation are necessary to obtain detailed information about the internal spatial organization of the individual buildings. Only one site stands out as an olive oil farm without residential accommodation: the building with two presses at site 205 (see Fig. 6.9a–b).[112] In a nearby farm (site 207) three presses were arranged side-by-side from the beginning (see Fig. 6.10). Other farms or agglomerations of farms with between two and twelve presses have no organizational logic; the presses are built on different alignments without any order or overall planning

---

108 Carcopino (1906: 370, III.4).
109 De Vos (2000: 35, fig. 57.5; 2004: 44.)
110 De Vos (2000: 35, fig. 57.5; 2004: 44); Sanz Palomera (2007: 383).
111 De Vos (2000: figs 78, 80; 2008: 208–9, fig. 25a).
112 De Vos (2000: 26–9, figs 36.1–7, 77–80).

(see Fig. 6.11). It seems that every farmer had his own press, and built another as the olive grove yielded more fruit (the trees reach their bulk production between twenty-five and sixty years), or as the family or clan grew.

We may interpret this unorganized distribution as a possible consequence of the eventual success of the *lex Manciana*, enshrined in the *lex Hadriana de rudibus agris*, in stimulating the exploitation of marginal land on imperial estates. The *lex Manciana* was still in force in AD 496, as the *cultores manciani* cited in the Albertini tablets demonstrate.[113] Until recent times similar rural labour conditions existed in the Mediterranean area, such as the sharecropping arrangements known as *mezzadria* in Italy and *khammās*[114] in the Maghreb. The *mezzadro* is entitled to one-half of the crop, the *khammās* to a fifth, hence their name. The Decree of 13 April 1874 regulated the *contrat de khammessat* in Tunisia.[115] A law of 2009 abolished this decree, substituting *métayer* for *khammās*, and determining that he could retain from a fifth to a half share of the harvest or more, according to the type of produce and local practice.[116]

Some farms preserve the huge kerbstones of a large carriage entrance, to prevent carts (*plaustra*) from damaging the doorposts. The kerbstones also contain a pivot mortise for the timber door leaf; that of farm site 570 measures 79 × 51cm, height 29 cm (Fig. 6.20).[117] Similar kerbstones are also present in urban houses at Thugga, Thuburbo Maius, Bulla Regia, and Madauros and in the service entrance of the Licinian Baths at Thugga. Smart doorposts are provided with a sculpted hook for tethering draft animals (Fig. 6.21); normally a hole is drilled diagonally in the edge of an ashlar block. Windows are secured by a grate of metal bars and stripes (*fenestra clatrata*): the example from the farm of the Gabinii had six horizontal square-sectioned bars framed by five double stripes (Fig. 6.22a–b). In addition, the window was closed with a horizontal wooden bar (*sera*), which was put in the L-shaped slot (*claustrum*, Fig. 6.22a), and with a vertical bar (Fig. 6.22b). The same system was used to lock doors from inside, its bars in addition being blocked by a diagonal bar of which the lower end was fixed in the entrance pavement while the upper bifurcated end (hence its name *furca* or *patibulum*) embraced the two crossed bars at the centre of the door leaf. The window over

[113] Mattingly (1988a); Weßel (2003).

[114] Hopkins (1977: 455, 463 with n. 9, 464, 466, 474, 478) for *khammās* arrangements at Testour and surroundings (20 km east of Dougga) in the 1970s.

[115] Bompard (1888: 3–9, articles 25–69).

[116] Code of Obligations and Contracts <http://www.jurisitetunisie.com/tunisie/codes/coc/Coc1191.htm> (accessed 3 Sept. 2012).

[117] The example is from farm site 570. Other items in farm sites 21, 31, 175, and 378. For site 31 see de Vos (2008: 279, fig. 29).

Fig. 6.20. Aïn Zillig, farm site 570: kerbstone with pivot mortise for carriage door (M. de Vos)

the door of the oil farm at site 205 was also barred (see Fig. 6.9a–b).[118] These lock systems indicate that the content of the farms and the presses was worth some investment in its protection. But this effective protection was not enough for the farmers: they also needed symbols or charms to keep away the evil eye, not only on the entrance door (Fig. 6.23), but also on the press elements (Fig. 6.24), particularly exposed to the risk of being broken during the pressing activities: 'the tenant was liable for damage done to the landlord's equipment destroyed through his fault', *quod si culpa coloni quod eorum corruptum sit, ex locato eum teneri.*[119] Many mortise blocks are indeed broken in the centre where they are weakened by the cavity of the mortise and where the greatest pressure is exercised during the lowering of the lever by the counterweight. It was very expensive to replace a mortise block mortared in the bottom of the wall or even a lintel with a mortise for the upper tenon of the vertical lever beam (Fig. 6.24).

THE INVESTORS

Who paid for the farm, press, and mill buildings? The *condicio Manciana* (mentioned in the Henchir Mettich inscription of the Traianic period), later

---

[118] De Vos (2000: figs 36.2, 36.7, 80.1).
[119] Ulp. 32 *ad Digestam* 19.2.19.2: Frier (1979: 204, 206, 210).

Fig. 6.21. The farm of the Gabinii, site 47: doorposts of *torcularium* with sculpted hook for tethering animals; clandestine excavation in foreground (M. de Vos)

incorporated in the *lex Hadriana de rudibus agris*, mentions *coloni* who *habent* or *habebunt aedificium*.[120] The *coloni* are to be considered as an economically independent class of farmers.[121] But, if they did not cultivate the fields in two successive years, they lost the tenancy (and their own farmstead?). Generally the landlords built the farm (as described by Cato, Cicero, Pliny the Younger, and the legal Codes, e.g. *Digest* 19.2[122]), and chose the building materials and techniques; the sharecroppers maintained their farmsteads out of their own resources.[123] Juridical texts concerning the lease conditions of farms and oil presses are explicit about the responsibilities of landlord and tenant. They inform us that:

---

[120] Henchir Mettich *CIL* 8.25902, 1.20–4 and 4.9; Kehoe (1988).
[121] Kehoe (1988: 71).
[122] The rights and duties of landlords and tenants described in *Digesta* 19.2 are analysed by Heitland (1921: 362–78) and Frier (1979: 216).
[123] Kehoe (1988: 98).

Fig. 6.22. The farm of the Gabinii, site 47: (a) post of window frame with holes for six horizontal square-sectioned bars of an iron security grille; (b) window lintel or sill with holes for five vertical double strips framing the bars (Fig. 6.22b) of the iron security grille (M. de Vos)

Fig. 6.23. Oued Khalled, site 597: threshold with apotropaic phallus (M. de Vos)

Fig. 6.24. Oued Khalled, site 69: lintel with mortise for vertical beam in which the lever beam was fixed, with apotropaic phallus (M. de Vos)

the landlord supplied all the durable equipment which the tenant did not already have, while the tenant both supplied the ephemeral equipment (e.g. the *fisci*, or pressing baskets, to be renewed after every pressing: Columella 12.52.10) and made ready all the equipment for its immediate use. The landlord had to furnish his tenant with a farm in good operating condition, ready to produce the crop. The tenant had to deliver the seed in the case of cereal cultivation or new cuttings to replace exhausted vines in the case of viticulture. The landlord was obliged to replace his equipment if it became defective [. . .] the tenant was liable for damage to the landlord's equipment through his fault (*culpa*) [. . .] the landlord bore the loss of his equipment deteriorated through normal wear and tear during the term of lease.[124]

Tenant indebtedness was common by the second century AD at Rome, either from a natural catastrophe (they were legally protected by automatic remission of rent), or from poor husbandry, or from market factors such as sudden depression of market prices.[125] The social conditions in Italy during the first

---

[124] Servius in Ulp. *Digesta* 19.2.15.2; Frier (1979: 209–10).
[125] Frier (1979: 221).

and second centuries AD cannot be applied to North Africa, but the juridical conditions may be pertinent, such as the rule that the olive mill (*mola olivaria = olearia*) and the press (*praelum*) are included in the *instrumentum* of a farm.[126]

Epigraphic evidence in the survey zone can shed some light on the land-owners in different periods of the first centuries of Roman occupation, which are the best represented (see Fig. 6.4). The oldest *terminus* (boundary stone) bearing the name of a landowner is the one of T. Statilius Taurus *imp(erator) iter(um)* (see Fig. 6.3);[127] Statilius Taurus, Octavian's general, was *imperator* for the second time in 34 BC after his triumphs over Sextus Pompeius at Naulochos in 36 and in Africa in 34 BC. In 36–34 BC he was *proconsul* of Africa Vetus and Africa Nova (Dio 49.14.6), as successor of M. Lepidus. He built the walls of Carthage (Tertullian, *de pallio* 1: *moenia Karthagini imposuit*).[128] His estate of *c*.3,636 ha was later transformed into the *saltus Neronianus* (see Fig. 6.4 and below).[129] Funerary inscriptions allow us to attribute smaller estates to the families of the Passieni (1,000 ha), of M. Licinius Rufus (250 ha), who *pago dedit macellum* AD 54;[130] and to some of the thirty-three leading and well-to-do families of Thugga (many of them native), known between the reign of Tiberius and the Tetrarchs (Table 6.5).[131]

These local families paid for various public buildings at Thugga. The Gabinii built six temples between AD 120 and 230, at a cost of 50,000–70,000 HS each.[132] Two families, the Magnii and the Remmii, linked by intermarriage, had adjacent small rural plots. At Thugga, Magnius Felix Remmianus offered a statue to Juno.[133] Between AD 180 and 192 the Pacuvii paid for the temple of Mercury, its portico, and the *area macelli* at a cost of over 120,000 HS.[134] A cistern and a fountain house on their estate, 3.5 km from Thugga, enabled the cultivation of irrigated vegetables and fruit to sell in the marketplace; and the same can be supposed of the estate of the sponsor of the *macellum* M. Licinius Rufus, where a water conduit carved in long ashlar limestone blocks collected the many water flows descending from Djebel Cheidi. Transport to market was facilitated throughout the year by the position of the estate along the *via a Karthagine Thevestem*,

---

[126] Pomponius, *Digesta* 33.7.21.

[127] Height 72 cm, width 38 cm, height of letters: first line, 5 cm; second and third lines, 4 cm. The lower part of the *terminus* that was hidden in the soil is not dressed.

[128] One of the slaves in the tomb of the Statilii at Porta Maggiore (Rome) was Punic: *Hannibalis ossa hic* (*CIL* 6. 6461). There are no archaeological traces of this city wall: Santangelo (2008: 462).

[129] Area calculated from Fig. 6.4.

[130] De Vos (2008: 284, fig. 32).

[131] Jacques (1984: 538–48); Ben Abdallah and Maurin (2002: 310–11).

[132] Ben Abdallah and Khanoussi (2000: 194–8).

[133] Maurin (2000: 253–4).

[134] *CIL* 8.26482.

Table 6.5. Family domains and estate sizes attested by inscriptions in the surroundings of Thugga

Family	Estate size (ha)	Inscription	*Reference*
Gabinii	0.2	*CIL* 8.27348	de Vos (2004: 48)
Magnii	0.3	*CIL* 8.27349–52	de Vos (2004: 49)
Remmii	0.4	*CIL* 8.27163	de Vos (2004: 12)
Pacuvii	0.8	*CIL* 8.15325	
Aburnii	0.3	*CIL* 8.26447b, c, e	de Vos (2004: 50)
Calpurnii	2.0	*CIL* 8.27369	
Labennii	1.0	*CIL* 8.27379, *AE* 1991, 1667	
Pullaieni	0.8	*CIL* 8.26415	de Vos (2000: 34, fig. 56.1–2; 2004: 32–3)
Statilii	3.6		See below, pp. 196–200.
Passieni	1.0		See pp. 193–6.

4.5 km from Thugga (see Fig. 6.2). Calpurnius Faustinus was honoured by the *civitas* of Thugga because he sold grain below the market price (*frumentum multo minore pretio*) in a time of shortage,[135] and L. Calpurnius paid in AD 163–6 the sum of 150,000 HS for the temple now known as 'Dar El-Acheb'.[136]

On the surface, there is no material difference visible between imperial, private, and urban property. The small size of the estates is striking, perhaps because suburban fields were more expensive. The native families may have owned estates elsewhere. The most important family, the Gabinii, who dominated Thugga's elite over two centuries and twenty-five members of which are known, owned, for example, the limestone quarry in which later the circus was built, left in the will of Gabinia Hermiona *ad voluptatem populi reipublicae*.[137] Probably they supplied building material from this quarry for the constructions of Thugga and environs.

Epigraphy helps in understanding and interpreting the survey data and the settlement distribution system. T. Statilius Taurus obviously obtained the best allotment of the region provided with a rich spring (Aïn Zeroug), nummulitic limestone outcrops exploited as quarries for building material and millstones, and probably a lead and zinc mine at Thigibba Bure (Djebba) on the north slope of Djebel Gorraa, re-exploited during the Turkish and the French Protectorate. The epitaph of Statilia Secunda found at Djebba (*CIL* 8.26214)

[135] *AE* 1997.1651; Tran (2008: 346 n. 93).
[136] *CIL* 8.26527.
[137] *CIL* 8.1483 = 15505 = 26546 = 26639 = 26650 = *AE* 1997.1654 = *AE* 2003.2013. For the modest dimensions of their farm (or one of their farms?), see above, n. 32.

may support this hypothesis. There has been a recent initiative to begin exploiting the mineral deposits again.

The boundary stone of T. Statilius Taurus *imp(erator) iter(um)* now incorporated into a modern wall at Henchir Chett (site 66) (see Fig. 6.3) may explain the initial Roman occupation of the Arkou valley, west of Dougga. The Taurian estate must have become imperial property either in AD 53, when Agrippina confiscated the *horti Tauriani* in Rome (Tacitus, *Ann.* 12.59), or in AD 66 on the occasion of Nero's marriage to Statilia Messalina. It became known as the *saltus Neronianus*, mentioned as *vicinus* in the Aïn Djemala inscription. The two copies of the *lex Hadriana de rudibus agris* at Aïn Wassel and Lella Drebblia confirm the transformation into an imperial estate.

The eastern part of the imperial estate was identified in 1999 thanks to the discovery of a copy of the *lex Hadriana de rudibus agris* near the *hawitha* of Lella Drebblia (a small rural shrine consisting of a circular dry stone enclosure with a niche inside for offerings and candles), 7 km east of Henchir Chett and a very abundant spring (Aïn Fawar).[138] During the Middle Empire and the Byzantine period the *saltus Neronianus* contained the highest concentration of presses of the whole region surveyed, of which six are multiple press installations, a marker of the estate's productive potential. The water flowing down, thanks to a drop of 85 m from Aïn Zeroug on Djebel Gorraa to Henchir Chett, created a fertile zone of richly irrigated and variegated vegetation now and in the past. Today the area includes olives, figs, poplars, carobs, pomegranates, cereals, and, along the wadi, thorns.

The long wall (site 132) that divides the estate of the Djebel Gorraa into two parts might be the northern boundary wall of the Taurian estate. The western neighbour of the Taurian estate *saltus Neronianus* consists of the *praedia* (estates) of the Pullaieni, a family from Uchi Maius. The two brothers mentioned as *clarissimi* in the inscription on the lintel of the entrance door were the first members of the family who succeeded in entering the senate: their father was still an equestrian.[139] The estate is relatively small for such an important family, but it might have extended further west, towards their city of residence. The family enriched itself by market cultivation and the export of olive oil and other products: lamps stamped with their *gentilicium* are distributed throughout the western half of the Mediterranean basin.[140] These lamps will have filled the space left between the amphorae packed on ships. In the *praedia* we found no sherds with Pullaieni stamps, but African lamps of the type produced by the Pullaieni have been collected everywhere in the survey area.

---

[138] De Vos (2000: 35, figs 57–8.1–3; 2004: 42–5).
[139] *CIL* 8.26415; de Vos (2000: 34, fig. 56.1–3); de Vos (2004: 32–3).
[140] Sotgiu (1968: 129).

The southern boundary of the Taurian estate *saltus Neronianus* is formed by the natural obstacle of the Arkou torrent. The southern bank of the river was occupied by other, smaller estates delimited with boundary stones, bearing different names on two sides: MTFC//LRSF[141] and AA//LO. AA can be interpreted as *agri accepti* or *attributi*;[142] the bottom of the stone is broken, so the toponym remains unknown, but might refer to Thugga (Fig. 6.4).

The fifteen boundary stones found around Thugga are nowadays stored in the cisterns of Dougga without record of their exact provenance. Only in rare cases is it possible to expand the initials, for example, on the stone from near Kern el Kebch inscribed RPA//CRR, where the first part may be expanded as *Res Publica Aunobaritanorum*.[143] So, the territory of Aunobari towards the north-east was only 800 m wide. A dispute about land only 100 m west of Aunobari between Iulius Regulus and the inhabitants of the town was arbitrated by the proconsul Marcellus (*ILAf* 591); the territory on this side was even smaller. The territory of Dougga included the entire width (7 km) of the Oued Khalled east of the city, and was limited by the *fossa regia* marked by thirteen boundary stones. A boundary marker (*ILAf* 509) between an imperial estate (AVGG NN) and a senatorial estate P(ublii) F S C(larissimi) V(iri) 3.5 km south-east of Thubursicu Bure delimits the territory of the city. The *pagus Assallitanus* and *civitas Mizigitanorum*[144] may be rural communities of native origin of Roman citizens (*pagus*) and Berbers. Mizig is linked with the word for 'Berber' (pl. *Imazighen*, possibly meaning 'free people'): many Berbers identified themselves with *Imazighen*, and *Mazices*[145] was the Romanized name of some Berbers at various places on the northern Mauretanian coast. Thus, a Berber clan remained in the fertile plain of the Khalled valley (contrast the situation of the French occupying the whole Khalled valley, driving the Tunisians out to the stony mountains). The Mizigitani also marked the dimensions of their *civitas*: 1,200 *passus* (1.776 km), or the *civitas*'s distance from the Carthage–Theveste road. Assallitanus derives from the root SLSU, a tribal name.[146]

The property of 1,000 ha of the senatorial Passieni adjacent to the *fossa regia* on the east bank of the Oued Khalled changed ownership in the fourth century AD, and passed to another senatorial family. On the (now lost) entrance inscription of the *praedia Rufi Volusiani*, the *praefectus urbi* in AD 365 and

---

[141] De Vos (2000: fig. 54.1–2).

[142] Cf. *Agri Accepti Cirtensium* or *Agri Attributi Milevitanis*: interpretation of Cuomo (2007: 126).

[143] De Vos (2000: fig. 55; 2004: 46).

[144] Poinssot (1920) introduced the erroneous spelling Assalitanus; see de Vos and Attoui (2011: 41, fig. 14).

[145] Ammianus Marcellinus 29.5; Ghazi-Ben Maïssa (2006).

[146] Jongeling (1994: 125), cf. *SLT* Chabot (1940–1: 618, 771, 894) and Salasus in *CIL* 8.2056 and 2057 = *ILAlg* 1.3649–50.

his wife Caecinia Lolliana are mentioned by their procurator Thiasus (*CIL* 8.25990). The estate may have been granted by Augustus to L. Passienus Rufus, proconsul of Africa in AD 3, for whom the city of Thaenae struck a *sestertius* with his portrait and that of *Divi fil Imp Caes* with *lituus*. After the *Bellum Gaetulicum*, Passienus earned not only the *ornamenta triumphalia* but also an imperial salutation. In a vow paid to Livia Iuno, *L. Passieno Rufo imperatore Africam obtinente* (*ILS* 120), he bore a title (*imperator*) no longer granted to private individuals during the empire. The dedication to 'Jupiter Optimus Maximus Aug(ustus)' for the health of his uncle Passen(i)us and his children (Fig. 6.25a–b),[147] in a settlement (site 390) near the *fossa regia*, was probably made by C. Passienius Septimus, whose epitaph (Fig. 6.26)[148] is the oldest epigraphic indication of this property; its mausoleum (*mesolaeum*, in the inscription) is still standing south of the farm and the Byzantine fortress that includes the epitaph and the *praedia* inscription.[149] The spelling Passenus (without i) occurs in epitaphs of the three cities around the estate: *L. Pasenius Aruntius* (*CIL* 8.27112) at Thugga, *L. Passenus Restu(tus)* and *L. Pas[senus] Feli[—]* (*CIL* 8.15327 and 8.26057) at Thubursicum Bure, and *L. Passenus Ingenuus Scapella* (*CIL* 8.15251) at Aïn Golea.[150] The names Passienus and Passenus are also interchangeable in the potter's stamps of Samian Ware. Brenda Dickinson[151] anticipated me in her observations on these stamps:

> As far as we can see from the evidence of our stamps, Passienus and Passenus are variants of the same name. Both versions appear on stamps from a group of samian found in the Oberwinterhtur Keramiklager[152] and both are sometimes prefixed by O (for officina) instead of the more usual OF. On the whole, the Passienus stamps tend to be slightly earlier than the Passenus ones, to judge by the vessel types on which they are found and the decoration with which they are associated. Frequently the spellings of stamps which are clearly by the same potter vary in their spellings. This may be due to the different workmen who cut the dies.

[147] *Iovi Optimo | Maximo Aug | sacrum | pro salute Pa[s] | s(i)eni patru[i/ et] liberor[um - | - e] ius*; height 39 cm, width 42 cm, height letters 4.5 cm.

[148] *C. Passienius Septimus mesolaeum feci mihi et | coniugi posterisque meis itemque dedicavi*; height 20 cm, width 106 cm, height letters 6.5 cm.

[149] De Vos (2004: 51).

[150] The three epitaphs contain the *praenomen* Lucius. Poinssot (1911: 175, 903) considers that Passenus, Pas(s)ienus, Pas(s)enius, Pas(s)ienius, Pas(s)inius relate to the same onomastic family. Khanoussi and Maurin (2002: 662) maintain that persons bearing these names may not be relatives.

[151] Hartley and Dickinson (2011). I thank Brenda Dickinson for generously communicating her observations to me.

[152] Ebnöther *et al.* (1994); Mees (forthcoming).

Fig. 6.25. Djebel Cheidi, Henchir Batoum, *fossa regia*, site 390, dedication: *Iovi Optimo | Maximo Aug | sacrum | pro salute Pa[s] | s(i)eni patru[i | et] liberor[um - | – e]ius* (M. de Vos, M. Andreoli)

Fig. 6.26. Oued Khalled, Bir Tersas, site 388: inscription of the mausoleum of C. Passienius Septimus, reused in Byzantine fortress: *C. Passienius Septimus mesolaeum feci mihi et | coniugi posterisque meis itemque dedicavi* (M. de Vos)

The dedication (and the temple) presumably marked the boundary of the estate, at the watershed between the Khalled and the Siliana valley. If this reconstruction is correct, it means that the Passieni succeeded in maintaining the African property, although C. Sallustius Passienus Crispus, the son of L. Passienus Rufus (*consul ordinarius* 4 BC and *proconsul Africae* AD 3), adopted by Sallustius Crispus, married first Nero's aunt Domitia and then his mother Agrippina, who inherited Passienus' fortune after his death in AD 47.[153] Nero was also enriched by this inheritance, as Passienus Crispus was his stepfather.[154] The *Thuggenses* erected a statue to Passienus Rufus, *tribunus militum* of the XII legion *Fulminata*, thanking his father, who had contracted an agreement of *amicitia* with them, a privilege granted only to senators (*CIL* 8.26580). Maurin suggests that the reason for the honour of a statue was the rain miracle that helped the *Fulminata* to win the war against the Quadi in AD 171, and was represented on the column of Marcus Aurelius in Rome.[155] This interpretation fits well with the military character of the dedication to IOM. The eastern boundary of the estate of the Passieni includes the site of the inscription.

[153] Scol. on Juv. 4.81; Syme (1982: 79 n. 106). Containing the fortunes of the historian Sallustius.
[154] Suet., *Ner.* 6.3.
[155] Bouard *et al.* (1997: 225).

During the Byzantine period the farm was transformed into a fortress, including the funerary and entrance inscriptions. It is the only site with all the seven phases represented in surface scatters.[156]

COMMUNICATION NETWORKS

The *via a Karthagine Thevestem*

The agricultural production and distribution system, which the ceramic record from the Dougga survey suggests was very dynamic until late antiquity, required a well-functioning road system. In the Roman period the area benefited from the dense road system of the Carthage region, which facilitated the export of the region's surplus produce to more distant markets (see Fig. 6.2).[157] The important military highway Carthage–Ammadaera–Theveste, 191.7 *milia* long, which crosses the region surveyed for 17 *milia*, was paved under Hadrian by the *Legio III Augusta*. It was an imperial inter-provincial road linking Africa Proconsularis (later Byzacena) to Numidia.[158] Sixty milestones have been discovered so far along the 17 Roman miles from the 71st to the 87th mile from Carthage:[159] they include ten milestones set up by Hadrian in 123,[160] four by Caracalla in 216,[161] and two by Maximinus and his son in 237;[162] some of these are still preserved at or near their original location. These milestones mention the emperors in the nominative case; they refer to three great operations of road

---

[156] Polla (2004–5: 94).

[157] Salama (1951).

[158] Salama (1987: 46). The highway formalized an old route.

[159] See Bigalke's useful website <http://www.bigalke-schmiedekunst.de/images/shop/meilensteine_an_der_via_numidica.htm> (accessed 3 Sept. 2012), containing a survey of the Carthage–Theveste road and its many unpublished milestones on Tunisian territory. Twelve fragments are fragmentary: four contain only the distance from Carthage.

[160] *CIL* 8.22039, 22040, 22042, 22050, 22062, 22063, 22071, 22080: distance from Carthage: 74, 76, 77, 81, 86 miles (three examples with the distance not preserved). The total number of Hadrianic milestones recorded along the Carthage–Theveste road is twenty-six: Bigalke 45 must be added to the twenty-five counted by Salama (1987: 56). The building of a bridge at Ammaedara (now Haïdra) by the Third Legion during the third consulate of Hadrian is commemorated in the recently found inscription *AE* 1995, 1652 (Ben Abdallah 1997).

[161] *CIL* 8.22041, 22048, 22064, 22072. Salama (1987: 56) says that fifty-two milestones of Caracalla are recorded between Carthage and Theveste; altogether there are sixty, adding the four examples Bigalke 14, 31, 55, 58 and the four milestones published by Kallala (2006: nn. 4, 6, 9, 10).

[162] *CIL* 8.22056 (= *ILBardo* 471), 22073. So far, a series of thirteen milestones mentioning the repairs of Maximinus and his son has been found along the Carthage–Theveste road: Bigalke 29 and 30 (at the 66th and 68th mile from Carthage) are to be added to the eleven examples counted by Salama (1987: 56).

making and repairs from one end to the other of the road, on imperial initiative. If the three emperors mentioned erected a *miliarium* at each mile, theoretically the total number of milestones would originally have been 573.[163] The total number of recorded milestones, including the examples of the third and fourth centuries, is 271.[164] Indeed, at some points in and around our surveyed area two, three, or four milestone sockets and/or milestones were preserved.[165] Hadrian first paved the road from Carthage to Tébessa (*viam a Karthagine Thevestem stravit*); nearly a century later Caracalla restored it (*restituit*); only twenty years later Maximinus and his son had to restore the road again, as it had been left unmaintained for a long time (*longa incuria corruptam adq[ue] dilapsam restituerunt*). The milestone texts emphasize the inter-regional character and the imposing character of the enterprise, stating that the repairs went as far as the frontier of the province of Numidia: *viam a Karthag[ine] usque ad fines Numidiae provinc[iae]*. A few years later, five milestones mention Gordian III in the nominative case and one in the dative;[166] five other milestones of Gordian were found between the 43rd and 69th miles. They probably refer to a partial repair of some 40 miles of highway between Vallis, Coreva, and Agbia. From this period onwards the nature of the intervention was no longer specified. The frequent repairs were necessary because of the heavy traffic, the geomorphology of the hilly terrain with many thalwegs, and the rough climate, especially in the autumn when heavy rains and swollen torrents may sweep away bridges and roads, often built across dams and in thalwegs. A monumental wall at the 72nd mile was built in the bed of a stream near Aïn Younes as a substructure to carry the road (Fig. 6.27). Earthquakes may also have damaged the roads, as the region is seismic and Teboursouk is situated on a fault line. Indeed, the survey team experienced an earthquake in August 1995. An inscription of Aunobaris, unfortunately undatable, mentions the restoration of a temple *[per te]rrae motum dilabsum*.[167]

Four milestones of Philip the Arab[168] and one of Decius[169] also contain the name of the emperor in the nominative case. The next two milestones of Decius[170] contain his name in the genitive, a rare practice in the Early and

---

[163] Salama (1987: 131 n. 215).

[164] To the 246 milestones counted by Salama (1987: 84 n. 4), must be added a further 12 discovered by Kallala (2006: 1823), and 13 others discovered in the Dougga survey.

[165] Davin (1928–9: 676), 71st mile, three milestones (Hadrian, two fragments with different diameter); 677, 72nd mile, three sockets, two milestones (Gordian, fragment); 73rd mile, two milestones (Gordian—*CIL* 22037—and fragments); 679, 74th mile, four sockets. The *limes* road from Bostra to Petra in Arabia even had ten to fifteen milestones at some points: Kroll PW s.v. *miliarium* c. 425.

[166] *CIL* 8.22037, 22043, 22046, 22061; de Vos (2000: fig. 24).

[167] *CIL* 8.15562, near the 86th mile.

[168] *CIL* 8.22057, 22059; Davin (1928–9: 678); de Vos (2000: fig. 26).

[169] *CIL* 8.22065: the 85th mile from Carthage.

[170] *CIL* 8.22066, 7th line: LXXXV must be corrected to LXXXVI and in *CIL* 8.22081 the distance figure is on the fracture line: LXXX, restored by Poinssot (1885: 103) as LXXXV, and by the *CIL* editor as LXXXVIIII, according to its find spot near Aïn Garsallah.

Fig. 6.27. *Via a Kartagine Thevestem*, roadway substructure near Aïn Younes (M. de Vos)

Middle Empire, explicable by the fact that the road crossed an imperial estate, as two unpublished inscriptions in the vicinity indeed confirm.[171]

The next emperors (Claudius II Gothicus excepted)[172] have their name in the dative; these inscriptions are to be considered dedications offered by the cities and the population: one to Valerianus,[173] three to Aurelian,[174] one to Probus,[175] one to Carinus and his sons,[176] one to Diocletian,[177] one to Constantius and Galerius Caesares (Fig. 6.28), one to Constantius I or II,[178] one to Maxentius,[179] one to Constantine,[180] one to Constantine II,[181] and one to Valentinian I.[182] But these votives are not merely praise or propaganda for

[171] Interpretation proposed by Salama (1987: 59 and n. 231) for two milestones near Timici in Mauretania Caesariensis bearing the names of Gordian III and Philip the Arab in the genitive.
[172] *CIL* 8.22052.   [173] *CIL* 8.22051.
[174] *CIL* 8.22058, 22067 and Bigalke 43.
[175] *CIL* 8.22074 = *ILPBardo* 532.
[176] *CIL* 8.22047.   [177] *CIL* 8.22068; Salama (1987: 67).
[178] *CIL* 8.22035 and Bigalke 49 (instead of 39), erroneously attributed to Constantine.
[179] *CIL* 8.22038.   [180] *CIL* 8.22075.   [181] Bigalke 44.
[182] Bigalke 42 attributes the milestone to Valentinian II, but it concerns rather his father, the last great western emperor: *D N Vale(ntin)* | *iano Maxim(o)* | *P(io) F(elici) Vic(t)or(i) LXXXV*; cf. the same sequence of titles in the *vota quinquennalia* and *decennalia* on the slabs of the *pons Valentiniani* on the Tiber in Rome (*CIL* 6. 31405) and in a dedication of Thibilis (*ILAlg* 2.2.4675). Lizzi Testa (2004: 403–6, app. II 452).

Fig. 6.28. *Via a Kartagine Thevestem*, Aïn Younes, column or milestone with dedication to Constantius and Galerius *Caesares* of the First Tetrarchy (293–305): *C. Flavio | Galerio | Constan | tio et | C. Galerio | Valerio | Maximi | no nobili | ssimis | C[a]esaribus* (M. de Vos, M. Andreoli, C. Favretto)

the emperors; they attest real restoration work. At the same time, they will have conditioned heavily and in different ways the perception of the landscape by travellers, Roman citizens, and the local population. A column with a dedication to Constantius and Galerius, *Caesares* of the First Tetrarchy (293–305), without subject (probably the city of Aquae) nor indication of the distance from Carthage (*c.*72nd mile), might be considered an honorific pillar related to the construction or an important repair of the road's substructure: *C. Flavio | Galerio | Constan | tio et | C. Galerio | Valerio | Maximi | no nobili | ssimis | C[a]esaribus* (Fig. 6.28). But it could also be a normal milestone: from the Tetrarchic period more than half of the milestones omit the mileage figure.[183] Beware the *error quadratarii*: the correct name of the first prince, Constantine's father, is C. Flavius Valerius Constantius, not Galerius.

[183] Salama (1987: 61–2).

The Roman road system affected identity: it 'displayed power over land-scape', and was an imprint of domination of the landscape; the names on the milestones can be seen as self-advertisement[184] by the rulers, meticulously updated through the setting-up of a second, third, and fourth milestone on the same spot and through the erasure of names owing to *damnatio memoriae*. After the mid-third century, at least, the local population paid for the road system and its functioning.

Pekáry argued that emperors did not usually finance road building and upkeep; when, exceptionally, it did happen, it was mentioned *expressis verbis*, and so far there is no evidence for it in northern Africa, except for the *pons novus* by Trajan at Simitthus.[185] This thesis, accepted also by Radke, Chevallier, and Salama,[186] is based not only on epigraphic and numismatic silence—if the emperor had spent enormous sums, he would not have let slip the opportunity to underline his generosity; he was used to doing so, even for more modest funding—but also on a calculation of the entities of the *aerarium Saturni* and *fiscus* that could not afford the expensive road building. The paving of one mile of *via publica* cost more than 100,000 *sestertii* in Italy;[187] the *via a Karthagine Thevestem*, 191.7 *milia* long, would have required 19.2 million *sestertii*. Including the erection of milestones, the building of bridges, *substructiones, praetoria, mansiones, mutationes*, and spaces for the *cursus publicus*, the estimated costs are 500,000 *sestertii per mile*, totalling 96 million *sestertii*. The yearly army costs in Augustan times are estimated at 500 million, and two or three times as much under Vespasian.[188] The network of *viae publicae* in the whole Roman empire totalled 120,000 km.[189] Eck rejects Pekáry's interpret-ation,[190] discussing only the epigraphic evidence, not the cost estimates. These authors are almost exclusively concerned with Italy in the Early Imperial period. Research on the plethora of provincial roads is needed. In the copious bibliography on Roman roads, nobody except the authors cited—as far as I know—has probed the economic aspect of road building. As extenuating circumstances, it can be adduced that evidence on funding is very scarce

---

[184] Potter (1987: 134); Purcell (1990: 15, 23); Witcher (1998).

[185] *CIL* 8.10117; Pekáry (1968: 97–102, 113, 169–71); cf. the milestone recently found near Aptera (Crete), which names Trajan in the nominative with the verb 'dedit', Baldwin Bowsky and Niniou-Kindeli (2006: 419–20).

[186] Pekáry (1968); Radke (1973: 1445–6); Chevallier (1998); Salama (2010: 42–3).

[187] Pekáry (1968: 94–5).

[188] Pekáry (1968: 96, citing Frank 1940: 4, 53).

[189] Quilici and Quilici Gigli (2004: 129).

[190] Eck (1979: 75–9) advances evidence for three other cases of epigraphic omission in Italy of *sua pecunia* in the Flavian period and by Nerva and Trajan. Eck (1979: 72 n. 228) admits, however, that the nominative of the emperor in building inscriptions and milestones cannot always be interpreted as imperial funding. The rate of landowner participation in road building in Italy is minor compared to that in the provinces, even if the army seems less involved in road building in Italy (Eck 1979: 73, 75).

and of difficult interpretation. The costs may have been lower in the Roman provinces, and the involvement of the army in building the *via a Karthagine Thevestem* will have further lowered the costs. The achievement of building 191.7 miles in one year supposes a massive participation of local *possessores agrum*, who had to supply at least building material and labour. The *munitio viarum* (road building and repair) was a *munus publicum*, and a *munus possessionum*, calculated on the dimensions not only of the estate surface but also of the crops. Cities and local landowners (and tenants?)[191] had to pay not only for the roads but also for most of the transport costs of the *cursus publicus* and *cursus clabularis*.[192] The milestones attest the continuous concern of emperors, cities, and landowners (*possessores agrorum*) for this strategic road not only for military and administrative but also for commercial reasons. The accumulation of milestones also suggests the intensive use of the road. Julian reminded the *vicarius* of Africa in 362 (*CT* 15.3.2) that the maintenance of roads had for a long time been the responsibility of the landowners and the cities. How and when the roads were repaired after the fourth century is not attested epigraphically. In other parts of the empire too the epigraphic evidence diminishes and stops dramatically in the fifth century: in Asia Minor the last few milestones date from the reign of Honorius and Theodosius II.[193] But the codes of Theodosius and Justinian contain several laws concerning road making, repairing, and transport.[194]

Secondary roads

The south-west/north-east orientation of the communication network is determined by geology and water systems. Grain and oil destined for the food distributions, as tax in kind, were transported to the *horrea fiscalia* in the provincial centres or in the *stationes* or *mansiones* along the road by the owners themselves with their own vehicles or beasts of burden,[195] and from there to the ports by means of the *cursus clabularis*, heavy wagon transport, also financed by the provincial population.[196] Various secondary roads or tracks linked rural settlements to the many cities in the region. Three milestones of the road from Thubursicu Bure to Bulla Regia and Thabraca are known (the road passed through the *saltus Neronianus* in the Fawar and Arkou valleys): one milestone is recorded at Bir Lafou, and two at Uchi

---

[191] So Pekáry (1968: 171) in the last sentence of his monograph on Roman roads, without citing sources.
[192] Pekáry (1968: 113–17).
[193] For North Africa, see Salama (1987: 210; 2010); for Asia Minor, see French (1988: 486–7).
[194] Pekáry (1968); Herz (1991); Kolb (2000).
[195] Salama (1987: 77–8 and nn. 294–5); Herz (1991: 169).
[196] Herz (1991: 170); Sirks (1991: 147); Peña (1998: 163).

Maius.[197] The first French explorers noticed conspicuous remains of these secondary roads; they have since disappeared, because of more intensive use and the consolidation works of recent times.

River transport

Nothing is known about possible river transport down the perennial Bagradas (Medjerda). The meandering course of the river would have tripled the distance, and bank erosion might have made difficult the use of rafts, *scaphae*, and *naves caudicariae*. The river's flow is slow (*lento pede*).[198] But the same may be said of the Tiber, yet there we are sure that river transport was common, although an extensive canal system was lacking.[199] Gascou considers that the Bagradas was navigable in antiquity as it is now.[200]

Although positive evidence of river transport in Africa Proconsularis is lacking, an iconographic source may partially and hypothetically fill this gap. A mosaic in the baths of a rich house at Althiburus, 200 km from the eastern coast and 90 km to the south-east of Thugga along the Carthage–Tébessa highway, represents a detailed catalogue of some twenty-five sea and river boats, each with its technical denomination—for example, *stlatta* (from *latus*, 'wide'); another one transporting amphorae has not preserved its name.[201] The mosaic is framed at one end by the mask of Ocean, and at the other by a river god. The image of the detailed and labelled catalogue located so far from the sea evokes the idea of river transport to the coast, even if Althiburus is situated in the centre of the fertile plain between the rivers Sarrath (34 km distant) and Siliana (58 km distant), tributaries of the Medjerda. Another marine mosaic in the *triclinium* of the same house represents a merchant ship loaded with *amphorae*; the emphasis on the realistic iconography of the boats suggests that the owner, probably an estate *possessor*, was involved in the shipping business. If this is correct, he was representing his *munus navicularium*—that is, his duty to deliver ships and equipment for food transport in the service of the *annona* of Rome. In return, legal privileges, exemption from tax, and local *munera* were granted to the *navicularii*; in compensation for overhead costs they also received 4 per cent of the cargoes and 1 *solidus* for each 1,000 *modii* of grain transported.[202] The *navicularii* who invested at least half of their wealth in ships belonged to the local elites.

---

[197] *CIL* 8.21990a, Bir Lafou (site 22) disappeared; Mastino and Khanoussi (2000: 1320–3).
[198] Silius Italicus, *Punica* 6.140.   [199] Laurence (1999: 121–2).
[200] Gascou (1991).
[201] Duval (1949); Dunbabin (1978: 127, 248, fig. 122). The mosaics are dated to the second half of the third century.
[202] Herz (1991: 171–3); Sirks (1991: 128–9).

In the region surveyed there are no traces of *horrea*. However, some 25 km to the north of the investigated area, at the foot of Djebel Skhira near Tichilla (now Testour, to the east of the Sidi Salem dam), is epigraphic evidence of a *horreum publicum*, presumably a state warehouse,[203] just where two tributaries (Siliana and Khalled) join the main river Medjerda (Bagradas), and where the *diverticulum* (a secondary branch, to the west of the main highway) Vallis–Tichilla–Agbia also reaches the Medjerda. The commodities produced in these valleys could be shipped here along the Medjerda in order to be transported to the Mediterranean ports at Utica, or Carthage. At Utica an imperial slave was guardian of the *horrea Augustae* (*CIL* 8.13190); from the end of the third century onwards oil from the Bagradas valley was stored in the *conditorium Zeugitanum* on the Îlot de l'Amirauté at Carthage.[204] For the settlements to the north of Thugga it was more convenient to convey their produce by this *diverticulum*, which halfway, at Tichilla, reaches the right bank of the river Bagradas. The *diverticulum* was monumentalized fifty years after the paving of the highway: the most recent milestone contains a dedication to Theodosius.[205] The highway *a Karthagine Thevestem*, probably used for transport by the settlements to the south of Thugga, runs parallel to the Bagradas at a distance of 10 km to the east.

Transport networks and the Church in late antiquity

It cannot be excluded that in late antiquity, when the roads were no longer maintained as intensively as before, transport increasingly relied on dromedaries. Two dromedary skulls excavated in the Byzantine farm of Aïn Wassel may be an indication for the (partial?) substitution of the wheel by camels, as attested in the eastern Mediterranean in late antiquity. A tariff of the ferry between La Goulette and Radès, near Carthage's harbour, datable after the end of the fourth century, mentions horsemen, muleteers, donkey- and camel-drivers with and without cargo: *camellus carricatus cum camelario f(ol)l(es) V, camelus levis cum camelario f(ol)l(es) III*.[206] The tariff shows that the dromedary had become common by late antiquity. Indeed, in the fourth and fifth centuries caravans of dromedaries transporting oil in skins from inland

---

[203] *CIL* 8.25895 = *AE* 1893, 61; Cagnat (1916: 264), also for *horrea* at Carthage and Utica. The inscription *AE* 2002: 1670 found at Henchir el Oust in the Miliana Valley mentions a *[h]orreum oliarium adq[ue] frumentarium*.

[204] Peña (1998: 216).

[205] *CIL* 8.10058–60, 21996–22001, 22019, Salama (1987: no. 165); the ten milestones mention emperors from Gordian to Theodosius, the last emperor on the highway milestones is Valentinian I: see n. 182.

[206] *CIL* 8.24512, *AE* 1906,138, *ILPBardo* 403; on the (pre)history of the dromedary in N. Africa: Shaw (1979).

Tunisia to the coast were such a common and familiar scene in the landscape
that they appear in appliqué decoration representing dromedaries loaded with
four skins on two different ARS dish forms produced at Oued el Guettar;
one dromedary with four skins appears on the discus of a lamp (type Atl.
XA, group C2 or Bonifay 54) found near Gabès and on two lamps with the
heads of the twelve Apostles on the shoulder.[207] Until recent years, transhumant cattle moved every summer from the steppes in central Tunisia to
the mountains of the Tell in the north, in order to graze stubble in the High
Tell,[208] where the nomads worked as harvesters using their dromedaries for
ploughing. These lamps offer a nice illustration of the progressive role of the
Church in *annona* supply.[209] Indeed, five out of six churches surveyed in
371 km[2] lay amid farms provided with presses (sites 5, 282, 565, 572,
586)[210]—a feature shared with more monumental settlements in central
Tunisia, as El Gousset near Haïdra, Kasr el Guellal, and Bir el Hfay near
Sbeïtla.[211] All the churches are located along roads, and they are rationally
distributed throughout the valleys (see Fig. 6.1): a church (site 5) in the
Arkou valley, another (site 282) in the Guetoussia valley, and one (site 565)
that dominates the Nemcha valley and the pass between the Khalled and
Bagradas valleys, near a monumental farm with a triple press.[212] The only
exception is a concentration in the Maatria valley, where three churches are
situated around Numluli. The most modest church (site 5), built with *spolia*
from the nearby temple of Fortuna, belonged to the (ex?) *saltus Neronianus*
and is situated near two farms each with a single press.[213] The church site
282 is built near an anti-erosion wall on a river bank below a settlement that
contained funerary inscriptions of five different well-to-do families of African origin living at Agbia, Thugga, and Uchi Maius: the Arsacii, Asicii, Iulii,
Morasii, and Mucii, who were owners or *conductores* of the estate.[214] It is
interesting to note the high rank of these estates before their passage to the
Church. It is possible that the imperial or private owner after his conversion
to the Christian religion bequeathed his goods to the Church, as Melania
did.[215] In the other three sites no names are available; the *trifolium* church

---

[207] Marlière and Torres Costa (2007: 90–3, figs 4–6, with bibliography).

[208] Clarke (1955).

[209] Reynolds (2010: 69, 130).

[210] Carton (1895: 242–3, fig. 80; 231, fig. 78; 291–2, figs 94–6; 281–4, fig. 91); de Vos (2000: 21,
figs 29–31; 2004: 12).

[211] Duval (1990); Béjaoui (2002: 205, 209, figs 21, 29): one building phase of the El Gousset
church is dated in the 26th year of king Thrasamund: AD 521.

[212] De Vos (2008: 278–9, fig. 26).

[213] De Vos (2000: 21, figs 30, 31.1–2).

[214] *CIL* 8.27406 is the only one still *in situ*; 8.27407, 8.27408, 8.27410, 8.27411; de Vos (2000:
21, figs 29, 1–2, 65).

[215] Chavarría and Lewit (2004: 38); for Melania, see Giardina (1988).

(site 572) is associated with a multiple press farm and the church (site 586) seems the most elaborate, with a circular baptistery.

CONCLUSIONS

This overview of the investigated region of the ancient landscape surrounding Thugga and Thubursicu Bure shows the complex structure of the various communities who lived and produced there. The overview is more a presentation than a detailed interpretation of the data. To deepen and sharpen the interpretation further excavations are necessary. The only excavation carried out so far concerns a Byzantine farm. The collected evidence offers much—but chronologically limited—epigraphic information about the second to fourth centuries AD; the surface pottery reflects better the ups and downs of the region's economy, and may over-represent the more recent periods, but suggests a slow start to the intensive agricultural exploitation of the landscape and a gradual increase from the pre-Roman to mid-Roman periods, and then a dramatic and rapid climax from the Late Roman period to the Byzantine period (see Table 6.3, Fig. 6.12), corresponding with the general dynamic ceramic productions, exportations, and seaborne trade in the Mediterranean.[216]

The first great properties beyond the *fossa regia* to the south of the river Bagradas were created by Octavian/Augustus for his generals,[217] and the largest became an imperial estate under Nero. In the second century AD the tenants were empowered by the *lex Hadriana de rudibus agris*, when A. Gabinius Datus (*AE* 1921, 24)[218] divided with his fellow countrymen the management of the imperial estates: the *conductores praediorum regionis Thuggensis* offered a statue for his merits to Gabinius.

Where epigraphic evidence is missing, the maps (see Figs 6.1, 6.4, and 6.12) show a pattern of holdings equally distributed over all types of soils and geomorphology; on the surface, they are not distinguishable from the imperial and aristocratic properties. Dependent and independent farmers did their best

---

[216] Reynolds (2010: 76, 100–5, 124, 126–8, 130, 146–8).

[217] Cf. the parallel case of the famous *fundus Villae Magnae Varianae sive Mappalia Siga* (at Henchir Mettich, 7 km north of the surveyed area), granted by Augustus to his potential successor P. Quinctilius Varus, proconsul of Africa *c.*7–4 BC, and which presumably reverted to imperial ownership after Varus' death in AD 9. The three estates are just beyond the *fossa regia*. After his victory at Thapsus in 46 BC, Julius Caesar annexed the Numidian kingdom as the province of *Africa Nova*. In this way the region became *ager publicus populi Romani*; evidently Octavian/Augustus could dispose to his liking.

[218] Khanoussi (2000: 159–60).

to maximize production. In late antiquity the imperial estates gradually passed back into private or ecclesiastical ownership.

Notwithstanding the distance of 100 km from the coast, the region seems to have produced a surplus of commodities as tax-in-kind and for the local and overseas markets. There is no material proof that the region's commodities arrived at Rome, but the case of the equestrian Q. Acilius Fuscus suggests a link. *Civis* and *patronus* of Thubursicu Bure, *procurator annonae* at Ostia under Septimius Severus, he earned a statue offered by the *corpus me(n)sorum frument(ariorum)* of Ostia (*CIL* 8.15255, 14.154). Acilius Fuscus belonged to the conspicuous group of Africans engaged in the *annona* transport between Africa and Rome in the second and third centuries AD and must have been involved in grain supply and transport. The transport of commodities of the Thugga and Thubursicu region to Carthage was facilitated by the road network around the *via a Karthagine Thevestem*, and by the river Bagradas from Tichilla down to the coast at Utica.

Investment in intensive agriculture seems to start in the second half of the first century AD, thanks to the passing under Vespasian of the *lex Manciana* and, later, the *lex Hadriana*. The area is famous because of the concentration of inscriptions related to the *lex Manciana* found at Henchir Mettich (property of Trajan in AD 117, when the inscription was carved and exposed) and the *lex Hadriana de rudibus agris et iis qui per X annos continuos inculti sunt*, found at Aïn Djemala, Lella Drebblia (both Hadrianic), and Aïn Wassel (Severan). Only the imperial estates could guarantee such perpetual leases, so *coloni* were motivated to maximize their efforts in their own interest, in the interest of their children and that of the emperor. They invested in new plantations and breeding livestock and sometimes also in buildings;[219] some of them already had a farm.[220] Normally the landlord had to supply the farm with all that was needed to run it. The improvements realized by the *coloni* could be bequeathed to their legal sons, and all the leased goods could be used as pledge—for example, to fund improvements of the farm.[221] One of the principal aims of the research was to compare the detailed information given by the 'great inscriptions' with the archaeological evidence emerging from survey and excavation. The monumental style of the farms in general and the worn-out aspect of pressing stones, sometimes readapted to the same or a similar function, the abundance of table- and cooking wares, do suggest a relatively well-to-do standard of life. White mosaic is often used to pave the pressing room. The standard of the building techniques implies skilled

---

[219] *aedificium deposuit posuerit CIL* 8.25902, IV.11: the tenant who has set or will set a building on the leased land.

[220] *qu[i i]n f[undo] Villae Magnae aut Mappalie Siga villas [habe]nt habebunt CIL* 8.25902, I.20–1.

[221] Kehoe (1988: 103, 168, 176).

stonecutters, masons, and architects. The rather scarce availability of these artisans can be deduced from the epitaph of Licinia Attica (site 82) in which her children beg their mother's pardon for the delay with which they erected her tomb, owing to *artificis morae*.[222] The private landlords and the *conductores*, managers of the imperial estates and tax collectors, considered municipal aristocrats, used their profits not for building luxurious villas but for euergetism in the towns to acquire prestige and offices in the municipal administration and government. The concentration of imperial estates in this part of North Africa will have contributed to the construction and repairs of the roads necessary for *annona* transport and later in the Vandal and Byzantine periods for the intra- and inter-regional trade communications, perhaps partially by river. In these periods many settlements were reorganized and also expanded with presses, using large blocks (funerary altars, thresholds, doorposts) side-by-side in double-faced walls instead of the regular and distanced use of orthostats between *opus vittatum* of the Middle and Late Empire. The good preservation of the landscape and the many details contained in the 'great inscriptions' make the Bagradas valley a unique test case where archaeologists can collect and test data very near to the reality of daily urban and rural life in antiquity.

REFERENCES

AAT = Atlas archéologique de la Tunisie. Paris 1892–1913.

Abu Zahra, N. (1982). *Sidi Ameur, a Tunisian Village*. Oxford and London.

Ahmet, K. (2001). 'A Middle Byzantine Olive Press Room at Aphrodisias', *Anatolian Studies* 51: 159–67.

Akerraz, A., and Lenoir, M. (1981–2). 'Les Huileries de Volubilis', *Bulletin d'archéologie marocaine*, 14: 69–101.

Amit, D., and Baruch, Y. (2009). 'Wine Presses with Stone Rollers—An Ancient Phenomenon Seen in a New Light', in E. Ayalon, R. Frankel, and A. Kloner (eds), *Oil and Wine Presses in Israel from the Hellenistic, Roman and Byzantine Periods* (BAR International Series 1972). Oxford, 429–40.

Amouretti, M.-C. (1986). *Le pain et l'huile dans la Grèce antique: De l'araire au moulin*. Paris.

Aounallah, S. (2010). Pagus, castellum *et* civitas. *Étude d'épigraphie et d'histoire sur le village et la cité en Afrique romaine* (Scripta antique 23). Bordeaux.

Attoui, R. (2004). 'Il progetto di conservazione come strumenti di riqualificazione economica e sviluppo sostenibile: Il parco archeologico di Dougga (Tunisia)', in de Vos (2004), 56–84.

Attoui, R. (2011) (ed.). *When did Antiquity End? Archaeological Case Studies in Three Continents* (BAR International Series 2268). Oxford.

---

[222] De Vos (2008: 282).

Baldwin Bowsky, M. W., and Niniou-Kindeli V. (2006). 'On the Road Again: A Trajanic Milestone and the Road Connections of Aptera, Crete', *Hesperia* 75.3: 405–33.

Balut, G. (1903). *Le Pays de Dougga et de Téboursouk à travers les ruines de vingt cités antiques*. Tunis.

Béjaoui, F. (2002). 'État des découvertes d'époque chrétienne des dix dernières années en Tunisie', *AnTard* 10: 197–211.

Ben Abdallah, Z. B. (1986). *Catalogue des inscriptions latines païennes du Musée du Bardo*. Rome.

Ben Abdallah, Z. B. (1997). 'À propos d'un pont de la voie de Carthage à Theveste construit, sous Hadrien, à l'entrée d'Ammaedara', *Bulletin Archéologique du Comité des Travaux Historiques et Scientifiques, Afrique du Nord* 24 (1993–5 [1997]): 95–100.

Ben Abdallah, Z. B., and Khanoussi, M. (2000). 'Les Gabinii', in M. Khanoussi and L. Maurin (eds), *Dougga, fragments d'histoire*. Bordeaux and Tunis, 194–8.

Ben Abdallah, Z. B., and Maurin, L. (2002). 'Notables de Dougga', in M. Khanoussi and L. Maurin (eds), *Mourir à Dougga: Recueil des inscriptions funéraires*. Bordeaux and Tunis, 310–11.

Ben Baaziz, S. (1991). 'Les huileries de la Tunisie antique', *CT* 43.155–6: 39–64.

Ben Hassen, H. (2006). *Thignica (Aïn-Tounga): Son histoire et ses monuments*. Ortacesus.

Ben Moussa, M., Ramon Torres, J., Revilla, V., Sanmartí, J., Maraoui Temini, B., Touihri, C., Ben Jarbai, I., and Ben Tahar, S. (2011). 'Catalogue du mobilier', in N. Kallala and J. Sanmartí (eds), *Althiburos I : La Fouille dans l'aire du Capitole et dans la nécropole méridionale*. Tarragona, 263–391.

Biagini, M. (2007), 'Reperti ceramici dalle aree 22.000 e 24.000: Ceramiche africane da cucina, ceramiche grezze, ceramiche comuni', in Vismara (2007), 372–428.

Bigalke, U. <http://www.bigalke-schmiedekunst.de/images/shop/meilensteine_an_der_via_numidica.htm> (accessed 3 Sept. 2012).

Bompard M. (1888). *Législation de la Tunisie*. Paris.

Bouard, V., Demaison, N., and Maurin, L. (1997). 'CIL, VIII, 26580 et l'écriture "africaine"', in M. Khanoussi and L. Maurin (eds), *Dougga (Thugga): Études épigraphiques*. Paris, 209–36.

Brun, J.-P. (2004). *Archéologie du vin et de l'huile dans l'Empire romain*. Paris.

Cagnat, R. (1916). 'L'Annone d'Afrique', *Mémoires de l'Académie des Inscriptions* 40: 247–77.

Carcopino, J. (1906). 'L'inscription d'Aïn-el-Djemala: Contribution à l'histoire des *saltus* africains et du colonat partiaire', *MEFRA* 365–481.

Carton, L. (1895). *Découvertes épigraphiques et Archéologiques faites en Tunisie (région de Dougga)*. Paris.

Chabot, J.-B. (1940–1). *Recueil des inscriptions libyques*. Paris.

Chavarría, A., and Lewit, T. (2004). 'Archaeological Research on the Late Antique Countryside: A Bibliographic Essay', in W. Bowden, L. Lavan, and C. Machado (eds), *Recent Research on the Late Antique Countryside*. Leiden and Boston, 3–51.

Chevallier, R. (1998). *Les voies romaines*. Paris.

Chouchane, A., and Maurin, L. (2000). 'Dédicace de l'aqueduc de Dougga', in M. Khanoussi and L. Maurin (eds), *Dougga, fragments d'histoire*. Bordeaux-Tunis, 102–9.

Ciotola, A. (2004). 'Le Ceramiche rinvenute nell'insediamento rurale di Aïn Wassel e nella ricognizione intorno a Dougga: Analisi funzionale dei contesti di scavo e sviluppo cronologico dei materiali', in de Vos (2004), 85–110.

Clarke, J. I. (1955). 'Summer Nomadism in Tunisia', *Economic Geography* 31.2: 157–67.

Cuomo, S. (2007). *Technology and Culture in Greek and Roman Antiquity*. Oxford.

Curtis, R. I. (2001). *Ancient Food Technology*. Leiden, Boston, and Cologne.

Davin, P. (1928–9). 'La voie romaine de Carthage à Theveste entre Ad Atticillae et Agbia', *BCTH* 665–82.

De Ligt, L. (2008). Review of Kehoe, D., *Law and the Rural Economy in the Roman Empire*, Ann Arbor, *JRS* 98: 208–9.

De Vos, M. (2000). *Rus Africum: Terra acqua olio nell'Africa settentrionale: Scavo e ricognizione nei dintorni di Dougga (alto Tell tunisino)*. Trento.

De Vos M. (2004) (ed.). *Archeologia del territorio: Metodi materiali prospettive Medjerda e Adige: Due territori a confronto*. Trento.

De Vos M. (2005). 'Ricerche archeologiche recenti dell'Università di Trento', in *Studi storico-archeologici in memoria di Adriano Rigotti, Rovereto, 19 novembre 2004* (Atti Accademici Roveretana degli Agiati di Scienze. Lettere ed Arti 5A, f. II vol. 255), 71–91.

De Vos M. (2007). 'Olio per Roma e per il mercato intraregionale', in E. Papi (ed.), *Supplying Rome and the Roman Empire* (JRA Suppl. 69). Portsmouth, RI, 43–58.

De Vos M. (2008). 'Caratteristiche della costruzione degli impianti produttivi rurali nell'*Africa Proconsularis*', in S. Camporeale, H. Dessales, and A. Pizzo (eds), *Arqueología de la construcción I: Los procesos constructivos en el mundo romano: Italia y provincias occidentales (Merida, Instituto de Arqueología, 25–26 de Octubre de 2007)* (Anejos de AEspA 50). Mérida, 269–84.

De Vos, M., and Attoui, R. (2011). 'Paesaggio produttivo: Percezione antica e moderna. Geografia della religione: Un case-study nell'Africa del Nord', in Attoui (2011), 31–89.

De Vos, M., Attoui, R., and Andreoli, M. (2011). 'Hand and "Donkey" Mills in North African Farms: Ubi Lapis Lapidem Terit (Plaut. Asin. 32)', in D. Peacock and D. Williams (eds), *Bread for the People, a Colloquium on the Archaeology of Mills and Milling, The British School at Rome, 05–07.11.2009* (BAR University of Southampton, Series in Archaeology 3). Oxford, 131–50.

De Vos, M., and Polla, S. (2005). 'Ceramica dai siti rurali intorno a Dougga (Tunisia settentrionale)', in J. Ma. Gurt i Esparraguera, J. Buxeda i Garrigós, and M. A. Cau Ontiveros (eds), *LRCW 1: Late Roman Coarse Wares, Cooking Wares and Amphorae in the Mediterranean: Archaeology and Archaeometry*. Oxford, 483–91.

Dunbabin, K. M. D. (1978). *The Mosaics of Roman North Africa: Studies in Iconography and Patronage*. Oxford.

Duval, N. (1990). 'Les nouveautés de l'archéologie tunisienne: Le Site d'Hr el Gousset', *Revue des Études Augustiniennes*, 36: 315–27.

Duval, P.-M. (1949). 'La forme des navires romains, d'après la mosaïque d'Althiburus', *MEFRA* 61: 119–49.

Ebnöther, C., Mees, A. W., and Polak, M. (1994). 'Le dépôt de céramique du vicus de Vitudurum-Oberwinterthur (Suisse). Rapport préliminaire', in L. Rivet (ed.), *Actes du Congrès de Millau, 12–15 mai 1994: Société française d'étude de la céramique antique en Gaule: Les Sigillées du sud de la Gaule, actualité des recherches céramiques*. Marseilles, 127–31.

Eck, W. (1979). *Die staatliche Organisation Italiens in der hohen Kaiserzeit*. Munich.

Falchi, I. (1894). 'Vetulonia: Scavi della necropoli vetuloniese durante l'anno 1893', *Notizie degli Scavi*, 335–60.

Fiorelli, G. (1873). *Gli scavi di Pompei dal 1861 al 1872*. Naples.

Flach, D. (1978). 'Inschriftenuntersuchungen zum römischen Kolonat in Nordafrika', *Chiron* 8: 441–92.

Flach, D. (1982). 'Die Pachtbedingungen der Kolonen und die Verwaltung des kaiserlichen Güter in Nordafrika', in H. Temporini (ed.), *ANRW* 2.10.2, Berlin–New York, 427–73.

Flach, D. (1990). *Römische Agrargeschichte*. Munich.

Foxhall, L. (1990). 'The Dependent Tenant: Land Leasing and Labour in Italy and Greece', *JRS* 80: 97–114.

Frank, T. (1940). *An Economic Survey of Ancient Rome*, 5. Baltimore.

Frankel, R. (1999). *Wine and Oil Production in Antiquity in Israel and other Mediterranean Countries*. Sheffield.

French, D. H. (1988). *Roman Roads and Milestones of Asia Minor* (BAR International Series 302). Oxford.

Frier, B. W. (1979). 'Law, Technology, and Social Change: The Equipping of Italian Farm Tenancies', *Zeitschrift der Savigny-Stiftung für Rechtsgeschichte. Romanistische Abteilung* 96: 204–28.

Gascou, J. (1991). 'Bagrada', *Encyclopédie Berbère*. 9. Aix-en-Provence, 1310–12.

Ghazi-Ben Maïssa, H. (2006). 'Et si on désignait ces fameux *Berbères* par leur vrai nom?', in *L'Africa Romana* 16.3: 2089–108.

Giardina, A. (1988). 'Carità eversiva: le donazioni di Melania la Giovane e gli equilibri della società tardoantica', *Studi storici*, 1: 127–42.

Gradgueb, A., Camps, G., Harbi-Riahi, M., M'Timet, A., and Zoughlami, J. (1987). *Atlas préhistorique de la Tunisie*, 5. Tunis (Collection de l'École française de Rome 81). Rome.

Hartley, B. R., and Dickinson, B. M. (2011). *Names on Terra Sigillata: An Index of Makers' Stamps and Signatures on Gallo-Roman terra sigillata (Samian Ware)*, vol. 7 (Bulletin of the Institute of Classical Studies, Suppl. 102.7). London.

Heitland, W. E. (1921). *Agricola: A Study of Agriculture and Rustic Life in the Greco-Roman World from the Point of View of Labour*. Cambridge.

Herz, P. (1991). 'Organisation und Finanzierung der spätantiken *annona*', in A. Giovannini (ed.), *Nourrir la plèbe*. Basle and Kassel, 161–88.

Hitchner, R. B. (1995). 'Irrigation, Terraces, Dams and Aqueducts in the Region of Cillium (mod. Kasserine): The Role of Water Works in the Development of a Roman–African Town and its Countryside', in P. Trousset (ed.), *Productions et exportations africaines: Actualités archéologiques en Afrique du Nord antique et médiévale. VIe colloque international sur l'histoire et l'archéologie de l'Afrique du Nord (PAU, octobre 1993 – 118e congrès).* Paris, 143–57.

Hopkins, N. (1977). 'The Emergence of Class in a Tunisian Town', *International Journal of Middle East Studies* 8.4: 453–91.

Israel, Y. (2009). 'A Byzantine Oil Press at Ashqalon', in E. Ayalon, R. Frankel, and A. Kloner (eds), *Oil and Wine Presses in Israel from the Hellenistic, Roman and Byzantine Periods* (BAR International Series 1972). Oxford, 355–8.

Jacques, F. (1984). *Le privilège de liberté: Politique impériale et autonomie municipale dans l'Occident romain (161–244).* Paris.

Jacquest, H. (2009). 'Les céramiques du site de la Basilique VII', in F. Baratte, F. Bejaoui, and Z. Ben Abdallah (eds), *Recherches archéologiques à Haïdra* 3. Rome, 181–99.

Jongeling, K. (1994). *North-African names from Latin Sources.* Leiden.

Kallala, N. (2006). 'Nouvelles bornes milliaires de la voie Carthage-*Theveste* découvertes dans la région du Kef (*Sicca Veneria*) en Tunisie', in *L'Africa romana* 16. Rome, 1795–1824.

Kassab, A., and Sethom, H. (1980). *Géographie de la Tunisie. Le pays et les hommes.* Tunis.

Kehoe, D. (1988). *The Economics of Agriculture on Roman Imperial Estates in North Africa* (Hypomnemata 89). Göttingen.

Kehoe, D. (1996). 'Roman-Law Influence on Louisiana's Landlord-Tenant Law: The Question of Risk in Agriculture', *Tulane Law Review*, 70: 1053–68.

Khanoussi, M. (2000). 'Hommage à A. Gabinius Datus', in M. Khanoussi and L. Maurin (eds), *Dougga, fragments d'histoire.* Bordeaux and Tunis, 159–60.

Khanoussi, M., and Maurin, L. (2002) (eds). *Mourir à Dougga: Recueil des inscriptions funéraires.* Bordeaux and Tunis.

Kolb, A. (2000). *Transport und Nachrichtentransfer im römischen Reich.* Berlin.

Kolendo, J. (1968). 'La Hierarchie des procurateurs dans l'inscription d'Aïn-el-Djemala (C.I.L., VIII, 25943)', *REL* 46: 319–29.

Kolendo, J. (1991). *Le colonat en Afrique sous le Haut-Empire*, 2nd edn. Paris.

Lancel, S. (1984). 'Études sur la Numidie d'Hippone au temps de saint Augustin', *MEFRA* 96.2: 1085–1113.

Lanfranchi, R. (2004). 'I torchi per la pressatura delle olive, i ritrovamenti nel territorio di Dougga.' MA thesis, Università di Trento.

Laurence, R. (1999). *The Roads of Roman Italy: Mobility and Cultural Change.* London and New York.

Lepelley, C. (1979). *Les Cités de l'Afrique romaine au Bas Empire*, vol. 1. Paris.

Lepelley, C. (1981). *Les Cités de l'Afrique romaine au Bas Empire*, vol. 2. Paris.

Ling, R. (1997). *The insula of the Menander at Pompeii*, vol. 1. Oxford.

Lizzi Testa, R. (2004). *Senatori, popolo, papi: Il governo di Roma al tempo dei Valentiniani.* Bari.

Marlière, E., and Torres Costa, J. (2007). 'Transport et stockage des denrées dans l'Afrique romaine: Le rôle de l'outre et du tonneau', in Mrabet and Remesal Rodríguez (2007), 85–106.

Mastino, A., and Khanoussi, M. (2000). 'Nouvelles découvertes archéologiques et épigraphiques à Uchi Maius (Henchir ed-Douâmis, Tunisie)', *CRAI* 1267–1323.

Mastino, A., and Porcheddu, V. (2006). 'L'*Horologium* offerto al *Pagus Civium Romanorum* ed alla *Civitas* di Numluli', in M. G. Angeli Bertinelli and A. Donati (eds), *Misurare il tempo, misurare lo spazio: Atti del Colloquio AIEGL, Borghesi 2005.* Faenza, 123–62.

Mattingly, D. J. (1988a). 'Olive Cultivation and the Albertini Tablets', in *L'Africa romana* 6: 403–15.

Mattingly, D. J. (1988b). 'Oil for export? A Comparison of Libyan Spanish and Tunisian Olive Oil Production in the Roman Empire', *JRA* 1: 33–56.

Mattingly, D. J. (1988c). 'Olea mediterranea?', *JRA* 1: 152–61.

Mattingly, D. J. (1988d). 'Megalithic Madness and Measurement. Or how Many Olives could an Olive Press Press?', *OJA* 7.2: 177–95.

Maurin, L. (1967). 'Thuburbo Majus et la paix vandale', *CT* 15: 225–54.

Maurin, L. (2000). 'Dédicace d'une statue de Junon reine par Magnius Felix Remnianus', in M. Khanoussi and L. Maurin (eds), *Dougga, fragments d'histoire.* Bordeaux and Tunis, 253–4.

Maurina, B. (2000). 'I contenitori di trasporto e da conserva', in de Vos (2000), 50–7.

Maurina, B. (2004). 'Aïn Wassel: Contenitori di trasporto e da conserva', in de Vos (2004), 111–29.

Maurina, B. (2005). *Aïn Wassel: Un insediamento rurale dell'Africa settentrionale fra l'età romana e l'alto medioevo*, Ph.D. thesis, Università di Siena.

Maurina, B. (2010). 'Anfore tipo Sidi Jdidi 14.9 dal territorio di Dougga (Tunisia)', in S. Menchelli, S. Santoro, M. Pasquinucci, and G. Guiducci (eds), *LRCW 3: Late Roman Coarse Wares, Cooking Wares and Amphorae in the Mediterranean: Archaeology and Archaeometry: Comparison between Western and Eastern Mediterranean* (BAR International Series 2185). Oxford, 525–30.

Maurina, B. (2011). 'Alcune considerazioni sulle ultime produzioni di anfore africane e sull'articolazione dei circuiti commerciali nel Mediterraneo del VII secolo', in Attoui (2011), 105–19.

Maurina, B., and Fermo, P. (2011). 'Studio analitico e multivariato di frammenti anforacei provenienti da Aïn Wassel (Tunisia)', in Attoui (2011), 121–7.

Mees, A. W. (forthcoming). *Vitudurum 10. Die reliefverzierten Terra sigillata—Schüsseln aus dem Keramiklager von Vitudurum.*

Mommsen, T. (1880). 'Decret des Commodus für den saltus Burunitanus', *Hermes* 15: 385–411.

Moritz, L. A. (1958). *Grain Mills and Flour in Classical Antiquity.* Oxford.

Mrabet, A., and Remesal Rodríguez, J. (2007) (eds). *In Africa et in Hispania: études sur l'huile africaine.* Barcelona.

Peacock, D. P. S. (1980). 'The Roman Millstone Trade: A Petrological Sketch', *World Archaeology* 12.1: 43–53.

Pekáry, T. (1968). *Untersuchungen zu den römischen Reichsstraßen.* Bonn.

Peña, J. T. (1998). 'The Mobilization of State Olive Oil in Roman Africa: The Evidence of Late 4th-c. *ostraca* from Carthage', in *Carthage Papers* (JRA Suppl. 28). Portsmouth, RI, 117–238.

Poinssot, C. (1983). *Les Ruines de Dougga.* Tunis.

Poinssot, J. (1885). 'Voyage archéologique en Tunisie exécuté en 1882–1883', *Bulletin trimestriel des antiquités africaines* 3: 103–4.

Poinssot, L. (1911). 'Les Inscriptions de Thugga', *Revue Tunisienne* 18: 169–77.

Poinssot, L. (1920). 'La *civitas Mizigitanorum* et le *Pagus Assalitanus*', *CRAI* 286–7.

Polla, S. (2004–5). *Dai cocci al paesaggio: Ceramica e territorio nella regione di Dougga (Alto Tell tunisino)*, Ph.D. thesis, Università di Siena.

Polla, S. (2006). 'Territorio e ceramica nella regione di Dougga (Alto Tell tunisino)', *Territorio e produzioni ceramiche: Atti del Convegno Internazionale, Pisa 20–22.10.2005* (Instrumenta 2). Pisa, 147–51.

Polla, S. (2011). 'Il paesaggio economico della regione di Dougga (Alto Tell Tunisino): Il dato della ceramica', in Attoui (2011), 91–104.

Potter, T. W. (1987). *Roman Italy*. London.

Purcell, N. (1990). 'The Creation of Provincial Landscape: The Roman Impact on Cisalpine Gaul', in T. Blagg and M. Millett (eds), *The Early Roman Empire in the West*. Oxford, 7–29.

Quilici, L., and Quilici Gigli, S. (2004). *Introduzione alla topografia antica*. Bologna.

Radke, G. (1973). 'Viae publicae Romanae', *RE Supplementum* XIII: 1415–1686.

Reynolds, P. (2010). Hispania *and the Roman Mediterranean*, AD *100–700. Ceramics and Trade*. London.

Ritter, S., and Khanoussi, M., with von Rummel, P. (2004–5). 'The German–Tunisian Project at Dougga: First Results of the Excavations South of the Maison du Trifolium', *Antiquités africaines* 40–41: 43–66.

Salama, P. (1951). *Les voies romaines de l'Afrique du Nord*. Algiers.

Salama, P. (1987). *Bornes milliares d'Afrique Proconsulaire: Un panorama historique du Bas Empire Romain*. Roma.

Salama, P. (2010). *Carte des routes et des cités de l'Est de l'Africa à la fin de l'Antiquité* (Bibliothèque de l'Antiquité Tardive 17), new ed. by J. Desanges, N. Duval, C. Lepelley, and S. Saint-Amans. Turnhout.

Santangelo, F. (2008). 'Le quotidien d'une cité exceptionnelle: Élites et évergétisme dans la Carthage romaine', in C. Berrendoner, M. Cébeillac-Gervasoni, and L. Lamoine (eds), *Le quotidien municipal dans l'Occident romain*. Clermont- Ferrand, 459–71.

Sanz Palomera, G. (2007). 'Nuevos fundamentos sobre la lex Hadriana: La Inscripción de Lella Drebblia', *Gerión* 25.1: 371–90.

Sethom, H., and Kassab, A. (1981). *Les Régions géographiques de la Tunisie* (Université de Tunis, Faculté des Lettres et Sciences Humaines, Deuxième Série: Géographie 13). Tunis.

Shaw, B. D. (1979). 'The Camel in Roman North Africa and the Sahara: History, Biology, and Human Economy', *Bulletin de l'Institut Fondamental d'Afrique Noire* 4, Ser. B, no. 4: 663–721, repr. in B. D. Shaw, *Environment and Society in Roman North Africa* (1995), IV.

Shaw, B. D. (1991). 'The Structure of Local Society in the Early Maghrib: The Elders', *Maghrib Review* 16.1–2: 18–55, repr. in B. D. Shaw, *Environment and Society in Roman North Africa* (1995), III.

Sirks, A. J. B. (1991). *Food for Rome: The Legal Structure of the Transportation and Processing of Supplies for the Imperial Distributions in Rome and Constantinople*. Amsterdam.

Sotgiu, G. (1968). *Iscrizioni latine della Sardegna* II.1. *L'*instrumentum domesticum: *lucerne*. Padova.

Stone, D. L. (2004). 'Problems and Possibilities in Comparative Survey: A North African Perspective', in S. E. Alcock and J. F. Cherry (eds), *Side-by-Side Survey: Comparative Regional Studies in the Mediterranean World*. Oxford, 132–43.

Stone, D. L. (2007). 'Monuments on the Margins: Interpreting the first millennium B.C.E. Rock-Cut Tombs (Haouanet) of North Africa', in D. L. Stone and L. M. Stirling (eds), *Mortuary Landscapes of North Africa*. Toronto, Buffalo, and London, 43–74.

Syme, R. (1982). 'The Marriage of Rubellius Blandus', *AJP* 103: 62–85.

Syme, R. (1986). *The Augustan Aristocracy*. Oxford.

Thomas, R. G., and Wilson, A. I. (1994). 'Water Supply for Roman Farms in Latium and South Etruria', *PBSR* 62: 139–96.

Tran, N. (2008). 'Les cités et le monde du travail urbain en Afrique romaine', in C. Berrendoner, M. Cébeillac-Gervasoni, and L. Lamoine (eds), *Le quotidien municipal dans l'Occident romain*. Clermont-Ferrand, 333–48.

Vismara, C. (2007) (ed.). *Uchi Maius 3. Frantoi, Miscellanea*. Sassari.

Waelkens, M., de Paepe, P., and Moens, L. (1988). 'Patterns of Extraction and Production in the White Marble Quarries of the Mediterranean: History, Present Problems and Prospects', in J. Clayton Fant (ed.), *Ancient Marble Quarrying and Trade* (BAR International Series 453). Oxford, 81–116.

Weßel, H. (2003). *Das Recht der Tablettes Albertini* (Freiburger Rechtsgeschichtliche Abhandlungen, Neue Folge 40). Berlin.

Williams-Thorpe, O. (1988). 'Provenancing and Archaeology of Roman Millstones from the Mediterranean Area', *Journal of Archaeological Science* 15: 253–305.

Williams-Thorpe, O., and Thorpe, R. S. (1989). 'Provenancing and Archaeology of Roman Millstones from Sardinia', *OJA* 8.1: 89–113.

Wilson, A. I. (1999). 'Deliveries *extra urbem*: Aqueducts and the Countryside', *JRA* 12.1: 314–31.

Witcher, R. E. (1998). 'Roman Roads: Phenomenological Perspectives on Roads in the Landscape', in C. Forcey, J. Hawthorne, and R. Witcher (eds), *TRAC 97: Proceedings of the Seventh Annual Theoretical Roman Archaeology Conference, which Formed Part of the Second International Roman Archaeology Conference, University of Nottingham, April 1997*. Oxford, 60–70.

7

Agricultural Production in Egypt

Alan Bowman

INTRODUCTION

Compared to other parts of the Mediterranean world, there is a massive amount of detailed evidence for the agricultural economy of Egypt between *c.*100 BC and AD 350. Our approach to dealing with this in a way that we think is fruitful for our larger context has already been outlined.[1] A move from this to a more detailed analysis presents its own problems of scale and perspective. There is far too much detailed evidence for proper presentation and analysis in the space available here. Even a summary account of modern syntheses would be likely to exceed it, would probably require more than a single monograph, and would not yield a convincing consensus. There is, furthermore, a real methodological difficulty in extrapolating from a series of microcosmic scenarios to a general synthesis or a model that is plausible, an observation that can be exemplified in recent scholarship.[2] The more generalized the calculations or models become, the less contact they seem to have with any reality, as the number of assumptions or speculations increases to fill the gaps in the evidence. On the other hand, the reader may well feel frustrated at being offered a series of methodologies and recommendations as to how the material might be analysed without finding that any of them have actually been implemented. Our aim here is, or should be, to attempt to maintain some contact with the reality of the surviving bodies of evidence, as the building blocks of our economic analysis. The present attempt therefore inevitably has to steer a course between Scylla and Charybdis and aims to offer some plausible speculations within reasonable parameters, along with a number of

---

[1] Bowman (2009); Bagnall (2009). I am grateful to Dominic Rathbone for his comments on an earlier draft of this chapter.

[2] For examples in the form of models that can accommodate a number of not wholly consistent datasets, or are based on arbitrary premises, or are capable of explaining any evidence at all, or are not tested against data, see Bagnall (2002a: 115; 2007: 641).

more detailed, illustrative scenarios (in which it is important not to conflate or confuse 'validity' and 'typicality').[3]

A further constraint on what can be done here is imposed by our having adopted an approach to quantifying the documentary evidence for the Egyptian economy that is essentially cumulative. Understanding population and settlement patterns, as far as is possible, is an essential prerequisite for analysing the agrarian regime in a quantified manner, and we have attempted that in an earlier volume.[4] But there are still many major issues on which certainty and consensus have not been achieved. Despite that, quantifiable data for various aspects of agricultural activity can now usefully be assembled and analysed. A fuller understanding of the economics of Egyptian agriculture can be obtained only in the context of governmental fiscal mechanisms and institutions (for example, taxation and coinage), the operation of transport networks, trade, markets, and so on, and this remains to be done.[5] Nevertheless, if we build on what we analysed in looking at land and settlement, it is possible to approach a quantified analysis of agricultural activity in Egypt by considering detailed evidence for some key systemic features of the agrarian sector and for a series of individual, smaller scenarios, which offer plenty of quantifiable data. All these elements are capable of expansion into longer individual studies (which some have already received), and there is room and evidence for still more.[6] A central and recurring question will, of course, be how far these smaller scenarios will help us to understand general trends in the bigger picture. The problem in using these as evidence for the macroeconomic picture over time lies, as ever, in reconciling data that are diverse and specific to different regions, periods, and units of production and represent different facets of the agrarian economy or activities in it. The judgement as to which bodies of data may plausibly be generalized from one scenario is bound to be to some extent intuitive and subjective, but it is inevitable and (it is hoped) transparent.

The basics are undisputed. Egypt was exceptionally productive and yielded significant surpluses throughout the period we are considering.[7] At no time in the Ptolemaic or Roman periods, as far as we can see, did overall internal demand come close to matching or exceeding supply, however we analyse the possible fluctuations of population and any theoretical Malthusian constraints

---

[3] The metrics on which these calculations are based are set out in the Appendix to this chapter.

[4] Bowman (2011).

[5] This will be the subject of Bowman (forthcoming).

[6] For a recent survey, see Bagnall (2005), and, for a new database for the Fayum, Winkler (2008) <http://www.agre.uni-tuebingen.de> (accessed 12 Aug. 2009).

[7] For recent summaries, see Rathbone (2006, 2007); and cf. Rathbone (1989).

(even if some areas suffered significant downturns in productivity).[8] There was significant expansion of the agricultural economy from the early Ptolemaic period onwards, at least into the middle of the second century AD; the effects of and recovery from the Antonine plague are still in debate, with some claiming that there is no useful proxy evidence at all—and closer study of the evidence from the Mendesian Nome in the Delta might suggest that depopulation had begun to set in *before* the plague struck.[9] In the sixth century Egypt was still sending large quantities of tax in kind to Constantinople (though in the fourth century the latter required very much less for a smaller population than Rome had needed in the earlier empire).[10] The detailed documentary evidence, and some potentially useable archaeological evidence, for the agricultural economy is not evenly spread in time and space. There are also serious doubts about some of the major features we need to know about (for example, population size and fluctuation), macro-estimates of which might be generally accepted (or not).

It will be obvious that any attempt to provide a balanced picture of the agricultural economy needs to take account of quantifiable evidence for production and consumption. Given the amount of quantifiable documentary evidence offered by the papyri, it is hardly possible to do that in the space available here. This chapter therefore considers only one side of the supply-and-demand chain in detail, offering some analysis of the shape of agricultural production (mainly arable) in Egypt with attention to diachronic changes and the relationship between metropoleis and villages in the larger contexts of their administrative districts (nomes). Full discussion of the demand side would require at least as much space again and is therefore postponed for future study, the possible direction of which is indicated briefly at the end of the chapter.

---

[8] By 'internal demand' I mean the needs of the population of the kingdom/province and of the administrative and military personnel who managed it, and the phrase 'at no time' should, of course, be understood as referring to averages smoothed over the period: the variability of the flood levels did create shortages in particular years (see Bonneau 1964). For decline in the Fayum villages, see Bowman (2011) and below. It should be noted that, even if the whole of the productive land in the Fayum were lost after *c.* AD 300, that would still account for only about 5% of the total area under cultivation in Egypt, though we should allow for the probability that levels of yield and production were more intensive than elsewhere. The demands of managing the irrigation system in the Fayum presumably meant that land could more easily become unproductive than elsewhere. An overall decline in population levels from the late third through to the fifth century and beyond is certainly not to be assumed, perhaps the reverse (or at least steady state); see Bowman (2011). Rathbone (1990: 137) summarizes the evidence for severe depopulation in the late second century in the Delta (see also Blouin 2005), but that does not preclude the possibility of some recovery in the course of the next 100 years or so.

[9] Rathbone (1990: 118); Greenberg (2003).

[10] Rathbone (1989); Bowman (2011).

THE NOMES

In the Ptolemaic and Roman periods the number of nomes fluctuated between thirty and forty (Fig. 7.1). There is nothing like a complete picture for any one region, but there is good, detailed evidence for several features of individual nomes, principally the Arsinoite (Fayum), the Oxyrhynchite, and the Hermopolite in Middle Egypt and the Mendesian Nome in the Delta. Estimates of the sizes of these and other nomes in Middle and Upper Egypt may be seen in

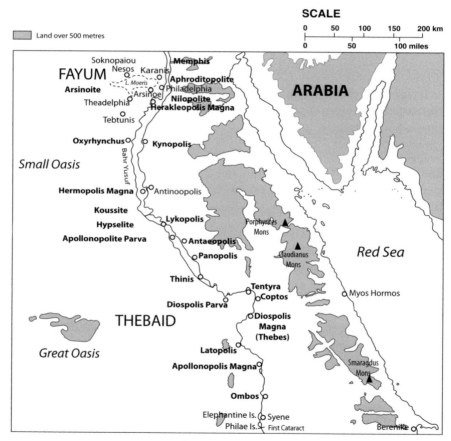

Fig. 7.1 The Nomes of Middle Egypt

Note: The precise locations of nome boundaries are uncertain. The individual nomes are indicated either by the name of the capital (metropolis) where known, or by the name of the nome. Both forms of toponym are in boldface. This version follows the information recorded on the maps in the Barrington Atlas, except that it omits another 'Aphroditopolite Nome' marked in Barrington on the West Bank between Panopolis and Antaeopolis. The names of the main Fayum villages, discussed below, are also marked. (A. Kotarba-Morley)

Table 7.1 (for the Delta there are at present no useful data except perhaps for the Mendesian Nome[11]). For several of these nomes the numbers and relative sizes of the towns and villages can be deduced, albeit somewhat hypothetically, and we have already made the case for considerable population growth from the Ptolemaic period into the 'high' empire (mid-second century, before the onset of the Antonine plague).[12]

Villages were certainly numerous in all nomes for which we have sufficient information,[13] and for the **Oxyrhynchite Nome** we can hypothesize a schematic distribution of amounts of territory attached to villages based on tax registers, which has no implication as to the status of ownership of the land in that territory (see Table 7.3).

The distribution is based on the estimate of 203,861 arouras of grain land (Table 7.1), which in turn is very close to the precisely attested figure (202,534 arouras) for the amount of grain land under cultivation in (probably) the first half of the fourth century.[14] This has also to be used as a basis for estimated calculations of the distribution of land in the neighbouring Hermopolite Nome, where similar conditions may be presumed.[15] The more detailed evidence for landholding in the Oxyrhynchite, which has been subjected to exhaustive analysis, reveals much about the nature and the mechanisms of landownership and tenancy (of both public and private land) and the ways in which these patterns changed over time, as the quantities of royal and public land diminished with the Roman annexation and were further reduced, effectively to zero, over the course of the Roman period.[16] Evidence is unfortunately lacking for the Ptolemaic period, but it has been estimated that around two-thirds or more of the land in these areas might have been in private ownership in the Early Roman period.[17] Both public and private landholdings were predominantly exploited through tenancy, which by and large guaranteed a better return to the owner. Private leases for relatively short terms and multiple, small parcels of land are evident throughout the period, even in the cases of wealthy landowners such as Claudia Isidora and Calpurnia Heraklia, whose families clearly actively acquired and disposed of land over

---

[11] See Rathbone (1990: 134–7); Blouin (2010; Chapter 8, this volume).

[12] This is the level at which Bagnall (2009) suggests we can find the best opportunity to extrapolate a useful model. I have here used some of the data to which he refers, and some other material, though space does not permit exhaustive analysis. There is scope for much further work.

[13] Bowman (2011: 333–40).

[14] Bagnall and Worp (1980).

[15] See Bagnall (1992).

[16] Rowlandson (1996, 2006).

[17] Rowlandson (1996: 63–9), but with considerable variation from region to region and even within regions. The proportion of public land is generally thought to be higher in the Fayum. What follows is essentially a summary of her main conclusions. For a different perspective, which cannot be discussed in detail here, see Monson (2008).

Table 7.1. Estimates of land use in nomes of Middle Egypt

Nome	A Surface area (ha)	B[*] Inhabited/cultivated area = 90% of A (ha)	=ar.	C[†] Grain land in = 80% of B (ha)	=ar.	D[‡] Garden and vineyard = 12% of B (ha)	=ar.	E[§] Other = 8% of B (ha)	=ar.
Ombite	7,200	6,480	23,563	5,184	18,850	777	2,827	518	1,885
Apollonopolite	13,700	12,330	44,757	9,863	35,806	1,479	5,380	986	3,586
Latopolite	22,500	20,250	73,507	16,199	58,806	4,920	17,893	1,620	5,890
Diospolite	28,400	25,560	92,782	28,448	74,226	3,067	11,153	2,044	7,435
Koptite	33,100	29,790	108,137	23,832	86,510	3,574	12,999	2,383	8,666
Tentyrite	30,000	27,000	98,010	21,600	78,408	3,240	11,781	2,160	7,854
Diospolite Parva	30,600	27,540	99,970	22,032	79,976	3,304	12,017	2,203	8,011
Thinite	61,300	55,170	200,267	44,136	160,214	6,620	24,074	4,413	16,049
Panopolite	57,500	51,750	187,852	41,400	150,282	6,210	22,581	4,140	15,054
Antaiopolite	53,100	47,790	173,477	38,232	138,782	5,734	20,853	3,823	13,902
Hypselite	12,500	11,250	40,837	9,000	32,670	1,350	4,909	900	3,272
Apollonopolite Parva	20,600	18,540	67,300	14,832	53,840	2,224	8,090	2,749	9,999
Lykopolite	25,000	22,500	81,675	18,000	65,340	3,000	10,909	1,800	6,545
Koussite	27,200	24,480	88,862	19,583	71,090	3,264	11,869	1,958	7,121
Hermopolite	114,000	102,600	372,438	82,080	297,950	12,312	44,770	8,208	29,847
Kynopolite	11,000	9,900	35,937	7,920	28,750	1,188	4,320	792	7,880
Oxyrhynchite	78,000	70,200	254,826	56,160	203,861	8,424	30,632	5,616	20,421
Herakleopolite	64,300	57,870	210,068	48,706	168,054	6,944	25,252	4,629	16,834
Arsinoite	150,000	135,000	490,909	108,000	392,707	16,200	58,909	10,800	39,272
Nilopolite	13,300	11,970	43,511	9,575	34,809	1,436	5,223	957	3,482
Aphroditopolite	20,000	18,000	65,340	14,400	52,272	2,160	7,854	1,440	5,236
Memphite	28,100	25,290	91,802	20,232	73,442	3,034	11,035	2,023	7,357

Note: ar. = arouras; ha = hectares.

[*] Column B: this calculation is very much a compromising though not arbitrary approximation, representing roughly 28,000 of 32,000 km². It is within the range of the recent macro-estimates, for a summary of which see Bowman (2011: table 11.1). The sites of the towns and villages will constitute a small percentage of the inhabited area and are envisaged as subsumed in E ('Other'). 'Cultivated area' should be taken to indicate the extent of cultivation rather than the area actually sown in any particular year or season. The model as a whole relies heavily on extrapolation from the Oxyrhynchite evidence (Bagnall and Worp 1980), which alone gives us a firm figure for the amount of grain land in the fourth century (202,534 arouras, comparing with my approximation of 203,861 arouras).

[†] Column C: the areas available for grain or other high-value crops, rather than the areas actually sown with cereals or rotated.

[‡] Column D: this figure is somewhat arbitrary but at the upper end of the range of 8–12% that is attested (see below, pp. 238–9).

[§] Column E: This figure is simply the remainder and will include, for example, town and village sites, temples, necropoleis, military sites, grazing land, and land used for other economically productive activities.

Sources: Surface areas (Column A): Butzer (1976); basis for calculating land under cultivation after Bagnall (1993).

centuries.[18] As for public land, a distinction must be made between the *katoikoi*, descendants of privileged military allotment-holders of the Ptolemaic period, who were effectively transformed into a class of private landowners, with alienation of land effected in technical terms of cession rather than sale, and the tenants of public land (called *demosioi georgoi* in the Arsinoite Nome), who are on the whole smaller fry.[19] Over the period, the evidence shows enhancement of the status of the private landowner and diminution of that of the tenant, and this is further intensified in the Later Roman period, as public land is transferred (by various mechanisms including imperial initiative to sell, absorption of smallholdings by the wealthy, and reclassification) into private ownership—the term being retained in the fourth century only to designate a higher rate of taxation.[20] Finally, two points to emphasize. First, that there is no sign of the leases specifying an increase in rents in kind in the later third century (when the currency is supposed to have collapsed) and second that, as we move into the fourth century, when private ownership is virtually universal, the lease is replaced by the rent-roll, as a symptom of the 'fiscalization' of estates.[21]

In the neighbouring **Hermopolite Nome** at the same period we are able to calculate the distribution of land among urban landowners resident in Hermopolis and Antinoopolis on the west bank (although the picture is skewed by the absence of the register of landholdings in the district closest to the metropolis) and to move from that to a speculative comparative estimate for the distribution of land among village landholders, which shows a lesser degree of inequality than among their urban counterparts. (In this respect there are interesting comparisons to be made with the fourth-century census records from Asia Minor analysed by Thonemann).[22] Once again the number of small to medium-sized holdings is striking, as are the fragmentation of the landholdings and the continuation of traditional patterns of leasing by large owners. Of particular value is the fact that the two contemporary Hermopolite registers allow us to quantify the amount of land changing hands, presumably by sale, which indicates a market that was still active and open. A synopsis of the key points of Bagnall's speculative model[23] for the Hermopolite Nome as a whole is as follows:

---

[18] For Calpurnia Heraklia, see Table 7.2.

[19] It is, however, important not to see them simply as subsistence-level peasants, and many landholders held amounts of both public and private land; see the analysis of landholdings at Krokodilopolis (below). and Rowlandson (1996: 93–6).

[20] Bowman (1985); Rowlandson (1996: 101); Schubert (2007).

[21] Rowlandson (1996: 276–8).

[22] Bowman (1985); Bagnall (1992); Thonemann (2007).

[23] Bagnall (1992: 137–9). Cf. my estimate (Table 7.1) of 297,950 arouras of grain land, essentially identical. His figure for village residents is a rounded 180,000 arouras.

- Total area: 1,140 km^2 = 413,820 arouras.
- Grain land: 298,000 arouras (reduced by 10 per cent, which was detached in the fourth century to form the Antinoopolite Nome) = 270,000 arouras,[24] of which:
- 95,000 arouras are owned by urban residents, 175,000 by village residents.
- A model population consists of 7,400 rural landholders with an average of 24.3 arouras each and 1,208 urban landholders, broken down as 952 Hermopolites with an average of 89.3 arouras and 256 Antinoites with an average of 39.0 arouras each. Men own 86 per cent and women 14 per cent of the total land.[25]

Evidence for conditions of this type in the other nomes of Middle Egypt is much more sporadic and for Upper Egypt virtually non-existent.[26] Bagnall's speculative attempt to quantify the holdings of vineland in the **Panopolite Nome** is broadly within the parameters of what can be deduced elsewhere.[27] More informative and from the mid-first century AD is a detailed though incomplete register of 163 holders of various categories of land, royal (*basi-like*), private (*idiotike*), and sacred ('¾ artab land'), around the village of Krokodilopolis in the **Pathyrite Nome**, close to Thebes, which is important simply because there is so little evidence of this kind for this area.[28] The equality of distribution within this category is more or less what one might expect in a village context, but it is striking that only 10 per cent of the 124 holders of royal land possessed more than 20 arouras (the largest being 46 arouras), whereas 45 per cent of the owners of private land have more than 20 arouras (the largest being 127 arouras). Thirty-five per cent of the holders of sacred land have more than 20 arouras (the largest 80+ arouras), which may reflect the traditional strength of the temples in landholding in this region.

In the **Arsinoite** (Fayum), conditions appear to have been rather different (as they surely were, in other ways, in the Delta too[29]). Unlike the other areas discussed, the Arsinoite is exceptionally well represented in our Ptolemaic evidence and several individual villages are also very well attested in the

---

[24] As an approximation, this figure is derived as: cultivated/inhabited land = 90% of total area, grain land = 80% of cultivated land/inhabited land, minus 10% for Antinoopolite (Bagnall 1992: 137).

[25] See the model of Tacoma (2006: 92–114) and cf. Bagnall (2007).

[26] There is important evidence for the Apollonopolite Nome in the late Ptolemaic period in a papyrus analysed in the unpublished thesis of Christensen (2002), showing a high proportion of privately owned land.

[27] Bagnall (2002b).

[28] *P.Lond.* III 604A (pp. 71 ff.), with discussion by Sharp (1998: 37), augmented by my own calculations. See also Monson (2008).

[29] There is no good evidence for the Delta except in the case of the Mendesian Nome (second century AD), discussed by Rathbone (1990), Rowlandson (2006), and Blouin (2005, 2007, 2008, 2010, and Chapter 8, this volume).

Roman period and down to the fourth century AD (see below).[30] The overall picture has to be understood in the context of consistent expansion and intensification of the agrarian economy and heavy settlement by the Greek immigrant population both in the metropolis (Krokodilopolis, later named Ptolemais Euergetis) and the villages. The latter have traditionally been regarded as large by Egyptian standards, but it is no longer so clear that this was true except in a very few cases. It is likely that the proportion of public land in various categories was greater in the Arsinoite than in other nomes, perhaps approaching 50 per cent.[31] Here, as elsewhere, there is some evidence for increasing concentration of landownership in private hands in the third century, particularly those of the descendants of veteran settlers of the Roman period.[32] As has already been noted, decline in some of the Fayum villages from the early fourth century is starkly evident, and it may be that the high proportion of public land contributed to this by failing to attract private investment as the government withdrew from direct ownership and leasing of land to public or royal tenants. Another important factor will have been the need to maintain the artificial irrigation system, which must have been a greater burden than in those areas that were directly inundated. In its heyday in the Roman period, the Arsinoite was vastly productive, as is suggested by the quantity of tax in kind assessed on one of the three divisions of the Arsinoite, 814,862 artabas for the year AD 184/5, when (it may be supposed) the effects of the Antonine plague have still to be taken into account.[33]

How can we use use such a figure?[34] There are various ways in which we can extrapolate from this evidence as an exercise in estimating orders of magnitude, none of them completely robust and all with some degree of approximation, but it is perhaps not too misleading to offer a simple calculation of its implications on the understanding that it might represent an expectation in 'normal times'.[35]

---

[30] For a gazetteer of Fayum villages, see <http://www.trismegistos.org/fayum> (accessed 12 Aug. 2009).

[31] Bagnall (1979/82 = 2003; 1992).

[32] Schubert (2007).

[33] *P.Oxy.* LXVI. 4527; see Schubert (2007: 149). Not that they are obvious: on the relationship of the figures to the effects of the plague, see Bagnall (2000); Van Minnen (2001).

[34] Against Bagnall's minimizing view of the effects of the plague, Van Minnen argues for a restoration of line 15 of the text, which would show that the amount actually collected up to the end of the year was only 223,581 artabas and therefore the area was in deep economic trouble. Self-evidently, the restoration (which suits the lacuna) cannot be verified or falsified, and we can make use of this evidence only by treating the larger figure as representing the official assessment and expectation, regardless of its realization. If the gap between the two were as striking as Van Minnen's argument implies, the government would have had plenty of time to adjust the assessment to a realistic level based on the amount of land still in production.

[35] This is the method I have used for the calculations on the Oxyrhynchite and the Fayum villages (below), applying the figures explained in the Appendix. They are evidently fairly crude, and there must be margins of error. If they can have no claim to accuracy, it is my intention that

The Herakleides division, which includes the metropolis, represents about 40 per cent of the population in the Arsinoite Nome (which may, but need not, imply 40 per cent of the cultivated land).[36]

Average tax rates across the various categories of land in wheat equivalent are 4.6 artabas/aroura.[37]

The amount of grain land represented by the tax assessment is approximately 177,143 arouras (814,862/4.6), c.45 per cent of the total estimated Arsinoite grain land (Table 7.1).

Total tax on grain land for the whole Arsinoite Nome is 1,806,452 artabas (392,707 arouras × 4.6).

Total grain yield is 4,712,484 artabas (392,707 arouras × 12).

Deduct 4.6 artabas/aroura for tax + 1 artaba/aroura for seed (2,199,159 artabas).

Remainder: 2,513,325 artabas, which would provide the basic wheat requirement for 76,161 families of 5.0—that is, close to 0.38 million people—at 33 artabas per family (wheat constituting 70 per cent of total caloric intake); on a total inhabited area of 1,350 km², this yields a population density of 282/km².

It should be obvious that this is merely an exercise in probabilistic estimation but not, I suggest, totally without value. The figures can be adjusted within plausible parameters and will then naturally afford different results. Of the quantified assumptions in the calculation, the most fragile or improbable will probably be the figures for population and density (particularly the latter),[38] but a main impact of the calculation is the demonstration that under 'normal' conditions the government might expect a level of grain production that could support close to 0.4 million people after taxes and seedcorn were deducted.[39] If this probably exceeds the likely actual population even at its height (which was

they should be transparent enough to make it clear what the consequences would be of adjusting any of the basic metrics (e.g. population size, yield, or tax rate).

[36] For population in the Ptolemaic period, see Clarysse and Thompson (2006: 102–13 and n. 111; table 4.7) showing 43% of attested Arsinoite villages in Herakleides; for a schematic map, see <www.trismegistos.org/fayum> (accessed 12 Aug. 2009). I assume that the proportion was maintained through population growth into the Roman period, when the population of the metropolis was perhaps 40,000+ (Bowman 2011). Note that the distribution of vineland between the 3 *merides* in the Roman period shows 50% in Herakleides (Ruffing 1999: 438).

[37] For the tax rates, see Bagnall (1979/82 = 2003) and below (pp. 240–2) on Karanis. It is generally agreed that the proportion of public land (and hence the tax yield) was higher in the Fayum than elsewhere, see above, n. 17.

[38] The figure is within the parameters of 200–300 proposed by Scheidel, but estimates for regions vary widely from over 400 to under 100; see the summary by Monson (2008).

[39] It is important to emphasize that the grain tax was not the only form in which taxes were raised, so this constitutes only a part of the state's revenue from this area. This subject will be analysed in more detail in Bowman (forthcoming).

presumably **not** the situation in AD 184/5) by some margin, it will thus be affording a significant 'surplus' (before deduction of transaction costs and so on). Whether such a level of production could be sustained with a lower population as a result of the impact of the plague is, of course, a different matter, and such evidence as there is certainly suggests that the population decline in the second century entailed an increase in unproductive land in the Mendesian Nome and presumably elsewhere too.[40] The corollary of this will be that, if the figure for AD 184/5 is a real one, the corresponding figure and its extrapolation thirty years earlier will be even larger.

Discussion of the actual cash value of this Arsinoite surplus may be postponed for the time being. On the one hand, it will, of course, be reduced by the need to take into account labour and transaction costs. On the other, the grain is only a part of the (in principle) quantifiable surplus: the food-stuffs that constitute the other 30 per cent of the human diet and caloric intake may also have yielded significant surpluses. This was certainly the case with wine, according to a recent calculation that predicts an annual production of around 0.25 million hectolitres per annum in the Ptolemaic period, a figure that is likely to have increased significantly in the Roman period as wine gained in popularity against the traditional Egyptian beer.[41] This will have produced a significant cash return, as was surely the case in the third-century AD Appianus estate.[42] Detailed evidence for individual communities, which is further considered below, is consistent with the general inference that in the Arsinoite (as elsewhere) the proportion of land under arable cultivation was between 70 per cent and 80 per cent and certainly not normally less than about 70 per cent. This is the picture that emerges from a text of the later third century BC giving us the crop schedule for an area of 180,000 arouras: 74.6 per cent wheat, 14.5 per cent barley, the remainder fodder and legumes.[43]

---

[40] Rathbone (1990).

[41] Vandorpe and Clarysse (1997), and, for more detail below, Rathbone (1991: 247); cf. Ruffing (1999). The rate of yield in both calculations is 25 hectolitres/ha, which means that the annual production requires 10,000 ha under cultivation. This can be accommodated within the estimate in Table 7.1 of 16,200 ha of garden land and vineyard and is consistent with the ratio of 2:1 for vineyard and garden land at Theadelphia suggested by Sharp (1998: 61). For comparative orders of magnitude note the estimate of 1.5 million hectolitres p.a., the produce of over 50,000 ha, for the city of Rome in the first century AD, see Tchernia (1986: 21–7).

[42] Rathbone (1991) and, for comparison with the Byzantine period, Banaji (2002: 18–19). Ruffing (1999: 405) offers a calculation of the profits in Arsinoite wine production for the first three centuries AD.

[43] *P. Petrie* III .75, 235 BC, cf. *P. Lille* I. 30–33 (Ghoran): cereals 75%, the remainder almost all *arakos*, a fodder crop. It is, of course, necessary to allow for local specialization of the kind identified by Crawford (1973).

THE METROPOLEIS

As regards the **nome capitals or metropoleis**, we naturally have less detail about the fundamental operations of the agricultural economy and we again rely on information from a very few (and the same) places: Oxyrhynchus, Hermopolis, Arsinoe (Ptolemais Euergetis), and a limited amount from Panopolis. We are mainly confined to evidence for urban landownership and for consumption of agricultural products, but this should not mislead us into clichés that emphasize the dominance of absentee urban landlords or the character of urban centres as parasitic and simply draining the wealth from the agrarian sector. The relationships are more complex and reciprocal. On the one hand, the urban centres supply a great deal of the technological and commercial infrastructure, which enables the agricultural product to be turned into tangible wealth. In addition, some significant proportion of the urban population is directly involved in the agricultural economy, sometimes as tenants, sometimes directly involved in the details of estate management, as is evident from many personal letters.[44] On the other, a significant number of the larger villages are socially stratified and provide facilities and administrative services characteristic of complex population centres.[45]

The patterns and configuration of landownership and land exploitation have been exhaustively dealt with from various points of view in recent publications, and much of the detail need not be repeated here.[46] The metropoleis naturally contained a concentration of wealthier landowners, and this must have intensified as the amount of land in private ownership increased, as the metropoleis grew in size and effectively became (under Roman rule) more status-based and stratified, with the emergence of a 'Hellenic' local elite. The exact relationship between the owners and the metropoleis is somewhat complicated (as it also is in the case of some of the Fayum villages) by the ownership of land by Alexandrians:[47] these may be either Alexandrians by *origo* who have acquired land in the *chora*, or metropolites by *origo* who have acquired Alexandrian citizenship, which was an integral part of upward mobility in Roman Egypt. The extensive fourth-century Hermopolite landlists also register landowners resident in Antinoopolis whose holdings lie in the Hermopolite Nome but unfortunately do not include landholdings in the district closest to Hermopolis itself.[48] Though there are some distinctions between these groups, from the present perspective it is clear

---

[44] Some evidence cited by Rowlandson (1996: 265) and Parsons (2007: chs 6 and 7).
[45] See Rowlandson (2007).
[46] Bowman (1985); Rathbone (1991); Rowlandson (1996); Bagnall (1992, 2002a, 2002b, 2007); Tacoma (2006: esp. 76–113).
[47] Cf. Tacoma (2006: 95).
[48] Bowman (1985).

that, as one would expect, wealthy landowners are concentrated in the urban centres and that the inequality of distribution within the urban landholding population is very great and likely to be increasing in the later Roman period.[49] Data from the earlier periods and from the later Roman period suggest that the degree of inequality of distribution was much less marked in the village landowning community.[50]

From the perspective of quantification and strategies of production, the fourth-century evidence from Hermopolis seems to support two relevant and related conclusions. First, that, although the concentration of land in the hands of fewer wealthier owners is evident, as it is elsewhere,[51] it is difficult to discern any movement towards geographical concentration and consolidation of 'large estates'—wealthy owners tended to own multiple plots in diverse locations. Second, that there is still a significant amount of market movement of land at this period by sale.[52] Other evidence indicates that, although there are significant changes in the modes of documentation, tenancy still remained the dominant feature of the exploitation of land.[53] Whether this concentration of landownership led to greater productivity (in terms of reduction of overheads, if not increased yields) is an interesting question that deserves further investigation.

The structural role of the urban communities in the agrarian economy is clearly a complex one. A very great deal of the business, commercial, and artisanal activity located in the metropoleis was integrally connected to the agrarian sector in one way or another. Despite the fact that many of the large villages had administrative institutions and offices, the metropoleis were the main centres of administration, documentation, and management for the land, as the large volume of relevant papyrological material found in or deriving from the major towns shows. This was true not only for the governmental administrative institutions but also for private estate management. The scattered *phrontides* of the Appianus estate in the Arsinoite Nome each had a manager (*phrontistes*), but the headquarters of the whole operation was in the nome capital Arsinoe, where the senior administrators presumably lived.[54]

---

[49] Tacoma (2006: 94) concludes that the majority of urban inhabitants in Hermopolis did not own land.

[50] Bagnall (1992).

[51] Cf. Schubert (2007), on Philadelphia.

[52] Bowman (1985).

[53] Rowlandson (1996).

[54] Rathbone (1991: 24–5). In this case, much of the production was achieved by wage labour, but there is no reason to assume a different pattern for large fragmented estates, which were mainly tenanted.

It has been estimated that, in Hermopolis, between 10 per cent and 15 per cent of the residents could feed themselves from the produce of their land,[55] leaving (presumably) a large number of urban residents for whom land was not their only or main source of livelihood and who needed to purchase much or all of what they consumed. Although the total of such landholdings was not inconsiderable and the average holdings in Bagnall's model (above) were certainly many times more than subsistence level,[56] there were a very few whose land yielded an extremely handsome surplus and remained in their family's possession for many generations. Examples from all three areas here under discussion are easy to identify but present diverse obstacles to precise quantification: Claudia Isidora, the Ti. Julii Theones, Calpurnia Heraklia (Oxyrhynchus);[57] Hyperechios, Aurelia Charite (Hermopolis);[58] the Appianus estate (Arsinoite).[59] It is again worth emphasizing, however, that such holdings of individual landlords were typically widely spread and often comprised land in different categories in the earlier periods when terminological distinctions between the categories were substantive. In almost all cases we cannot be sure that the data we have for individual landowners are complete, but the orders of magnitude revealed nevertheless have illustrative value. I cite examples of larger landowners (three from the above list) that cannot be generalized but, on the other hand, are not likely to be wholly exceptional either:

1. A declaration of only part of the property of Calpurnia Heraklia in AD 245/6 shows land in five separate villages in the eastern part of the Oxyrhynchite Nome totalling around 1,683 arouras and comprised of individual parcels ranging in size from a few arouras to several hundred (Table 7.2). All of the land is leased out, and the pattern of acquisition by purchase is particularly notable: the earliest is in the reign of Tiberius, then there is a gap before further increases under Commodus, the Severi, and Gordian III.[60]

2. The will of the Oxyrhynchite *bouleutes* Aurelius Hermogenes-Eudaemon, dated AD 276, bequeaths grain land in six villages of the nome, vineyards in three villages, a house with appurtenances, and slaves in the metropolis.[61]

3. About a century later, the two more or less contemporary Hermopolite landlists show property belonging to Aurelia Charite in four or five

---

[55] Sharp (1998: 45).
[56] As is also true for village landholders.
[57] All discussed by Rowlandson (1996: see index *svv*).
[58] Lewuillon-Blume (1988); Harrauer (2008: *P. Charite*).
[59] Rathbone (1991).
[60] *P. Oxy.* XLII.3047–8.
[61] *P. Oxy.* VI.907; cf. Tacoma (2006: 69–70).

Table 7.2. The assets of Calpurnia Heraklia

Village	Land area* (ar.)	Land value[†] (tal.)	Grain stock (art.)	Grain value (1)[‡] (dr.)	Grain value (2)[‡] dr.)
Thmoenacom	219				
(...)					
Thmoenopsobthis	909		460	7,360	11,040
Schoebis	256				
Osoronnophrios	69				
Tychinnecotis	230				
Suis			3,020	48,320	72,552
Dositheou			245	3,920	5,880
Iseum Tryphonis			220	3,520	5,280
Lile			280	4,480	6,160
Satyrou[§]			820 (533)	13,120 (8,528)	19,680 (12,792)
Total	1,683	28.5	5,045	80,720 (72,192)	120,592 (113,704)

Note: ar. = arouras; art. = artabas; dr. = drachmas; tal. = talents (1 talent = 6,000 dr.).

* Much of the declared land was uninundated, presumably because of a poor flood or a series thereof. This should not affect the capital value of the land over time, and one would assume that a wealthy landholder would not normally need to sell land when prices were depressed.

[†] The figure calculated for the capital value of the land is purely theoretical. It assumes that 1 aroura of saleable grain land at this period was worth around 1,000 drachmas (see Rowlandson 1996: 320–1, table 11). But prices vary considerably according to location and quality. Not all of the land declared was private and straightforwardly saleable, but the value is assessed as if it were.

[‡] The 'normal' value (value (1)) of 16 drachmas per artaba is derived from the figures given by the editor of *P.Oxy.* XLII. 3047–8 and Rathbone (1997: 193–4) for the mid-third century. The compulsory purchase price of 24 drachmas per artaba (value (2)) is very high and clearly indicates severe shortage. The amounts of grain stocks available for purchase need to be reduced by unquantified deductions for rations of employees and wage labourers on the estates.

[§] For Satyrou, the figures in parentheses account for the amount of 287 artabas already pledged to individuals in the city.

Sources: *P.Oxy.* XLII. 3047–8, AD 245/6; Rathbone (1997).

separate districts (*pagi*) as 61 and 60¾ arouras of 'public' land and 193 and 314 arouras of 'private' land. We do not know which of the lists is the earlier, but it is evident that there was significant movement of her 'private' holdings by purchase or sale. An archive of her documents contains leases of parts of her holdings (the sizes of the parcels leased are unfortunately not preserved).[62]

4. The Hermopolite lists also show the diverse holdings of the family of the descendants of Hyperechios, amounting to at least *c.*4,000 arouras, more probably a minimum of 5,509 and possibly as much as 6,760.[63] As may be seen from Table 7.3, this is well in excess of the estimated total land in the territory of most villages in the Oxyrhynchite Nome.

[62] Lewuillon-Blume (1988: *P. Charite*).
[63] Bowman (1985: 144 n. 45); Lewuillon-Blume (1988); Harrauer (2008).

THE VILLAGES

It is both legitimate and revealing to extend some of these methods and calculations to the **village communities,** where the patterns of distribution of landownership among individuals are different and somewhat less un-equal.[64] But the evidence for the relative size of villages and their territories in the Oxyrhynchite based on tax assessments (Table 7.3) again shows a marked inequality in territorial size, with few large and many small villages with no implication here as to who actually owned the land in these territor-ies—in many cases presumably urban residents such as Calpurnia Heraklia.

In the present context, which will not permit exhaustive analysis, there is much to be gained from a handful of case studies that throw light on different aspects of the agricultural economy in a quantitative perspective. It needs to be borne in mind, however, that almost all this evidence comes from villages in the Fayum, which have been analysed in detail in some excellent recent studies and cannot simply be mapped onto other regions. Nevertheless, such spots of evidence as we do have from elsewhere suggest that the agricultural regime in villages of Middle, Upper Egypt, and the Delta was not totally different in kind. The presentation follows a more or less chronological order as far as evidence permits.

I offer first of all a table (Table 7.4) with some orders of magnitude for population, site size, and land at various periods. Many of these are quite sizeable villages with some administrative facilities of their own. Idiosyncrasies, which are probably attributable to unreliable evidence and should therefore be set aside, include some *huge* figures (for example, for the population of Narmouthis and the territory of Bacchias). A general picture emerges of significant growth from the first two centuries of Ptolemaic rule to the mid-second century AD, and significant decline in the period after AD 300.[65] Some of the villages listed in the table provide illustrative or diagnostic evidence for particular features of the agricultural regime, which can be analysed in more detail.

Although the agricultural regime in the Ptolemaic period certainly differed in important respects, it is nevertheless worth a prefatory look at some quantifiable evidence for that period, for comparative purposes. **Kerkeosiris** appears to have been in a less than wholly healthy economic condition in the late second century BC. We have a good idea of the territory and population size and can now compare them with data from elsewhere in the Ptolemaic Fayum. Careful analysis of the crop regime and rent returns by Dorothy Crawford (Thompson), augmented by evidence subsequently published, shows that the data for cleruchic land (that is, that allotted to the more

---

[64] Bagnall (1992).
[65] More detail, particularly bibliographical, is available in the database entries in <http://www.trismegistos.org/fayum> (accessed 12 Aug. 2009).

Table 7.3. Relative sizes of Oxyrhynchite villages based on tax payments

Village*	A† Payment figure applied (dr.)	B Payment A as % of total payment (%)	C‡ Area of grainland represented by % payment in B (ar.)	D Total cultivated land assuming grainland in C = 80% of the whole (ar.)	E§ Toparchy
Nesmimis	1,024	3.54	4,816.40	6,020.50	U
Chysis	828	2.87	3,894.51	4,868.14	U
Sinkepha	568	1.97	2,671.60	3,339.49	U
Athychis	712	2.46	3,348.90	4,186.13	U
Enteiis	300	1.04	1,411.05	1,763.82	U
Thosbis	70	0.24	329.25	411.56	U
Mermertha	1,068	3.70	5,023.35	6,279.19	U
Monimou	872	3.02	4,101.46	5,126.83	U
Kerkemounis	360	1.25	1,693.26	2,116.58	U
Episemou	846	2.93	3,979.17	4,973.96	U
Nigrou	80	0.28	376.28	470.35	U
Iseion Panga	371	1.28	1,745.00	2,181.25	U
Sadalou	236	0.82	1,110.03	1,387.54	U
Xenarchou	72	0.25	338.65	423.32	U
Nesla	64	0.22	301.02	376.28	U
Senyris	116	0.40	545.61	682.01	U
Archibiou	72	0.25	338.65	423.32	U
Kerkethyris	441	1.53	2,074.25	2,592.81	W
Senekeleu	236	0.82	1,110.03	1,387.54	W
Senokomis	1,296	4.49	6,095.75	7,619.69	W
Syron	560	1.94	2,633.97	3,292.46	W
Senao	100	0.35	470.35	587.94	W
Pela	1,018	3.52	4,788.18	5,985.22	W
Paeimis	100	0.35	470.35	587.94	W
Seryphis	1,940	6.71	9,124.81	11,406.02	W
Herakleidou ep.	108	0.37	507.98	634.97	W
Paneuei	516	1.79	2,427.01	3,033.77	W
Lenon	72	0.25	338.65	423.32	W
Mouchinaxap	45	0.16	211.66	264.57	W
Leukiou	324	1.12	1,523.94	1,904.92	W
Petemounis	108	0.37	507.98	634.97	W
—	63	0.22	296.32	370.40	E
Psobthis	356	1.23	1,674.45	2,093.06	E
Taampemou	630	2.18	2,963.21	3,704.02	E
Ophis	500	1.73	2,351.76	2,939.70	E
Satyrou	68	0.24	319.84	399.80	E
Posompous	72	0.25	338.65	423.32	E
Adaiou	200	0.69	940.70	1,175.88	E
Terythis	223	0.77	1048.88	1,311.10	E
Pakerke	342	1.18	1608.60	2,010.75	E
Phoboou	900	3.11	4233.16	5,291.45	E
[Lile]	88	0.30	413.91	517.39	E
[Sarapionos Chaeremonos]	176	0.61	827.82	1,034.77	E
[Th . . .]	272	0.94	1,279.36	1,599.19	E
Sento	108	0.37	507.98	634.97	M
Tanais	438	1.52	2,060.14	2,575.17	M
Ieme	100	0.35	470.35	587.94	M
Istrou ep.	380	1.32	1,787.33	2,234.17	M
Senepta	100	0.35	470.35	587.94	M

Continued

Table 7.3. *Continued*

Village[*]	A[†] Payment figure applied (dr.)	B Payment A as % of total payment (%)	C[‡] Area of grainland represented by % payment in B (ar.)	D Total cultivated land assuming grainland in C = 80% of the whole (ar.)	E[§] Toparchy
Nomou ep.	622	2.15	2925.58	3,656.98	M
Taampitei	540	1.87	2,539.90	3,174.87	M
Herakleion	265	0.92	1,246.43	1,558.04	M
Takolkeilis	156	0.54	733.75	917.18	M
[Pou.eo]	48	0.17	225.77	282.21	M
[Koba or Koma]	68	0.24	319.84	399.80	M
[Petne]	300	1.04	1,411.05	1,763.82	M
[Artapatou]	54	0.19	253.99	317.49	M
[Plelo]	48	0.17	225.77	282.21	M
[Nemera]	242	0.84	1,138.25	1,422.81	M
[Mastingophorou]	78	0.27	366.87	458.59	M
[Psobthis]	98	0.34	460.94	576.18	M
[Kerkeuros]is	145	0.50	682.01	852.51	M
[Texei]	36	0.12	169.33	211.66	M
[Petenouris]	29	0.10	136.40	170.50	M
Teis	1,308	4.53	6,152.19	7,690.24	T
Paomis	496	1.72	2,332.94	2,916.18	T
Palosis	208	0.72	978.33	1,222.91	T
Tholthis	72	0.25	338.65	423.32	T
Kesmouchis	117	0.40	550.31	687.89	T
Sepho	72	0.25	338.65	423.32	T
Iseion Tryph.	213	0.74	1,001.85	1,252.31	L
Sinary	340	1.18	1,599.19	1,998.99	L
Souis	160	0.55	752.56	940.70	L
Talao	379	1.31	1,782.63	2,228.29	L
Tholthis	225	0.78	1,058.29	1,322.86	L
Sesphtha	796	2.75	3,744.00	4,680.00	L
Takona	632	2.19	2,972.62	3,715.78	L
Tychinphagon	300	1.04	1,411.05	1,763.82	L
[Iseion Kato]	20	0.07	94.07	117.59	L
[c.6]aur.[. (Psobthis?)	300	1.04	1,411.05	1,763.82	L
[Kosmou]	101	0.35	475.05	593.82	L
[Mouchinar]yo	188	0.65	884.26	1,105.33	L
[Dositheou]	700	2.42	3,292.46	4,115.57	L
[Total]	28,895		135,908.00	169,885.00	

Note: ar. = arouras; dr. = drachmas.

[*] The villages are listed in the order in which they appear in *P. Oxy.* X. 1285. The hypothesis is that the total number of villages recorded with payments preserved (n = 83) is about two-thirds of the total number of villages in the Oxyrhynchite (see Rathbone 1990). There are some significant omissions of well-known larger villages (notably Sko).

[†] The payment figures, some of which might be modified by re-reading, basically follow those used by Rowlandson (1996: 288–90). I here assume that this has not caused significant statistical distortion. The total (28,895 drachmas) is the cumulative total of the preserved payments and not the total of the subtotals given for each toparchy in the text.

[‡] The total amount of grain land is two-thirds of the figure in Table 7.1, on the assumption that the total number of villages with preserved payments represents approximately two-thirds of the total number of villages in the Oxyrhynchite (see[*]).

[§] Abbreviations of the names of toparchies (subregions): U = Upper, W = Western, E = Eastern, M = Middle, T = Thmoisepho, L = Lower.

Sources: *P. Oxy.* X. 1285, with Rathbone (1990) and Rowlandson (1996) used as a basis for calculating amounts of land attached to the villages.

Table 7.4. Population, site size, and land in Fayum villages

Village	A Population	B Site area (ha)	C Land Area ha. = ar.	Date of evidence for area in C	Source
Karanis	3,600 (I/II AD)	80	3,176 = 11,549	*c.* AD 170	Davoli (1998: 74)
	2,300 (II/III AD)		1,160 = 4,219	AD 308	Bagnall (2003)
	400 (IV AD)				Bagnall (1992)
Bacchias		34			Davoli (1998: 117)
Euhemeria		65			Bagnall (1993)
Hiera Nesos			1,117 = 4,062	AD 167	Rathbone (1990)
Kerkeosiris	1,200 (II BC)		1,297 = 4,716	118 BC	Rathbone (1990)
Philadelphia	3,300 (I/II AD)	50	2,750+ = 10,000	AD 167	Rathbone (1990) Hanson (2007)
Soknopaiou Nesos	1,100 (I/II AD) 760>420>0 (II/III AD)	22			Rathbone (1990) Davoli (2005) Messeri Savorelli (1989)
Theadelphia	2,300 (I/II AD) 80 (IV AD)	25	*c.*1,874 = 6,814*	*c.* AD 150	Rathbone (1990); Davoli (1998); Sharp (1999)*; Bagnall (2003)
Narmouthis	(6,500) (I/II AD)	60			Rathbone (1990) Davoli (1998: 223)
Tebtunis	4/5,000 (I/II AD)	57			Davoli (1998: 179) Rowlandson (1999)
Dionysias	1,150 (III BC)	40			Rathbone (1990); Davoli (1998: 301)
Philoteris	1,100 (III BC)	10.7			Römer (2004)
Oxyrhyncha	*c.*1,000 (?) (II BC)		*c.*2,180 = 6,000 (min.)	2nd c. BC	Clarysse (2008)

Note: ar. = arouras; ha = hectares.
* France (1999: 309) has a higher estimate of *c.*9,400 arouras for the second century AD.

privileged landholders)[66] include a much higher proportion of unproductive or derelict land and suggest that the relatively more privileged cleruchs were actually in a worse situation than the crown tenants at this time. For land held by the latter, the statistics emphasize the relative stability of the crop regime and the tax yield. The high-value crops (wheat, barley, lentils) predominate, occupying an average of 76.6 per cent of the land under cultivation, and this

[66] Crawford (1971: 53–85).

may be compared with data from *P. Petrie* III 75 of 235 BC (cited above). The average tax yield across all land and crops hovers around 4 artabas/aroura and a further deduction of 1 artaba/aroura should be made for seed in calculating surpluses. Unfortunately, we do not know for certain what proportion of the average total yield 5 artabas/aroura will have represented, but it is very unlikely to have been as high as 50 per cent and was probably quite signifi-cantly lower.

Evidence from **Philadelphia** for the third century BC shows wine produc-tion on a significant scale, a Ptolemaic innovation that is not part of the picture in the preserved records from Kerkeosiris. The calculations of wine produc-tion at Philadelphia by Vandorpe and Clarysse[67] imply a production of 5,760 hectolitres on 234 arouras at 25 hectolitres/ha, to which they compare a yield at Bubastos of 1,920 hectolitres on *c.*77 ha. This they extrapolate to a yearly production for the Arsinoite of 220,000 hectolitres on 8,800 ha = 32,000 arouras, calculating a market value for the total Arsinoite wine production of 1.34 million drachmas per annum. This is evidently speculative and seems to me suspiciously optimistic, not least because the amount of vineyard land obviously must vary from place to place.[68] For comparison, the Appianus estate of the mid-third century AD, based at Theadelphia, shows twenty attested vineyards but nothing on size or productivity. Rathbone's estimate is calculated on the basis of 7,000/7,500 mon. p.a. = 500 hectolitres at 100 monochora/aroura = *c.*25 hectolitresl/ha—that is, *c.*72 arouras.[69] These orders of magnitude, perhaps a little reduced, can be measured against the broad picture suggested in Table 7.1 above, which posits perhaps *c.*60,000 arouras (16,200 ha) of productive non-arable land in the Arsinoite. The other period for which we have good quantifiable evidence, the third century AD, shows that in AD 215/16 there were 3,826 arouras of privately owned grain land and 757 arouras of garden land (vineyards and orchards), 83.5 per cent and 16.5 per cent respectively. Detailed analysis of the level of equality of distribution reveals a Gini coefficient of 0.532, greater (more unequal) than Ptolemaic Kerkeosiris, less than fourth-century Hermopolis. This is part of the picture adumbrated by Schubert, analysing the build-up of larger estates, a process in which the descendants of veteran families played a prominent role.[70]

Here it is perhaps convenient to compare other evidence for **Theadelphia**, which has been analysed in great detail by Sharp.[71] His estimate of *c.*6,800 arouras (= 1,874 ha.), is argued to have included about 7–8 per cent of vineyard and garden land. Of the arable land, the pattern of cultivation

---

[67] Vandorpe and Clarysse (1997).
[68] For detailed analysis of data for the Roman period, see Ruffing (1999).
[69] Rathbone (1991: 247).
[70] Schubert (2007).
[71] Sharp (1998, 1999). Also for the location of major parts of the Appianus estate, see Rathbone (1991). See also France (1999); Van Minnen (2000: 214–15).

(with some double cropping and rotation) in the mid-second century AD shows:

> Wheat: under 40 per cent
> Lentils: 22 per cent
> Barley: unknown (some hundreds of arouras)
> Fodder: 10 per cent

Here the wheat proportion is strikingly low (and perhaps untypically so even for this village) but from an economic point of view compensated to some extent by lentils, which are a high-value crop (1:1 with wheat). If the unknown figure for barley were 10 per cent (within the known ranges from other places), the high-value crops would comprise over 70 per cent, consistent with patterns elsewhere. It is noteworthy that by AD 216 the amount of land under cultivation was comparable but the proportion of vineyard and orchard land seems to have risen to almost one-third (3,600 arouras of arable, 1,500 arouras of garden and orchard), and the proportion of vineyard to garden land may also have increased. Again, this may reflect a tendency to concentration of land in the hand of wealthier owners, and it has also been suggested that the production and consumption of wine tend to increase in the course of the Roman period. It is well known that by the early fourth century Theadelphia had suffered drastic depopulation and decline, apparently to a greater extent than Karanis (see below).[72]

There are good quantifiable data from **Tebtunis** for the Ptolemaic and the Roman periods, and Rowlandson provides an excellent sketch of the latter with emphasis on the social relations of the agrarian economy in which the balance of crop distribution was probably much the same as that elsewhere: predominantly arable, with some alternation of fodder crops, and a small percentage of vineyard and garden land.[73] Unfortunately, there is no hard evidence for population or size of territory, but, if Rowlandson's guesses are close to the mark, it will have been significantly larger than any of the other villages listed in Table 7.4. In the present perspective, some of the best material is derived from the Grapheion Archive of the reign of Claudius, which has been subjected to some analysis, though perhaps not exploited as fully as is possible. The full range of documents associated with Tebtunis and the grapheion runs from AD 8 to AD 56, and it provides the most detailed evidence we have for the ways in which the management of property (domestic as well as agricultural) was documented, including sales, leases, and subleases of land, which may partly be viewed as strategies or mechanisms for the division or redistribution of agricultural resources, in the form of both private and state land. In fact, this body of material offers an excellent opportunity to quantify

---

[72] Bagnall (1979/82 = 2003).
[73] Toepel (1973); Rowlandson (1999); Lippert and Schentuleit (2005).

Table 7.5 Movement of land at Tebtunis
(a) Individual documents

Transaction type	Transaction (n)	Date range	Size range (ar.)	Average size (ar.)
Sale/cession	18	AD 25/6–48	0.5–10	3.66
Lease/sublease	12	AD 8–46/9	2.5–26	11 (rounded)

(b) Registers

Transaction type	Transaction (n)	Date range	Size range (ar.)	Average size (ar.)
Sale/cession	20	AD 42–45/7	0.5–10	4.3
Lease	144	AD 42–45/7	0.5–24	5.8

Note: ar. = arouras.
Source: Material from the Leuven database (http://www/trismegistos.org/) accessed and compiled in 2006/7 by Dr Myrto Malouta.

'transaction costs' in the definition cited by Lo Cascio—the costs associated with defining, protecting, and exchanging property rights.[74] Leasing was clearly the predominant mode of exploitation. The documents summarized in Tables 7.5a and 7.5b show a high level of activity in moving control of small amounts of land (*c.*23 per cent of all contracts), many with metropolitan landlords leasing to villagers.[75] It is worth quoting Rowlandson's conclusion that at Tebtunis we find leases of land made for every tenurial category and every type of crop (with fodder particularly prominent for reasons that she attempts to explain), with all sections of the population involved, whether as landlords, tenants, or (significantly) both.[76] It is in this body of evidence that we find very high wheat rents, which imply yields that may be as much as twentyfold. There is no reason to suppose that Tebtunis was wholly exceptional in these respects, but the evidence from family archives of the second century AD, subjected to careful analysis by Rowlandson, suggests some different nuances: combination of leasing and direct paid labour (the 'Laches archive'); metropolitan landowners with holdings in several villages including Tebtunis (*P. Fam. Teb.*), a pattern well attested at Oxyrhynchus; an independent village family acting as both lessors and lessees and partly financing their operations by loans (Kronion archive).[77]

There is no reason to assume that things were substantially different at **Karanis** in the north-east Fayum, at least in the period up to *c.* AD 150. This is undoubtedly the best-attested village over the first four centuries of the Roman period, with both documentary evidence and a significant, even if partial,

---

[74] Lo Cascio (2006: 218–19).

[75] Based on material compiled by Dr Myrto Malouta from the text database in <www.trismegistos.org> (accessed May 2006).

[76] Rowlandson (1999: 155).   [77] Rowlandson (1999: 152–4).

Table 7.6. Land and taxes at Karanis and neighbouring villages, mid-second to early fourth century AD

(a) Mid-second century

Area/payment	Karanis	Horiodeiktia	Total
Land area (ar.)	11,549	14,986	26,535
Tax paid (art. of wheat)	54,457	67,690	122,147
Tax rate (art./ar.)	4.7	4.5	4.6

(b) Mid-second century, dependent villages

Area/payment	Ptolemais Nea	Hiera Nesos
Land area (ar.)	3,924	4,061
Tax paid (art. of wheat)	16,891	15,797
Tax rate (art./ar.)	4.3	3.9

(c) Early fourth century

Area/payment	Karanis	Horiodeiktia	Total
Land area (ar.)	1,198	3,020	4,218
Tax paid (art. of wheat)	2,092	4,447	6,539
Tax rate (art./ar.)	1.74	1.47	1.55

Note: ar. = arouras; art. = artabas.
Source: after Bagnall (1985 = 2003).

archaeological record.[78] These in conjunction indicate that, as elsewhere, there was a significant sector of the population engaged in non-agricultural activities and also give us some hints of the scale of land in the surrounding territory (the villages in the *horiodeiktia* of Karanis). The evidence for orders of magnitude in production and consumption in the period before the Antonine plague of the mid-second century and in the early fourth century afford a striking contrast that is certainly paralleled in some other villages (Table 7.6).[79] Following Bagnall, my calculations are based on an estimated pre-Antonine

[78] There is a large bibliography that cannot be cited here. For the archaeological evidence, see Davoli (1998: 73–116). Geremek (1969) provides a synthesis of the documentary evidence, which has much increased in the past four decades.

[79] The data in Table 7.6 (a–c) are derived from original calculations by Bagnall (1985 = 2003), but with correction of one significant statistical error. The figure given at Bagnall (1985: 293) for the total land at Karanis should be 11,549 arouras rather than 7,855 (cf. Rathbone 1990: 134); Bagnall has failed to add the further estimate (1985: 292) of 3,694 arouras for the *ousiai* (the total of 12,204 for the *horiodeiktia* **does** include the *ousiai*). The effect of this correction is to reduce the overall average taxation rate from about 5 artabas/aroura to 4.6 artabas/aroura. The figures tabulated for the *horiodeiktia* on the basis of *P. Bour.* 42 by Rowlandson (2006: 177) are somewhat smaller, because of choices made as to how to estimate (or not) missing figures. For Karanis, see Rathbone (1990: 132).

population for Karanis of *c.*3,600 people, which I reckon as *c.*700 families, *c.*2,300 (*c.*450 families) in the 170s, showing the effects of the Antonine plague, and an early fourth-century population of 420 (*c.*80 families). The population of the villages in the *horiodeiktia* (of which at least three were substantial) is unknown. The evident drastic reduction in population, land, and tax yield is very striking, but detailed discussion of what the latter, in particular, means must be postponed. The obvious question is whether the levels of government revenue from this area really did decline so drastically, from an overall average rate of *c.*4.5 artabas per aroura to 1.55 artabas per aroura, or whether the reduction in this mode of taxation was compensated by other modes of revenue extraction, and, if so, whether this also applied elsewhere in Egypt. For the earlier period, it should be noted that the overall figures for tax yield are of the same order of magnitude as those derived for crown land at Kerkeosiris in the second century BC, an apparent stability (if that is the case) that is maintained through a period of significant demographic expansion.[80]

From the point of view of estimating production, consumption, and subsistence, it is interesting to compare the second-century and the fourth-century data with an emphasis that is slightly different from that of Bagnall, who correctly points out a huge quantitative decline both at **Karanis** and at **Theadelphia** (Table 7.7).[81]

These figures are again in some cases highly hypothetical or speculative,[82] but, if we assume (and it *is* a big assumption, given the severe reduction in population that might affect ability to sustain intensity of production) a consistent twelvefold yield, we can see that the percentage 'surplus' is considerable in both periods, even in that of 'decline'. Self-evidently, adopting the estimate of a total area of 11,549 arouras of grain land for the 170s, when the population is presumed to have declined to *c.*2,300, would yield a more favourable outcome, if the levels of cultivation and of production were maintained at pre-plague levels, but this seems inherently unlikely.[83] In any event, the 'surplus' is not a real surplus in the sense of profit, merely a figure after deduction of tax, seed, and subsistence requirement in wheat equivalent and would need to be reduced by further considerations:

---

[80] Bowman (forthcoming).

[81] A very crude sighting shot for subsistence may be derived from the statement that five arouras will provide subsistence for a family in the Ptolemaic period (*P. Teb.* I. 5).

[82] In particular it should be noted that the fourth-century figures for Theadelphia are calculated from the known figures of taxes collected in AD 312 of *c.*363 artabas (*P. Sakaon* 5), on the basis of a rate of 1.55 artabas/aroura; applying the figure of 451 artabas for AD 336 (Bagnall 1985 = 2003: 295) would increase the results proportionately.

[83] Cf. Rathbone (1990: 134–6) (Mendesian Nome); Bagnall (2002a).

Table 7.7. Production and consumption

(a) Mid-second century AD

Land/product	Karanis	Theadelphia
Land (ar.)	11,549	6,814
Yield (art.)*	137,508	81,768
Tax (art.)[†]	54,457	31,344
Seed (art.)[‡]	11,549	6,814
Balance (art.)	71,592	43,610
Total subsistence (art.)[§]	32,900	21,150
Actual wheat consumption (art.)	23,100	14,850
'Surplus' (art.)	38,692 (= 28%)	22,460 (= 27.5%)

(b) Early fourth century AD

Land/product	Karanis	Theadelphia
Land (ar.)	1,198	[235]
Yield (art.)*	14,376	2,820
Tax (art.)[†]	2,092	363
Seed (art.)[‡]	1,198	[235]
Balance (art.)	11,086	2,222
Subsistence (art.)[§]	3,760	940
Actual wheat consumption (art.)	2,640	660
'Surplus' (art.)	7,326 (= 51%)	1,880 (= 66%)

Note: ar. = arouras; art. = artabas.
* The rate of yield applied is 12 art./ar.
† The rate of tax applied in wheat equivalent is 4.6 (mid-second cent.) and 1.6 (early fourth cent.) art./ar.
‡ The sowing rate is standardly 1 art. of seed per ar.
§ The subsistence requirement is calculated in wheat equivalent.

- effect of crop rotation;
- transaction costs;
- labour costs.

Such a scenario ideally needs more precision, however, and by analogy it would in principle be better to consider Karanis and its *horiodeiktia* together, since Karanites may well have owned or held land in the district. Unfortunately, we are hampered by the absence of any grounds for an estimate of the population of its *horiodeiktia* that would enable us to estimate subsistence requirements and surpluses. Even with all these caveats, however, it seems possible to conclude that the inhabitants of the 'declining' villages of the early fourth-century Fayum were not in fact individually impoverished to the point of non-viability.

CONCLUSIONS

The selection of data presented here in this compressed form is by no means exhaustive, but it is hoped that it gives some sense, albeit patchy and selective, of the scale and shape of various features of the agrarian economy in Egypt. Although I have claimed some level of general validity, even if crude and speculative, for some of the data, I have not attempted large-scale agglomeration or extrapolation to a pan-Egyptian picture. It would not be difficult to do that on the basis of transparent methods of calculation and data, some of which at least are robust. But, as stated at the outset, it is difficult to avoid the feeling that greater generalization leads us further away from any testable reality and I suspect that such conclusions would at this stage merely complement our pre-existing ideas of context and scale. At a later stage, where we do have some evidence on which to base large-scale calculations,[84] we can attempt to see how the balances of individual elements might have changed or fluctuations in the level of production might have occurred within the agrarian sector in a way that is consistent with (let us say) the levels of revenue known under Augustus and under Justinian.[85] That might be a next step in the chain.

As indicated earlier, a complete picture with a proper estimate of generation of surplus wealth needs to consider the balance between supply and demand or production and consumption and it has not been possible to deal with the latter in any detail here. If arable production supplies an estimated 70 per cent of subsistence requirements, we need to add consideration of viticulture and oleoculture, livestock, and other agricultural products, balanced against the costs of labour, animal power, fodder, transport, and so on. Thus far, we can offer only a crude and unrefined illustration of orders of magnitude for the metropoleis. They were concentrated centres of consumption that offer some quantifiable evidence, part of which has already been addressed.[86] We here proceed on the basis that the total populations of Arsinoe, Oxyrhynchus, and Hermopolis in the period up to *c.* AD 150 consisted of up to 9,000, 6,000, and 7,000 families respectively, with a family average of five individuals.[87] It is a simple matter to estimate basic subsistence requirements for these population levels, but this will leave us no wiser than we were with the knowledge that the product of these regions far outstripped the basic subsistence needs. For Oxyrhynchus in the later third century (*c.* AD 270), we also have the evidence for the 'corn-dole', the output of which can be quantified at a maximum of around 48,000 artabas per annum (though it remains unclear exactly where

---

[84] e.g. Bagnall (1979/82 = 2003); Rathbone (1989).
[85] Rathbone (1989).   [86] Bowman (2011).
[87] In this calculation, 'family' = 'household', including all consumers (e.g. slaves).

the expense of this benefit fell).[88] It is not clear whether this allowance was calculated in the form of milled or unmilled wheat (more probably the latter), but we do know that thirty loaves could be made from an artaba of (milled) wheat and how many the bakeries could produce per day.[89] On this basis, as a very rough approximation, we could calculate the annual subsistence requirements in wheat equivalent for a metropolitan population of 6,000 families at *c.*242,000 artabas and the actual wheat consumption, assuming it constitutes 70 per cent of diet, at *c.*198,000 artabas. Any estimate for the nome is bound to be purely speculative, since we lack the means to estimate population. If 30,000 families were taken as a maximum and a twelvefold yield applied to a rounded 203,000 arouras of grain land (Tables 7.1 and 7.8), the results would be large 'surpluses', which would need to be reduced by calculation of overhead costs and other factors mentioned above in order to achieve a more realistic picture of the excess value of supply over consumption.[90]

The belief implicit in the approach adopted here is that the individual scenarios of regions, towns, and villages analysed do have something to tell

Table 7.8. Oxyrhynchite cereal production

Wheat usage	II AD	IV AD
Yield*	2,436,000	2,436,000
Tax†	609,000	324,800
Seed‡	203,000	203,000
Wheat consumption§	990,000	990,000
'Surplus'	634,000 (26%)	918,200 (37.7%)

* The rate of yield applied is 12 artabas/aroura.

† The average figures used for tax on all categories of grain land are 3 artabas/aroura for the second century and 1.6 artabas/aroura for the fourth (Bagnall 1992). For further discussion of the earlier figure and the discrepancy, see Appendix, n. 6.

‡ The sowing rate is standardly 1 artaba of seed per aroura.

§ The calculation is based on a purely illustrative estimate of 30,000 families in the Oxyrhynchite Nome (of which 6,000–7,000 are in the metropolis) at a consumption rate 33 artabas of wheat per family per annum (see Appendix).

[88] 12 artabas p.a. for a maximum of 4,000 adult males; see *P. Oxy.* XL.

[89] *P. Oxy.* VI.908, XII.1454, cf. Sharp (1998: 153, 156). The figure suggests a direct relationship between the artaba, the number of loaves, and the grain dole, in that the individual allowance of one artaba per month is equivalent to one loaf per day. See also Bagnall (2001).

[90] This is, of course, an oversimplification, and several of the figures are subject to margins of error. Some may think a twelvefold yield too high (see Appendix), and it is applied across the total of grain land without taking account of crop rotation. This is clearly a crucial element, and the estimate used here is derived from Rowlandson's calculation (1996: 215) of yields derived from rent levels in leases. For the pre-AD 300 average tax rate of 3 artabas/aroura assuming a ratio of 2:1 private to public land, see Appendix, note 6). The surplus cannot be pure profit, since it does not take account of labour and transaction costs. Nevertheless, it is still substantial, even allowing for rotation and for extra costs, and represents, of course, only a proportion of the agricultural surplus. It hardly needs to be pointed out that, if the population were higher, the 'surplus' would be correspondingly lower.

us about the structural features and the overall scale of the agrarian economy, even if they each have their own idiosyncratic elements. We might also have added individual estates, except that the present scale would allow only the briefest summary of syntheses already available that have undermined the idea of a primitive and small-scale subsistence economy in the agrarian sector.[91] But, if this approach seems valid for the sets of Egyptian data, I believe it is also legitimate to hypothesize along the same lines when trying to set Egypt (or any other province) in the broader context of the Hellenistic world or the Roman empire. That is not the same as a claim of 'typicality' for Egypt. Apart from the obvious geographical and ecological differences that profoundly condition the agrarian regime and set it apart from other regions, idiosyncratic features such as the very low level of slave labour also need to be taken into account. It may, however, be suggested that one could allow for these differences without ignoring the significance of the modes in which agrarian behaviour fits into the social and economic patterns of the Hellenistic and Roman states.

This chapter has compiled evidence that suggests some such changes over the period under consideration, some possibly contingent and temporary (the effects of plague), others more fundamental and longer term (the effective privatization of land). There is evidence for exploitation though direct labour, but tenancy is predominant. The indebtedness of tenants seems more prevalent later, entailing a need for greater security of tenancy, a widening of the gap between the status of the tenant and landlord as rent rolls replace leases on private or fiscal estates (which may be seen as the Egyptian form of what is usually called the late Roman colonate). All this points to a greater equality of distribution in the Ptolemaic and early Roman periods (except for imperial estates) and growing inequality into the later Roman period. It is relevant for all periods that slave labour on the land plays little or no role except as an occasional substitute for 'wage labour'. This suggests, overall, an agrarian economy that is flexible, entrepreneurial, and deeply monetized, even at the village level, as the significant number of cash payments for rents and purchases shows.

We can enrich the picture by looking at the Egyptian agrarian economy in a broader political and institutional context, considering how, for example, the average tax rates on land can be increased or decreased by the state by manipulating the balance of other modes of taxation and raising revenues that have to be paid in cash and at least partly, in effect, by commutation of the agricultural 'surplus'. Although it remains to be tested in detail, this is the most obvious explanation for the dramatically lower rates of grain tax after AD 300. We can also consider the relationship between our quantifiable data and the possibility of constructing some sort of a generic model that would take

---

[91] Świderek (1960); Rathbone (1991).

account of amount and use of land, average yields, various deductions for tax, seed, labour, transport costs, subsistence requirements, and so on. This type of analysis has already been fruitfully applied to some bodies of evidence and suggests an approach in which the model can be successfully created only if it is driven by a clear sense of the questions that the existing evidence can address and an iterative process that allows the incorporation of new evidence to modify it.[92]

APPENDIX

The basic figures used for my calculations are as follows:

1. Aroura, unit of land measurement: 0.68 acre, 0.275 ha (1 feddan = 1.524 arouras = 0.42 ha).
2. Artaba, dry measure: 38.78 litres = 4.5 *modii Italici* = 30.2 kg of milled wheat.
3. *Modius Italicus*: 8.62 litres = 6.7 kg wheat.
4. Cereal yields: twelvefold average yield over time. This is a critical issue on which is it very difficult to achieve certainty. In Egypt yields varied greatly according to the level of the Nile flood and the consequent quality of the harvest. An average tenfold yield has often been assumed, but my estimate is rather higher, following the evidence analysed by Rowlandson (1996: 247–9) (for the Oxyrhynchite Nome, normal yields of 10 artabas per aroura and more). For comparative estimates for Italy (much lower), see Spurr (1986: 82–8).
5. Seed: 1 artaba per aroura is standard sowing rate.
6. Taxation rates in kind (wheat or wheat equivalent). The figures applied are crude but likely to be of the right order of magnitude. For the period before Diocletian rates of tax on private land are 1 artaba/aroura or a bit more, on the various categories of public land 5 or 6 artabas/aroura. For the Fayum (Arsinoite), where there is assumed to be significantly more public land, than elsewhere (perhaps 50/50), following the calculations of Bagnall, as corrected in n. 79 above), I apply an overall average rate of 4.6 artabas/aroura. For Middle Egypt and the Oxyrhynchite, where the ratio of private to public land was perhaps more like 2:1 (Rowlandson 1996), I apply an overall average rate of 3 artabas/aroura. For the post-Diocletianic period, when all land was effectively in private ownership, I apply an overall average of 1.55 artabas/aroura (fuller discussion of the significance of this difference in rates must be postponed).
7. Subsistence and consumption needs in wheat equivalent, established by Foxhall and Forbes (1982):
   i. Average for wheat: 3,340 calories/kg.
   ii. Average for barley (60/70 per cent extraction of meal from hulled barley): 3,320 calories/kg.

---

[92] See Van Minnen (2000); Winkler (2008), describing the database at http://www.agre.uni-tuebingen.de.

iii. Male requirements per diem: 3,822 (exceptionally active), 3,337 (very active), 2,852 (moderately active). So 1 artaba wheat per month = subsistence for a 'very active' male.

These are the basis for calculating household requirements per diem: 15,494 calories for six-person household unit (Foxhall and Forbes 1982), scaled down to a maximum of $c.$13,000 for Egyptian household of 5.0 persons = approx 3.9 kg = $c.$0.58 modius = 0.129 artabas = 47 **artabas per annum in wheat equivalent; 33 artabas wheat per family per annum in actual consumption**, assuming that 70 per cent of calorie requirements are provided by wheat in the diet.

REFERENCES

Atkins, M., and Osborne, R. G. (2006) (eds). *Poverty in the Roman World*. Cambridge.

Bagnall, R. S. (1979/82). 'The Population of Theadelphia in the Fourth Century', *BSAC* 24: 35–57 (= Bagnall 2003, VI).

Bagnall, R. S. (1985). 'Agricultural Productivity and Taxation in Later Roman Egypt', *TAPA* 115: 289–308 (= Bagnall 2003, XVII).

Bagnall, R. S. (1992). 'Landholding in Late Roman Egypt: The Distribution of Wealth', *JRS* 82: 128–49.

Bagnall, R. S. (1993). *Egypt in Late Antiquity*. Princeton.

Bagnall, R. S. (2000). 'P. Oxy. 4527 and the Antonine Plague in Egypt: Death or Flight?', *JRA* 13: 288–92.

Bagnall, R. S. (2001). 'A Heavy Artaba and its Ninety-Six Loaves', *BSAA* 46: 7–12 (= *Alexandrian Studies in Honour of Mostafa el Abbadi*).

Bagnall, R. S. (2002a). 'The Effects of Plague: Model and Evidence', *JRA* 15: 114–20.

Bagnall, R. S. (2002b). 'Public Administration and the Documentation of Roman Panopolis,' in A. Egberts, B. P. Muhs, and J. van der Vliet (eds), *Perspectives on Panopolis: An Egyptian Town from Alexander the Great to the Arab Conquest: Acts from an International Symposium Held in Leiden on 16, 17 and 18 December 1998* (Papyrologica Lugduno-Batava 31). Leiden, 1–12.

Bagnall, R. S. (2003). *Later Roman Egypt: Society, Religion, Economy and Administration* (Variorum Collected Studies Series 758). Aldershot.

Bagnall, R. S. (2005). 'Evidence and Models for the Economy of Roman Egypt', in Manning and Morris (2005), 187–204.

Bagnall, R. S. (2007). 'The Bouleutic Merry-Go-Round', *JRA* 20: 639–42 (review of Tacoma 2006).

Bagnall, R. S. (2009). 'Response to Alan Bowman', in Bowman and Wilson (2009), 205–9.

Bagnall, R. S., and Frier, B. W. (1994). *The Demography of Roman Egypt*. Cambridge.

Bagnall, R. S., and Worp, K. A. (1980). 'Grain Land in the Oxyrhynchite Nome', *ZPE* 37: 263–4.

Banaji, J. (2002). *Agrarian Change in Late Antiquity: Gold, Labour, and Aristocratic Dominance*. Oxford.

Bang, P. F., Ikeguchi, M., and Ziche, H. G. (2006) (eds). *Ancient Economies, Modern Methodologies. Archaeology, Comparative History, Models and Institutions*. Bari.

Blouin, K. (2005). *Homme et milieu dans le nome mendésien à l'époque romaine (1er au 6e s.)*, Ph.D. thesis, Université Laval and Université de Nice Sophia Antipolis.

Blouin, K. (2007). 'Environnement et fisc dans le nome mendésien à l'époque romaine: Réalités et enjeux de la diversification', *BASP* 44: 135–66.

Blouin, K. (2008). 'De Mendès à Thmouis (delta du Nil, Égypte): Hydrologie mobile, société mobile?' in E. Hermon (2008) (ed.). *L'eau comme patrimoine—de la Méditerranée à l'Amérique du Nord* (Quebec), 107–28.

Blouin, K. (2010). 'Topographie et cartographie du nome mendésien à l'époque romaine', in T. Gagos (ed.), *Proceedings of the Twenty-Fifth International Congress of Papyrology, Ann Arbor 2007* (American Studies in Papyrology). Ann Arbor, 85–96.

Boak, A. E. R. (1955). 'The Population of Roman and Byzantine Karanis', *Historia* 4: 157–62.

Bonneau, D. (1964). *La crue du Nil, divinité égyptienne, à travers mille ans d'histoire (332 av.–641 ap. J.-C.) d'après les auteurs grecs et latins, et les documents des époques ptolémaïque, romaine et byzantine*. Paris.

Bowden, W., Lavan, L., and Machado, C. (2004) (eds). *Recent Research on the Late Antique Countryside* (Late Antique Archaeology 2). Leiden.

Bowman, A. K. (1985). 'Landholding in the Hermopolite Nome in the Fourth Century AD', *JRS* 75: 137–63.

Bowman, A. K. (2009). 'Quantifying Egyptian Agriculture', in Bowman and Wilson (2009), 177–204.

Bowman, A. K. (2011). 'Ptolemaic and Roman Egypt: Population and Settlement', in Bowman and Wilson (2011), 317–58.

Bowman, A. K. (forthcoming). 'The State and the Economy: Fiscality and Taxation', in A. I. Wilson and A. K. Bowman (eds), *Trade, Commerce, and the State in the Roman World* (Oxford Studies on the Roman Economy). Oxford.

Bowman, A. K., and Wilson, A. I. (2009) (eds). *Quantifying the Roman Economy: Methods and Problems* (Oxford Studies on the Roman Economy 1). Oxford.

Bowman, A. K., and Wilson, A. I. (2011) (eds). *Settlement, Urbanization, and Population* (Oxford Studies on the Roman Economy 2). Oxford.

Butzer, K. W. (1976). *Early Hydraulic Civilization in Egypt: A Study in Cultural Ecology*. Chicago.

Christensen, T. (2002). *The Edfu Nome Surveyed: P.Haun.Inv.407 (119–118 BC)*, Ph.D. thesis, University of Cambridge.

Clarysse, W. (2003). 'The Archive of the *praktor* Milon', in W. Clarysse and K. Vandorpe (eds), *Edfu, an Egyptian Provincial Capital in the Ptolemaic Period*. Brussels, 17–27.

Clarysse, W. (2008). 'Graeco-Roman Oxyrhyncha, a Village in the Arsinoite Nome', in Lippert and Schentuleit (2008), 55–73.

Clarysse, W., and Thompson, D. J. (2006). *Counting the People in Hellenistic Egypt*. Cambridge.

Crawford, D. J. (1971). *Kerkeosiris, an Egyptian Village in the Ptolemaic Period*. Cambridge.

Crawford, D. J. (1973). 'Garlic Growing and Agricultural Specialization in Graeco-Roman Egypt', *CE* 48: 350–63.

Davoli, P. (1998). *L'archeologia urbana nel Fayyum di età ellenistica e romana*. Naples.

Davoli, P. (2005). 'The Temple Area of Soknopaiou Nesos', in Lippert and Schentuleit (2005), 97–124.

Foxhall, L., and Forbes, H. A. (1982). '*ΣΙΤΟΜΕΤΡΕΙΑ*: The Role of Grain as a Staple Food in Classical Antiquity', *Chiron* 12: 41–90.

France, J. (1999). *Theadelpheia and Euhemereia: Village History in Greco-Roman Egypt*, Ph.D. thesis, University of Leuven.

Garnsey, P. (1983). 'Grain for Rome,' in P. Garnsey, K. Hopkins, and C. R. Whittaker (eds), *Trade in the Ancient Economy*. London, 118–30.

Geremek, H. (1969). *Karanis, Communauté rurale de l'Égypte romaine au IIe–IIIe siècle de notre ère*. Wroclaw, Warsaw, and Krakow.

Greenberg, J. (2003). 'Plagued by Doubt: Reconsidering the Impact of a Mortality Crisis in the 2nd C. AD', *JRA* 16: 413–25.

Hanson, A. E. (2007). 'Estimate for Capitation Tax of Philadelphia', in A. J. B. Sirks and K. A. Worp (eds), *Papyri in Memory of P. J. Sijpesteijn (P. Sijp.) (American Studies in Papyrology* 40.26), 172–84.

Harrauer, H. (2008). 'Hyperechios und seine Familie,' in F. A. J. Hoogendijk and B. P. Muhs (eds), *Sixty-Five Papyrological Texts Presented to Klaas A. Worp on the Occasion of his 65th Birthday* (Papyrologica Lugduno-Batava 33). Leiden, 181–94 (no. 25).

Hermon, E. (2008) (ed.). *L'eau comme patrimoine : De la Méditerranée à l'Amérique du Nord*. Quebec, 107–28.

Hillman, G. (1973). 'Agricultural Productivity and Past Population Potential at Aşvan', *Anatolian Studies* 23: 225–40.

Hobson, D. W. (1984). 'Agricultural Land and Economic Life in Soknopaiou Nesos', *BASP* 21: 89–109.

Humphrey, J. H. (2002) (ed.). *The Roman and Byzantine Near East* (JRA Suppl. 49). Portsmouth, RI.

Keenan, J. G. (2003). 'Deserted Villages: From the Ancient to the Medieval Fayyum', *BASP* 40: 119–39.

Kirby, C., and Rathbone, D. W. (1998). 'Kom Talit: The Rise and Fall of a Greek Town in the Fayum', *Egyptian Archaeology* 8: 29–31.

Lewuillon-Blume, M. (1988). 'Enquête sur les registres fonciers (P. Landl.) : La Repartition de la propriété et les familles des propriétaires', in V. G. Mandilaras (ed.), *Proceedings of the XVIII International Congress of Papyrology, Athens 25–31 May 1986*, vol. 2. Athens, 279–86.

Lippert, S., and Schentuleit, M. (2005) (eds). *Tebtynis und Soknopaiou Nesos: Leben im römerzeitlichen Fajum*. Wiesbaden.

Lippert, S., and Schentuleit, M. (2008) (eds). *Graeco-Roman Fayum: Texts and Archaeology: Proceedings of the Third International Fayum Symposion, Freudenstadt, May 29–June 1, 2007*. Wiesbaden.

Lo Cascio, E. (2006). 'The Role of the State in the Roman Economy', in Bang, Ikeguchi, and Ziche (2006), 215–34.

Mango, M. (2011). 'Byzantine Settlement Expansion in North Central Syria: The Case of Androna/Andarin', in A. Borrut, M. Debié, A. Papaconstantinou, D. Pieri, and J.-P. Sodini (eds), *Le Proche-Orient de Justinien aux Abbassides: Peuplement et dynamiques spatiales* (Bibliothèque de l'Antiquité Tardive 19). Turnhout, 93–122.

Manning, J. G. (2007). 'Hellenistic Egypt', in W. Scheidel, I. Morris and R. Saller (eds), *The Cambridge Economic History of the Greco-Roman World*. Cambridge, 434–59.

Manning, J. G., and Morris, I. (2005). *The Ancient Economy, Evidence and Models*. Stanford.

Messeri Savorelli, G. (1989). 'La popolazione di Soknopaiou Nesos nel 178/9 d.C.', *APapyrol* 1: 7–14.

Miller, R. L. (1991). 'Counting Calories in Egyptian Ration Texts', *JESHO* 34.4: 257–69.

Monson, A. (2008). 'Communal Agriculture in the Ptolemaic and Roman Fayum', in Lippert and Schentuleit (2008), 173–86.

Oates, J. F. (1976). 'Census Totals; Nemesion's Notes', in A. E. Hanson (ed.), *Collectanea Papyrologica: Texts Published in Honour of H. C. Youtie*, vol. 1 (Papyrologische Texte und Abhandlungen 19). Bonn, 189–96.

Padró, J. (2007). 'Recent Archaeological Work', in A. K. Bowman, R. A. Coles, N. Gonis, D. Obbink, and P. J. Parsons (eds), *Oxyrhynchus, a City and its Texts* (Egypt Exploration Society, Graeco-Roman Memoirs, No. 93), London, 129–38.

Parsons, P. J. (2007). *City of the Sharp-Nosed Fish: Greek Lives in Roman Egypt*. London.

Pollard, N. D. (1998). 'The Chronology and Economic Condition of Late Roman Karanis, an Archaeological Reassessment', *JARCE* 35: 147–62.

Rathbone D. W. (1989). 'The Ancient Economy and Graeco-Roman Egypt', in L. Criscuolo and G. Geraci (eds), *Egitto e storia antica dall'ellenismo all'età araba: Atti del colloquio internazionale, Bologna, 31 Agosto–2 Settembre, 1987*. Bologna, 159–76.

Rathbone, D. W. (1990). 'Villages, Land and Population in Graeco-Roman Egypt', *PCPS* 36: 103–42.

Rathbone, D. W. (1991). *Economic Rationalism and Rural Society in Third-Century A.D. Egypt: The Heroninos Archive and the Appianus Estate*. Cambridge.

Rathbone, D. W. (1994). 'Settlement and Society in Greek and Roman Egypt', in A. Bülow-Jacobsen (ed.), *Proceedings of the XXth International: Congress of Papyrologists, Copenhagen 23–29 August 1992*. Copenhagen, 136–45.

Rathbone, D. W. (1997). 'Prices and Price Formation in Roman Egypt', in *Économie antique, prix et formation des prix dans les économies antiques* (Entretiens d'archéologie et d'histoire). Saint-Bertrand-de-Comminges, 183–244.

Rathbone, D. W. (2006). 'Poverty and Population in Roman Egypt', in M. Atkins, and R. G. Osborne (eds), *Poverty in the Roman World*. Cambridge, 100–14.

Rathbone, D. W. (2007). 'Roman Egypt', in W. Scheidel, I. Morris, and R. Saller (eds), *The Cambridge Economic History of the Greco-Roman World*. Cambridge, 699–719.

Römer, C. (2004). 'Philoteris in the Themistou Meris: Report on the Archaeological Survey Carried out as Part of the Fayum Survey Project', *ZPE* 147: 281–305.

Rowlandson, J. L. (1996). *Landowners and Tenants in Roman Egypt: The Social Relations of Agriculture in the Oxyrhynchite Nome*. Oxford.

Rowlandson, J. L. (1999). 'Agricultural Tenancy and Village Society', in A. K. Bowman and E. Rogan (eds), *Agriculture in Egypt from Pharaonic to Modern Times*. Oxford, 139–58.

Rowlandson, J. L. (2006). 'The Organisation of public land in Egypt', in J. C. Moreno Garcia (ed.), *L'Agriculture institutionelle en Egypt ancienne: État de la question et perspectives interdisciplinaires* (Cahiers de recherches de l'Institut de papyrologie et d'égyptologie de Lille 25). Villeneuve-d'Ascq, 173–94.

Rowlandson, J. L. (2007). 'Oxyrhynchus and its Hinterland', in A. K. Bowman, R. A. Coles, N. Gonis, D. Obbink, and P. J. Parsons (eds), *Oxyrhynchus: A City and its Texts* (Egypt Exploration Society, Graeco-Roman Memoirs, No. 93). London, 205–17.

Ruffing, K. (1999). *Weinbau im römischen Ägypten*. St Katharinen.

Scheidel, W. (1999). 'Salute, agricoltura e popolazione in Egitto nell'età romana e nel XIX secolo', in D. Vera (ed.), *Demografia, sistemi agrari, regimi alimentari nel mondo antico: Atti del convegno internazionale di studi: Parma, 17–19 ottobre 1997* (Pragmateiai 3). Bari, 309–24.

Scheidel, W. (2002). 'A Model of Demographic and Economic Change in Roman Egypt after the Antonine Plague', *JRS* 15: 97–114.

Scheidel, W. (2004). 'Demographic and Economic Development in the Ancient Mediterranean World', *Journal of Institutional and Theoretical Economics*, 160: 743–57.

Schubert, P. (2007). *Philadelphie: Un village égyptien en mutation entre le IIe et le IIIe siècle ap. J.-C.* (SBA, Band 34). Basel.

Sharp, M. (1998). *The Food Supply in Roman Egypt*, D.Phil. thesis, University of Oxford.

Sharp, M. (1999). 'The Village of Theadelphia in the Fayyum: Land and Population in the Second Century,' in Bowman and Rogan (1999), 159–72.

Spurr, M. S. (1986). *Arable Cultivation in Roman Italy c.200 B.C.–c. A.D. 100* (JRS Monographs 3). London.

Świderek, A. (1960). *La propriété foncière privée dans l'Égypte de Vespasien et sa technique agricole d'après P.Lond. 131 recto*. Wroclaw.

Tacoma, L. E. (2006). *Fragile Hierarchies : The Urban Elites of Third-Century Roman Egypt* (Mnemosyne Suppl. 271). Leiden.

Tchernia, A. (1986). *Le vin de l'Italie romaine: Essai d'histoire économique d'après les amphores* (Bibliothèque des écoles françaises d'Athènes et de Rome 261). Rome.

Thonemann, P. (2007). 'Estates and the Land in Late Roman Asia Minor,' *Chiron* 37: 435–78.

Toepel, L. R. (1973). *Studies in the Administrative and Economic history of Tebtunis in the First Century A.D.*, Diss. Duke University.

Vandorpe, K., and Clarysse, W. (1997). 'Viticulture and Wine Consumption in the Arsinoite Nome (P.Köln V 221)', *AncSoc* 28: 67–73.

Van Minnen, P. (1995). 'Deserted Villages: Two Late Antique Sites in Egypt,' *BASP* 32.1–2: 41–56.

Van Minnen, P. (2000). 'Agriculture and the "Taxes-and-Trade" Model in Roman Egypt', *ZPE* 133: 205–20.

Van Minnen, P. (2001). 'P.Oxy.LXVI 4527 and the Antonine Plague in the Fayum', *ZPE* 135: 175–7.

Vera, D. (1999) (ed.). *Demografia, sistemi agrari, regimi alimentari nel mondo antico: Atti del convegno internazionale di studi: Parma, 17–19 ottobre 1997* (Pragmateiai 3). Bari.

Winkler, A. (2008). 'The Database AGRE—Agriculture in Greco-Roman Egypt', in Lippert and Schentuleit (2008), 223–4.

8

The Agricultural Economy of the Mendesian Nome under Roman Rule

Katherine Blouin

1. INTRODUCTION

The agricultural economy of Roman Egypt is mostly known through papyri and archaeological remains from the Fayum, the Oxyrhynchite Nome, and the oasis sites of Douch (Kharga) and Kellis (Dakhla). This documentation shows how, in these regions, the agricultural production was characterized by a quantitative preponderance of wheat farming, followed by a variety of other crops (other cereals, legumes, grapevines, olive trees, fruits, vegetables, and forage) and non-agricultural activities (breeding, hunting, fishing, harvesting).[1] While the farming strategies prevalent in the Roman Nile valley and oases are fairly well documented, much less is known of the situation prevailing in the Nile Delta at the time. However, as this chapter will show, the documentary papyri related to the Mendesian Nome shed light on the reality of agrarian life in the eastern part of the Delta.

The Mendesian Nome, one of ancient Egypt's districts, was located in the north-eastern Delta (Fig. 8.1). For most of antiquity, it was traversed by a branch of the Nile called, like the nome itself, 'Mendesian', in reference to Mendes, the nome's pre-Roman capital. This territory, which borders part of today's Menzaleh Lake, was also rich in marshy zones and had direct access to the Mediterranean Sea. Such hydrological features allowed for the development of a variety of food production and industrial activities, which, together with the nome's strategic maritime and fluvial location, made Mendes one of the most prosperous commercial and religious centres in the Delta and even, under the twenty-ninth dynasty (399–380 BC), the capital of Egypt.[2]

---

[1] Schnebel (1925) (general); Rathbone (1991: 212–64) (Fayum); Rowlandson (1996: 19–26) (Oxyrhynchite); Bousquet (1996) (Douch); Bagnall (1997) (Kellis).
[2] Redford (2004, 2005, 2009, 2010).

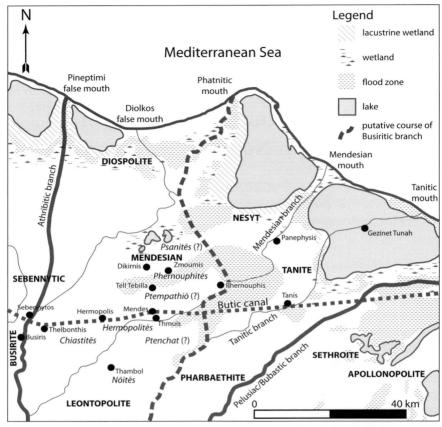

Fig 8.1 Map of the Mendesian Nome (K. Blouin and D. Nakassis)

The Mendesian Nome is also one of the very few deltaic zones documented by a significant papyrological corpus,[3] most of which consists of the carbonized archives from Thmuis. These archives found in Thmuis, the nome's Roman *metropolis*, are composed of cadastral registers, tax arrears registers, and fiscal reports dating from the end of the second to the beginning of the third century AD.[4] Altogether, the data preserved in these and in other papyri document the chief characteristics of the Mendesian agricultural economy from the second to the early fourth century AD. The present chapter aims at

---

[3] The only other substantial papyrological corpora found in the Delta are the carbonized papyri from Bubastis (*P. Bub.* I and II) and Tanis (Chauveau and Devauchelle 1996). In addition to these, many papyri from elsewhere in Egypt (for instance, the Zenon and Theophanes archives) deal in one way or another with the Nile Delta.

[4] Kambitsis (1985); Blouin (2007a: annexe 2).

identifying these characteristics, and at getting a better understanding of their socio-economic relevance within the imperial context of the time. To do so, I shall first discuss the Mendesian agrarian and fiscal terminology preserved in the carbonized archives from Thmuis. I shall then turn my attention to *P. Oxy.* XLIV.3205, a sowing survey, which offers a unique glimpse into the agrarian landscape of a Mendesian village at the turn of the fourth century AD.

2. LAND CLASSIFICATION: WHAT THE AGRARIAN TERMINOLOGY SAYS

In total, Mendesian papyri contain nearly 200 references to land categories. These are essentially preserved in three documents: *P. Thmouis* 1, *P. Mendes. Genev.*, and *P. Ryl.* II.426. *P. Thmouis* 1 is a register of taxes in arrears written in AD 170–1 by the nome's *basilikos grammateus* (lit. 'royal scribe', a nome-level adminis-trator). The document deals with tax payments that were suspended in AD 170–1, after they had been subject to a moratorium of one to several years;[5] these include land taxes, poll taxes, as well as a variety of sums (*hypokeimena kai alla*) owed by deserted villages for the financing of civil servants and official duties. All plots listed in the register are said to be 'dry' (χέρσαι)—that is, barely productive or sterile. *P. Mendes. Genev.* consists of a list, compiled according to topographic criteria, of not flooded (ἄβροχαι) or artificially irrigated (ἐπηντλημέναι) land declarations submitted to the local administration by private landowners and public tenants in a village of the Phernouphites toparchy (administrative subdiv-ision of a nome) around AD 200. *P. Ryl.* II.426, which is very mutilated, is made up of seventeen fragments belonging to a similar register dated from the same period.

These documents are not without limitations. First, they deal only with specific categories of land: dried-up land in the case of *P. Thmouis* 1, and not flooded or artificially irrigated land in the cases of *P. Mendes. Genev.* and *P. Ryl.* II.426. Second, the nome's toparchies are very unequally represented; in reality, certain activities—for instance, cattle breeding—were certainly more widespread than the preserved data lead us to believe. Third, Mendesian papyri are silent on the actual organization of agricultural work, on harvesting, or on systems such as fallowing, rotating, and mixed cropping. Fourth, and this no doubt results from the fragmentary nature of the available documentation,[6] some Mendesian productions attested in third-century BC papyri—harvesting

---

[5] The earliest preserved moratorium is dated from AD 128–9; Kambitsis (1985).

[6] The much awaited edition of the unpublished fragments belonging to *P. Thmouis* 1, which are for the most part housed in Florence, would certainly improve the representativeness of these data and fill some lacunas.

and farming of papyrus and lotus, as well as sesame and castor-oil plant cultivation—are not mentioned in Roman evidence.[7] In spite of such biases, the large number of agrarian categories, toparchies, and villages preserved in the carbonized archives of Thmuis encourages me to think that this corpus is generally representative of the nome's qualitative and quantitative agrarian profile.

Table 8.1 lists all the categories of land attested in the Mendesian Nome under Roman rule whose general (or particular in the case of the *ousiai*—land belonging to former imperial estates[8]) agricultural designation is known, for a total of forty-two distinct categories. Three main types of farmland are represented: cereal (wheat), vineyards, and pastures.

The primacy of grain land over vineyards and pastures is clear and seems symptomatic of the preponderance of grain cultivation within the territory of the nome. This is all the more plausible since, in the case of *P. Thmouis* 1, only monetary arrears are compiled. Indeed, since vineyards, orchards, and gardens were mostly taxed in money, whereas, apart from payments in wine or oil, taxes in kind applied only to grain or legume land, one would logically expect a greater presence of vineyards, garden, and orchards in a register of monetary taxes than in one of taxes in kind. Yet this is not the case: except for vineyards, no category of land specifically dedicated to gardens and orchards (including olive growing) is attested. Finally, references to pastures most probably concern arid, salty, or humid plots unsuitable for grain farming; fodder cultivation, to which an important part of the Arsinoite and Oxyrhynchite nomes seem to have been dedicated, might well have been practised on those plots.[9] The Mendesian agrarian vocabulary is hence comparable to other Egyptian data, which clearly assert the quantitative predominance of grain land in the province, but are rather evasive when it comes to other types of farming activities.[10] This phenomenon is generally understood as echoing the centrality of cereals in ancient Egyptian and Mediterranean diets, their high speculative value, and the importance of Egyptian wheat in Mediterranean food supply networks.[11] The reduced number of land categories specifically

---

[7] *P. Cair. Zen.* II.59470 (papyrus); *P. Cair. Zen.* II.59292, 661–2, and *P. Lond.* VII.1995, 180 (lotus); *P. Lond.* VII.1995, 183, and *P. Rev. Laws* 62, 17 (sesame); *P. Lond.* VII.1995, 181; *P. Rev. Laws* 62, 22 (castor-oil plant).

[8] On *ousiai*, see Crawford (1976); Parássoglou (1978).

[9] Cf. Rowlandson (1996: 22). Rathbone (1991: 214) believes that fodder was, after wheat and barley, the third most heavily cultivated crop on the Appianus estate. Rowlandson (1996: 20–1) estimates that, in the Oxyrhynchite Nome, fodder came second, just after wheat.

[10] Bagnall (1993: 24–5); Rathbone (1991: 213–14); Rowlandson (1996: 19).

[11] I will not discuss here the substantial role of Egypt in the grain supply of Rome and other Mediterranean cities, nor examine the debated question of the relationship between its contribution and that of Africa; on these issues, which have given rise to an abundant bibliography, see notably Rickman (1980); Garnsey (1996); De Romanis (2002, 2003); Erdkamp (2005).

Table 8.1. Agrarian typology and land classification in the Mendesian Nome under the Principate

Land category/Classification	Cereal	Vineyards	Pastures
Private land			
ἰδιωτική	X		
ἰδιω[τικ	X		
(μονάρταβος)	X		
σ(ιτικῆς) αδ	X		
ας΄ χερσάμπελος	X		
(ἡμιτεταρταβίας) (δεκαρούρων)	X		
(δεκαρούρων)	X		
λιμνιτικὴ (δεκαρούρων)	X		
(δεκαρούρων) Ἰετηριτῶν	X		
εΙ (δεκαρούρων) Ἰετηριτῶν	X		
εΙ (δεκαπενταρούρων)	X		
(ἑπταρούρων)	X		
[.](ἀρταβ) ῥαβδοφόρων	X		
ἡμι[.....]ιως	X		
βα( ) ἀπογρ(αφομεν)	X		
πρότερον κληρουχικῆς	X		
ας΄ ἰδιόκτητος	X		
ἰδιόκτητος ἐκ (δρ.) κ		X	
(μονάρταβος) ἐωνημένη	X		
λιμνιτικὴ (μονάρταβος) ἐωνημένη	X		
λιμνιτικὴ ἐωνημένη χέρσου	X		
ἐωνημένη	X		
ἐωνημένη ἀπὸ ἱερατικοῦ ὑπολόγου	X		
ἐωνημένη ἀπὸ βασιλικοῦ ὑπολόγου	X		
ἐωνημένη ἀπὸ ὑπολόγου χερσαμπέλου	X	X	
ἐωνημένη ἀπὸ λιμνιτικῆς προσόδου	X		
χέρσου ὑπολόγου			X
ἀπὸ ἱερατικοῦ ὑπολόγου	X		
ἀπὸ βασιλικοῦ ὑπολόγου	X		
ἀπὸ λιμνιτικοῦ ὑπολόγου	X		
χερσαμπέλου = ~ χερσαμπέλου ὑπολόγου	X		
~ ἱερά = ~ ἱερὰ ἐπὶ καθήκουσι	X		
χερσάμπελος, χέρσος ἐπὶ ναυβίῳ, or χέρσος		X	
Public land			
ἱερὰ ἐν ἐκφορίῳ	X		
ἱερὰ (διάρταβος) μεμισθωμένη may belong to ἱερὰ ἐν ἐκφορίῳ	X		
ἱερὰ (μεμισθωμένη), may belong to ἱερὰ ἐν ἐκφορίῳ		X	
διοικήσεως	X		
βασιλικὴ γῆ διοικήσεως	X		
διοικήσεως ἐν ἐκφορίῳ	X		
οὐσιακή	X	~X	X
νομαὶ κτηνῶν			X
πλεονασμός	X		

dedicated to other farming activities should not, however, be seen as a token of their economic marginality, as we shall see in the following section.

Until recently, it was generally assumed—essentially on the basis of Fayumic evidence—that most of Egypt's agrarian land was public.[12] Private land, which was taxed at a lower rate than publicly owned land, seems usually to have been of a poorer agricultural quality and, as such, to have contributed in a lesser way to the fiscal revenues of the province. Mendesian papyri, like those from the Nile valley,[13] do not conform to this model. Rather, they mostly deal with private plots, and notably with *kleruchic* land—that is, parcels that were granted to native army or police veterans and their descendants under the Ptolemies, and whose denomination and taxation rates were maintained by the Romans, but henceforth attached to the land itself.[14] How can we explain this phenomenon? Two main factors could be evoked: the nature of the documentation—one can indeed suppose that a great part of the dry, not flooded, and artificially irrigated plots attested in the carbonized archives from Thmuis was located in less agriculturally suited areas—and, concomitantly, the abundance of dry or damp areas resulting from both the region's environmental idiosyncrasies and the difficult agrarian context of the time.[15]

3. TAXES ON WHAT GROWS: THE MENDESIAN FISCAL TERMINOLOGY

The fiscal terminology preserved in the carbonized archives from Thmuis provides us with a more detailed portrait of the Mendesian agricultural reality. I have identified more than 100 different taxes or fees—mostly monetary but some in kind—in the Mendesian papyri.[16] Among these, thirty-five pertain to land, or agricultural production or transformational activities. Data come primarily from the carbonized archives from Thmuis and date mostly from the second half of the second century AD. Table 8.2 lists all known taxes on agriculture by crop, providing for each of them the number of occurrences. In the case of payments in kind, the reference is provided. Finally, taxes levied on 'limnitic' land (*limnitike*)—that is, originally damp or submerged land)—are enclosed in curly brackets, to distinguish them from 'regular' taxes.[17]

---

[12] See Rowlandson (1996: 63 n. 116).
[13] Rowlandson (1996: 63–9); Monson (2012: 96–102).
[14] See, on that matter, Martin (1967); Rowlandson (1996: 41–55).
[15] On the context of socio-economic crisis, which shows through the carbonized archives from Thmuis, see Kambitsis (1985); Blouin (2007a).
[16] See Blouin (2007a: annexe 5).
[17] Blouin (forthcoming).

Table 8.2. Taxes on agriculture in the Mendesian Nome under the Principate according to papyri

Crop	Tax (*source for non-fiscal or general references*)	Number of entries
(a) Cereals (wheat and barley)	ἀλλαγή	24
	εἰκοστή	39
	{εἰκοστὴ (λιμνιτικά)}	5
	ἡμιαρταβία ποδώματος	1
	[κοσ]κινία ἁλώνων	1
	{[ ]ν κοσκινία ἁλώνων}	1
	ναύβιον	36 (13 = a or c; 2 = a and c)
	{ναύβιον (λιμνιτικά)}	6 (a or c)
	παράναυλον	46
	χωματικόν	24
	BGU III. 976–80 (payments in kind)	—
(b) Lentils	τέλος φακοῦ ἐρείξεως	1
	BGU III. 977 (payments in kind)	—
(c) Grapevine	ἀλλαγή	24
	ἀπόμοιρα	9 (7 c or d)
	{ἀπόμοιρα (λιμνιτικά)}	1 (c or d)
	β· τριώβ. ᾿Αλεξανδρέων	3 (c or d)
	γεωμετρία	2 (c or d)
	~δεκάδραχμος	1 (c or d)
	ἑξάδραχμος Φιλαδέλφου	1
	ἐπαρούριον	5 (3 = c or d)
	{ἐπαρούριον (λιμνιτικά)}	1 (c or d)
	ναύβιον	22 (13 = a or c; 2 = a and c)
	{ναύβιον (λιμνιτικά)}	6 (a or c)
	οἴνου τέλος	5
	ὀκτάδραχμος	7
	τέλεσμα ἀμπέλου	1
	τρίδραχμος/τρίδραχμος μητροπολιτῶν	22 (c or d)
	{τρίδραχμος (λιμνιτικά)}	2 (c or d)
	φόρος ἀμπέλου	8
	{φόρος ἀμπέλου (λιμνιτικά)}	1
	P. Ryl. II.213 and 217	—
(d) Fruits and vegetables	ἀπόμοιρα	7 (c or d)
	{ἀπόμοιρα (λιμνιτικά)}	1 (c or d)
	β· τριώβ. ᾿Αλεξανδρέων	3 (c or d)
	γεωμετρία	2 (c or d)
	~δεκάδραχμος	1 (c or d)
	ἐπαρούριον	3 (c or d)
	{ἐπαρούριον (λιμνιτικά)}	1 (c or d)
	~μονόδραχμος	3
	~πεντάδραχμος	2
	τρίδραχμος/ τρίδραχμος μητροπολιτῶν	22 (c or d)
	{τρίδραχμος (λιμνιτικά)}	2 (c or d)

Continued

Table 8.2. *Continued*

Crop	Tax (*source for non-fiscal or general references*)	Number of entries
(e) Olive tree	ἐλαϊκή	13
	τέλος ἐλαιουργικῶν/τέλεσμα τῶν ὀργάνων	3
(f) Flax	μερισμὸς ἐνδεήματος ὀθονηρᾶς/ ὀθονηρά	4
	τιμὴ λινοκαλάμης	1
(g) Castor oil	τέλεσμα κικιουργικοῦ ὀργάνου	2

Note: The data on the tax assessments collected in this table are derived from the commentaries on the sources concerned as well as from Wallace (1938).

By counting once occurrences that could apply to two types of agricultural land (vineyards and gardens mostly, but also grain land), I have numbered a total of 313 entries, referring to 8 types of crops: cereals (wheat and barley), lentils, vines, fruits and vegetables, olive, flax, and castor-oil plant. The activity referred to by the highest amount of taxes (13) is vine growing, followed by fruits and vegetables (8, 6 being shared with vineyards), cereals (7, 2 of which also apply to vineyards, olives (2), flax (2), lentils (1), and castor-oil plant (1) cultivation.

Taxes on cereal farming are attested in twelve of the nome's fifteen, perhaps sixteen, toparchies. It is worth noticing that wheat cultivation was even practised in the Ptempathio and Ptenchat toparchies (see Fig. 8.1), on originally humid plots called 'limnitic'. Given that wheat does not thrive in damp soils, one must suppose that the parcels in question had been anthropically or geomorphologically drained, or both.[18] In addition to the general taxes applied to cereal and lentil farming, taxes in arrears and fees on wheat (πυροῦ), barley (κριτῆς),[19] and beans (φακῆς)[20] are listed. In Egypt, barley was significantly less cultivated than wheat, of which it was generally worth half.[21] However, since it was more resistant to drought land and salinity than wheat, it seems to have been favoured in the case of drier or more saline parcels.[22] Taxes on lentils remind us of the importance of legumes in ancient Mediterranean diets. Rich in proteins and in essential nutrients that are not heavily present in cereals,

---

[18] Blouin (forthcoming).

[19] *BGU* III. 976, 12; 977, 7, 14; 978, 4, 21, 22; 979, 3, 7, 9, 16; 980, 2, 7, 9, 12, 15, 17.

[20] *BGU* III. 977, 2. There is no reference to olyra, which is mentioned neither in the Heroninos archives nor in the Oxyrhynchite papyri: Rathbone (1991: 214 n. 3, 219); Rowlandson (1996: 20). See also Schnebel (1925: 98–9) and Bagnall (1993: 24).

[21] Bagnall (1985: 7); Rathbone (1991: 214); Rowlandson (1996: 20). Bagnall (1993: 25) estimates that about 20% of grain land was dedicated to barley.

[22] Bonneau (1987: 189; Hayes *et al.* (2005); Thanheiser (1992b).

more tolerant of aridity than wheat, and very suitable for long-distance transportation, they also offered a valuable substitute to meat, which was more expensive and scarce, and a complement to cereals.[23]

Several taxes on fruits and vegetables are also attested. However, apart from olive farming and viticulture, they are of a general nature, and hence do not provide us with more details than the agrarian terminology discussed above. The paucity of details available on gardens and orchards may be due to the fact that they were often smaller-scale productions destined for domestic or local consumption; in other words, their 'niche' economic profile did not require the same detailed agro-fiscal treatment as grain land, vineyards, and olive farms.[24] Nevertheless, fruits and vegetables were an interesting investment for farmers, who could thereby diversify their diet and generate sizeable revenues from the sale of fresh products in local and peripheral markets. For in antiquity as today, the interdependency between rural peripheries and urban centres enhances the profitability of perishable commodities.

Viticulture was practised in at least nine toparchies. In addition to thirteen taxes, payments or fees paid in jars of wine ($\kappa\epsilon\rho\acute{\alpha}\mu\iota\alpha$) are listed.[25] In Egypt, vines had to be planted above the floodplain (that is, on higher ground less suited for cereal farming), and needed artificial irrigation and specialized care. The energy and time viticulture required were compensated for by the profits this essentially commercial activity generated.[26] It is also reasonable to believe that intercropping involving vines and other mixed procedures, which are otherwise attested in Egypt and elsewhere in the Mediterranean,[27] was also in use in the nome. The mention of a plot planted with trees ($\delta\epsilon\nu\delta\rho o\phi\acute{\upsilon}\tau o\upsilon$) in fragment 29 of *P. Ryl.* II.427, where there is also reference to vineyards, could support this hypothesis. More generally, practices of this type may explain why numerous taxes and monetary fees were applied to both vine cultivation and other fruits and vegetables.

Three oleaginous plants are attested in the fiscal terminology: olive tree, flax, and castor-oil plant.[28] The few mentions of olive farming may testify to the relative marginality of this activity in Egypt, and all the more so in the Delta. Like vines, olive trees will not grow in flooded land, and thus can be

[23] Garnsey (1998: 214–25; 1999: 12–21).

[24] Crawford (1971: 130–1); Rathbone (1991: 381); Thanheiser (1992a: 118); Bagnall (1993: 25–7); Garnsey (1996); Horden and Purcell (2000: 203); Scheidel (2001: 237).

[25] *P. Ryl.* II.213 (204, 210, 215, 295, 300, 304) and 217 (9, 19, 21, 69, 91, 111, 112). Sums are associated with plots located in the Ptempathio (see Fig. 8.1), Neomare, Thmoibastites, and Pheopites toparchies.

[26] Schnebel (1925: 239–92); Rathbone (1991: 212–13); Brun (2004: 143–68).

[27] Bousquet (1996); Rowlandson (1996: 19); Brun (2004: 144).

[28] On oleaginous production in Hellenistic and Roman Egypt, see Schnebel (1925: 197–203); Sandy (1989); Bagnall (1993: 29–31); Brun (2004: 169–84) (olive oil mostly).

farmed only above the floodplain.[29] Apart from cities and villages proper, such areas were few in the Mendesian Nome. The taxes listed as τέλος ἐλαιουργικῶν / τέλεσμα τῶν ὀργάνων (thus far unique to the Mendesian Nome) and τέλεσμα κικιούργικος ὀργάνου indicate that olive and castor-oil[30] presses were located in many settlements belonging to at least two toparchies. As for flax, its farming—essentially for textile production—remained an important sector of non-food activity in Egypt, and particularly in the vast humid zones of the northern Delta, throughout antiquity and well into the medieval period. The lack of fiscal data on flax farming is certainly due to the fact that the carbonized archives from Thmuis deal mostly with land that was too dry for this activity.[31]

Finally, although it goes beyond the subject matter of this chapter, the economic importance of certain non-arable activities, to which the fiscal data testify, must be underlined.[32] Cattle breeding (pig, sheep, goat, poultry, and cows) seems to have been widespread in the nome, at the very least on a domestic level.[33] Further, the importance of hunting, fishing, fish farming, and gathering, which visibly played a significant economic role in the nome's lacustrine, palustrine, lagoonal, and coastal settlements, might well be a deltaic specificity, like the abundance of private land categories discussed earlier.[34]

Apart from that, though, the agro-fiscal terminology preserved in the carbonized archives from Thmuis is generally consonant with other Egyptian evidence: it documents both the preponderance of cereal farming and the concomitant diversity of agricultural strategies implemented in the nome during the second century AD. *P. Oxy.* XXIV.3205, which shows how this agrarian trend continued through the beginning of the fourth century AD, allows us to gauge its magnitude more precisely.

4. A LOCAL SAMPLE: *P. OXY.* XLIV.3205

P. Oxy. XLIV.3205 is one of only two fourth-century AD sowing surveys known in Egypt.[35] It offers invaluable insights into the agrarian dimensions

---

[29] See Rathbone (1991: 244–7) and Rowlandson (1996: 24), who underline the rarity of sources regarding olive growing in Theadelphia and in the Oxyrhynchite nome.

[30] On the different names given to this plant and its uses in Egypt, see Pliny the Elder, *HN* XV.7. On the hieroglyphic, Coptic, Greek, and Aramaic forms of *kiki*, see Vycichl (1983: 74).

[31] Blouin (2007b; 2012).

[32] On this matter, see Blouin (2007c).

[33] Blouin (2007c, 2010).

[34] Blouin (2007b, 2010).

[35] At present, only one other register of this kind and period is known. It is *P. Ryl.* IV.655, which is unfortunately very fragmentary; cf. Świderek (1971: 32).

of the fiscal reforms introduced in Egypt under Diocletian. More specifically, it is the only source documenting the typology of land in the Mendesian Nome at the turn of the fourth century AD.[36] The document includes two registers written most probably between the general land censuses of AD 301 and 308: the first one is a list of land situated in the Phernouphites toparchy; the second is a topographical list of land belonging to a Phernouphite village named Ψεν[. . .] (Psen-). The first section having been discussed elsewhere,[37] I will focus on the second one.

The register as a whole illustrates how the complex terminology in use under the Principate gave way to a much simpler vocabulary in the fourth century AD.[38] Land is indeed chiefly categorized according to its yield and agrarian vocation. Two main categories are listed: cultivable (ἐνεργός)—that is, potentially productive—land, and dry (χέρσος)—that is, that has been unproductive for many years and is consequently exempt from taxes—land.[39] Cultivable land is also subdivided, according to the type of crop: we find grain land (τάξις ἰδιωτική) and orchards (τάξις παραδείσων). Grain land is comprised of royal land (βασιλικὴ γῆ), private land (ἰδιωτικὴ γῆ), and a category of land designated by a mutilated term (θεω[.] [ ]ερ[ ]ικη), possibly privately owned land that was said to be 'sacred'. Royal land, which was public under the Principate, seems to have been in large part privatized at the time when the register was written. The legal distinction between public and private land established under the Principate—both categories including grain land, vineyards, gardens, orchards, and pastures—started to blur under Hadrian. With time, the terms 'royal land' and 'private land' became indiscriminately used to designate private grain land.[40] As for the subcategory called 'orchards', it included vineyards (ἄμπελος φόριμος), actual orchards (τάξις παραδείσων—these also subdivided into 'productive orchards' (παράδεισοι ἐνάρετοι) and bean fields (κυάμων)), and a type of land corresponding perhaps to reed plantations (χαρακὼν ἔμφυτος).[41]

This new land classification system was deliberately introduced under Diocletian, with the aim of it being more reflective of the agrarian reality,

---

[36] Świderek (1971: 31–2). On Diocletian's fiscal and monetary reforms, cf. among others Carrié and Rousselle (1999: 190–5, 593–615).

[37] Blouin (2008).

[38] On that matter, see more generally Bonneau (1971).

[39] See Bonneau (1971: 202).

[40] Rowlandson (1996: 77–9). The expression 'royal land' completely disappears from papyri after the fourth century AD: Bonneau (1971: 201–2). The continued use of the former agrarian terminology (royal, public, and perhaps sacred land) over quite a long period after Diocletian's reforms might result from the temporary maintenance of the fiscal modalities associated with these types of land.

[41] The word χαρακὼν also appears in *BGU* III.961, 1 and *P. Ryl.* II.427, fr. 19 and 39. Świderek (1971: 44, n. to l. 41), thinks that the definition provided by *LSJ* ('vineyard containing staked vines') does not fit with the context of the present document; I agree with her.

and thus fairer to taxpayers.[42] In fact, however, the dissociation of the annual variability of the Nile flood from the assessment of land taxes that came with this reform had the opposite effect: by ignoring the Nilotic variable, it abstracted the agrarian management of Egypt.[43] This new conception of the relationship between territory and taxation, which broke away from the fiscal customs in place since pharaonic times, lasted through to the Arab period. This is not to say though that *P. Oxy.* XLIV.3205 is a worthless piece of evidence. Indeed, since the survey was compiled shortly after the reform was introduced, we can assume that the data it contains are roughly representative of the reality on the ground.

The second section of the register consists of two parts: a sowing survey of the land belonging to the village of Psen- (69–77; henceforth called 'general survey') (Table 8.3), followed (64–100) by a list by *koite* (cadastral division) of land belonging to the village's *koinon* (a group consisting of officials and members of the village's elite) (Table 8.4). Given that the latter list is quasi-identical to the former one, we can safely deduce that it too deals with Psen-'s agricultural land.[44] Tables 8.3 and 8.4 present a ranking of the totals by yield (productive or dry) and agrarian vocation (royal/sown land = grain land, orchard, and legume land).

According to this document, the agricultural territory of Psen- covered between 483 and 484 arouras—that is, about 1.33 km^2. Of this total, approximately 95.5 per cent was considered to be productive, and 4.5 per cent dry. Considering the propensity of government officials to list unproductive plots as productive, the effective proportion of fertile land was certainly lower than the official numbers suggest.[45] Yet these data are significantly more polarized than the ones regarding the Phernouphites toparchy as a whole (74 per cent productive versus 26 per cent dry).[46]

Unsurprisingly, the agricultural territory of Psen- was essentially composed of grain land: 93.77 per cent in the general survey, 94.06 per cent in the list by *koite*. When including dry land, which was also dedicated to cereal farming, these totals respectively increase to 98.22 per cent and 98.49 per cent. What was left of the of the village's agrarian territory amounted to less than 2 per cent (1.78 per cent and 0.51 per cent) and was made up of orchards. In the general survey, these include both actual orchards and bean fields; this seems to indicate that, in the context of this document, *paradeisoi* were planted with fruit trees and beans. The mixed culture of other crops such as vegetables,

---

[42] Bonneau (1971: 199–201); Carrié and Rousselle (1999: 193).

[43] The fact that cadastral records were in all likelihood not updated every five years as was originally planned also contributed to aggravate the situation; Carrié and Rousselle (1999: 194–5). See also *P. Cair. Isid.* 1.

[44] Świderek (1971: 35).

[45] Van Minnen (2001: 175–7).

[46] Van Minnen (2001: 175–7).

Table 8.3 The agricultural land of Psen- (Phernouphites toparchy) at the turn of the fourth century AD according to *P. Oxy.* XLIV.3205

State	Category	Subcategory	Arouras	%
Productive			461.78125	95.55
	Royal (cereals)		453.1875	93.77
	Orchards		8.59375	1.78
		Orchards	*3.46875*	*0.72*
		Kuamon	*5.125*	*1.06*
Dry	Royal (cereals)		21.5	4.45
Total			**483.28125**	**100**

Source: Świderek (1971).

Table 8.4 The agricultural land of Psen-'s *koinon* at the turn of the fourth century AD according to *P. Oxy.* XLIV.3205

State	Category	Arouras	%
Productive		462.84385	95.57
	Sown (cereals)	455.546975	94.06
		+ [. . .]*	
	Orchards	2.171875+	0.45
		[. . .]	
	Kuamon	5.125	1.06
Dry		21.4375	4.43
Total		**484.28135**	**100**

* The total calculated by Świderek (1971) in her summary table is 455 and 3/64 (1/32 + 1/64) arouras. The difference results from the fact that, in the section dealing with the fourth *koitè*, she reads 37 arouras ¼ + 1/8 + 1/64. However, her edition of the papyrus gives 37 arouras ¾ + 1/8 + 1/64; A verification of the digitized original reveals that the mistake lies in the table; cf. *P. Phernouphitès* 88 and Świderek (1971: 36).

fodder, or flowers, though not documented, is at the least conceivable. In any case, here too totals are clearer cut than those related to the Phernouphites toparchy,[47] which lists approximately 77 per cent of grain land. Vineyards, orchards, and the farming of beans and reeds occupied approximately 22.7 per cent of the territory, the rest of the toparchy corresponding to uncultivated sandy or scrubland (χέρσος ἁλμυρὶς καὶ ξυλῖτις). However, if we take into account only cultivable land, the proportion of grain land increases to 95.45 per cent. Vineyards, orchards, and leguminous plants follow far behind, with respectively 3.49 per cent and 0.55 per cent. Even considering the unavoidable optimism of official surveys, the orders of magnitude at the toparchy and village level are such that there cannot be any ambiguity.

[47] Blouin (2008).

The existence of categories called ἄμπελος φόριμος and χερσάμπελος in the Phernouphites survey indicates that vineyards were classified separately. How should we interpret the absence of such categories in the section dedicated to Psen-? The inclusion of vineyards in the category of orchard land seems unlikely, given the existence of wine-growing categories at the toparchy level. Data regarding dry land are on that matter illuminating. Indeed, whereas the village's dry land was entirely composed of grain land, dry grain land represented only 6.35 per cent of the toparchy's land, but dry vineyards nearly 15 per cent. Orchards, which covered less than 1 per cent of the territory, officially consisted of 81.28 per cent of dry land; in the case of vineyards, the percentage climbs to 85.21 per cent. This phenomenon could evidence the constraints associated with vine cultivation and the priority given to cereal farming on more fertile plots. It is thus probable to suppose that Psen-'s land was simply not suited for viticulture.

Lastly, the papyrus also states that a portion of Psen-s' land consisted of 'added' land (πλεονασμός); in fact, *apo pleonasmou* land represents the largest category of marginal land in the document (26.42 arouras, that is close to 5.5 per cent of the village's land). According to S. L. Wallace, the term *pleonasmos* is a synonym of ἐπιβολή.[48] In papyri, *epibole* designates public parcels of land attached to private plots.[49] Wallace's definition has since been further refined by H. C. Youtie, who believes that the term designated land that was once infertile, but became productive owing to Nile flood(s) (and hence was literally 'added').[50] *Pleonasmos* also appears in the carbonized archives from Thmuis (cf. Table 8.1): *P. Ryl.* II. 213 (82, 108, 140) lists a *phoros pleonasmos* three times in the Ptempathio toparchy section, and *P. Thmouis* 1 (97, 10) mentions 5 and 47/128 arouras of land 'added' to a 20-aroura taxable wheat-growing plot in the same toparchy (village of Pois). This category of 'liturgical' land continued to exist after the Diocletianic agrarian reform, as our document shows.[51] It can finally be likened to land referred to as χα^λ or χάλασμα, which appears thirty-five times in *P. Mendes. Genev.*[52]

5. CONCLUSION: THE MENDESIAN AGRICULTURAL ECONOMY IN CONTEXT

The agrarian and fiscal terminology preserved in the carbonized archives from Thmuis and in *P. Oxy.* XLIV.3205 shows that, during the Roman period, the

---

[48] Wallace (1938: 21).
[49] Bonneau (1971: 187); Kambitsis (1985: 89 n. 12); Blouin (2007a: 182 n. 276).
[50] *P. Cair. Isid.* 3 intro.: 39.
[51] See also *P. Cair. Isid.* 73, 8; *P. Corn.* 20 a III.
[52] Martin (1967: 32–3).

nome's agricultural territory was in greater part dedicated to cereal farming (essentially wheat, but also barley); vine cultivation, which was arduous but potentially very lucrative, comes in second place. The paucity of evidence regarding the farming of fruits and vegetables (including olive growing), lentil, and flax seems to result from the bias of the documentation, and the particular conditions in which these activities were practised (essentially domestic or small-scale production) and taxed (common taxes for vineyards/orchards). Lastly, we must note the peculiar economic role activities such as flax growing and transformation, cattle breeding, fish farming, hunting, fishing, and gathering seemingly had in the areas of the nome—and notably its abundant marshy zones—not suited for farming.[53]

As underlined earlier, the preponderance of wheat cultivation is no doubt due to a combination of factors: the suitability of Mendesian land for grain farming; the advantages of wheat in terms of food risk management and, hence, its high speculative value; finally, the role of Egypt in imperial grain supply networks. Several phenomena evidenced in the Mendesian papyri tend to show that the Roman fisc tried to maximize the extension and intensification of land farming: the preponderance of wheat in the agrarian and fiscal data discussed above; the predetermined and fixed agricultural use of land plots; incentives for the cultivation of marginal land (auctions, fiscal exemptions, and rent/tax holidays) or assignations for compulsory farming, more often than not for wheat farming;[54] instances of (then dry) grain land in the northernmost—thus wettest—areas of the nome (notably on lots called 'limnitic').[55] Apart from 'limnitic' land, which is so far attested only in the Mendesian Nome, these managerial practices fit with what we know of those implemented in the Fayum and the Nile valley. They can also be paralleled with procedures ascribed in the *lex Manciana* and the *lex Hadriana de rudibus agris* to the imperial domains of Africa, as well as with the data preserved in Cadaster B from Orange. These inscriptions advertise reduced taxation rates for irrigated land, sales of uncultivated land by the state, and tax holidays for newly farmed plots.[56] The similarities between these measures and those attested in the Mendesian Nome and elsewhere in Egypt show how the fiscal management of Egypt's territory resulted from a pragmatic conception not only of local and provincial, but also of imperial agrarian, economies.

The concomitant persistence of several types of farming practices that is attested in Mendesian papyri, however, illustrates how the quantitative

[53] Blouin (2007b, forthcoming).
[54] On that matter, see Blouin (2007a: 167–90).
[55] Blouin (forthcoming: n. 11).
[56] *Lex Manciana: CIL* 8.25902; 8.25943; 8.26416; 8.10570 (14464); 8.14428; 8.14451. *Lex Hadriana de rudibus agris: CIL* 8.25943; 8.26416. See, among others, Kehoe (1984: 241–63; Chapter 2, this volume); Hitchner (1995: 124–42); Scholl and Schubert (2004: 79–84); de Vos (Chapter 6, this volume). Cadaster B from Orange: Favory (2004: 95–118).

prevalence of wheat farming did not preclude a diversified agricultural regime. The limited quantity of land officially dedicated to these activities must not prevent us from recognizing their essential alimentary role on local levels and their profitability as cash crops. Agricultural diversification in the nome most probably resulted, as was also concluded in the case of the Fayum and the Nile valley, from an 'opportunistic' adaptation to local environmental specificities. Yet Mendesian data are also symptomatic of a competition between the interests of the economically powerful (state, large landholders, merchants) and those of small owners and tenants, for whom diversification was not only advantageous, but vital.

REFERENCES

Bagnall, R. S. (1985). *Currency and Inflation in Fourth Century Egypt*. Atlanta.
Bagnall, R. S. (1993). *Egypt in Late Antiquity*. Princeton.
Bagnall, R. S. (1997) (ed.). *The Kellis Agricultural Book* (P. Kell. *IV Gr 96*). Oxford.
Blouin, K. (2007a). *Homme et milieu dans le nome mendésien à l'époque romaine (1er au 6es.)*, Ph.D. thesis, Université Laval and Université de Nice Sophia Antipolis.
Blouin, K. (2007b). 'La Gestion patrimoniale de l'eau dans l'Égypte romaine: Le cas des milieux humides mendésiens', *Revue d'histoire comparée de l'environnement* <http://www.chaire-rome.hst.ulaval.ca/revue_point_vue.htm> (accessed 5 Mar. 2012).
Blouin, K. (2007c). 'Environnement et fisc dans le nome mendésien à l'époque romaine: Réalités et enjeux de la diversification', *BASP* 44: 135–66.
Blouin, K. (2008). 'De Mendès à Thmouis (delta du Nil, Égypte): Hydrologie mobile, société mobile?', in E. Hermon (ed.), *L'eau comme patrimoine – de la Méditerranée à l'Amérique du Nord*. Quebec, 107–27.
Blouin, K. (2010). 'La Révolte des Boukoloi (delta du Nil, Égypte, ∼166–172 de notre ère) : regard socio-environnemental sur la violence', *Phoenix* 64.3–4: 386–422.
Blouin, K. (forthcoming). 'Régionalisme fiscal dans l'Égypte romaine: Le cas des terres limnitiques mendésiennes', in F. De Angelis (ed.), *Proceedings of the Conference Regionalism and Globalism in Antiquity*. Leuven.
Blouin, K. (2012). '*Minimum firmitatis, plurimum lucri*: Le cas du "lin mendésien"', in *Proceedings of the 26th International Congress of Papyrology*. Geneva, 219–318.
Bonneau, D. (1971). *Le Fisc et le Nil: Incidences des irrégularités de la crue du Nil sur la fiscalité foncière dans l'Égypte grecque et romaine*. Paris.
Bonneau, D. (1987). 'Les Hommes et le Nil dans l'Antiquité', in A. De Réparaz (ed.), *L'eau et les hommes en Méditerranée*. Paris, 187–98.
Bousquet, B. (1996). *Tell-Douch et sa région: Géographie d'une limite de milieu à une frontière d'Empire*. Cairo.
Brun, J.-P. (2004). *Archéologie du vin et de l'huile dans l'Empire romain*. Paris.
Carrié, J.-M., and Rousselle, A. (1999). *L'Empire romain en mutation: Des Sévères à Constantin, 192–337*. Paris.

Chauveau, M., and Devauchelle, D. (1996). 'Rapport sur les papyrus carbonisés de Tanis', *BSFFT* 10–III: 107–11.

Crawford, D. J. (1971). *Kerkeosiris: An Egyptian Village in the Ptolemaic Period.* Cambridge.

Crawford, D. J. (1976). 'Imperial Estates', in M. Finley (ed.), *Studies in Roman Property.* Cambridge, 35–70.

De Romanis, F. (2002). 'Gli *horrea* dell'urbe e le inondazioni d'Egitto: Segretezza e informazione nell'organizzazione annonaria imperiale', in J. Andreau and C. Virlouvet (eds), *L'information et la mer dans le monde antique.* Rome, 279–98.

De Romanis, F. (2003). 'Per una storia del tribute granario africano della Roma imperiale', in B. Marin and C. Virlouvet (eds), *Nourrir les cités de la Méditerranée. Antiquité – Temps modernes.* Paris, 691–738.

Erdkamp, P. (2005). *The Grain Market in the Roman Empire: A Social, Political and Economic Study.* Cambridge.

Favory, F. (2004). 'L'évaluation des compétences agrologiques des sols dans l'agronomie latine au 1er siècle après J.-C.: Columelle, Pline l'Ancien et le cadastre B d'Orange', in M. Clavel-Lévêque and E. Hermon (eds), *Espaces intégrés et ressources naturelles dans l'Empire romain.* Besançon, 95–118.

Garnsey, P. (1996). *Famine et approvisionnement dans le monde gréco-romain: Réactions aux risques et aux crises.* Paris.

Garnsey, P. (1998). 'The Bean: Substance and Symbol', in W. Scheidel (ed.), *Cities, Peasants and Food in Classical Antiquity.* Cambridge, 214–25.

Garnsey, P. (1999). *Food and Society in Classical Antiquity.* Cambridge.

Hayes, A., Verhallen, A., and Taylor, T. (2005). 'Cultures couvre-sol: L'Orge', Ministère de l'Agriculture, de l'Alimentation et des Affaires rurales de l'Ontario <http://www.omafra.gov.on.ca/french/crops/facts/cover_crops01/barley.htm> (accessed 5 March 2012).

Hitchner, R. B. (1995). 'Historical Text and Archaeological Context in Roman North Africa: The Albertini Tablets and the Kasserine Survey', in D. Small (ed.), *Methods in the Mediterranean: Historical and Archaeological Views on Texts and Archaeology.* Leiden, 124–42.

Horden, P., and Purcell, N. (2000). *The Corrupting Sea: A Study of Mediterranean History.* Oxford.

Kambitsis, S. (1985). *Le Papyrus Thmouis 1, colonnes 68–160.* Paris.

Kehoe, D. P. (1984). 'Private and Imperial Management of Roman Estates in North Africa', *Law and History Review* 2.2: 241–63.

Martin, V. (1967). 'Un document administratif du nome de Mendès', *SPP* 17: 9–48.

Monson, A. (2012). *From the Ptolemies to the Romans: Political and Economic Change in Egypt.* Cambridge.

Parássoglou, G. M. (1978). *Imperial Estates in Roman Egypt.* Amsterdam.

Rathbone, D. (1991). *Economic Rationalism and Rural Society in Third-Century A.D. Egypt: The Heroninos Archive and the Appianus Estate.* Cambridge.

Redford, D. B. (2004). *Excavations at Mendes. Volume 1. The Royal Necropolis.* Leiden and Boston.

Redford, D. B. (2005). 'Mendes: City of the Ram-God', *Egyptian Archaeology* 26: 8–12.

Redford, D. B. (2009). *Delta Reports: Research in Lower Egypt* I. Oxford.

Redford, D. B. (2010). *City of the Ram-Man.* Princeton.

Rickman, G. (1980). *The Corn Supply of Ancient Rome*. Oxford.

Rowlandson, J. (1996). *Landowners and Tenants in Roman Egypt*. Oxford.

Sandy, D. B. (1989). *The Production and Use of Vegetable Oils in Ptolemaic Egypt*. Atlanta.

Scheidel, W. (2001). *Death on the Nile: Disease and the Demography of Roman Egypt*. Leiden.

Schnebel, M. (1925). *Die Landwirtschaft im hellenistischen Aegypten*. Munich.

Scholl, R., and Schubert, C. (2004). '*Lex Hadriana de rudibus agris* und *Lex Manciana*', *Archiv für Papyrusforschung* 50.1: 79–84.

Świderek, A. (1971). 'The Land-Register of the ΦΕΡΝΟΥΦΙΤΟΥ Toparchy in the Mendesian Nome', *Journal of Juristic Papyrology* 17: 31–44.

Thanheiser, U. (1992a). 'Plant-Food at Tell Ibrahim Awad: Preliminary Report', in E. C. M. Van Den Brink (ed.), *The Nile Delta in Transition: 4th.–3rd. Millennium B.C.* Tel Aviv, 117–21.

Thanheiser, U. (1992b). 'Plant Remains from Minshat Abu Omar: First Impressions', in E. C. M. Van Den Brink (ed.), *The Nile Delta in Transition: 4th.–3rd. Millennium B.C.* Tel Aviv, 167–70.

Van Minnen, P. (2001). '*P. Oxy.* LXVI 4257 and the Antonine Plague in the Fayyum', *ZPE* 135: 175–7.

Vycichl, W. (1983). *Dictionnaire étymologique de la langue copte*. Leuven.

Wallace, S. L. (1938). *Taxation in Egypt from Augustus to Diocletian*. Princeton.

9

Mechanical Irrigation: Water-Lifting Devices in the Archaeological Evidence and in the Egyptian Papyri

Myrto Malouta and Andrew Wilson

INTRODUCTION

Attempts to quantify agricultural output in antiquity face major problems; we lack records of harvests or yields, and we often have little evidence for what land was planted to what crops, although this makes a vast difference to estimates of GDP, as Helen Goodchild shows in Chapter 3 of this volume. Even the durable remains associated with agricultural production are generally associated with the processing of particular kinds of crops rather than their initial production—notably presses for wine or olive oil, or mills for grain. While wine and olive presses were generally sited on or near the estates that produced the crops, the same is not necessarily true for grain mills. Because grain keeps better than does flour, it is usually ground into flour close to the point of consumption, rather than on the farm where it was grown, and the distribution of grain mills thus says more about consumption than production. This chapter, therefore, considers other ways of exploring possible improvements in agricultural yield, analysing some evidence for the development and application of irrigation techniques.

Some recent research has argued for both demographic growth in the early Roman empire *and* rising output and standards of living, perhaps from the Augustan period to the mid-second century AD.[1] If these indicators are to be seen as valid, then we need some way of explaining how the Roman world was apparently able to escape Malthusian checks for a period of perhaps two centuries, with demographic growth and per capita growth running in parallel.

---

[1] e.g. de Callataÿ (2005); Jongman (2007a, 2007b); Bowman and Wilson (2009, 2011).

The answer seems to lie in the way that both the Malthusian model and new economic growth theory tend to assume that one of the main input factors, land, is essentially fixed and unchanging.[2] Karl Persson indeed queries whether the quantity of land was ever a binding constraint, and points out that the Malthusian model takes no account of technological progress in agriculture that might improve the efficiency of land use.[3] The idea that the quantity of useable land was constant, and that there was no progress in agricultural techniques, is demonstrably not the case for the classical world, and especially for the period 200 BC to AD 150. This period saw intensive colonization and population expansion, especially into areas of North Africa and western Europe, which were underpopulated and not intensively farmed. In North Africa, apart from the Punic littoral, most societies were transhumant or semi-nomadic pastoralists until the incipient adoption of agriculture by the Numidian kingdoms in the early second century BC, and then the intensive expansion of agriculture under Roman colonization. Important introductions in irrigation enabled the bringing of large tracts of land under cultivation. In an initial shift from pastoralism to agriculture, it becomes possible to see how both population and per capita incomes might rise together. On this view, then, the Malthusian equilibrium could be reset by shocks such as the introduction of particularly important new technologies affecting land use and carrying capacity—in this case, agricultural ones—that enable the bar of carrying capacity to be raised; population expansion and per capita growth can then occur together until the new limit is approached. In a sense, the Industrial Revolution was another such major shock, the first of a succession of major modern technological shocks that have so far kept the bar out of reach of expanding modern economies. Time lags in the Malthusian system thus could enable periods of simultaneous population growth and per capita economic growth following such technological shocks. Persson, indeed, argues that technological progress went beyond mere periodic shocks and was progressive and cumulative, so that the effects of technological progress, coupled with the efficiency gains from regional specialization and trade, and fertility strategies consciously adopted by households, was such as to invalidate the Malthusian model entirely.[4] If we are looking for technological innovations that might be thought to have the greatest impact in antiquity, we should look for those that directly affected agricultural productivity, at the start of the production chain, by increasing the amount or the fertility of available land. Geoffrey Kron has drawn attention to the improvements in crop rotation systems in the Roman period.[5] We can identify several technological advances in the ancient world that increased the availability of *useable*

---

[2] But a review by Bauer (1956: 635) of Lewis (1955) makes the point about land clearance and reclamation in the early stages of growth of principally agricultural economies.
[3] Persson (2010: 42–52).   [4] Persson (2010).   [5] Kron (2000).

or *cultivable* land by the development of agricultural landscapes through irrigation, drainage, and land reclamation schemes. In this sense technology can be considered to have had an important impact on the availability of the land input factor. Here, we concentrate on irrigation technologies.

IRRIGATION TECHNOLOGY AND THE AVAILABILITY OF USEABLE LAND

Irrigation was essential to agriculture in much of the ancient Mediterranean world.[6] It might take the form of channel irrigation systems deriving from springs or water courses—the *lex rivi Hiberiensis*, a Hadrianic regulation governing the use of a large channel irrigation system in the Ebro valley north of Zaragoza in Spain, is a striking example of the scale and complexity of such systems.[7] If it relates to the known archaeological remains of a major irrigation system further upstream in the Ebro valley, the whole system must have been over 100 km long; if, as is more likely, it does not, the middle Ebro valley had at least three systems each of over 20 or 30 km long (including the separate system further downstream mentioned in the much earlier *Tabula Contrebiensis*[8]). Other very large systems are known from North Africa (for example, the Lamasba irrigation decree, and the remains of many medium-sized systems in Algeria and Tunisia) and Syria.[9] Most of these used technology that was not new at the time of their construction; what does appear to be new in the Roman period is the scale of the application of such technologies outside Mesopotamia and Egypt—notably in Syria, North Africa, and Spain—and the widespread use of dams.[10] The effectiveness of such systems relied not only on the surveying and construction technology involved, but also on a developed framework of irrigation law and water rights, exemplified by the *Tabula Contrebiensis*, the *lex rivi Hiberiensis*, and the Lamasba decree.

Channel and dam irrigation technology enabled intensive cultivation of regions in the drier circum-Mediterranean areas. In some extremely arid zones, run-off collection and wadi wall technology enabled the cultivation of land that otherwise could not have been cultivated at all.[11]

---

[6] Oleson (2000a).   [7] Beltrán Lloris (2006).
[8] Richardson (1983); Birks *et al.* (1984).
[9] Lamasba: Shaw (1982). Algeria: Fentress (1979). Syria: Decker (2009b: 177–89).
[10] Dams: Smith (1971); Schnitter (1978, 1992); Garbrecht (1987, 1991); Kamash (2006: 54–73).
[11] Gilbertson *et al.* (1984); Barker *et al.* (1996).

THE EVIDENCE FOR WATER-LIFTING MACHINES

These irrigation systems, ranging from the small scale to the massive, depended on gravity flow. But to irrigate land above the level of locally available water, the water has to be raised, and this is usually prohibitively difficult to do manually in anything but the smallest quantities. The irrigation—and in some regions therefore the cultivation—of land higher than a local water source is therefore possible only through the use of water-lifting machines.[12] This chapter examines the archaeological evidence for the use and spread across the empire as a whole of the water-lifting machines used in the Roman world—*shadufs*, Archimedes screws, animal-driven and water-driven wheels with compartmented rims, animal-driven pot garlands, and force pumps—and the papyrological evidence for their use in Egypt. We shall argue that many different kinds of water-lifting devices were in use throughout the Mediterranean provinces of the empire, and not just in Egypt or the east; and that the uptake of these technologies was widespread well before the late antique period.

Between 260 and 240 BC there seems to have been a spate of invention at Alexandria of water-lifting devices.[13] Several water-lifting devices are mentioned in the writings of Philo of Byzantium—either in the original Greek, or in Arabic translations of lost Greek portions of the work that can nevertheless be shown to be original through the use of the Greek alphabetic order rather than the Arabic alphabetic order of the lettering of accompanying diagrams.[14]

The mid-third century BC, when many of these devices were invented, is a period when papyri show a drive by the Ptolemaic rulers of Egypt to increase agricultural yields, and archaeology shows expansion of agriculture in the Fayyum, irrigated by lifting water from canals onto adjacent fields. The new water-lifting devices—the Archimedes screw, the water-driven wheel with compartmented rim, the animal-driven wheel with compartmented rim, and the animal-driven pot garland—appear to be the result of royal sponsorship of technological research aimed at increasing production, and this forces us to consider the achievements of the Alexandrian Museum as more than mere abstract academic research.[15]

The archaeological evidence for water-lifting devices, and particularly for the Early Roman period, indicates widespread use throughout the empire. The full dataset of archaeological and literary evidence builds on the fundamental study by John Oleson of Greek and Roman water-lifting devices, published in 1984, with the addition of a large number of new archaeological finds

---

[12] Oleson (1984, 2000b).
[13] Lewis (1997); Wilson (2002).
[14] e.g. Philo *Pneumatica* 5, 62, 65; Lewis (1997: 20–32).
[15] Lewis (1997); Wilson (2002).

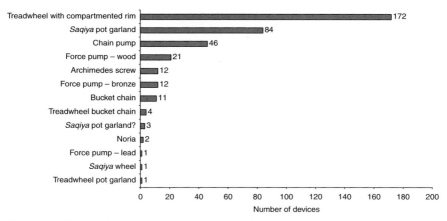

Fig. 9.1. Different functions of water-lifting devices represented in the archaeological evidence (n = 370)

discovered since, and the elimination of dubious cases. As Fig. 9.1 shows, the most common categories represented in the 370 sites known from archaeological evidence are accounted for by treadwheels for mine drainage works, bilge pumps (chain pumps) on ships, and pot-garland irrigation machines—overwhelmingly productive or useful functions, therefore.

In the papyri, as we shall see, irrigation machinery constitutes the overwhelming bulk of attestations of water-lifting devices. In order to analyse them we compiled a database of all direct references to water-lifting devices in the papyri of the third century BC to the eighth century AD—all except one from Egypt—as well as references to water-lifting and artificial irrigation, even when the actual device used for that purpose is not specified.[16] As it stands, the database contains 298 texts with 658 references to a minimum of 583 machines.[17] The machines may in fact be many more, but we have chosen to count unspecified plurals as two, whereas specified plurals are occasionally a lot more numerous.[18]

The main complication when trying to establish the nature of each device is that the terminology of the device itself and of many of the parts it comprises is still a subject of debate.[19] As the following discussion shows, it is clear that one must allow for regional or chronological variations in that terminology.

---

[16] This MySQL database is available on the OXREP website at <http://oxrep.classics.ox.ac.uk/>.

[17] Oleson's study included 184 papyri and 8 ostraca (Oleson 1984: 129).

[18] A reference to 100 devices (*organa*) in *P. Petr.* III. 43 is, however, possibly an erroneous reading.

[19] Oleson (1984: 127, 131–71); Bonneau (1993); Rathbone (2007).

The *shaduf*

Before the third century BC, the only such machine available in the ancient world was the swape-well or *shaduf*, called in Greek *kelon* or *keloneion*, in Latin *telo* or *tolleno*, a swing beam with a bucket on one end and a counter-weight on the other.[20] Its advantage was that it allowed the operator to pull *downwards* on the bucket to immerse it in the water, using the stronger back and leg muscles to raise the counterweight; on releasing the rope, the counter-weight raised the container of water, which the operator simply tipped into a receiving container or channel. This was a relatively simple machine with a low lift and a fairly low output.

There are no certain archaeological finds of *shadufs* from the ancient world, since the device itself was made of perishable materials and the only fixing necessary was a post in the ground. Iconographically they are represented in ancient Egyptian wall paintings; for the Roman period, there is one depiction of a *shaduf*, on a mosaic floor from the House of the Laberii at Oudna in Tunisia (Fig. 9.2).[21] Pliny (*NH* 19.20.60) regards the *tolleno* (*shaduf*) as a normal part of garden irrigation equipment, and Isidore of Seville, writing in the seventh century AD, records that in Spain *shadufs* were called *ciconiae* ('storks'), confirming their use there at that period.[22] In fact, given their low cost and relative simplicity, they are likely to have been widespread in the Roman world, and their modern distribution supports this view—they are still widespread in parts of Africa, were common in medieval and early modern Europe, and are still to be seen in Romania today.[23]

The *keloneion* or *shaduf* is the type of water-lifting device best attested in the earliest papyri from Egypt. As opposed to the other machine types that are predominantly attested in the Roman period, the *keloneion* is attested throughout the Ptolemaic period, until the second century AD, at which point we find the highest concentration of references. After the second century, however, references to the *keloneion* cease (Fig. 9.3). This sudden apparent disappearance of the *keloneion* from our sources is one of the main reasons to consider the correspondence between the ancient terms for water-lifting devices and modern interpretations carefully: if one were to take the papyrological evidence at face value, one would conclude that the *shaduf*, although prominent throughout the Ptolemaic and early Roman times, ceased to be used in Egypt at some point in the second century AD. This cannot be

---

[20] Oleson (2000b: 225–9).　　　[21] Gauckler (1896).

[22] *Origines* 20.15.1: *hoc instrumentum Hispani ciconiam dicunt, propter quod imitetur eius-dem nominis avem, levantes aqua ac deponentes rostrum, dum clangit*; Oleson (1984: 56–7); Adams (2007: 238–9).

[23] Cf. *OED s.v. swape-well* for its use in nineteenth-century Britain. Romania: Wilson (2002: plate I.1).

Fig. 9.2. Mosaic from the House of the Laberii, Oudna (Tunisia) showing a rural scene with a *shaduf* (Musée du Bardo, Tunis)

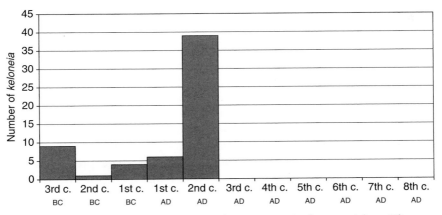

Fig. 9.3. Number of *kelôneia* attested per century in the papyri (n = 59)

true. The *shaduf* is still in use today in Egypt, and, as it is one of the simplest and cheapest water-lifting devices, it would be hard to imagine that it gave way to its more costly and labour-intensive counterparts. Moreover, Oleson refutes Bonneau's suggestion that the disappearance from the documents of certain kinds of devices depends on whether or not they were taxed, pointing out that water-lifting devices feature in the papyri regardless of their status as taxable goods.[24] We hear of them when they are sold or hired, damaged and repaired, when labourers must be remunerated for operating them, or when accidents happen with them. One might, of course, choose to argue that eventual increase in prosperity may have led to the greater affordability of more complex machines. While not impossible, this argument would assume sustained economic growth, the indication for which lies in evidence such as the kind under scrutiny here, and would therefore beg the question. How do we solve this conundrum? The predominance of unspecified types of water-lifting devices after the second century AD may in fact be due to such a switch in terminology that has not yet been accurately detected; we will return to this possibility in the discussion below.

The water-powered waterwheel

The new Hellenistic devices of the third century BC included the water-lifting wheel driven by the current of a stream or river with compartments on the rim, which filled as they dipped under the water and emptied near the top of the cycle into a collection trough. A high lift and large output could be achieved—somewhat less than the diameter of the wheel, which could be many metres across—and it required no human or animal labour to operate. There is a representation of such a water-driven wheel on a mosaic from Apamea (dated to AD 469), in which the stepped axle support still characteristic of water-driven wheels at Hama in Syria is clearly visible (Fig. 9.4).[25] The device is still in use in parts of Syria, notably Hama (Fig. 9.5), and on the Euphrates; also in the Fayyum in Egypt, in Morocco, and in the Iberian peninsula (for example, Cordoba), where its use is definitely attested from the Middle Ages onwards.[26] (In the Near East it is called a *noria*, although in Spain this term refers to an animal-driven wheel.)

The evident continuity of use in the East has led to a widespread presumption that in antiquity the water-driven wheel was used principally in the Eastern provinces, but there are indications that its introduction to North

---

[24] Bonneau (1970: 49); Oleson (1984: 131).
[25] Oleson (1984: 185–6 and fig. 41).
[26] Zaqzouk (1990); Wilson (2003: 123–5); Rathbone (2007: 254).

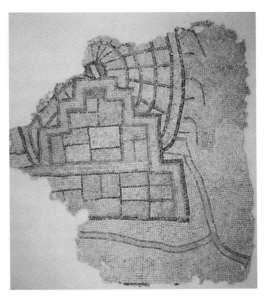

Fig. 9.4. Mosaic from the colonnaded street at Apamea (Syria), showing a water-driven water-lifting wheel (*noria*), AD 469 (Z. Kamash)

Fig. 9.5. Water-lifting wheel (*noria*) at Hama (Syria) (A. Wilson)

Africa and Spain occurred before the Islamic period.[27] As early as the first century BC Lucretius uses the water-driven wheel as an analogy for cosmic rotation—*ut fluvios versare rotas atque austra videmus* ('as we see rivers turning wheels and their scoops')—which must suggest that it was familiar to audiences in Italy; if they had never seen such a machine, the analogy would be ineffective as an explanatory device.[28] Elagabalus is said to have tied court sycophants to such wheels and called them his *Ixiones amicos* ('Ixionian friends'), or perhaps even his *Ixiones amnicos* ('stream-driven Ixions').[29] Since the source is unreliable and Elagabalus himself was from Syria, where he must have been familiar with such wheels, this attestation does little to prove the use of the water-driven wheel in Italy, but if any doubts persisted about its use in the central Mediterranean they have been recently dispelled by the discovery at Salona in Dalmatia of the installation for a water-powered lifting wheel in an ecclesiastical complex of the sixth century AD. A waterwheel driven by a branch of the aqueduct within the city lifted water into a reused sarcophagus, which served as a tank to feed a nearby ornamental fountain.[30] That the only known archaeological find of a Roman or Byzantine water-powered water-lifting wheel is from an urban context, where it was clearly not used for irrigation, is again explicable by the relatively slight foundation traces these machines would leave in an uncanalized rural watercourse, their vulnerability to destruction by erosion over the centuries, and the low likelihood of coming upon isolated rural installations like these by chance.

In the Egyptian papyri there is no unambiguous reference to water-powered water-lifting wheels: the terms *trochos* and *tympanon* can refer to wheels of various types, including the animal-driven pot-garland machine described below, or components of it. The probable invention of the water-powered water-lifting wheel in Hellenistic Egypt (on the basis of sources connected with the Museum at Alexandria) and the existence of water-powered wheels today in the Fayyum suggest they they were used there,[31] and some of the instances of the terms *trochos, mechane,* or even *organon* may refer to these machines.

Ulpian indicates that there was some legal debate over whether the drawing of water from a river by means of a wheel (type unspecified, and irrelevant to the legal point at issue) constituted a legal servitude; a rescript of the emperor

---

[27] Watson (1974: 13, 28; 1983: 104–5, 191–2 n. 15) played down the pre-Islamic use of the *noria*, although Glick (1970: 178–80) and Butzer *et al.* (1985: 482) acknowledged the use of this device in Roman Spain.

[28] Lucretius, *De Rerum Natura* V. 515–16.

[29] *SHA, Heliogabalus* 24.5; Oleson (1984: 96–7).

[30] Morvillez *et al.* (2005).

[31] Lewis (1997); Rathbone (2007: 254).

Antoninus (probably Caracalla) established that it did not, but existing rights should be protected.[32]

The animal-driven wheel and bucket-chain/pot-garland machines

Where a flowing current was not available to turn a wheel, animal-driven wheels might be used to lift water out of canals, wells, or cisterns. For low lifts, of a metre or so, one might use a wheel with wooden compartments on the rim, or later with pots lashed to the rim, powered via a right-angled gearing by an animal walking in circles around a drive wheel.[33] This again allowed a lift somewhat less than the wheel diameter, perhaps a metre or two, generally enough to lift water out of a canal onto an adjacent field. Archaeologically there are no certain examples of this type of installation known; before the introduction of pots lashed to the rim of the wheel, the entire machine consisted of perishable elements of wood and rope, and where pots are preserved they may equally, or more likely, have come from animal-driven pot-garland machines. A painting in a tomb chamber from Wardian in the suburbs of Alexandria shows such a wheel in a rural context evidently used for

Fig. 9.6. Painting from a tomb at Wardian (Alexandria, Egypt), showing oxen working a water-lifting wheel (A. Wilson; Greco-Roman Museum Alexandria)

---

[32] Ulpian, *Digest* 8.4.2; cf. Bruun (2012: 29).
[33] Schiøler (1973); Oleson (1984: 350–85).

irrigation (Fig. 9.6).[34] The painting is variously dated on the uncertain basis of artistic style to the first century BC or first century AD.

A variant of this machine with the same drive arrangement, but allowing the lifting of water to a greater height, is that of the bucket chain or pot garland looped over the wheel, where the wheel is used not to lift water directly, but rather to set in motion a long rope or chain from which hang a series of containers (wooden, bronze, or ceramic) that reach the water level below.[35] This mechanism, and by extension the whole system of cog wheels and waterwheel(s), is today known in many parts of the Arabic-speaking world as a *saqiya*, although in the Iberian peninsula it is often called a *noria*. In the Greek of the papyri the bucket chain was probably referred to by the term *kulle kuklas*, but the whole machine seems to be commonly referred to simply as *mechane*.

Archaeologically this device is better represented than the others considered so far, and is known both from installations and from the characteristic *saqiya* pots that appeared in later versions of the device. Again, though, most of the identifiable examples are from urban contexts rather than being rural devices used for irrigation; this reflects the pattern of modern investigation rather than ancient usage.

The bucket chain is one of the mid-third-century BC inventions mentioned by Philo of Byzantium (*Pneumatica* 65, an impractical water-powered version),[36] and is first attested archaeologically at Cosa in Italy, where in the second century BC a bathhouse on the acropolis was supplied using a bucket chain to raise water from a cistern to the baths.[37] In the early first century BC, a bucket-chain device, with wooden buckets on a rope chain, was installed at the spring house by the port of Cosa to raise water through 16 m probably to a villa or amphora factory connected with the port nearby.[38] Four other early instances of water-lifting wheels, though probably treadwheel-driven, rather than driven by a right-angled gearing, are known from baths in Herculaneum and Pompeii, all dating from the late second/early first century BC.[39] These examples are all urban, and used for the supply of baths or other buildings rather than for agricultural purposes, reflecting the bias towards excavation of urban sites noted earlier, but they do demonstrate that the technology was in use in Italy by the second century BC, even if we cannot see its use for irrigation.

Bucket-chain water-lifting technology had spread to Britain by soon after the middle of the first century AD, as shown by finds from excavations in

---

[34] Oleson (1984: 184–5); Venit (1988, 1989).
[35] Oleson (1984: 350–70; 2000b: 251–63, 267–72).
[36] Lewis (1997: 32).
[37] Oleson (1984: 201).
[38] Oleson (1984: 201–4; 1987).
[39] Oleson (1984: 213–15, 242–8).

Gresham St, in the central part of Roman London. These revealed two large square wells, with remains of water-lifting devices. One was built just after the Boudiccan revolt, *c.* AD 63; and was in use for about ten years before being filled in. Instead of buckets, it used wooden boxes linked together probably by iron links. The second well was dug in the early second century AD, and the device used here had wooden boxes connected by cranked iron chain links, some of which survived, enabling the reconstruction of a full-sized working replica at the Museum of London.[40] These finds enabled the reinterpretation of an earlier discovery made in the 1950s, of a similar large square well with the find of a wooden box compartment similar to those from the earlier of the two Gresham St wells; it seems to have supplied the public baths at Cheapside. The drive mechanism was not preserved, but an animal-driven right-angled gearing is the most likely solution. Again, these devices demonstrate that water-lifting bucket-chain technology existed in Britain within twenty years of the Roman conquest. Once more, these are urban finds, but their use in a civilian context shows that there is no need to see the army as an agent of technological diffusion here.

The archaeological finds of water-lifting bucket chains in Italy and Britain demonstrate the use of this water-lifting technique in the western empire, and show that it would have been available as an irrigation technology here if needed, but the known finds are all urban and were used to supply water to buildings, principally baths. However, the suspicion that the device would also have been used for irrigation is confirmed by the discovery at the Villa de Careiron et Pesquier, in southern Gaul, of an oval well dated to the first century AD. The dimensions, 3.80 × 1.56 m in plan, indicate that a wheel was installed in the well, and this must have been a wooden bucket chain or pot garland (probably the former, as no *saqiya* pots were found). It fed water to a series of channels with sluice gates for control of distribution. Some water may have gone to parts of the villa, but the channel arrangements and the layout of the site also suggest that the water was used to irrigate gardens.[41] This discovery appears to confirm the use of pot-garland irrigation in Gaul in the first century AD.

The well at the Villa de Careiron et Pesquier shows how the shape and size of wells may be used as diagnostic features for identifying pot-garland installations. Normal domestic wells in the ancient world tended to be circular or square, about 0.80–1 m across—large enough for the digger to work in, but minimizing the work needed to dig it. Wells that are substantially larger than this in plan require some explanation for why the extra effort has been expended on their excavation. In the case of a series of wells whose dimensions in plan approximate 3 × 1 m, the answer is obvious; they were intended to

[40] Blair (2004); Blair *et al.* (2005, 2006).
[41] Conche *et al.* (2005).

accommodate a pot-garland wheel over the mouth of the well. There are several examples in Syria, most obviously the rectangular well excavated as part of the mid-sixth-century AD bathhouse at Al-Anderin (Androna); numerous fragments of the characteristic *saqiya* pots were also found in the excavation of the baths.[42] A well of similar dimensions was noted on the outskirts of the settlement at Al-Anderin, and another at the mid-sixth-century 'palace' of Qasr Ibn Wardan, outside the main building.[43] These latter two examples may possibly have been used for the irrigation of gardens.

At Ptolemais in Cyrenaica there is a brick-lined well in the middle of the Square of the Cisterns, at least 11 m deep (to the present fill), with a rectangular opening measuring 3 × 1 m. Structurally it antedates the construction of the main group of cisterns under the square, and may belong to the Early Roman period. A well of this depth and size was clearly fitted with a water-lifting machine, and must have served for the purpose of public water supply, perhaps before the construction of the city's aqueduct.[44] A rectangular well at Tocra (ancient Taucheira) of similar size in plan may also have had a pot-garland machine.[45] Again, neither of these two examples was for irrigation, but they attest the use of the technology in Cyrenaica.

Further west in North Africa, there is some evidence for the use of pot-garland devices on the subterranean Roman aqueduct that ran from La Soukra towards Carthage. This aqueduct collected and transported groundwater from the Ariana plain to the west of Carthage. Some of the access or inspection shafts are *c.*3 × 1 m in plan (Fig. 9.7), much larger than normal access shafts for underground aqueducts, and, given their rural location, they probably served for animal-driven pot-garland machines to lift water for irrigation in the surrounding fields; interestingly, in the early twentieth century, French colonists installed wind pumps over these shafts to use them for the same purpose.[46] These indications of the use of pot-garland machines in North Africa reinforce the idea that the reference by Tertullian (a North African writer) in his *De Anima* (33.7) to *aquilegas rotas* (water-lifting wheels) driven by mules and donkeys was drawn from personal familiarity with the machine.

The foregoing discussion has argued that the use of bucket-chain or pot-garland types of water-lifting technology was widespread throughout the Roman empire, for irrigation and other purposes, and not just confined to Egypt and the provinces of the Near East. These water-lifting machines were not an early medieval introduction into Spain and North Africa from the Arab world, but long predated the Arab conquest of these regions.[47] Necessarily,

---

[42] Mango (2002: 313).   [43] Personal observation; cf. Wilson (2003: 120).
[44] Wilson (2003: 121).   [45] Wilson (2003: 121).
[46] Renault (1912: 471–5); Fornacciari (1928–9); Wilson (2003: 121).
[47] *Contra* Watson (1974:13; 1983: 104–5, 191–2 n. 15); Glick (1979: 74 ('the noria revolution' in Islamic Spain), 235–8 (= Glick 2005: 258–61)) and Butzer *et al.* (1985: 496), who regarded the pot garland (*saqiya*) as 'a bonafide Islamic introduction' to Spain.

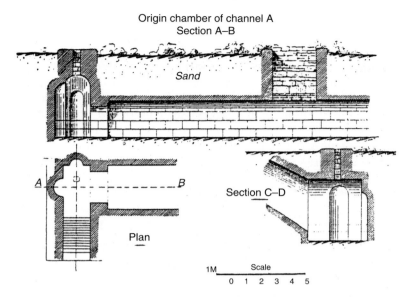

Origin chamber of channel A
Section A–B

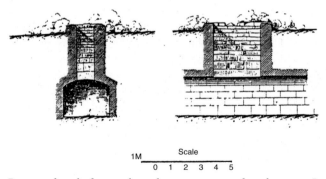

Sections through one of the inspection shafts (Channel B)

Fig. 9.7. Rectangular shafts on the subterranean aqueduct between La Soukra and Carthage, probably for *saqiya* irrigation of the Ariana plain (after Renault 1912: 473–4)

given the urban focus of most excavations, the argument has had to proceed by establishing the use of the technology in urban contexts for uses other than irrigation, and then adducing supporting evidence that confirms the use of such water-lifting machines in rural contexts for irrigation.

The early versions of bucket-chain machines, as described by Philo of Byzantium in the third century BC and by Vitruvius in the first century BC,[48] had bronze buckets linked with an iron chain, and the finds from Cosa and London used wooden buckets or compartments linked together by ropes or an iron chain; leather bags may also have been used for installations in Egypt.[49] The survival of these elements is rare, given the recuperation and reuse of the metal elements in antiquity and the perishability of the wooden and rope elements, which survive only in waterlogged contexts. But at some point in the Roman period the design of these water-lifting machines, at least in Egypt and the Near East, was re-engineered to replace the wooden buckets or leather bags with ceramic pots, tied onto ropes.[50] In the south-eastern Mediterranean, where wood was scarce and expensive, this development dramatically reduced the cost of this device. It also greatly increases the archaeological visibility of the device; the characteristic *saqiya* pots, with a knob at the base to facilitate their lashing to the rope garland, have been found in wells, as surface scatters, and as grave goods in Israel, Egypt, and Nubia.[51]

The date of the introduction of *saqiya* pots is being pushed back by new research. At least eighty-two sites in Egypt, Nubia, and the Levant have yielded finds of *saqiya* pots dating between the third and seventh centuries AD, although in many cases the dating is imprecise (a range of several hundred years within this period).[52] Finds from Israel indicate that such pots were already in use in the third century AD.[53] But the fourth-century peak in the number of known sites does support the long-held view that pot-garland devices became popular as a result of Diocletian's introduction of tax relief on irrigated land.[54] The combination of this state move encouraging irrigation and the re-engineering of elements of the machine in cheaper materials appears greatly to have encouraged the uptake of the device in the eastern provinces in the Late Roman period.

The problem of archaeological visibility means that the contrast between the third and the fourth centuries could be largely due to the introduction, perhaps in the third century, of pots rather than wooden buckets, and the subsequent uptake of this new design. The combined evidence of the papyri, as we shall see, and of rectangular wells, and the related wooden bucket evidence from Cosa and London for essentially the same technology in non-irrigation contexts, suggests that the basic machine was not rare before the fourth

---

[48] Philo, *Pneumatica* 65; Vitruvius, *De Architectura* 10.4.4; cf. Oleson (1984: 75–9, 116–17).
[49] Oleson (1984: 216).
[50] Oleson (1984: 354–5, 366–7); Ayalon (2000).
[51] Ayalon (2000); Decker (2001: 375–6; 2009b: 199–202); Kamash (2006).
[52] Decker (2009b: 201) refers to forty-six sites in the Near East that have yielded *saqiya* pots of Byzantine date, many of which are included in the total of eighty-two.
[53] Ayalon (2000); cf. Rathbone (2007).
[54] Bonneau (1970: 49); Oleson (1984: 379–80).

century AD, and was probably used extensively outside Egypt. Its use in irrigation contexts in Roman Gaul and North Africa appears to be established; its use in Spain is also therefore very likely well before the Arab conquest.

There is plentiful papyrological evidence for the use of the pot garland in Egypt, although it is rather complicated by the variety of terminology used, and in some cases uncertainty over which type of device is meant by some of the terms. In the case of *kukleuterion* and *kulle kuklas*, it is clear that we are dealing respectively with the entire animal-driven water-lifting installation and the pot-garland element of the machine; the terms *trochos, tympanon,* and *mechane* seem also to have been used, sometimes or often, to refer to pot-garland machines or their components.

The word *kukleuterion*, interpreted as either animal-driven waterwheel or pot-garland installations, emerges in the Early Roman period; there are no Ptolemaic references to *kukleuteria*. All attestations fall between the first and seventh centuries AD, and within those confines their pattern of attestation displays the usual sixth- and seventh-century peaks, as well as a notable peak in the second century (Fig. 9.8). It is noteworthy that the attestation of the device by this term occurs long before the introduction of *saqiya* pots.[55]

The term *kulle kuklas* is interpreted as bucket chain or pot garland;[56] it is not attested in the papyri before the fourth century AD (Fig. 9.9), and its

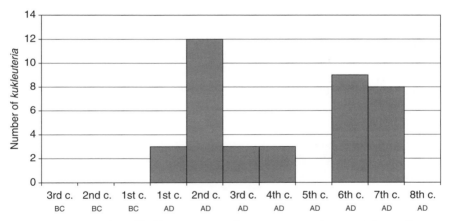

Fig. 9.8. Number of *kukleuteria* attested per century in the papyri (n = 38)

---

[55] A related term, *kukleutikon*, occurs in several ostraca, dating from the first and second centuries AD, from the fort at Maximianon on the route between Coptos and Myos Hormos in the Eastern Desert. The *kukleutikon* was apparently a salary paid to women for operating a waterwheel, either directly or by driving the animals that powered the wheel. The waterwheel installations presumably served the *hydreumata* or watering points that catered to the desert traffic on this route (Cuvigny 2003: 389–94).

[56] Oleson (1984: 133–4).

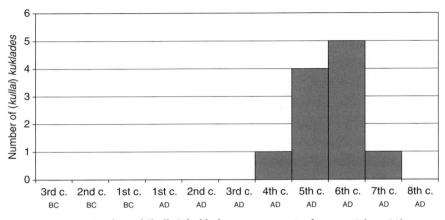

Fig. 9.9. Number of (*kullai*) *kuklades* per century in the papyri (n = 11)

introduction coincides with the earliest finds of *saqiya* pots in Egypt, suggesting that it was used specifically to mean 'pot garland' rather than 'bucket chain'.

Trochoi, which are taken to mean waterwheels, show a very pronounced concentration in the Roman period, with no references before the first century BC or after the fourth century AD. It must be stressed that we understand the term in a generic sense, referring to a wheel for lifting water; it might refer either to water-powered waterwheels, or to a bucket-chain or pot-garland machine (or a component of one), or the animal-driven wheel with compartmented rim, but, because it is impossible to ascertain this from the context, we have presented *trochoi* here as a separate group (Fig. 9.10).

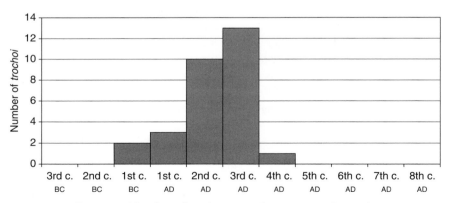

Fig. 9.10. Number of *trochoi* attested per century (n = 29)

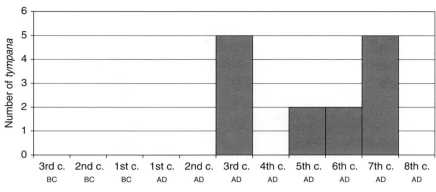

Fig. 9.11. Number of *tympana* attested per century (n = 14)

As with the *kulle kuklas*, the term *tympanon* has been graphed separately (Fig. 9.11), although it seems most likely that it too refers to a part of a pot-garland machine, either the hollow bobbin-type wheel over which the pot garland was looped (its meaning in texts of the third-century AD Heroninos archive), or perhaps sometimes a cog wheel.[57] It is interesting to observe that the emergence of the term *tympanon* in the third century almost coincides with the disappearance of the term *trochos*; does one term effectively replace the other?

Archimedes screw

The Archimedes screw or 'Egyptian screw', invented apparently by Archimedes in the third century BC, is a kind of displacement pump that used a rotating screw fitted within an inclined cylinder with one end immersed in the water, to lift and push up blocks of water through an angled tube.[58] This achieved a fast discharge but a relatively low lift, in the order of a metre or so. Literary references attest its use in Egypt for irrigation—indeed Polybius refers to the device as 'the Egyptian screw'[59]—and by the second century BC in the Carthaginian mines of southern Spain, where they were used for draining underground galleries. The archaeologically preserved examples are all found in mines, where the underground conditions and inaccessability have preserved them. No rural examples for irrigation have been found, but this again is unsurprising given the perishability of the wooden elements and the

---

[57] Rathbone (2007: 260). Cf. Vitruvius' use of *tympanum dentatum* to refer to a toothed cog wheel (e.g. *de Arch.* 10.5.2; 10.9.1–7).

[58] Oleson (1984: 296).

[59] Posidonius, quoted in Diodorus Siculus 5.37.3–4 and Strabo 3.2.9 (Oleson 1984: 91–2).

Fig. 9.12. Wall painting from the House of Publius Cornelius Teges in Pompeii, showing an Egyptian genre scene with a man operating an Archimedes screw to water crops (A. Maiuri, *NSA*, 1927, pl. IX)

recyclability of the metal parts of the machine. An inscription from Syria records the construction of a water screw (*kochlias*) on the Euphrates between AD 72 and AD 74, which from its situation seems to have been for irrigation.[60] Iconographic sources do, however, show the machine used for irrigation in genre scenes of the Egyptian countryside, notably in a wall painting from the House of Publius Cornelius Teges in Pompeii (Fig. 9.12), and a series of terracottas showing a man treading an Archimedes screw.[61]

Yet, although the use of Archimedes screws is a *topos* associated with the Egyptian rural scene, we have not a single explicit reference in the papyri to Archimedes screws used for irrigation. Only nine Archimedes screws are attested in the papyrological evidence, and these are all in the same document (*P. Lond.* III.1177 of AD 113), which relates to the urban water supply of Arsinoë.[62] The term used in that document is *kochlias*, and searches of the papyrological corpora for other terms that might signify an Archimedes screw (*helix*, for example) have not yielded any further examples. In this case, as with the *shaduf*, one has to wonder whether one or more of the more generic terms

---

[60] *ILS* 8903; Oleson (1984: 55–6).
[61] Oleson (1984: 207–8, 227, 241–2).
[62] Habermann (2000).

for a water-lifting device, such as *mechane* or *organon*, for example, might also be used to refer to the Archimedes screw.

Force pump

The force pump was invented by Ctesibius in the second century BC, and was originally made of bronze, requiring precision engineering in a relatively costly material.[63] The written sources attest its use for fire-setting in mines, fire-fighting, and spraying perfumed water on crowds in circuses and amphi-theatres,[64] but not in irrigation. At some point in the Early Roman period, perhaps the first or second centuries AD, the force pump was re-engineered to use a single block of wood, hollowed out where necessary, making it more affordable and encouraging uptake in the northern provinces; there are several finds from Germany and Britain (Fig. 9.13).[65] The wooden force pumps appear in a variety of contexts, used mainly for urban and domestic villa supply, but some garden irrigation is possible in some instances, although limited to small plots. The evidence for force pumps—*siphones*—is quite scant in the papyri (five mentions in three different papyri, of which one is from Nessana in Palestine).

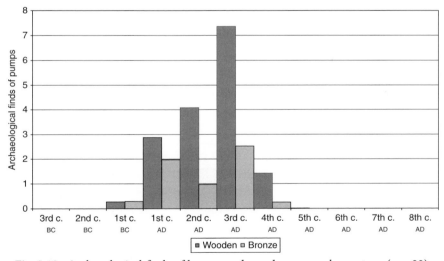

Fig. 9.13. Archaeological finds of bronze and wooden pumps by century (n = 22)

---

[63] Oleson (1984: 301–25); Stein (2004).

[64] Cf. the discovery of elements of a wooden force pump in the basement of the amphitheatre at Trier: Oleson (1984: 275–6).

[65] Stein (2004).

Indeterminate devices

The term for a water-lifting device that appears in the papyrological evidence most often is *mechane*. From the context in which it appears it would seem that the term usually refers to animal-driven bucket-chain and pot-garland machines.[66] The chronological distribution is shown in Fig. 9.14. In general terms, the *mechane* is well attested between the first and eighth centuries AD, with one solitary reference in the third century BC. While this isolated instance might at first seem suspicious, it is not problematic in general, since the animal-driven bucket-chain machine appears to have been known as early as the middle of the third century BC.[67] However, *mechane* is an unspecific term and in some instances may refer to other kinds of devices, including probably the Archimedes screw.

Another well-attested but vague term is *organon*. There are numerous references to *organa* that have been interpreted as probably parts of water-lifting devices, but may in fact refer to a specific kind of device that has not so far been identified (Fig. 9.15). The spread, as with the *mechanai*, is concentrated between the second and seventh centuries AD. There are three attestations in the third century BC, one in the first century AD, and none in between. It is worth wondering whether the term, which becomes suddenly very popular after the second century AD, may have been used to denote the *shaduf*, whose mysterious disappearance we wondered about before, or even a number of devices including the *shaduf*. Similarly, the term *mechane*, which, when that can be ascertained, means the bucket-chain or pot-garland machine, should

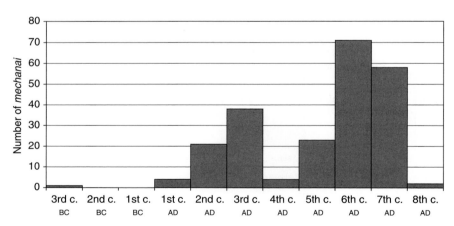

Fig. 9.14. Number of *mechanai* attested per century in the papyri (n = 222)

---

[66] Cf. Rathbone (2007).   [67] Lewis (1997: 32).

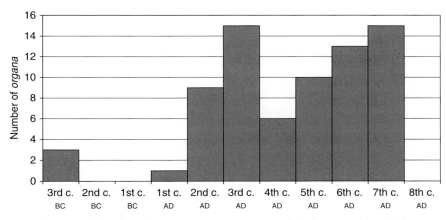

Fig. 9.15. Number of *organa* per century attested in the papyri (n = 72)

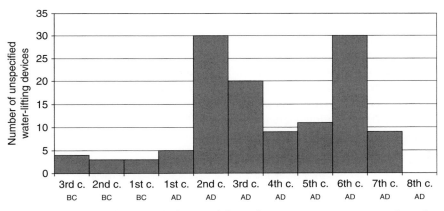

Fig. 9.16. Number of unspecified water-lifting devices per century attested in the papyri (n = 124)

perhaps be interpreted more flexibly, especially in view of the high number of pot-garland machines and the low number of Archimedes' screws found in the surviving published papyri.

Other than the above-mentioned water-lifting devices, there are a few references to mechanical parts that definitely belong to water-lifting devices, which however remain unidentified (Fig. 9.16). As these unidentified types of devices are expected to have been one or another of the devices mentioned above, the pattern that emerges in this graph is not surprising, with marked peaks in the second, third, and sixth centuries.

DISCUSSION

The documentary evidence, as stated above, consists of 298 texts with 658 references to a minimum of 583 machines. In 124 cases the exact type of device is unclear, although there is little doubt that we are indeed dealing with a water-lifting device, and in many of these we can tell whether that device was used for irrigation, or for furnishing water for baths and so on. In a further 13 cases, usually because of damage to the papyrus, a reference to a part of the device is preserved, but again without allowing us to draw a secure inference as to which device we are dealing with. Of the rest, 222 can be interpreted as *saqiyas*, 29 as waterwheels, 14 as possible waterwheels, 38 as either water-wheels or *saqiyas*, 11 as pot garlands, 25 as possible pot garlands, 59 as *shadufs* (Fig. 9.17). We also find 5 pumps and 9 Archimedes screws.

The vast majority (225) of the devices attested come from the Oxyrhynchite Nome; 94 are from the Arsinoite Nome, 71 from the Hermopolite, and, of the rest, 60 are of unknown origin, and there are 6 from Alexandria and one from Nessana in Palestine—our only attestation from outside Egypt. The picture is similar if we look for the origin of the papyri that carry the attestations rather than the attestations themselves: 103 from the Oxyrhynchite Nome, 52 from the Arsinoite, 54 from the Hermopolite, 45 unknown, 2 from Alexandria, and 1 from Nessana.

The distribution of papyri that mention water-lifting devices by century and half-century units is shown in Figs 9.18 and 9.19. With the aid of Habermann's graph of the overall chronological distribution of papyri (Fig. 9.20), the percent-age of papyri containing references to water-lifting devices as a proportion of the total of surviving papyri can be calculated (Fig. 9.21). What is immediately

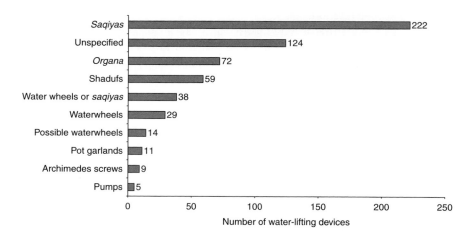

Fig. 9.17. Types of water-lifting devices attested in the papyri (n = 583)

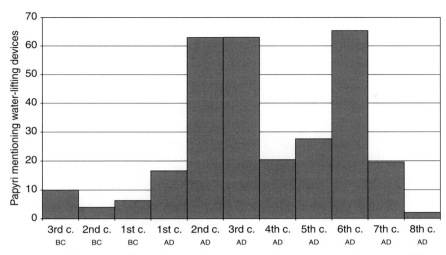

Fig. 9.18. Chronological distribution by century of papyri mentioning water-lifting devices (n = 298)

apparent is the massive peak that our data exhibit in the fifth and sixth centuries AD. Given the content of the documents in question, this is not difficult to explain: the vast majority of sixth-century texts included in this database belong to the archive of the Apiones, a wealthy landed family, much of which consists of estate accounts. It is to be expected that it would include many references to water-lifting devices, mainly relating to their maintenance. Besides, the archive comes from Oxyrhynchus, which goes some way to explaining the preponderance of Oxyrhynchite sources.

The complete picture of different machine types by century mentioned in the papyri is given in Fig. 9.22, showing peaks in attestations in the second, third, sixth, and seventh centuries AD. Collection of the literary, documentary, and archaeological evidence for water-lifting devices over time (Fig. 9.23) shows a clear difference between the two categories of evidence, each of which is individually problematic; but comparison between the categories is revealing about the nature of the datasets. The archaeological evidence increases sharply in quantity before the literary evidence does, in the second century BC, consistent with seeing the widespread diffusion of these technologies under the conditions of political unity and increased communication enabled by the Roman empire. The quantity of archaeological evidence drops considerably after the fifth century AD—in sharp contrast with the papyrological evidence for Egypt, which shows a major peak in the sixth and seventh centuries. The fifth- and sixth-century papyri seem to contain proportionately more references to water lifting than before, perhaps for reasons

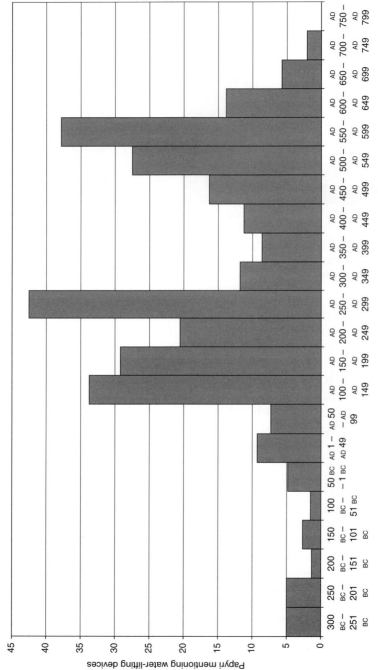

Fig. 9.19. Chronological distribution by half-century of papyri mentioning water-lifting devices (n = 298)

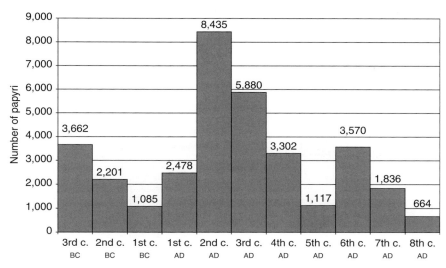

Fig. 9.20. Chronological distribution by century of all papyri from the third century BC to the eighth century AD (graph adapted from Habermann 1998: 147, fig. 1)

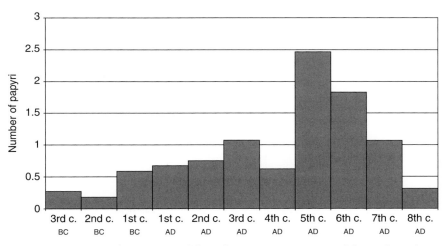

Fig. 9.21. Papyri mentioning water-lifting devices as a percentage of the total numbers of papyri, by century (total papyri data from Habermann 1998)

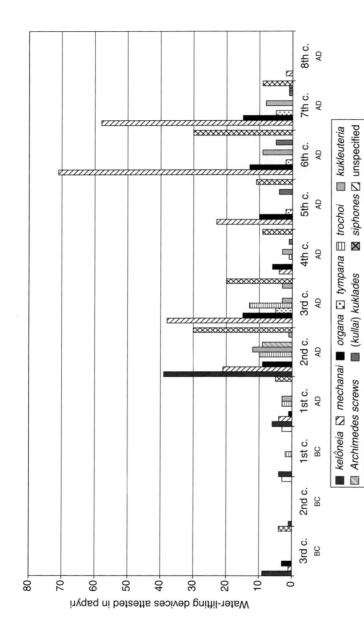

Fig. 9.22. Types of water-lifting devices attested in the papyri, over time (n = 583)

Legend:
kelôneia | *mechanai* | *organa* | *tympana* | *trochoi* | *kukleuteria*
Archimedes screws | (*kullai*) *kuklades* | *siphones* | unspecified

Y-axis: Water-lifting devices attested in papyri (0, 10, 20, 30, 40, 50, 60, 70, 80)

X-axis: 3rd c. BC, 2nd c. BC, 1st c. BC, 1st c. AD, 2nd c. AD, 3rd c. AD, 4th c. AD, 5th c. AD, 6th c. AD, 7th c. AD, 8th c. AD

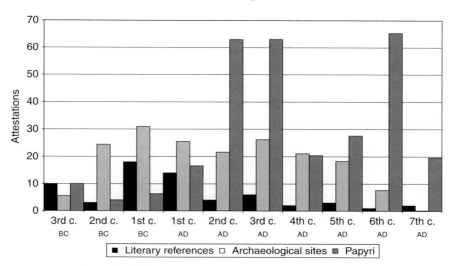

Fig. 9.23. Evidence for different categories of water-lifting devices over time—literary, papyrological, and archaeological

connected with the type of document containing the evidence. Because of different biases in the different kinds of evidence, and the changing visibility threshold of different devices over time, it is clear that no single type of evidence—archaeological, literary, or papyrological—gives a reliable picture of the trends in usage of water-lifting technology (and, by extension, probably of other technologies too), and that any real understanding of the phenomenon must come from an analysis of all the types of evidence. What is, however, evident from the papyri is that artificial irrigation was not only a significant component of agriculture in Byzantine Egypt, as is commonly thought, but also a prominent feature of the Egyptian agricultural economy of the Roman period, given the very large number of references to water-lifting machines in the second and third centuries AD. Where the context is given, the irrigation machines mentioned in the papyri were frequently watering intensively cultivated plots of high-value crops—orchards and vineyards.

The wider archaeological and literary evidence suggests that water-lifting machines were also used for irrigation in many of the other Mediterranean provinces across the empire, in the west as well as the east. The archaeological finds come from all around the Roman empire—the pot-garland or bucket-chain machines are not confined to Egypt, but are also represented by *saqiya* pots from Israel, and by wooden bucket chains from Cosa in Italy, and by no less than four first- and second-century AD devices from London. The Cosa and London devices were admittedly not for irrigation, but they illustrate the spread and rapidity of technological uptake—the earliest of the London machines was in place only twenty years after the invasion of Britain. As regards irrigation devices, there are compelling reasons to see the bucket chain/pot garland as being used in North Africa, and the water-driven water-lifting wheel in the Iberian peninsula in Roman times.[68] Although these machines are often regarded as an Islamic introduction to the western Mediterranean, especially Iberia, this seems unlikely in the face of the evidence of their ancient use in the western Mediterranean provinces. They must represent either a survival from Roman times, or a reintroduction after a period in Visigothic Spain when the technology had fallen out of use. In any case, Andrew Watson's idea of an agricultural revolution in the Islamic world relies heavily on the idea that the Arabs introduced irrigation devices and systems that had not been widely used in the Roman world; in the light of recent research on Roman channel irrigation in Spain, on water-lifting devices, and on crop diffusion in antiquity, this now seems unsustainable.[69] Instead, the evidence increasingly indicates that the diffusion and uptake of these irrigation technologies in the Hellenistic and Roman worlds boosted both the cultivable areas available within the Roman empire, and the per capita agricultural production of those areas.

REFERENCES

Adams, J. N. (2007). *The Regional Diversification of Latin, 200 BC–AD 600*. Cambridge.

Ayalon, E. (2000). 'Typology and Chronology of Water-Wheel (Saqiya) Pottery Pots from Israel', *IEJ* 50: 216–26.

Barker, G. W. W., Gilbertson, D. D., Hunt, C. O., and Mattingly, D. J. (1996). 'Romano-Libyan Agriculture: Integrated Models', in G. W. W. Barker (ed.), *Farming the Desert: The UNESCO Libyan Valleys Archaeological Survey* 1. Paris, Tripoli, and London, 265–90.

Bauer, P. T. (1956). 'Lewis' *Theory of Economic Growth*: A Review Article', *American Economic Review* 46.4: 632–41.

Beltrán Lloris, F. (2006). 'An Irrigation Decree from Roman Spain: *The Lex Rivi Hiberiensis*', *JRS* 96: 147–97.

Birks, P., Rodger, A., and Richardson, J. S. (1984). 'Further Aspects of the Tabula Contrebiensis', *JRS* 74: 45–73.

Blair, I. (2004). 'The Water Supply and the Mechanical Water-Lifting Devices of Roman Londinium: New Evidence from Three Archaeological Sites in the City of

---

[68] Wilson (2003).

[69] Watson (1974; 1983); with counter-arguments regarding irrigation machines in Wilson (2004), and regarding crops in Decker (2009a; 2009b: 201–2).

London', in F. Minonzio (ed.), *Problemi di macchinismo in ambito romano: Macchine idrauliche nella lettatura tecnica, nelle fonti storiografiche, e nelle evidenze archeologiche di età imperiale.* Como, 113–24.

Blair, I., Spain, R., and Taylor, T. (2005). 'The Technology of the 1st- and 2nd-Century Roman Bucket Chains from London: From Excavation to Reconstruction', in A. Bouet (ed.), *Aquam in altum exprimere: Les machines élévatrices d'eau dans l'Antiquité.* Bordeaux, 85–114.

Blair, I., Spain, R., Swift, D., Taylor, T., and Goodburn, D. (2006). 'Wells and Bucket-Chains: Unforeseen Elements of Water Supply in Early Roman London', *Britannia* 37: 1–52.

Bonneau, D. (1970). 'L'administration de l'irrigation dans les grands domaines en Égypte au VIᵉ siècle de N.E', in *Proceedings of the Twelfth International Congress of Papyrologists.* Toronto, 45–62.

Bonneau, D. (1993). *Le régime administratif de l'eau du Nil dans l'Égypte grecque, romaine et byzantine.* Leiden.

Bowman, A. K., and Wilson, A. I. (2009) (eds). *Quantifying the Roman Economy: Methods and Problems* (Oxford Studies on the Roman Economy 1). Oxford.

Bowman, A. K., and Wilson, A. I. (2011) (eds). *Settlement, Urbanization, and Population* (Oxford Studies on the Roman Economy 2). Oxford.

Bruun, C. (2012). 'Roman Emperors and Legislation on Public Water Use in the Roman Empire: Clarifications and Problems', *Water History* 4.1: 11–33.

Butzer, K. W., Mateu, J. F., Butzer, E. K., and Kraus, P. (1985). 'Irrigation Agrosystems in Eastern Spain: Roman or Islamic Origins?', *Annals of the Association of American Geographers*, 75: 479–509.

Conche, F., Plassot, É., and Pellecuer, C. (2005). 'Puiser, élever et distribuer l'eau dans la villa de Careiron et Pesquier à Milhaud (Gard): Premiers commentaires', in A. Bouet (ed.), *Aquam in altum exprimere: Les machines élévatrices d'eau dans l'Antiquité.* Bordeaux, 69–84.

Cuvigny, H. (2003). 'La société civile des praesidia', in H. Cuvigny (ed.), *La route de Myos Hormos : L'armée romaine dans le désert oriental d'Égypte.* Le Caire, 361–95.

De Callataÿ, F. (2005). 'The Graeco-Roman Economy in the Super Long-Run: Lead, Copper and Shipwrecks', *JRA* 18: 361–72.

Decker, M. (2001). *Agricultural Production and Trade in Oriens, 4th–7th centuries AD*, D.Phil. thesis, University of Oxford.

Decker, M. (2009a). 'Plants and Progress: Rethinking the Islamic Agricultural Revolution', *Journal of World History* 20.2: 187–206.

Decker, M. (2009b). *Tilling the Hateful Earth: Agricultural Production and Trade in the Late Antique East.* Oxford.

Fentress, E. W. B. (1979). *Numidia and the Roman Army; Social, Military and Economic Aspects of the Frontier Zone* (BAR International Series 53). Oxford.

Fornacciari, C. (1928–9). 'Note sur le drain romain de la Soukra [communication à la séance de la Commission de l'Afrique du Nord, 10 décembre 1929]', *BCTH* 413–15.

Garbrecht, G. (1987) (ed.). *Historische Talsperren.* Stuttgart.

Garbrecht, G. (1991) (ed.). *Historische Talsperren 2.* Stuttgart.

Gauckler, P. (1896). 'Le Domaine des Laberii à Uthina', *MMAI* 3: 177–229.

Gilbertson, D. D., Hayes, P. P., Barker, G. W. W., and Hunt, C. O. (1984). 'The UNESCO Libyan Valleys Survey VII: An Interim Classification and Functional Analysis of Ancient Wall Technology and Land Use', *LibStud* 15: 45–70.

Glick, T. F. (1970). *Irrigation and Society in Medieval Valencia*. Cambridge, MA.

Glick, T. F. (1979). *Islamic and Christian Spain in the Early Middle Ages*. Princeton.

Glick, T. F. (2005). *Islamic and Christian Spain in the Early Middle Ages*, 2nd edn. Leiden.

Habermann, W. (1998). 'Zur chronologischen Verteilung der papyrologischen Zeugnisse', *ZPE* 122: 144–60.

Habermann, W. (2000). *Zur Wasserversorgung einer Metropole im kaiserzeitlichen Ägypten: Neuedition von P.Lond. III 1177* (Vestigia 53). Munich.

Jongman, W. (2007a). 'The Early Roman Empire: Consumption', in W. Scheidel, I. Morris, and R. Saller (eds), *The Cambridge Economic History of the Greco-Roman World*. Cambridge, 592–618.

Jongman, W. (2007b). 'Gibbon was Right: The Decline and Fall of the Roman Economy', in O. Hekster, G. Kleijn, and D. Slootjes (eds) *Crises and the Roman Empire*. Leiden, 183–99.

Kamash, Z. (2006). *Water Supply and Management in the Near East, 63 B.C. – A.D. 636*, D.Phil. thesis, University of Oxford.

Kron, G. (2000). 'Roman Ley-Farming', *JRA* 13.1: 277–87.

Lewis, M. J. T. (1997). *Millstone and Hammer: The Origins of Water Power*. Hull.

Mango, M. M. (2002). 'Excavations and Survey at Androna, Syria: The Oxford Team 1999', *Dumbarton Oaks Papers* 56: 307–15.

Morvillez, É., Chevalier, P., Mardesic, J., Pender, B., Topic, M., and Causevic, M. (2005). 'La noria découverte à proximité de "L'oratoire A", dans le quartier épiscopal de Salone (mission archéologique franco-croate de Salone)', in A. Bouet (ed.), *Aquam in altum exprimere: Les machines élévatrices d'eau dans l'Antiquité*. Bordeaux, 153–69.

Oleson, J. P. (1984). *Greek and Roman Mechanical Water-Lifting Devices: The History of a Technology*. Toronto.

Oleson, J. P. (1987). 'The Spring House Complex', in A. M. McCann (ed.), *The Roman Port and Fishery at Cosa: A Center of Ancient Trade*. Princeton, 98–128.

Oleson, J. P. (2000a). 'Irrigation', in Ö. Wikander (ed.), *Handbook of Ancient Water Technology* (Technology and Change in History 2). Leiden, 183–215.

Oleson, J. P. (2000b). 'Water-Lifting', in Ö. Wikander (ed.), *Handbook of Ancient Water Technology* (Technology and Change in History 2). Leiden, 207–302.

Persson, K. G. (2010). *An Economic History of Europe: Knowledge, Institutions and Growth, 600 to the Present*. Cambridge.

Rathbone, D. W. (2007). 'Mêchanai (Waterwheels) in the Roman Fayyum', in M. Capasso and P. Davoli (eds), *New Archaeological and Papyrological Researches on the Fayyum*. Lecce, 253–62.

Renault, J. (1912). 'Les Bassins du trik Dar-Saniat à Carthage', *RT* 19/95 (September), 471–98.

Richardson, J. S. (1983). 'The *Tabula Contrebiensis*, Roman Law in Spain in the Early First Century BC', *JRS* 73: 33–41.

Schiøler, T. (1973). *Roman and Islamic Water-Lifting Wheels*. Copenhagen.

Schnitter, N. J. (1978). 'Römische Talsperren', *AW* 9.2: 25–32.

Schnitter, N. J. (1992). 'Römische Talsperren und Wehre auf der Iberischen Halbinsel', in *Geschichte der Wasserwirtschaft und des Wasserbaus im mediterranen Raum.* Braunschweig, 159–77.

Shaw, B. D. (1982). 'Lamasba: An Ancient Irrigation Community', *AntAfr* 18: 61–103.

Smith, N. A. F. (1971). *A History of Dams*. London.

Stein, R. (2004). 'Roman Wooden Force Pumps: A Case Study in Innovation', *JRA* 17: 221–50.

Venit, M. S. (1988). 'The Painted Tomb from Wardian and the Decoration of Alexandrian Tombs', *JARCE* 25: 71–91.

Venit, M. S. (1989). 'The Painted Tomb from Wardian and the Antiquity of the Saqiya in Egypt', *JARCE* 26: 219–22.

Watson, A. M. (1974). 'The Arab Agricultural Revolution and its Diffusion, 700–1100', *Journal of Economic History* 34: 8–35.

Watson, A. M. (1983). *Agricultural Innovation in the Early Islamic World*. Cambridge.

Wilson, A. I. (2002). 'Machines, Power and the Ancient Economy', *JRS* 92: 1–32.

Wilson, A. I. (2003). 'Classical water technology in the early Islamic world', in C. Bruun and A. Saastamoinen (eds.), *Technology, ideology, water: from Frontinus to the Renaissance and beyond*. Roma, 115–41.

Zaqzouk, A. R. (1990). 'Les norias: anciens moyens d'irrigation les plus importants dans la région de Hama', in B. Geyer (ed.), *Techniques et pratiques hydro-agricoles traditionelles en domaine irrigué: approche pluridisciplinaire des modes de culture avant la motorisation en Syrie: Actes du Colloque de Damas 27 juin – 1er juillet 1987*, vol. 2. Paris, 337–65.

10

Agriculture in the Faynan: Food Supply for the Mining Industry

Hannah Friedman

INTRODUCTION

Although agriculture and metallurgy have been treated as separate economies in the Roman world, they are actually closely linked. In mining zones, one cannot understand the industry without considering the agricultural sector. The ability to supply the essentials to a non-subsistence population is vital for the maintenance of large-scale industry. This was especially true for *metalla*, Roman state-run mining districts, which were large-scale industries that required correspondingly large quantities of supplies.[1] Rothenburg and Blanco-Freijeiro believed that the ability to organize and provide infrastructure and supplies, regardless of any environmental or economic constraints, was a true hallmark of imperial ownership.[2] One of these organizational needs was a dependable supply of food.

An excellent example of the relationship between agriculture and industry within imperial *metalla* is found in the copper-rich Faynan district in southern Jordan. Located in a semi-arid environment, it lies between the Jordanian plateau that receives relatively high levels of precipitation and the arid environment of the Wadi 'Arabah. Our best evidence of imperial ownership of this copper mine comes from the early Church father Eusebius, who described the specific punishment of *damnati ad metalla* and confirms the presence of convict labour in the Faynan.[3] Many authors agree that the presence of convicts condemned to the mines indicates imperial jurisdiction.[4] Eusebius'

---

[1] Good examples of other copper mines include Cyprus (Given and Knapp 2003).
[2] Rothenburg and Blanco-Freijeiro (1981).
[3] Eusebius makes multiple references to the Faynan in *Martyrs of Palestine*; the clearest are 7.2 and 8.1.
[4] Millar (1985: 142); Hirt (2010: 97).

account is corroborated by other sources of the third and fourth centuries, Athanasius (AD 293–373), Epiphanius of Salamis (*c.* AD 310/320–403), and Theodoret of Cyrrhus (AD 393–457).

The Faynan has evidence for a Roman presence from the second to the sixth centuries AD, the heaviest industry occurring at the end of the third and fourth centuries. The output of the smelting process is estimated at 2,500–7,000 tonnes for the Roman and Early Byzantine period, or an average of 6.25–17.5 tonnes per year. The population size of the Faynan is difficult to determine without excavation, but the Wadi Faynan Landscape Survey estimates based on settlement density and cemetery data suggested at most 1,500–1,750 individuals in the Faynan region.[5] I would argue, after reviewing the Jabal Hamrat Fidan surveys, that the figure is slightly higher—1,600–1,850.[6] In order to produce over 6 tonnes of copper per year, a substantial portion of this population would have had to have been employed in the industry, at least for much of the year. In order to feed such a workforce, the industrial administration would have taken steps to ensure an adequate supply of food. Evidence for this is seen in the organization of the agricultural resources of the region.

But how did this imperial ownership affect the basic food supply and the agriculture of the region? How many people could be fed from local sources? Do we detect any evidence that an overall administrative strategy was employed?

FIELD SYSTEMS OF THE FAYNAN

The Roman and Byzantine settlement in the Faynan clusters around the main wadi from which the region takes its name (Fig. 10.1). Wadi Faynan runs from the base of the foothills leading to the Jordanian Plateau, and, heading west, eventually becomes the Wadi Fidan. Khirbet Faynan was the largest settlement of the region in the Roman period. Directly to the west of this site is the Faynan agricultural field system, designated as WF4 in the excavation.

The Wadi Faynan is unique, with the largest floodplain of any wadi leading into the 'Arabah south of the Dead Sea.[7] The field system occupies this floodplain; composed of *c.*800 individual fields, it provided 209 ha of arable land and extended for 4 km along the wadi (Fig. 10.2).[8]

---

[5] Barker *et al.* (2007: 414).
[6] The population estimate is based on additional survey information and is, of course, an approximation.
[7] Newson (2002: 155).
[8] For description of the fields in detail, see Barker *et al.* (2007: 141–74, 327–32).

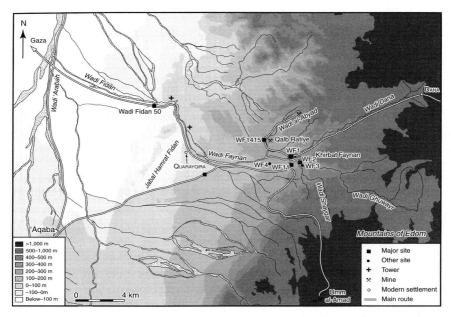

Fig. 10.1. The landscape of the Wadi Faynan region (Barker *et al.* 2007: 310)

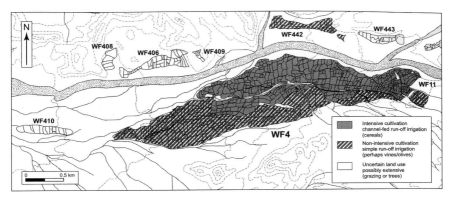

Fig. 10.2. Plan of the ancient field systems in the Wadi Faynan and summary of their uses (Barker *et al.* 2007: 331)

During the Roman and Byzantine periods the floodplain had a complex and highly sophisticated irrigation system. While higher precipitation levels were experienced throughout the Levant during the Late Roman/Early Byzantine period, rainfall was never sufficiently plentiful to water the fields directly.

The fields of WF4 were farmed using floodwater irrigation; rainwater was controlled by a series of walls and terraced units, redirecting water to maximum effect and distributing it over the fields.

The field system is not uniform; the northern fields were relatively flat ground with good soil. These were watered with channel irrigation (Fig. 10.2). The southern fields were rockier and more steeply sloping than their northern counterparts.[9] These fields were terraced and irrigated with run-off from some of the northern fields and localized water collection.

If agriculture and the copper industry are as linked as I suggest, then it is essential to discuss first the way the administration reorganized the fields for overall benefit. WF4 was a focal point for the wadi system. Excavation and analysis of the field walls and sherd scatter suggest that portions of the floodplain had been farmed from at least the Bronze Age.[10] It is significant that WF4 underwent extensive changes during the Roman period corresponding to the time when the imperial industry was most active.

The directing walls and channels in the fields are difficult to date securely by topology, and the tendency to reuse or modify existing walls further obscures the matter. Pottery sherds are found in the fields, but these indicate field usage, and, while they can be associated with hydraulic structures, they cannot be used to date them securely. Even with these caveats, some clear patterns of usage appear.

The flood walls and associated pottery indicate that during the Late Nabataean period, in the first century BC and first century AD, there were independent hydraulic systems working in WF4. The only exceptions were WF4.1/4.3, which were watered together as a unit, but these fields were only 187,191 m².[11] Other pottery scatters were clustered around structures contained within and directly to the south of WF4 (Fig. 10.3). Their location suggests that these may have been domestic structures used by agricultural workers for onsite observation and management of crops. Supporting the supposition of an agricultural focus for these structures, a subset of seven display complex features and have large enclosed yards. This aspect suggests that these seven were more than monitoring structures; rather, they were farmsteads where agricultural processing took place.[12]

By the Late Roman period, the field system had been altered substantially. Instead of a series of discrete adjacent irrigation channels, large areas of the plain were incorporated into an integrated system.[13] These were watered by a series of feeder channels, with associated Roman and Byzantine pottery, which

---

[9] Barker *et al.* (2007: 153).
[10] Newson (2002: 220).
[11] Wright *et al.* (1998); Newson (2002: 224).
[12] Barker *et al.* (2007: 295).
[13] Barker *et al.* (2007: 209).

fed secondary channels (see Fig. 10.2). These channels were of a greater technical complexity than those of the previous period, well organized and efficient with little water loss.

Accompanying this change, the number of domestic structures related to fields decreased. Fifteen out of the twenty-six domestic structures used in the Nabataean period were abandoned, and showed no evidence of continuing habitation. New cultivation practices suggest decreased independent farming by inhabitants in the region. The new system with its centralized irrigation strongly suggests increased regional control and a definite change in population with the arrival of a colonizing power.

In the Late Byzantine period, the field system was again adapted. Excavation shows that the feeder channels went through a period of modifications. The larger irrigation system changed into smaller independent systems, and some areas were abandoned or minimized.

There was relatively little copper production in the Nabataean period, before the province was annexed by Rome, and thus a centralized agricultural system was not required. However, once the Faynan became a *metallum*, the field system changed. The individual agricultural plots were amalgamated, more land was under cultivation, and it was more intensively farmed. Finally, the changes during the Late Byzantine period could be due to shifting water flow patterns across the floodplain, with redirection of the wadis' courses rendering some systems unuseable. Or, in a reversal of the earlier changes, this adaptation indicates a social or political change occurring within the Faynan. The copper industry was slowing and eventually ceased. The resumption of earlier decentralized farming practices suggests less regulated control, perhaps the absence of the centralizing administration that had previously accompanied the industry.

Why then might a change in irrigation patterns of field organization reflect the imposition of an imperial administration and a state-run copper industry? Land rights and especially control of irrigation systems in desert environments are generally not spontaneously abandoned by a community. The local population present in the Nabataean period agreed or was forced to give up previously private land rights and accept new collective ones. The likelihood of this happening without imperial intervention, and the application of economic and physical force, is low. A point of departure for this supposition is the ethnographic studies of agricultural disputes close to the region. In the early 1990s, the Rashaiyida and Shawabke tribes had a dispute over land rights in the Wadi Ghuwayr.[14] The wadi was divided into two sections, one for each tribe. However, only the Rashaiyida farmed theirs and eventually were allowed to be sharecroppers on the other half. The expansion of agriculture continued

---

[14] Lancaster and Lancaster (1999: 123).

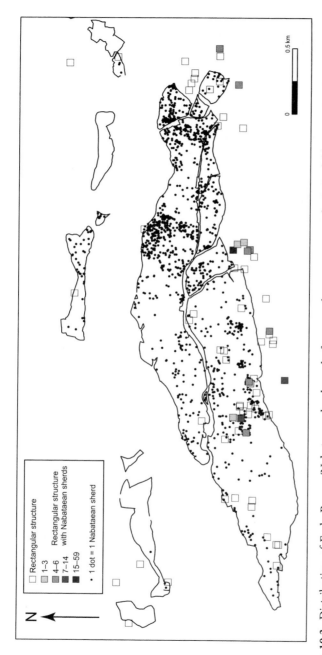

Fig. 10.3. Distribution of Early Roman/Nabataean sherds, and of rectangular structures, in the WF4 field system (Barker *et al.* 2007: 172, fig. 5.52)

with the creation of a new hydraulic system. The Shawabke protested against the building of permanent structures on their land and destroyed the pipes. This confrontation grew increasingly violent with armed opposition and destruction of crops and property.[15] Eventually the matter had to be settled with royal mediation by Crown Prince Hassan. If similar attitudes to property and water systems existed in the ancient Faynan, then the implementation of a centralized water system would have had serious social and cultural repercussions.

Although floodwater farming techniques were common during this period, WF4 was unique; no other system of integrated fields of such size and complexity is known in the entire Levant.[16] A reason to take such extraordinary measures would exist if the supply of food were important for more than just agricultural sale: being needed to supply the copper industries' workforce. The changes in the fields, although they cannot be dated very precisely, correspond to the changes in industry and the history of the region.

AMOUNT OF FOOD NEEDED

Why this centralized system? Simply put, it was to utilize the fields in the best way possible and to make them as productive as possible. The larger system meant that more land was under cultivation than in the Nabataean period and that this land was organized into types. The northern fields were watered with channel-fed irrigation; the southern fields had more simple constructions for directed run-off.[17] These differences allowed for the optimal usage of field morphology and soil types. The northern fields had a gentle gradient and contained better soil for cereal crops. Cereals require more attention, needing ploughing and higher amounts of fertilizer, and the northern fields were ideal. The pottery distribution in these fields reflects extensive manuring practices (see Fig. 10.3). The southern fields were terraced, and with their rockier soil were probably used for grape or olive crops, activities that required less ploughing. Sediment cores taken in the Wadi Faynan contain pollen from olive trees and grape vines, confirming their cultivation.[18] The fewer sherds found in these areas also point towards less manuring. The result of all these changes was that a larger area of the floodplain was intensively farmed and more food was produced.

---

[15] Lancaster and Lancaster (1999: 123).
[16] Barker *et al.* (2007: 327).
[17] Barker *et al.* (2007: 331).
[18] Barker (2002: 501).

Table 10.1. Yields of barley and wheat at Nitzana/Nessana according to *P. Ness.* 82

Crop	Place	Yield (multiples of quantity sown)
Wheat	Ragorion to Kat	6.8
	Malalkani	7.2
	Alphag	6.8
Barley	Alphag	8.0
	Berain	8.7

Table 10.2. Yields of barley and wheat at Avdat farm (Evenari *et al.* 1982: 122)

Season	Crop	Yield (multiples of quantity sown)
1959–60	Barley	10.4
1961–62	Wheat	7.2
1963–64	Barley	14.5
	Wheat	13.9

Estimations of the efficacy of this irrigation technique were explored by Evenari, Shanan, and Tadmor.[19] They tested experimental reconstructions using run-off technology in the Negev Desert, Israel, and these yielded substantial crops. Two experimental farms, Avdat and Shivta, were built and irrigated solely by run-off catchments. The farms were run over a number of years and successfully produced cereal and pasture crops as well as supporting orchards and vineyards.[20] The ability of this type of agriculture to withstand the effect of drought was quickly established, as the Negev experienced one of the worst droughts in modern history during the trials. These yields can be compared to those of an ancient model from Nitzana (ancient Nessana), a late Byzantine community in the Negev desert. Papyri discovered there documenting the community's land use and agriculture are particularly helpful in confirming predictions about the type of crops and how much could be produced in this climate. The Nitzana papyri record lower yields of cereal crops than those recorded on the experimental farms (Table 10.1). Evenari *et al.* speculate that the higher yields on the modern desert experimental farms are due to their use of modern fertilizer (Table 10.2).

HOW MANY PEOPLE?

The northern fields, as stated above, were probably used for cereal crops and measured 104 ha (see Fig. 10.2). A basic estimate of the potential productivity

---

[19] Evenari, Shanan, and Tadmor (1982).
[20] Evenari *et al.* (1982: 191–213).

of the fields can be produced. Flannery postulated that a hectare of wild barley and wheat in the conditions of the Levant would yield an estimated two million kilocalories (kcal) per annum, enough to feed a family of three.[21] Using Flannery's yield estimate, the northern fields of WF4 would have produced grain crops yielding 208,088,000 kcal per year.

The dietary standards issued by the Food and Agriculture Organization of the United Nations (FAO) estimate the daily caloric consumption by a 'very active male' is 3,337 kcal.[22] If a hectare can produce two million calories, then each hectare could support 1.6 'very active' males consuming 1,218,000 kcal per year, if they are subsisting on grain alone.

The 'active male' is an appropriate model, given the labour-intensive lifestyle that inhabitants of the Faynan were likely to be leading. However, there are other variables to be taken into account. Ancient authors such as Cato describe how diet varied depending on social class; he recommended slaves in chains be fed 4 or 5 pounds of bread a day.[23] Slaves or convicts in the Faynan may have subsisted on the poorest diet, one of only bread. However, this was rare for other social groups; even the lower classes had access to other sources of food such as meat, wine, and olive oil. For these populations, an estimated 75 per cent of calories were gained from grains.[24] Based on these data, the number of calories derived from grain needed for an active male would be reduced to 2,503 kcal/day. Thus, a hectare of cereals would support 2.2 active males.

The population was not likely to be composed entirely of active males; women and children were also condemned to mines.[25] These demographic groups would also have made up a portion of the free population and are represented in the cemetery evidence.[26] If, as Flannery believes, the two million calories produced by a hectare of wild grains could feed a family of three for a year, the figures in Table 10.3 are generated.

These figures are, of course, estimates, and many other considerations apply. For example, not all of the population of the Faynan, most especially the convicts, would have received a healthy diet containing enough calories. In addition, the WF4 fields would have contained domesticated grain species, not wild, as was the basis of Flannery's estimate. Domesticated grains should have increased productivity and yields.

---

[21] Flannery (1973: 278).
[22] Many estimates have been made—3,337 kcal is the figure used in Foxhall and Forbes (1982: 49) and does not differ substantially from the FAO (2004: table 5.5).
[23] *De Agri Cultura* 56.
[24] Foxhall and Forbes (1982: 56).
[25] Eusebius describes these unfortunates in *MP* 8.1.
[26] Karaki (2000: 46).

Table 10.3. Individuals supported annually from the northern fields based on calculations by Flannery (1973), and Foxhall and Forbes (1982), without taking account of pollution

Population	Annual caloric need from grain (kcal)	Persons supported per hectare of grain	Persons supported by northern fields per year
Active male (free) 75% of diet	913,500	2.2	228
Active male (slave) 100% of diet	1,218,000	1.6	171
Family (average 3) 100% of diet	2,000,000	3.0	312

POLLUTION

Yet a further complication must be taken into account when estimating the productivity of the Faynan fields. The link between industry and agriculture does not just stop at what the fields produced. Unfortunately, it was a reciprocal relationship; the industry produced pollution.

The act of smelting and ore processing generates heavy metals and environmental poisons. Pollutant concentrations were examined from several soil samples taken from Tell Wadi Faynan, in the centre of WF4 and several km downwind from the main industry site at Khirbet Faynan, using Energy Dispersive X-ray Micro-Analysis (EDMA). After measuring the amount of pollutants in different stratigraphic levels, the highest amounts of pollution were found in the Roman and Byzantine periods.[27] These levels probably correspond to the airborne pollution produced by smelting.[28]

Zinc, copper, and lead will inhibit or stop root growth and development, lowering productivity, and, in high enough concentrations, will lead to the eventual death of the plant.[29] The degree to which this soil pollution would have negatively affected crop productivity can be estimated from present-day studies of wild barley in the Wadi Faynan. A slagheap near Khirbet Faynan was examined to determine how pollutants affected the barley plants.[30] The authors found copper toxins present at 200 ppm (parts per million) on the surface of the slagheap. In this experiment, a transect was taken from the slagheap to a distance of 1,000 m, where there was no evidence of smelting activities. The seed potential, the number of seeds produced by each plant, was dramatically affected (Fig. 10.4).

[27] Barker *et al.* (1999: 265).
[28] Grattan *et al.* (2006).
[29] Bradshaw *et al.* (1965: 329); Lal and Sing (2008: 26).
[30] Pyatt *et al.* (1998: 306).

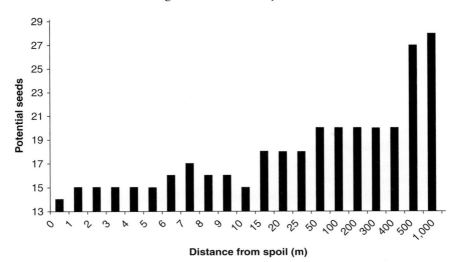

Distance from spoil (m)

Fig. 10.4. The effect of proximity to the Khirbet Faynan slagheap on seed productivity (Pyatt *et al.* 1999: 307, fig. 15)

In the dry environment of the wadi, the expected seed potential should be 50–60 seeds per plant. At 1,000 m from the slagheaps, the seed production was only 30 per cent of the expected figure per plant and it decreased further with increasing proximity to the pollutants. At 100 m, seed potential was only 20 per cent of the expected figure per plant.[31] This affects both the harvest and the next year's crop, because of the amount that needs to be retained as seedcorn for the next sowing.

Large quantities of pottery sherds are found in the northern fields (see Fig. 10.3). This finding suggests attempts to counteract massive degradation of the landscape with increased use of fertilizer, assuming the pottery derived from middens that were subsequently used for manuring. During the periods of the highest industrial productivity, from the Nabataean through the Byzantine ages, pottery counts from the fields increase dramatically. The low-lying lands, which were most likely used for cereals, were the most heavily manured. These cereal crops have more shallow root systems, which would have been seriously affected.

A further complication in sustaining the agricultural environment would have been the increasing bioaccumulation of toxins. Livestock consuming local vegetation would absorb toxins from them. Faeces containing these toxins would be used as fertilizer for the fields. Studies in the present-day Faynan indicate that goats are excreting high levels of toxic metals in milk, faeces, and urine.[32] If flocks were allowed to consume the remnants of cereal crops, and then their waste was used to manure the fields, they would create a continuing cycle of increasing environmental damage.

---

[31] Barker *et al.* (2000: 45).
[32] The average levels were 150 ppm of Cu in goat faeces: Grattan *et al.* (2003: 776).

WF4 may have experienced other problems requiring increased application of manure. These might have included decreasing soil productivity due to over-planting to compensate for low yields, or erosion of the wadi due to loss of trees consumed as fuel. It is likely that diminishing harvests were due to a combination of these factors, but the pollution would be the most detrimental.

Evenari's experimental farms are not as helpful in this regard, as they used both natural and modern fertilizers on unpolluted soil, limiting the analogy with the Faynan.[33] The Faynan would have had both its own animal populations and those of animal caravans to provide fertilizer. It is unlikely that they lacked this resource; but it does not seem to have been able to counter the effects of soil pollution.

Thus, the fields at Faynan were unlikely to have had the yields predicted for Flannery's unpolluted fields. A predictive model to estimate such crop yields comes from a study of sites in the United Kingdom that dealt with the potential damage caused by sewage sludge.[34] Sewage that has high concentrations of heavy metals has effects on crop productivity similar to those from smelting pollution. Researchers tested yields at two sites, Gleadthorpe and Rosemaund. At Gleadthorpe, crops could be established in the field, but they quickly became underdeveloped. When extractable zinc and copper concentrations were high, the reduction in crop yield was on the order of 16–47 per cent or an average of 1.5 tonnes per hectare for grain.[35] The Avdat farm had a grain yield of 4.8 t/ha (similar to Gleadthorpe with 4.93 t/ha of barley in untreated soils). A reduction in yield of 1.5 t/ha equates to a loss of 31.25 per cent of crops and of their potential grain calories. This is consistent with the 30 per cent reduction in seed potential at 1 km from the copper-smelting slagheap at Khirbet Faynan discussed above.

Taking this figure as a comparable estimate for reductions in crop yield from field pollution at Faynan, the yield of the northern field system would be reduced by 30 per cent. This would reduce the caloric yield per hectare from 2,000,000 kcal to 1,400,000 kcal annually, and the estimates of individuals who could be sustained from the northern field system at Faynan under these assumptions are shown in Table 10.4.

SOUTHERN FIELDS

The northern fields of WF4 were not the only agricultural lands. Added to the above figures are the calories produced by the southern fields of WF4 (105.2 ha). These fields may have had cereal crops as well, but this is not likely,

---

[33] Evenari *et al.* (1982: 191).
[34] Overall, Cu levels were 120–300 ppm, similar to those of the Faynan; Bhogal *et al.* (2003: 413).
[35] Bhogal *et al.* (2003: 419).

Table 10.4. Estimates of individuals supported annually by the polluted northern fields

Population	Annual caloric need (kcal)	Persons supported per hectare of grain	Persons supported by northern fields
Active male (free)	913,500	1.54	160
Active male (slave)	1,218,000	1.12	120
Family (average 3)	2,000,000	2.1	218

as the soil was not optimal for this type of agriculture. However, the pollen record does indicate the presence of another crop, *Olea*, olive trees.[36] Olive fields can have between 100 and 250 trees per hectare; each tree produces an average of anywhere from 15 kg to 50 kg of olives depending on age and environmental conditions.[37] Depending on the variety and the environmental conditions, it has been suggested that a hectare of olives can produce amounts of calories similar to those with cereal crops.[38] What effect the pollution had on olive crops or any other non-cereal crops is uncertain. Because of the diminished manuring and the fact that they were further away from the Khirbet smelting and had deeper roots, it can be argued that crops there were less affected by pollution. In this case, the 105 ha could have produced an additional 210,000,000 kcal or supported 172 active slave males.

Olives and other crops would provide valuable calories and nutrients, but it was likely they provided only a portion of the daily calories, the missing 25 per cent of the diet as estimated by Foxhall and Forbes. Using the earlier estimates, only 160 free males could have received their entire required caloric content (grain and other sources) from locally produced food.[39] The food for the remainder of the population must have been imported from further afield, unless they were being fed unbalanced diets, in which case 292 active slave males could have been supported from local production in the northern and southern fields combined. Food importation would have had to take place regardless, as the estimates above indicate that no more than 300 of the estimated 1,600–1,850 individuals could have been fed by WF4. Despite the best efforts of the administration, supplies of food must have been imported to the region. Mons Claudianus in Egypt is an example of another imperial *metallum* (in this case, a quarry site) that relied solely on imported supplies.

---

[36] Barker (2002: 501).
[37] Mattingly (1988: 41); Info Com (2006).
[38] Osborne (2004: 45).
[39] Assuming the polluted northern fields provided 75% of calories and the southern ones 25%.

CONCLUSION

While the industrial and agricultural sectors of the Roman economy are often viewed as unrelated activities, the example of the Faynan in the Roman era illustrates that they are co-dependent. The mining industry relied heavily on the agricultural sector to produce foodstuffs vital to the efficiency and success of metal production. This demand resulted in wholesale changes in the physical and political complexion of the agricultural sector of the region. In practice, this response resulted in the most important piece of arable land in the southern 'Arabah being changed dramatically through the implementation of a single, carefully constructed and executed plan of land usage coinciding with the periods of most intensive Classical-period copper production.

While increased metal production and increased agricultural production were co-dependent, ironically, success in metal production reduced agricultural productivity over time. While the thought exercise in this chapter probably does not capture all the nuances of pollution and agriculture in the Faynan, it clearly indicates that environmental damage caused by metal production had substantial effects on crop yields. Greater food production increased total supplies available to the region, helping to support larger non-subsistence populations, but this in turn led to more pollution and increasingly less food, the fields being adversely impacted by the industry they were enhanced to sustain. While local food production after imperial modification initially sustained population increases, it is likely that food importation became more necessary over time, as mining activity continued to increase while industrial pollution reduced crop yields.

REFERENCES

Barker, G. (2002). 'A Tale of Two Deserts: Contrasting Desertification Histories on Rome's Desert Frontiers', *World Archaeology* 33.3: 488–507.

Barker, G., Adams, R., Creighton, O., Crook, D., Gilbertson, D., Grattan, J., Hunt, C., Mattingly, D., McLaren, S., Mohammed, H., Newson, P., Palmer, C., Pyatt, F., Reynolds, T., and Tomber, R. (1999). 'Environment and Land Use in the Wadi Faynan, Southern Jordan: The Third Season of Geoarchaeology and Landscape Archaeology (1998)', *Levant* 31: 255–92.

Barker, G., Adams, R., Creighton, O., Daly, P., Gilbertson, D., Grattan, J., Hunt, C., Mattingly, D., McLaren, S., Newson, P., Palmer, C., Pyatt, F., Reynolds, T., Smith, H., Tomber, R., and Truscott, J. (2000). 'Archaeology and Desertification in the Wadi Faynan: The Fourth (1999) Season of the Wadi Faynan Landscape Survey', *Levant* 32: 27–52.

Barker, G., Gilbertson, D., and Mattingly, D. (2007). *Archaeology and Desertification: The Wadi Faynan Landscape Survey*. Oxford.

Bhogal, A., Nicholson, F. A., Chambers, B., and Shepherd, M. A. (2003). 'Effects of Past Sewage Sludge Additions on Heavy Metal Availability in Light Textured Soils; Implications for Crop Yields and Metal Uptakes', *Environmental Pollution* 121.3: 413–23.

Bradshaw, A., McNeilly, T., and Gregory, R. (1965). 'Industrialization, Evolution and the Development of Heavy Metal Tolerance in Plants', in G. Goodman, R. Edwards, and J. Lambert (eds), *Ecology and Industrial Society*. Oxford, 327–44.

Evenari, M., Shanan, L., and Tadmor, N. (1982). *The Negev: The Challenge of a Desert* (2nd edn). Cambridge, MA.

FAO (2004). 'Human Energy Requirements: Report of a Joint FAO/WHO/UNU Expert Consultation, Rome, 17–24 October 2001' <http://www.fao.org/docrep/007/y5686e/y5686e00.htm> (accessed 21 September 2011).

Flannery, K. (1973). 'The Origins of Agriculture', *Annual Review of Anthropology* 2: 271–310.

Foxhall, L., and Forbes, H. (1982). 'Sitometreia, the Role of Grain as a Staple Food in Classical Antiquity', *Chiron* 12: 41–90.

Given, M., and Knapp, B. (2003). *The Sydney Cyprus Survey Project: Social Approaches to Regional Archaeological Survey*. Los Angeles.

Grattan, J., Huxley, S., and Pyatt, F. (2003). 'Modern Bedouin Exposures to Copper Contamination: An Imperial Legacy?', *Ecotoxicology and Environmental Safety* 55: 108–15.

Grattan, J. P., Gilbertson, D. D., and Hunt, C. O. (2007). 'The Local and Global Dimensions of Metalliferous Pollution Derived from a Reconstruction of an Eight Thousand Year Record of Copper Smelting and Mining at a Desert-Mountain Frontier in Southern Jordan', *Journal of Archaeological Science* 34: 83–110.

Hitchner, R. (1993). 'Olive Production and the Roman Economy: The Case for Intensive Growth in the Roman Empire', in M.-C. Amouretti and J.-P. Brun (eds), *Oil and Wine Production in the Mediterranean Area*. Paris, 499–508.

Hirt, A. (2010). *Mines and Quarries in the Roman Empire: Organizational Aspects, 23BC–AD 235*. Oxford.

Info Com (2006). <http://www.unctad.org/infocomm/anglais/olive/crop.htm> (accessed 28 Dec. 2009).

Karaki, L. (2000). *Skeletal Biology of the People of Wadi Faynan: A Bioarchaeological Study*, Unpublished MA dissertation, Yarmouk University, Jordan.

Lal, R., and Singh, B. R. (1998). 'Effects of Soil Degradation on Crop Productivity in East Africa', *Journal of Sustainable Agriculture* 13.1: 15–36.

Lancaster, W., and Lancaster, F. (1999). *People, Land and Water in the Bilad-Ash Sham, the Arabian Peninsula: Indigenous Systems in the Countryside*. London.

Mattingly, D. J. (1988). 'Oil for Export? A Comparison of Libyan, Spanish and Tunisian Olive Oil Production in the Roman Empire', *JRA* 1: 33–56.

Millar, F. (1985). 'Condemnation to Hard Labour in the Roman Empire, from the Julio-Claudians to Constantine', *PBSR* 52: 124–47.

Newson, P. (2002). *Settlement, Land Use and Water Management Systems in Roman Arabia: an Integrated Archaeological approach*, Ph.D. thesis, University of Leicester.

Orejas, A., and Sánchez-Palencia, F. (2002). 'Mines, Territorial Organization, and Social Structure in Roman Iberia: Carthago Noua and the Peninsular Northwest', *AJA* 106: 581–99.

Osborne, R. (2004). *Greek History*. New York.

Pyatt, F., Barker, G., Birch, P., Gilbertson, D., Grattan, J., and Mattingly, D. (1999). 'King Solomon's Miners—Starvation and Bioaccumulation? An Environmental Archaeological Investigation in Southern Jordan', *Ecotoxicology and Environmental Safety* 43: 305–8.

Rothenberg, B., and Blanco-Freijeiro, A. (1981). *Studies in Ancient Mining and Metallurgy in South-West Spain: Explorations and Excavations in the Province of Huelva*. London.

Wright, K., Najjar, M., Last, J., Moloney, N., Flender, M., Gower, J., Jackson, N., Kennedy, A., and Shafiq, R. (1998). 'The Wadi Faynan Fourth and Third Millennium Project, 1997; Report on the First Season of Test Excavations at Wadi Faynan 100', *Levant* 30: 33–60.

Index

The index is not exhaustive and is intended only to direct the user to substantive discussion of the places and subjects indexed. Index references are *not* included for subjects which recur throughout the book (e.g. 'agriculture') or for chapters whose titles explicitly indicate their content.

Index